Christopher Harvie

THE
LIGHTS
OF
LIBERALISM

University Liberals
and the
Challenge of Democracy
1860-86

Allen Lane

First published in 1976

Allen Lane
Penguin Books Ltd
17 Grosvenor Gardens, London SW1

ISBN 0 7139 07185

Printed in Great Britain by
Lowe & Brydone (Printers) Ltd.,
Thetford, Norfolk.

Let's drink about,
and talk a little
of the state of the nation,
or some such discourse
that we all understand.

Squire Western, in *Tom Jones*,
quoted by Leslie Stephen, 1873.

CONTENTS

PREFACE

> It is now more than fifteen years since I exhorted my
> young literary and intellectual friends, the lights
> of Liberalism, not to be rushing into the arena
> of politics themselves, but rather to work inwardly
> upon the predominant force in our politics –
> the great middle class – and to cure its spirit. The great
> Parliamentary machine has gone creaking
> and grinding on ... and there one sees them now,
> helping to grind – all of them zealous, all of them
> intelligent, some of them brilliant and leading.
> What has been ground, what has been produced
> with their help? Really, very much the same sort of
> thing which was produced without it?

Thus Matthew Arnold in 1886 [1] The devil has had the best lines about the radical intelligentsia of the mid nineteenth century. Arnold found them ineffectual; Bloomsbury found them timid and dull. Yet if any acknowledgement ought to preface this book it is one of gratitude to the group of men whose personalities and achievements sustained and stimulated my research. Their failures and failings were considerable, but so were their accomplishments and ambitions. Moreover, in the years since 1966, when this book started as a postgraduate dissertation at Edinburgh University, their political preoccupations have acquired an increased relevance. The devolution of decision-making, the relationship of ethics to politics, the political implications of the extension of higher education, the continuing problem of Anglo – Irish relations: such concerns have demonstrated the limitations of the essentially manipulative 'welfare politics' of the 1960s, while the collapse of the ideology of economic growth has meant that the function of politics in promoting socialization and collective action must again be re-examined. George Brodrick's priorities are as important today as when he wrote his reform essay in 1867: [2]

9

The vice of despotic government, however paternal, and that which renders it as ruinous economically as it is morally degrading, consists not in its wilful neglect of popular interests, but in its contempt for popular opinions, in treating the people as passive materials for benevolent superintendence; and this vice must attach, more or less, to every government constituted with reference to the happiness only, and without reference to the voice, of the governed.

This book will stand or fall as history writing, but it has owed a great deal to personal involvement in politics and education. What Richard Crossman once called 'the charm of politics' – meaning fascination rather than aesthetic appeal – gave me, on doorsteps and in committee rooms, a forceful education in the mores of parties and voters, not to speak of the way in which the academic related, or did not relate, to them. Work for the Open University – the logical successor of the extension schemes pioneered by the university liberals – has helped me to understand both the relationships between higher education and politics, and the ideological tradition of the adult education movement.

To older universities I am no less grateful. Edinburgh funded, and generously rewarded, the writing of my postgraduate dissertation. Merton College, Oxford, elected me to a visiting Fellowship in the Michaelmas Term of 1973, enabling me to complete research work on the book. I am much indebted to their librarians and library staff, and their colleagues at the Bodleian and Balliol College libraries, Oxford, University College library, the British Library of Political Science, the British Museum library, the Bishopsgate Institute and the Greater London council archive in London, Trinity college and the university libraries in Cambridge, the University library, Bristol, and the National Library of Scotland in Edinburgh. They have been unfailingly courteous and helpful in meeting my requests for documents and printed material.

Many friends and colleagues have discussed this project with me; for their advice, criticism, assistance, and hospitality I am deeply grateful. For their help, in all its shapes and sizes, I thank (and this list cannot be as complete as ideally it ought to be): Geoffrey Best, Arthur Marwick, Brian Harrison, Kenneth Morgan, Roger Highfield, Norman Vance, Henry Pelling, Robert Robson, Iain MacLean, John Brown, Nicholas Phillipson, Owen Dudley Edwards, James Cornford, Victor Kiernan, Harry Hanham, Anand Chitnis, Iain MacDougall, William Marwick, John Simpson, George Cubie, Clive Emsley, Henry Cowper, Bob Bell, David Wright, Margaret Clarke, Margaret Keech and Dorothy Packard.

[1]

BRAINS
AND
NUMBERS

In the spring of 1867, at the height of the parliamentary struggle over the second Reform Bill, a group of young professional men, mainly from the two old universities, published *Essays on Reform* and *Questions for a Reformed Parliament*. Both books not only favoured the extension of the franchise but expressed sympathy with the ideal of democratic government, until then regarded as revolutionary by the educated classes. The reform essays had therefore a mixed reception, but on one thing all their reviewers were agreed: Oxford and Cambridge seemed to have emerged as seminaries for radical theorists.

The emergence of the radical don was commented on as much as the liberal politics of the essays. Robert Lowe, the most eloquent scourge of 'the evils of unbridled democracy',[1] found cause for concern in the failure of the universities to impart a proper conservatism to their graduates;[2] those who applauded his parliamentary stand agreed.[3] But enthusiasts for reform welcomed the accession to their ranks[4] and, far from regarding links between reform and education with suspicion, argued that opinion within the universities had significantly shifted and had now become an effective ally.[5] The editor of the radical *Fortnightly Review,* John Morley, an Oxford contemporary of several of the contributors, wrote:[6]

The extreme advanced party is likely for the future to have on its side the most highly cultivated intellect in the nation, and the contest will lie between brains and numbers on one side, and wealth, rank, vested interest, possession in short, on the other.

He emphasized that university liberals did not simply endorse other men's policies, but had evolved their own political perceptions. More, they could be counted on to participate in the political process themselves and make their ideals a reality.[7]

Distinction in career is only a partial indication of a group's achievement, but the essayists produced in later life a significant

11

number of authoritative and versatile public men: A.V.Dicey, constitutionalist and political theorist; Sir Leslie Stephen, biographer, intellectual historian and literary critic; Goldwin Smith, historian and controversialist; Viscount Bryce, jurist, historian, political theorist, politician, diplomat and traveller; Sir George Young and Sir Godfrey Lushington, senior civil servants; Frederic Harrison, journalist, historian, literary critic and trade union reformer; Charles Pearson, historian, politician and educationalist in Australia, Thorold Rogers, economic historian; the Hon. George Charles Brodrick, journalist, historian, authority on land and Warden of Merton College, Oxford. They were, in turn, the friends and colleagues of men like Henry Sidgwick, philosopher, economist and political scientist; Henry Fawcett and Lord Courtney, economists and politicians; Henry Jackson, classical scholar; James Stuart, physicist, pioneer of university extension and politican; Sir George Otto Trevelyan, politician and historian – all of these from Cambridge – and, from Oxford, T.H.Green and Edward Caird, philosophers; Lords Bowen and Davey, judges; Sir Thomas Holland and Sir William Anson, constitutionalists; Sir Mountstuart Grant-Duff, politician and Governor of Madras; Lord Goschen, politician; Lord Sheffield, politician and educational reformer; J.R.Green and E.A.Freeman, historians; and Sir Courtenay Ilbert, constitutionalist and Clerk to the House of Commons.

The achievement of the university liberals was respectable: in the long-term development of British society and politics it was something more. Yet their own summing-up was ambivalent. In the 1860s they had hoped to be, in Morley's words 'the influential and governing generation of thirty years hence',[8] but in the 1890s, with the exception of Morley himself, their role in Liberal politics was not an important one. Gladstone's successor as Liberal leader was the dilettante landowner Rosebery, sent down from Christ Church for owning racehorses just at the time when academic liberalism was at its most intense. His rival, Harcourt, an academic in name only, treated his Cambridge chair as a sinecure throughout a long and unproductive tenure. Sir Henry Campbell-Bannerman, who succeeded them, was an undistinguished and unenthusiastic graduate of Trinity.[9] Although James Bryce spoke of 'those men who came from the English universities into public life and infused into it the spirit of the high standards they owned' as 'an inspiration to the nation's life',[10] he and his friends regretted a deterioration in public life which it seemed they had been impotent to prevent: the coming men in parliament were much younger, or not from the universities at all. They did not bear comparison with 'the generation of the Liberal revival of the 1860s'. [11] The rejoinder of the younger men could be savage. 'James Bryce is only about 65,' Arthur Balfour wrote to Edmund Gosse in 1905,[12]

and I assure you his appearances in the House of Commons are those of a gabbling, foolish, muddled old man. Nobody could be older in mind, less elastic than Bryce ... Bryce is a standing instance of the uselessness of the higher education.

Parliament did not, however, monopolize British politics, and the apparatus of partisanship, criticism and self-justification which still, in biographies, invests Victorian and Edwardian parliamentarians with disproportionate significance, masks a wider and more complex commitment to politics among the British intellectuals. The civil service, education, voluntary organizations, journalism and litera-ture were in many ways as significant in forming political conscious-ness, and recent historical preoccupations – with the growth of the administrative state, or the evolution of the 'new liberalism' – have given such factors their due.[13]

In a sense the central failure of academic liberalism – its inability to appraise objectively its consciousness and role – contributed to its subsequent neglect. Academic liberals looked back on their careers with a mixture of pride and disillusion which, on the whole, undervalued their real achievement: the assimilation by the English upper middle class of the new vocabulary of political democracy, and the coordination of the endowed institutions of higher educa-tion with the new national politics. In fact the destruction of their own historiography has been a necessary preliminary to the rediscovery of their contribution to modern British politics.

'The evils one foresees are seldom the evils that actually arrive': Bryce's 'formula for cheerfulness' in the gloomy days of 1916 [14] was an appropriate comment on the political speculations of his colleagues fifty years earlier. The politics they attacked in the 1860s were sectional, deferential and sectarian, threatening the national community and its institutions, but they did not anticipate that a revived national homogeneity would provide the matrix for the politics of economic manipulation, welfare and class. They overesti-mated the stability of the 1860s situation, and when it dissolved they regretted its successor more than they attempted to understand it. Dicey's *Law and Public Opinion* (Macmillan, 1905) and Bryce's *Modern Democracies* (Macmillan, 1921) are alike monuments to this incom-prehension.

13

But the fact that *Law and Public Opinion* had, for about fifty years, the status of a classic treatment of nineteenth-century legislation testifies to the influence wielded by the rehabilitated universities. Before 1850 Oxford and Cambridge appeared in a state of psychopathic withdrawal from society: the ruling schools of political thought drew on the Scottish universities, if they drew on universities at all. By the end of the century the two old universities had 'nationalized' not only the education of the governing elite, but the content of its instruction, at the expense of provincial and non-university initiatives, a situation which even the impact of two total wars has failed to change. [15]

It would be possible to explain such developments in terms of the 'circulation of elites' [16] – the conscious creation of a secular clerisy for a nominal democracy – but this would be misleading. Theories of elite rule, evolved in a European or American context, are scarcely apposite to the politics of mid-nineteenth-century Britain, where class interest, or the threat of class interest, obsessed politicians and political theorists (see p.143). A small radical group, the Positivists, adopted a conscious and coherent elitism, but they remained distinctive; most academics saw the alternative to class rule as participatory government and were confident that precipitate change would be checked by the inertia of traditional institutions rather than by the manipulative skills of an elite. This accorded with their own entry into politics, not as potential rulers with programmes to hand, but as men escaping from an educational and intellectual impasse, forced to identify with groups seeking 'incorporation' in national institutions in order to legitimize their position in the new political settlement.

The coincidence of the academic crisis with the political crisis was of great importance for the evolution of modern British politics: an earlier, more comprehensive university reform might have produced a 'satisfied' academic intelligentsia, tied to an administrative, anti-democratic liberalism in the style of Robert Lowe, Walter Bagehot, or the German universities after 1848. Failure to secure the settlement of the 1860s might have put the old universities at risk, and transferred endowments to civic universities and technical colleges. Either way the twentieth-century British intelligentsia, and its politics, would have been different, certainly not Noel Annan's 'intellectual aristocracy', 'wedded to gradual reform of accepted institutions and able to move between the worlds of speculation and government ... unexcitable and to European minds unexciting ...' [17]

Since then the manipulative component in politics has steadily increased and the character of political leadership has become more significant. The elitist options inherent within the settlement of the 1860s have been taken up; the assumptions of the old universities maintained and enhanced. The importance of the college as a political community; education as intellectual stimulus rather than professional instruction; endowment of careers out of institutional funds; stress on social homogeneity rather than on the professional in-group: such factors have continued to secure to the graduates of Oxford and Cambridge an elite status while the social base from which they have been recruited has steadily been broadened. The effectiveness of a homogeneous elite is arguably contingent on the homogeneity of the electorate; [18] the academic liberals of the 1860s, if not a conscious elite, were determined to secure this. In the degree to which they identified national political problems with their own predicament and capabilities they anticipated elite responses which have persisted to the present day. At a time when national homogeneity can no longer be taken for granted, however, the nature of the elite is unlikely to remain unchanged. The ascendancy of the old universities, secured to them by the efforts of men like Bryce and Dicey, Stephen and Sidgwick, may now be coming to an end.

Because elitism in British politics has not been a constant but has varied – albeit in a highly distinctive way – with changes in politics, institutions and society, it has been as difficult to accommodate within traditional historiography as within classical sociology. Historical specialization has not helped. Educational history, where not concerned with techniques and organization, has tended to examine the academic world as a political microcosm, in which ideology plays a minor role compared with connection, patronage and manoeuvre, a tendency accelerated by Namier's contributions to political history. For most universities most of the time this is valid enough; for universities at a time of rapid social and political change, surely less so. The responses to such situations can, after all, determine the future structure of academic politics. [19] The inadequacies of traditional political science are more obvious and stem partly from the failure of academic consciousness noted earlier. Categories and conflicts derived from individual ethics – 'sovereignty', 'natural rights' and so on – survived; little attempt was made to show their relevance to the specific situations that confronted political thinkers. Reputations were assessed, and survived or perished, in terms of internal consistency; only recently has ideology been interpreted as the response of a group to shared preoccupations, and judged by its utility in specific situations. [20] Political history itself tended to be straightforwardly biographical, or devoted to specific issues in which ideology – in the traditional, formal sense – was naturally at a discount. Both Namier and the historians of nineteenth-century administration, in their revaluation of the politics of decision-making and organization, tended further to devalue ideology, which Marxism, at least the crudely activist version popular among British intellectuals in the 1930s, had already reduced to a ruling-class attachment to tangible economic interests. [21]

The application of interdisciplinary techniques to the study of the Victorian period, pioneered by G.M.Young, W.L.Burn and G.S.Kitson Clark, and consolidated and institutionalized by scholars in the 1950s, notably those involved with the journal *Victorian Studies* (1957), has altered this situation. Intellectual and educational history is now much more concerned with using 'political' criteria to establish the quantitative impact and specific influence of ideas, and pays particular attention to the nature of contemporary assessments, the role these played in conveying ideas to society at large, and the correspondence – by no means straightforward – between society's expectations and ruling intellectual preoccupations. [22] Likewise, political historians now tend to stress the role of politics in providing an identity for groups in society, rather than as a means of securing favourable legislative change by groups whose identity was already distinct. [23]

Because of this the role of ideology in nineteenth-century British politics is now seen as more important and more complex than a mere rationalization by groups of their situation and ambitions, even if it is still not an autonomous system, rationally coherent and self-contained, to be adopted or discarded at will: it influences the groups who profess it, not simply as a programme but as a factor within their own constitution which affects their perception of 'social reality'.

This means that it is difficult to appraise the ideology of a particular group objectively, and virtually impossible to disassociate it from the group's history. It is not surpising that two of the best studies of the ideology of the nineteenth-century intelligentsia – Noel Annan's *Leslie Stephen, His Life and Thought in Relation to His Time* (MacGibbon & Kee, 1951) and Melvin Richter's *The Politics*

16

of Conscience: T.H.Green and His Age (Weidenfeld, 1964) – are
biographical: an approach which attempts to comprehend the
subjective attitudes of individuals will find such a framework
congenial. But can it also work for groups? The contention of this
study is that it can, and, further, that unless the predicament and
philosophy of the liberal academics of the mid-nineteenth century
are studied as a collective response, our knowledge of the role of
ideology in modern British politics will be deficient.

The adoption of a biographical approach does not imply that the
academics' relationships and ideology remained constant; but it
provides a structure which demonstrates how, for a critical decade,
these were sufficiently integrated to create an organization and a
programme which transcended the capabilities of individuals and,
even while waning, continued to affect their political responses.
Agreement and identification were cumulative processes. There was
no preliminary assent to doctrine; only when the political situation
became critical was ideology projected beyond the immediate
concerns of the group, and it remained governed by its members'
desire to preserve their cohesion. But, if doctrine and membership
were flexible, the consciousness of who was, and who was not, a fit
member of 'the party of humanity' was more acute than any sense
of identification with other bodies.

This was seen at the time as implying a consciousness of
alienation (notably by J.R.Green, see p.97). In post-Marxist
political sociology this concept has become critical in explaining the
mobilization of social classes, but the situation in Britain in the
1860s has been recognized as unique. Marx envisaged the intelligentsia, 'a portion of the bourgeois ideologists who have raised
themselves to the level of comprehending theoretically the historical
movement as a whole', [24] as natural allies of the proletariat. Indeed,
when the word itself reached Britain from Russia in the wake of the
revolution, it carried this meaning. But, by then, it was also evident
that the nature of the intelligentsia varied from country to country.
In 1931, in his Italian prison, Antonio Gramsci considered this
problem. He divided the intelligentsia into two sections: 'organic'
intellectuals were the necessary educated part of the dominant social
organization – technicians, economists, managers; while 'traditional' intellectuals – clergymen, scholars, the older professions –
stemmed from earlier social systems and considered themselves
independent, obedient to the internal sanctions of their profession or
vocation. Marx had assumed that capitalism would bring the
'organic' intellectuals to the fore. Gramsci saw that this was far

from being the case, and that Britain in particular had managed to assimilate the organic to the traditional intellectuals: [25]

The old land-owning aristocracy is joined to the industrialists by a kind of suture which is precisely that which in other countries unites the traditional intellectuals with the new dominant classes.

Impediments to the progress of the organic intelligentsia Gramsci listed as 'a whole series of checks (moral, intellectual, political, economic, incorporated in specific sections of the population, relics of past regimes which refuse to die out)'. [26] In Britain academic liberals encountered these checks, not as organic intellectuals sustained by powerful innovating forces, but as individuals within, and constrained by, the traditional intelligentsia. The result of their struggle with their environment, the subject of the first half of this book, was the creation of an effective unity which pre-empted the relatively unfocused forces of the organic intelligentsia. The political success of the academics was momentary; long-term changes in education, politics and society, strengthening both the old governing class and new proletarian organisations, diminished their influence on policy. Their cohesion subsequently impeded individual careers and, in 1886, caused a distortion of political judgement which effectively isolated them from the Liberal party. But their central achievement endured: in the 1860s they realized, as their organic contemporaries – and even Gramsci – did not, the importance in British politics of institutional loyalties and initiatives, subordinate to national politics but still checking and directing them. The settlement they obtained balanced the power of institutions against the incorporation of the working class in national politics. The result, as Gramsci noted, was important in differentiating British from European politics, but it was not what the academics had desired: as a component of the governing class (which they still regarded with suspicion) their privilege and status was confirmed, but in the dynamic of national life they became intellectually restricted and politically weak. The experience of the academic liberals demonstrates how, within the old order and reacting to its constraints, a group could attain the status and influence of an elite, but then, by the very success and stability of the settlement it achieved, could lose its initiative and revert to being an interest within a class. If it contradicts the classic Marxist appraisal of the role of the intelligentsia in politics, it also opposes theories which see the manipulation of politics by an intellectual elite as a continuous and consistent process.

[2]

THE
LIBERAL
INTELLECT

To discover the principles which regulate the
progress of human society, which facilitate
the attainment of high ideals, all these enquiries
come within the sphere of our operations ... The
acquisition of truth can alone satisfy the human
mind, and slowly and surely each succeeding
generation comes nearer to the object of its quest.

Thus Lord Reay, its President, defined the philosophy of the newly
formed British Academy in 1903. [1] Of the forty-odd middle-aged to
elderly Academicians he addressed, all but a handful considered
themselves liberals. If many no longer voted Liberal, it was because
they thought the Liberal party had changed, not their own
convictions. [2] The causes to which they pledged their Academy – the
scientific study of history and archaeology, philology, philosophy,
jurisprudence and economics – reflected the concerns which had
preoccupied them for half a century: education, ideology and
politics. However academically specialized or politically conservative they now were, the Academy summed up their success in
implanting liberal inquiry at universities which Gladstone, only
recently dead, had once defended as the seminaries of the Church. [3]

The British Academy exemplified a mature academic community: its programme provides a definition – but a retrospective one –
of academic liberalism. But what that had meant at various times
during the preceding fifty years was often quite different. Academic
liberalism was protean; its stock of ideas and social preoccupations
changed over time. For this reason it is as difficult to accommodate
it within the traditional criteria of 'history of ideas' as it is to fit
university reform into the framework of educational or political
history. To attempt to do so would only distort the reality, in which

19

ideology engaged in a continual dialogue with predicament. A philosophical definition of academic liberalism, for example, runs into the problem that close political agreement could often stem from disparate philosophical convictions. As the 'impenitent Benthamite' A.V.Dicey wrote of his ally T.H.Green:

... almost all his definite opinions might be endorsed by Bright and Cobden but neither Bright nor Cobden could understand the process by which Green's opinions are obtained, nor the arguments by which they are defended.

If this was generally true of academic liberalism even at its period of maximum cohesion in the 1860s, when it united positivists, Christian Socialists, idealists and utilitarians, there was even less similarity of perception of educational theory, or the type of instruction to be offered, or the future organisation of the universities; institutional pressures and political agreement produced cohesion where the application of any logical educational theory would have produced disruption (see p. 95)

The political component of academic liberalism remains critical, but even this is complex. Attempts to analyse university politics which stress their autonomy, and the importance of manoeuvre at the expense of ideology – imposing, in other words, a Namierite pattern of interest and antipathy – can lead to insensitivity to the intellectual uniqueness of the period. [5] Too straightforward a Marxian thesis of social cause and institutional effect can, likewise, underestimate the complexity of the political process, inside and outside the universities. [6] This was after all a period in which the intellectual life of Britain was undergoing unprecedented, rapid and permanent change, which Leslie Stephen likened to the cataclysmic break-up of an ice-cap after the slow sapping action of warm currents had weakened it. [7] A generation faced with this, and engaged in the search for 'the principles which regulate the progress of human society' was not likely to be politically pliable and intellectually incurious.

Accepting, therefore, that academic liberalism was not a constant but an evolving force, it is as well to focus on the experience of the academics themselves, and to study the impact on them, over time and in an institutional context, of the ideas and attitudes that were subsequently to characterize the content and scope of their liberalism. This preference for a subjective approach may conflict with the traditional techniques of intellectual, educational and political history, but in recent years such disciplines have themselves come to pay as much attention to contingent relationships and contexts as to the internal consistency of their own methodologies. [8]

II

The commitment to liberalism was a complex one. Even Lewis Campbell, academic liberalism's first historian, oversimplified it in his *The Nationalisation of the Old English Universities* [9] by defining it as a constant spirit of free inquiry, growing in strength but unchanging in character. For the liberals of the 1860s were deeply and permanently influenced by factors which were ultimately irrational – the atmosphere of the home, the tastes, sensibilities and relationships produced by collegiate life, even the formal religion which so many of them were subsequently to treat with hostility or indifference. The men who took such things for granted were necessarily distinct from their external liberal allies. This also gave the liberal movement at the universities its distinctively political cast, not because it was a party affair, but because it was absorbed in the relationships of society and the intellectual life. This absorption pre-dated the impact of liberal ideas on the universities; in some ways it was, at the time, hostile to liberalism. Yet no study of the generation which matured between 1850 and 1865 can neglect the response of its forebears to intellectual and social change during the revolutionary period, and the dialectic of the resulting evangelical movement with the universities during a later period of political change.

In his L. T. Hobhouse Lecture, 'The Curious Strength of Positivism in English Political Thought', Noel Annan has remarked on the tendency of English social philosophers to conflate individual and social morality, and has contrasted this with the sociology of Max Weber, Durkheim and Pareto, who interpreted society as a 'nexus of groups'. Continental sociologists were not interested in how the individual was to live a 'moral' life, and how institutions ought to be arranged to facilitate this. The individual was, instead, [10]

... a bolt that might snap if the nut of society held it too tightly or too loosely. Institutions could never be explained solely in terms of their utility; they could be understood only by discovering how they corresponded to the general needs of society.

In the 1860s and 1870s, when the positivist tradition was in decline in France, and had never made much of an impact in idealist Germany, in England it was actually reinforced by the intellectual controversies of the time. [11] The academic liberals, then conspicuous as defenders of reason against clerical dogma, upheld the tradition so enthusiastically that the emphasis on individual morality transcended the differences between empiricist and idealist. Its source – the point at which England diverged from Europe in social and political thought – can be traced back to the reactions of the national communities to the upheavals of the revolutionary period. Germans, Frenchmen and Englishmen reacted against Enlightenment rationalism, but in different ways. In Germany the current set towards romantic and idealist nationalism, in France towards the 'scientific' study of the structure and mechanics of society, exemplified by the work of Saint-Simon. [12] England, affected neither by revolution nor invasion, did not directly feel the force of these traumas, but Englishmen of the upper classes realized that their society was rapidly, if peacefully, changing. As a class, their response took the form of the Evangelical movement. Leslie Stephen later christened it 'the religious reaction', favouring that 'sound common sense' of the eighteenth century which found room for Bentham as well as Burke and Johnson, but he implicitly bore witness to 'the single most widespread influence in Victorian England'. [13] As Annan has commented: [14]

> The peremptory demand for sincerity, the delight in plain speaking, the unvarying accent on conduct, and the conviction that he who has attained a Higher Truth must himself evangelise ... proclaim him a child of the Evangelical tradition.

Inculcated by home and family, the tradition penetrated deep into the psyche of most of his friends and contemporaries. When we look for the source of the individualist ethic in nineteenth-century English thought, we will find it here.

The Evangelical imprint had two main aspects – individual and social. The individual – the contrite sinner – experienced the grace of God, in repenting of his sins and throwing himself on the mercy of his Maker. So the responsibility for being born again rested with him, not with Calvin's omnipotent deity, who could consign good and evil together to Hell. A doctrine of such vagueness and illogicality, apparently depriving God himself of free will, would find it difficult to sustain itself in an age with the leisure and inclination for systematic theology. But with revolution in France, and Europe ablaze with war, the English governing classes regarded the religious revival with no unfriendly eye. [15] Moreover, with the potential domestic menace produced by the growth of an industrial society, the socially reconciling power of 'vital religion' took a new

22

significance. Professor Victor Kiernan has noted that to them it had [16]

the great merit, in face of egalitarian ideas, of throwing into relief the equality of souls without disturbing the inequality of ranks. All men were not equally good, as Rousseau had made people think, but they were all equally bad.

Kiernan notes that during the 1790s 'reasonable' interpretations of religion 'as the formulary of an established society,' [17] were dropped in favour of the direct appeal of the Wesleyan. A common religious language was a necessary social cement: 'if high and low were to join in worship, it must be 'the worship of the poor.' [18]

Goldwin Smith who, exceptionally, had been brought up in a Broad-Church household – Dean Milman and Bishop Blomfield were family friends [19] – reached a similar conclusion in his inaugural lecture as Regius Professor of History at Oxford, when he contemplated the eighteenth century: [20]

The people received the religion which the gentry and clergy had rejected; the people preserved the traditions of English morality and English duty; the people repaired, by their unflagging industry, the waste of profligate finance, and of reckless and misconducted wars.

Urging the universities to produce a national leadership equal to its task, Smith restated the democratic element in the Evangelical revival. Its emphasis on the equality of souls was comparable with his own appeal for civic and political equality within the nation. Politics had replaced religion as an instrument of class reconciliation. [21] The reverent manner in which many university men tried to adapt their lives to their politics – T.H.Green's preference for the society of 'plain people', his rough farmer's suits, his insistence on travelling third class – recalls Wesley on circuit, a secular Wesley whose gospel was the spiritual fulfilment of individuals in the cooperative effort of a political commonwealth. [22]

'Protestantism in one aspect', wrote Leslie Stephen in 1895, paraphrasing Bunyan, 'is simply rationalism still running about with the shell on its head.' [23] Clear away the impurities of superstition from it and you discover as your precipitate the essential Pilgrim – a robust and active conscience, serviceable but by no means transcendent. A.V.Dicey remarked of his mother, Anne Stephen, Leslie's aunt, that her Evangelicalism was 'closely connected, if not almost blended, with many features of Quakerism, and ... hardly tainted by Calvinism.' [24] The evangelical conscience and the

Quaker 'inner light' may have been close; the inner light and rationalist inquiry were closer still. In the words of Francis Newman, the Cardinal's brother: [25]

I was an Evangelical, but, like plenty of Evangelicals beside, both now and then, was resolved to follow the Truth *whithersoever it* led me; and was always indignant when told 'you must believe this or that' or you will find it 'will lead you further'. 'If that time comes, I shall go further' was my uniform reply.

Evangelicalism, however, took a personal toll. It seems directly to have imposed that element of rigour, of reserved, self-conscious detachment, that pervaded their lives. Thomas Hardy's comparison of Leslie Stephen to the Schreckhorn is telling: [26]

Aloof, as if a thing of mood and whim,
Now that its spare and desolate figure gleams
Upon my nearing vision, less it seems
A looming Alp-height than a guise of him ...

This was not the only time that Hardy, on the fringes of the group, imaginatively captured qualities of its character to which its members were oblivious. Their formal, undemonstrative, withdrawn natures were remarked neither by themselves nor by biographers who were close contemporaries. Their children, however, noticed. Austin Harrison, brought up in the 1880s and 1890s in a London composed of 'houses inhabited by queer, old, fierce, literary men ... dry and punctilious,' [27] remembered that his father 'did not wholly trust himself. He could not entirely unbend, hence he never appeared entirely natural.' [28] Frederic Harrison never smoked, never entered a pub or a music hall, regarded sex as 'not a subject that decent men discuss'. [29] The attitude of his friends varied – sex, in particular, posed problems (see p. 63) – but the defensive seriousness was general. Kindliness and generosity were, usually justly, commemorated in memoirs and obituaries; very seldom did a biographer probe further. One significant exception was Sir Henry Cunningham's portrait of Charles Bowen. Cunningham, exceptionally among his circle, was an imaginative writer of some merit. His sketch of Bowen's personality could well be taken as a commentary on that of the group as a whole: [30]

There are minds which are dominated by an instinctive reserve. They have intellectual and moral recesses, the gloom of which they themselves hardly venture to explore, problems which they give up as insoluble, depths which no plummet may sound, obstinate questionings to which no answer is forthcoming, mysteries of their

24

own consciousness before which they stand in mute bewilderment. The last thing which natures so constituted can endure is the prying eye and the officious tongue, which would destroy the privacy of existence, invade the recesses of thought and feeling and make their inner life the theme of common talk.

To J.H.Newman this reserve was the natural corollary of agnosticism, the reflex of men 'who do not look through and beyond their own minds to their Maker, but are engrossed in notions of what is due to themselves, to their own dignity and their own consistency'. [31] This was not wholly fair. Liberal academics were not immobilized and made miserable by their loss of faith. But they were handicapped in more indirect ways. Take James Bryce, for instance, scrupulous, benevolent, but utterly distanced from ordinary human sensibility – all of this patent in his letters. Surely this was a direct result of the individual's mind being loaded with the responsibility for its own salvation, which the secularization of the Evangelical impulse only increased, as the rational individual became the denominator of utilitarian politics. Individualization served the academics well in producing that strong, sharp intellect – what Leslie Stephen called the 'masculine' mind – which could plough its way through, in Stephen's case, ethics, politics, economics and literary criticism. However, it also separated them from the political mores of ordinary people. Graham Wallas exposed this gulf when, in *Human Nature in Politics*, he attacked political science teaching at the universities, and cited James Bryce's preface to Ostrogorski's *Democracy and the Organisation of Political Parties* as an example of it: [32]

Mr Bryce refers to 'the democratic ideal of the intelligent independence of the individual voter, an ideal far removed from the actualities of any State'.
What does Mr Bryce mean by 'ideal democracy'? If it means anything, it means the best form of democracy which is consistent with the facts of human nature. But one feels ... that Mr Bryce means by these words the kind of democracy which might be possible if human nature were as he himself would like it to be, and as he was taught at Oxford to think that it was.

But the blame rested less with the university, whose politics teaching in the 1850s was scarcely so effective, than with the belief in individual responsibility inculcated in the life of the home.

Evangelicalism was also an instrument of social control, and here again there was a correspondence between the academics' political ideal and their fathers' and grandfathers' conception of the function of religion. Looking back from the agnostic 1870s, Leslie Stephen and John Morley both commended the robust if naïve reinforcement it gave to civilized society. Stephen wrote of the Evangelicals: [33]

What, they seem to have tacitly inquired, is the argument which will induce an ignorant miner or a small tradesman in a country town to give up drinking and cock-fighting? The obvious answer was: Tell him that he is going straight to hell-fire to be tortured for all eternity ...

From Morley, whose lapse from belief while at Oxford had estranged him from his family and damaged his professional career, [34] the tribute was even more dramatic: [35]

Although the theology of a town like Blackburn is of a narrow, unhistoric and rancorous kind, yet one must give even this dull and cramped Evangelicalism its due, and admit that the churches and chapels have done a good service through their Sunday Schools and otherwise in impressing a kind of moral organisation on the mass of barbarism which surged chaotically into the factory towns. Lancashire theology does not make a man love his neighbour; but its external system promotes cleanliness, truth-telling and chastity; and the zeal of the clergy of all sects, however much we may wish that it had been connected with a more hopeful doctrine, has been a barrier, for which civilisation will always owe something to their name, against the most awful influx the world ever saw of furious provocatives to unbridled sensuality and riotous animalism.

Evangelicalism's power as a means of social control lay in its popular vocabulary, its simple message – 'Do not rest Christianity on argument but tell him dogmatically that every word of the Bible was dictated by God Almighty; and that every word is as plain as the ABC' [36] – and the ready availability of a code of conduct in the form of the Scriptures. Given the perils England faced, the movement had an obvious utility: it had helped save society from the mob. Academic reaction to civil disorder remained close, to the horror of the Evangelicals – those who revolted against society also offended against the providence of God, which was coordinate with the law. Imperfect law could be improved; nothing could restore the 'social tissue' once disorder had torn it apart. Fitzjames Stephen viewed the French Revolution of 1848 'with the feelings of a scandalized policeman towards a mob breaking windows in the cause of humanity': [37]

feelings ... of fierce unqualified hatred for the revolution and revolutionists; feelings of the most bitter contempt and indignation against those who feared them, truckled to them, or failed to fight them wheresoever they could and as long as they could: feelings of zeal against all popular aspirations and in favour of all established institutions whatever their various defects or harshnesses (which however, I wished to alter slowly and moderately).

He then went on to prescribe grapeshot, and the summary execution of Louis Philippe for not using it. Fitzjames admittedly carried 'masculinity' to excess, but his more pacific brother reacted similarly to the Draft Riots in New York in 1863: 'Some good volleys got the brutes under, but there should have been a real good massacre.' [38] The analogy with the earlier experience is obvious enough: disregard of law was not only troublesome and dangerous, it was a sin which cast those who committed it out of the society of men and the mercy of God. When in 1820 the Cato Street conspirators, still unrepentant, were executed in London, the great preacher Thomas Chalmers was appalled at their 'fierce and unfeeling hardihood' and equated their rebellion with 'a glimpse into Pandemonium'. For this there could be only one remedy: [39]

It is neither a system of unchristian morals, nor the meagre Christianity of those who deride, as methodistical, all the peculiarities of our faith, that will recall our neglected population ... Nothing will subdue them but that regenerating power which goes along with the faith of the New Testament, and nothing will charm away the alienation of their spirits but the belief in the overtures of redeeming mercy.

Chalmers articulated problem and prescription in the convention of the period. When the liberal academics faced the possibility of a similar situation, they repeated the diagnosis, but invoked as remedy not irrational dogmatics but an approach to politics which, while 'scientific', could draw from the mass of the people a 'religious' respect; conviction now inspired the individual to realize himself in the service of the community. Against Paley's conception of 'reasonable' religion as a social utility, the Evangelicals had propagated a 'new birth' which would unify the nation through a shared religious experience. [40] Later, against men like Robert Lowe, who looked on the franchise as something 'like every other political expedient', [41] the academic liberals argued for its extension on the grounds that political equality would convert a class society into a genuine commonwealth, by giving each voter a sense of individual responsibility to the community. Criticizing Matthew Arnold's 'reasonable' argument for culture 'as the great help out of our present difficulties', [42] Henry Sidgwick demonstrated the 'fire and strength' [43] of this new gospel, which combined rational inquiry with commitment: [44]

Mr Arnold may say that he does not discourage action, but only asks for delay, in order that we may act with sufficient knowledge. This is the eternal excuse of indolence – insufficient knowledge: still, taken cautiously, the warning is valuable, and we may thank Mr Arnold for it: we cannot be too much stimulated to study the laws of the social phenomena that we wish to modify, in order that 'reason the card' may be complete and as accurate as possible. But we remember that we have heard this all before from a very different sort of prophet. It has been preached to us by a school small, but energetic (energetic to a degree that causes Mr Arnold to scream 'Jacobinism!'): and the preaching has not been in the name of culture but in the name of religion and self-sacrifice.

III

Nothing in the Evangelical contribution related directly to the social function of the universities, beyond a general commitment to reform through existing institutions. Nevertheless the desire to proselytize at the universities produced, by reaction, a movement which assigned them a prominent place in its social thought. On its failure this concept was bequeathed to its liberal successors.

Cambridge had, at a distance, followed the general social tendencies of the eighteenth century. It tolerated, even in a quiet way encouraged, the Evangelicals. The initial hostility of the high-and-dry school was overcome, and when Charles Simeon, the Evangelical leader, died in 1836, Francis Thornton could write to his father at Clapham of [45]

the respect which had been gradually increasing, till it showed itself in full force yesterday – That was indeed a magnificent spectacle for those who knew in what circumstances Simeon began his course. *The heads of houses* attended *as a body*, and all undergraduates were admitted, in mourning.

Subsequently Cambridge faithfully reflected the steady decline of upper-class Evangelical fervour. By the time of Sir James Stephen and Sir Charles Trevelyan it had become 'an attitude of the soul rather than a dogmatic creed,' [46] which could comprehend Leslie Stephen's attempt to commit himself to the Broad Churchmanship of Maurice and Sidgwick's flirtation with Unitarianism; ultimately it lapsed into undogmatic theism, scepticism or agnosticism. The religious question was never central to university politics. 'Individuals might belong to what were then called the "high", "low" or "broad" parties,' Leslie Stephen recollected, 'but their differences did not form the ground for any division in University politics. We left such matters to Oxford.' [47]

The Oxford tradition had never been one of accommodation:

always High Church, recently Jacobite, it was uncongenial to Evangelicalism. More recently, fresh, more dangerous currents of opinion made themselves felt, associated with the small but active liberal party, the Noetics, who 'maintained a wholesome intellectual ferment in the Oriel common room'. [48] Despite a certain insularity they were, in Pattison's words 'distinctly the produce of the French Revolution. They called everything in question; they appealed to first principles and disallowed authority as a judge in intellectual matters.' Against the dialectic of Arnold, Whately and Coplestone, Hampden, Baden Powell and Blanco White, the formality and aridity of Evangelical dogma was no defence. [49] The more intelligent of its former adherents had to adopt a more sophisticated theology. But the conservative isolation of Oxford meant that this revulsion led to the reinforcement of the dominant high Church. Although well equipped to demolish scriptural fundamentalism, the Noetics, 'dry, cold, supercilious, critical, out of sympathy with religion and the religious temper', [50] were too few in number, too close to the Whigs. They bore a Tory university no particular loyalty; they could, and did, go elsewhere – Whately to Dublin, Arnold to Rugby, Coplestone to Llandaff. Just as, a generation later, Sidgwick rejected the 'reasonableness' of Matthew Arnold, the young Oxford Evangelicals – Faber, the Wilberforces, Newman, Gladstone [51] – rejected them and turned instead to the vital tradition of the High Church, currently threatened by the Reform Parliament. They saw that the traditional links between state and church could simply be used to tailor the authority and doctrine of the latter to suit the political convenience of the former. [52] Hence the peremptory demand of Tract i: [53]

> Should the government of the country so far forget their God as to cut off the Church, to deprive it of its temporal honours and substance, on what will you rest the claims to respect and attention which you make upon your flock?

John Morley, forty years later, counted this a distinct intellectual advance: [54]

> The whole strength of their appeal to members of the Church lay in men's weariness of the high and dry optimism which presents the existing order of things as the noblest possible, and the undisturbed way of the majority as the way of salvation ... Conspicuous as were the intellectual faults of the Oxford Movement, it was at any rate a recognition in a very forcible way of the doctrine that spiritual matters are not to be settled by the dicta of a political council.

By exalting personal conviction and rejecting acquiescence in a 'politique' settlement [55]

It acknowledged that a man is answerable at his own peril for having found or lost the truth. It is a warning that he must reckon with a judge who will not account the *status quo*, nor the convenience of a cabinet, a good plea for indolent acquiescence in error. It ended, in the case of its most vigorous champions, in final and deliberate putting out of the eyes of the understanding.

Even this final destructive act vindicated reason and logic: the tragedy was that these were used to defend archaic dogmatics. Newman, in Pattison's eyes [56]

threw off not only the scum of democratic lawlessness, but the allegiance which the individual understanding owes to the universal reason, and too hastily concluded that authority could supply a basis for philosophical belief.

But Newman's authority lay in the Roman Catholic Church, and his conversion in 1845 severely weakened the Anglican authority he and his allies had originally defended. Men like Morley, Pattison and Goldwin Smith regretted as tragic the rejection of 'the universal reason', but they welcomed the damage the secession did to the arguments of those who supported the religious exclusiveness of the universities. [57]

Pusey bluntly defined 'the problem and special work of a university' as [58]

not how to advance science, not how to make discoveries, not how to form new schools of mental philosophy, nor to invent new modes of analysis, not to produce works in Medicine, Jurisprudence, or even Theology; but to form minds religiously, morally, intellectually, which shall discharge a right whatever duties God, in his providence, shall appoint to them.

And Gladstone in 1834, opposing in the Commons a Bill to admit dissenters, was no less explicit, arguing that the universities could only be described as national institutions through their connection with the Established Church. Their purpose was 'the cultivation of its doctrines in the rising generation of the country': [59]

To attain this a certain fixed course of study and of discipline must be observed. But how could this be done when by the Bill before the house it was proposed to throw open their doors not only to Dissenting Christians of every sect and denomination, but also to all sorts of persons, be they Christians or not? This he hoped the Church would never allow.

After 1845 this argument lost much of its plausibility. Only two months after the trial before Convocation and Degradation of W.G.Ward for his Catholic manifesto *The Ideal of a Christian Church* ended the first phase of the Movement – Church called it 'the birthday of the modern Liberalism of Oxford' [60] – W.D.Christie, Liberal M.P. for Weymouth, a Unitarian who had been at Cambridge but had been unable to graduate, moved for a Royal Commission on the universities, adducing in support the theological turmoil at Oxford: [61]

What is the result of all your endeavours to unite the University and the Church in an indissoluble theological alliance? ... Learning has at last proclaimed her independence – burst your theological fetters – ay, and dragged the Church after the Universities into a latitude of theological speculation which well beseems a place of learning, but is utterly subversive of the foundations of the Church.

'His speech', commented Lewis Campbell, 'marks the beginning of an understanding between the Nonconformists ... and some of the younger liberals at Oxford.' [62]

The responsibility of the individual to his own conscience was, during the Movement, focused within the institution of the university, and on the problem of its social role. At the 'reasonable' level it showed the danger of maintaining the Anglican seminary concept when the Church was divided on the theological basis of Anglicanism, and itself represented only a minority of the nation. The university had to be made 'national' and its studies relevant, to avoid drastic parliamentary intervention. [63] This, by and large, was the position of Broad Churchmen, like Jowett, A.P.Stanley and most Cambridge reformers. But the younger men, seeking 'vital religion', a new *Weltanschauung*, now committed themselves to restructuring society through a secular liberalism deriving leadership from the universities. Both schools, however – the 'reasonable' school initially by far the larger – united in campaigning for change, and both were later to unite in paying tribute, without irony, to Newman as the man responsible more than any other for it. When he visited Oxford in 1878 an Anglo–Catholic clergyman, Frederick Meyrick, sourly observed: [64]

At dinner his health was given by Professor Bryce, who congratulated him on having brought about a state of theological liberalism or indifferentism in Oxford, the one thing which from the beginning of his life to its end he abhorred ... it was his old enemies, whom he had fought *à outrance*, and whose principles he hated now from the bottom of his heart, who flocked round him as their champion, and thanked him for what he had done in demolishing the power of the Church of England in Oxford.

IV

To Mark Pattison the Movement was at best an emetic. It purged the university of the malignant virus of clerical dogma. Until 1845 all was darkness, then [65]

the light was let in in an instant, as by the opening of the shutters in the chamber of a sick man who has slept till midday. Hence the flood of reform, which broke over Oxford in the next few years following 1845, and did not spend itself till it had produced two government commissions, until we had ourselves enlarged and remodelled all our institutions ...

This conclusion was questionable. The Movement was not wholly 'an eclipse which had shut out the light from heaven', especially to the generation who carried their liberalism into political activity. To Morley, for instance, Pattison was haunted by the 'embittering presence' of his dead enthusiasm. His reaction was vindictive rather than philosophical. [66] Further, there was no rush of intellectual freedom after 1845. Pattison took until 1850 to lapse from Tractarianism. 'The Liberals of his school', wrote Church of Stanley, 'were then [1845] still a little flock: a very distinguished and a very earnest set of men, but too young and too few'. [67] The Oxford of Matthew Arnold and Arthur Hugh Clough was a disoriented, unsettled place, plagued by 'the sick fatigue, the languid doubt' Arnold lamented in 'The Scholar Gipsy'. [68]

Twenty years later Henry Sidgwick wrote sympathetically of Clough's irresolution: [69]

He would not accept either false solutions or no solutions, nor, unless very reluctantly, provisional solutions. At the same time he saw just as clearly as other men that the continued contemplation of insoluble problems is not merely impractical but anti-practical; and that a healthy and natural instinct forces most men, after a few years of feverish youthful agitation, to turn away from it. But with this instinct Clough's passion for absolute truth conflicted ...

This was the critical dilemma of the liberal academic. Three years earlier, just after his discovery of Clough, Sidgwick wrote to a friend: 'In the present age an educated man must either be prophet or persistent sceptic – there seems no *media via*.' [70] Clough's relevance became even more obvious when the universities were freed from the clerical yoke, and the debate started in earnest on the future of university studies and the endowment of research. From that uneasy interlude of the 1840s, between the rout of the Movement and the advance of the liberals, he had predicted the ultimate break-up of the latter, the tension between prophet and sceptic, between teacher and scholar, between Jowett and Pattison, between T.H.Green and Henry Sidgwick (see pp.94, 200). But this was all in the future. Action, and the dispelling of the miasma of irresolute speculation, waited on the gradual grouping of the liberal forces.

Besides the collapse of the Movement, Pattison briskly claimed the Railway Mania and the continental revolutions of 1848 as the causes of the liberal advance. [71] Although he tended to generalize, there was an element of truth in both cases. The spectacle of dons turning railway financiers, swept from theology to the stock exchange, then cast down when the bubble burst, was not an apt overture to reform, but on 12 June 1844 the first train arrived at Oxford from Paddington. The Eastern Counties line reached Cambridge in 1845. The isolation of the university towns was ended. The newspapers reached them early on the day of printing. Fellows at the Bar or in London journalism could easily come up for dinner and consultation with their resident colleagues; the universities were pulled closer to the intellectual life of the capital. Admittedly the clerical party was now able to summon up country parsons by the trainload to vote down reform measures in Convocation and Senate, but the alliance of residents and London professional men, the axis on which the reform movement at both universities pivoted, was now physically feasible.

The revolutionary spirit of 1848 was also significant. According to Grant Duff: [72]

Those who were at Oxford in those days will not readily forget the abiding change which the events of that year produced, increasing tenfold the interest in and knowledge of the Continent – its social, political and religious modes of thought.

Lewis Campbell was more sceptical, but admitted that Jowett, who had visited Paris during the revolution, 'could not remain unaffected by a great European change which had come immediately under his view'. [73] More specifically the events of 1848 brought forth the Broad Church militant as Christian Socialism, and in so doing stimulated the social sympathies, and ultimately overtaxed the faith, of many devout and radically minded university men (see pp. 36, 149). The response was on the whole conservative. The extravagant enthusiasm of Flaubert's Parisian students in *L'Éducation Sentimentale* gave way in Britain to the men of King's College, London – many future university radicals among them – enrolling as special constables against the Chartists. [74] Fitzjames Stephen's prescriptions would probably have been endorsed by most had shooting actually started. But the year remained significant for many of the younger men, like A.V.Dicey, who dated from it their political conscious-ness. [75]

1848 was only one of several factors whose cumulative effect gave momentum to the liberal cause. The Corn Laws had just been repealed, and the resulting split in the Tory party led to the return of a Whig–Peelite majority in parliament, favourable to institution-al modernization. [76] The products of the reformed public schools, especially Rugby, were flowing into the universities. [77] Arnold himself had been appointed to the Regius Chair of History at Oxford in 1840, horrifying the High Church party. [78] His tenure was brief, as he died in 1842, but in 1844 Stanley published his *Life*, and created the Rugby legend. As far as liberalism was concerned, the legend had a solid basis of reality. The *Guardian* complained in 1848 of the school under Tait: 'Is there any political or religious theory on the so-called liberal side which might not find its supporters there?' [79] But, more important, the flight of the tractarians left college tuition to the young liberals. The Balliol of Oakeley and Ward became the Balliol of Lake, Edwin Palmer and Jowett. Ward's brilliant logical dogmatism – 'Believe in nothing or believe in the one true Church!' [80] – was replaced by Jowett's sympathetic cultivation of his pupils' abilities, and the wide speculation he at that time encouraged and himself indulged in. [81] Although the Oxford Greats course was conservative in its literary approach to the texts, its philosophical sections were increasingly studied, in the more progressive colleges, alongside and in the light of modern writers. The new generation of dons encouraged their charges, and kept them on a light rein. Along with the informality of studies, this led undergraduates into a latitude of speculation unthinkable a few years earlier. [82] The reliance an able undergraduate had to place on his own reading can be seen from the detailed book-lists which, fifteen years earlier, the young Gladstone kept. [83] Now that theology had been dethroned, this emphasis on self-culture led to the rapid absorption of contemporary liberal thought. The liberal lamp, slowly brightening at Cambridge among the Apostles, now began to flare up at Oxford. That 'young ardent soul looking with hope and joy into a world overclouded to the zenith and the nadir of it by incredible uncredited traditions, solemnly sordid hypocrisies, and beggarly deliriums old and new' [84] made his presence felt in common-rooms where only a year or so earlier the talk had been of Patristics and the Eucharist.

The secular intellect took time to establish itself. Meanwhile the 'healthy and natural instinct' to accept provisional solutions led many of the younger men to identify themselves with the theological and social views of the Broad Church. For five or six years after 1848 the influence, especially at Cambridge, of F.D.Maurice and the social and educational projects of the Christian Socialists demonstrated how the desire to realize a social role for the university temporarily overtook the progress of 'scientific' thought within it. It was the last attempt to envisage this role in religious terms.

V

Central to the Oxford Movement was the nature of religious authority. Its followers did not totally ignore social questions, but they pushed them to the side. There was no ideological connection between their theology and social intervention, no anticipation of the 'sacerdotal socialism' of late-nineteenth-century High-Churchmanship. Liddon was certainly a bitter opponent of the New Poor Law, [85] and Hurrell Froude apparently affected radicalism, [86] but their overall approach was not a distinctive one. In fact the leaders of the Movement – Marriott, Froude, Pusey and Keble – were, in 1836, active members of the Oxford Society for the Suppression of Mendicity, [87] formed with the best utilitarian and individualistic objects in view by the liberal Whately in 1828. [88]

On the other hand, social problems were a central concern of Broad Church theology. As Duncan Forbes has written, it sustained and befriended humanity where the Movement was disposed to oppose and correct. [89] Liberal Anglicans fused German idealist historical scholarship with the romantic conservatism of Coleridge to reject the concepts of 'progress' and 'civilization' associated with the Enlightenment, discovering instead merely a cyclical motion in which nations and civilizations arose, flourished, then fell back. [90] 'True progress' was therefore 'synonymous with the development of true religion, that is to say, with Christianity.' [91] The crises of the 1830s and 1840s seemed to indicate that the decline of English civilization was at hand, and that the responsibility for its redemption lay with the Church. 'Christianity is to be wrought out fully,' wrote Stanley, 'not by the destruction of the kingdoms of the world but by their adaptation with all their power, literature and institutions to its own divine ends.' [92] One such institution which could fruitfully be adapted was the university, and from its beginning in 1848 Christian Socialism – the practical embodiment of the Liberal Anglican ideal – drew heavily on the universities for its direction.

There was some enthusiasm for the industrial projects of the Christian Socialists at Oxford and Cambridge. Sympathizers wore strange clothes made by tailoring cooperatives,[93] which Edward Vansittart Neale of Oriel lost a fortune in promoting,[94] and several contributed to *Politics for the People*.[95] Christian Socialist ideas on cooperative production proved resilient, and recurred in the political schemes of academic liberals in the 1860s, but, on the whole, educational projects proved more attractive. Numbers of university men taught at the Working Men's College, founded by Maurice in 1854 – Chenevix-Trench, W.Johnson Cory, Nevil Story-Maskeleyne, Grant Duff, H.J.S.Smith, Charles Pearson[96] – and similar institutions were subsequently set up at Oxford and Cambridge. The Macmillan brothers, Montague Butler and Henry Sidgwick were involved in the Cambridge project[97] and Maskeleyne, Henry Smith, J.H.Bridges and George Brodrick in its Oxford counterpart.[98]

Christian Socialism marked a transitional stage in the liberalization of the universities. Politically, Maurice was a conservative who had rejected unitarian rationalism for the Coleridgeian concept of an ordered and organic community.[99] He was no subversive, wanting the Church 'fully to understand her own foundation, fully to work out the communism which is implied in her own existence.'[100] But he implied that it – and the university – should live up to the responsibilities they had previously shirked. The social implications of this were obvious.

Maurice's theology itself was attractive to a generation in recoil from dogmatism and beginning to worry about the effect of scientific method on religious belief. Leslie Stephen wrote that those of his contemporaries[101]

who were not prepared to 'swallow all formulas' and, like Herr Teufelsdroeck, strip themselves stark naked, read Coleridge, and found the most attractive contemporary leader in the admirable F.D.Maurice. He, they thought, might be taken as a guide to the promised land where orthodox dogma in alliance with philosophy could also be reconciled with science and criticism.

Despite his conservatism and timidity, Maurice was a sincere and attractive figure. He was also the victim of orthodoxy; in 1853 he was dismissed from the Chair of Theology at King's ollege, London. Persecution enhanced his appeal. Yet the affinity was temporary, the intersection of the constant of his mystic faith with the descending curve of their belief. Academics who were attracted to him because he promised to reconcile transcendent providence with humanist found that this merely became an act of semantic juggling: [102]

Look, he would say, at the plain words of scripture, and do you not find – it is hard to say what, but he used to imply, in various ways, that the simple natural sense of the words used was something quite different from what everyone habitually supposed it to be ... Does not Tweedledum rightly understood mean Tweedledee, and does not that make all the difference?

Liberal Anglicanism did not fail simply because its theology was inadequate. The crisis of civilization, which its ideologists believed to be impending, failed to materialize. The economy recovered from the depression of the forties, and, after the repeal of the Corn Laws and Navigation Acts, national prosperity seemed to vindicate rational liberalism. [103] The prophecies and programmes of the Liberal Anglicans 'ran into the sands'. [104] But the failure – unlike that of the Movement – caused little intellectual dislocation; among university men utilitarian logic, ethics and social philosophy were already elbowing out less systematic approaches.

Mark Pattison later claimed that there was a direct link between the domination of the clerical party at Oxford and the importance of intuitionism in the Schools: the secession of Newman meant the admission of Mill. In 1845 'Oxford repudiated at once sacerdotal principles and Kantian logic.' [105] While there is truth in this, the clinching argument the utilitarians could advance was one of practical success; and tutors like Jowett, alive to the future prospects of their charges, wanted to assimilate philosophy within the university to this prevalent pattern. Again the 'reasonable' argument: just as Paley regarded religion explicitly as a social control, so moderate reformers saw utilitarianism reinforcing existing institutions. Like their forebears, however, the younger academics were determined to 'go further'.

Herr Teufelsdroeck was Leslie Stephen's alternative to F.D. Maurice: evidence of a further powerful influence, Thomas Carlyle. Carlyle's view of society and his scathing indictment of the values of nineteenth-century liberalism – today possibly the most influential part of his writing – seem to have made little impression on the academics. But his reinterpretation of religion in terms of a secular standard of individual personality and effort struck home to the former Evangelical: [106]

You might return from the strange gleam and splendour of the

French Revolution or *Sartor Resartus* revolted or fascinated; but to read it with appreciation was to go through an intellectual crisis; and to enter into this spirit was to experience something like a religious conversion. You were not the same man afterwards. No one ever exercised such a potent sway over the inmost being of his disciples.

Stephen, although continually disagreeing with 'the old prophet', revered him, as did other university men whose philosophies differed widely from his, like T.H.Green and Edward Caird at Oxford. [107] Even Frederick Harrison, who regarded Carlyle's life as a tragedy of unbelief, wrote that 'in the period which separates the era of Bentham from the era of Darwin' his was the most potent and ennobling influence. [108] The disagreements were fundamental enough. When Leslie Stephen criticized his brother's anti-democratic polemic *Liberty, Equality, Fraternity* (1873) he attributed Fitzjames's backsliding to Carlyle's influence. [109] But the insistence on 'plain speaking', on casting off 'Hebrew old clothes', on fulfilment through personal effort rather than through obedience to received authority, both endorsed the developing case of the academic mind and provided significant additions to a new, secular vocabulary.

Carlyle's role in this development was not seminal, and less significant than his contribution to the criticism of industrial society by creative artists, writers and working-class leaders later in the century. [110] But at the universities his exhortations were listened to. He offered no solutions, but he adjured effort, truthfulness and moral courage. He was no friend to liberal individualism, but in the universities during the 1840s and 1850s he eased the transition to it.

VI

In 1843 John Stuart Mill published his *System of Logic*. Within a decade it had become, much to its author's surprise, the orthodoxy of reading men at the universities. [111] 'No-one', recalled the dying Henry Sidgwick in 1900, 'has ever had equal influence... since Mill's domination began to weaken.' [112] Leslie Stephen's Cambridge, John Morley's Oxford, alike regarded him as the ultimate court of appeal for all moral, political or philosophic questions: 'The summary answer to all hesitating proselytes was "read Mill!"' ' [113]

Why did Mill gain an authority denied to Bentham and his own father? This can only partly be explained by the increased receptivity of the universities to liberal ideas, what Mark Pattison called 'the slow process of innurition of the religious brain and development of the rational faculties'. [114] It also owed much to the relevance of Mill's own preoccupations, and the process by which he rationalized them into the agenda of the *Logic*, to the situation of the academics. [115]

The ideology Mill was subjected to in his youth was totally dissimilar to their own experience, [116] but the dislocation he suffered after his breakdown in 1826 resembled as well as anticipated their own situation a decade or so later, with one significant difference: Mill's own prescription for recovery was available to them. In revolt against the rigidity and philistinism of Benthamism, Mill encountered the same influences and 'provisional solutions' – the romantic poets, Coleridge, F.D.Maurice, Carlyle; he also involved himself, energetically though fruitlessly, in radical politics, on the ebb after 1832. [117] Out of this came his determination to formulate 'the logic of the moral sciences', to provide a more sophisticated groundwork for generalization about society and culture than Bentham or his father had done. [118] Mill had little respect for the universities, [119] but he was driven in this direction by the activities of three of Cambridge's ablest products, Macaulay, Adam Sedgwick and William Whewell. Macaulay's attack on James Mill's *Essay on Government* convinced him that 'my father's premises were really too narrow, and included but a small number of the general truths on which, in politics, the important consequences depend'. [120] The *Discourse on the Studies of the University of Cambridge*, published by the geologist Sedgwick in 1833 infuriated him by pre-empting the experimental sciences for intuitionism, a 'sentient principle within' the mind, arranging and therefore altering the stimuli it received. [121] To Mill, reared in the associationist psychology of David Hartley, intuitionism was 'the great intellectual support of false doctrines and bad institutions'. [122] Despite Sedgwick's liberalism, the prospect of the philosophy of science – at that time, in Britain at least, quite new – becoming dominated by intuitionism, appeared to Mill like a political defeat for radicalism. The appearance of Whewell's *History of the Inductive Sciences* strengthened this conviction. Whewell was a pioneer in the history of science, but he used intuitionism as an explicit reinforcement of his conservatism: 'I could not possibly believe', he wrote in 1842 to a friend, [123]

that Providence has thus enabled man to discover moral and social truth, and to embody it in his institutions, if I believed that man had as yet made no progress in doing this, and that the great step was still to be made – that we were to learn our duty and our work by some new lights entirely different from the old ones.

In comparison with Oxford conservatives Whewell was a moderate; as a scholar even Mill admitted himself in his debt. [124] But in terms of he organization and curriculum of the university he represented the limits of the old order: a little 'reverent' and (he hoped) final reform, and the avoidance for didactic purposes of 'subjects which were unsettled'. [125] To the younger academics he remained, first and foremost, the Master of Trinity.

With Mill, on the other hand, they could identify. Even if they subsequently disagreed with his interpretations and prescriptions, they shared his broad cultural and political concerns, attempted to emulate his powers of synthesis, and benefited by his range of reference, which his subsequent work on economics and ethics widened. He was, A.V.Dicey concluded, half a century later, 'a teacher created for, and assured of a welcome in, an age of transition'. [126] Dicey had reservations about Mill: his defence of intellectual liberty was energetic, but it appealed emotionally rather than convinced intellectually; his economics were vitiated by socialist and protectionist inconsistencies. [127] The approval of his juniors was itself ambiguous: reverence – notably for the *On Liberty* of 1859 – was combined with a highly selective endorsement of his ideas about politics and economics. [128] The influence of the *Logic* was itself idiosyncratic; it established the credentials of free inquiry, but it tended to inspire its readers to follow Mill's route out of mental and philosophical confusion rather than to re-examine his own premises and the utilitarian tradition on which he drew. The influence of Dicey's misleading account of Bentham in *Law and Opinion* is evidence enough of that. [129] The *Logic*, however, provided a synoptic view of authorities from whose influence the universities had too long been insulated; it was 'the opening of the shutters' on the new knowledge of Europe.

These authorities, in some cases, proved in the long run more influential than Mill himself; but his own approach both invited an 'experimental' commitment and paralleled the development of the academics' convictions. While working on the *Logic* he had been particularly intrigued by the Saint-Simonians and their division of history into critical and organic periods: critical periods occurred when an ideology which had made sense of the fixed relationships of an organic period no longer served, and had to be re-cast in the light of intellectual and social change. [130] Auguste Comte, Saint-Simon's disciple, elaborated this division by combining it with an evolutionary explanation of the development of human knowledge. Natural and social phenomena were interpreted first through theology, later through metaphysics, ultimately scientifically, or *positively*: [131]

The feudal and Catholic system was the concluding phase of the theological state of the social science, Protestantism the commencement, and the doctrines of the French Revolution the consummation of the metaphysical ... its positive state was yet to come.

Disenchanted with the conceptual narrowness of Benthamism, Mill believed that Comte's analysis indicated the possibility of real moral and intellectual progress. If squaring Bentham's politics with Coleridge's ideal of culture meant being inconsistent, this was a peculiarity of a critical period, which methodical research into science, ethics, psychology and society might overcome. Mill anticipated [132]

a future which shall unite the best qualities of the critical with the best qualities of the organic periods; unchecked liberty of thought, unbounded freedom of individual action in all modes not hurtful to others; but also, convictions as to what is right and wrong, useful and pernicious, deeply engraven on the feelings by early education and general unanimity of sentiment, and so firmly grounded in reason and in the true exigencies of life, that they shall not, like all former and present creeds, religious, ethical and political, require to be periodically thrown off and replaced by others.

There was a central inconsistency here, which Mill never really resolved, and which parted him from Comte. What was the connection between free inquiry and ethical conviction? If an ethical sense could be derived from fairly simple calculations of pleasure against pain, adapted into general sanctions by society, what value had speculation, which might unsettle society? Believing in the superior utility of intellectual cultivation, Mill followed Comte in arguing that 'the moral and intellectual ascendancy, once exercised by priests, must in time pass into the hands of philosophers', [133] but he drew back when faced with Comte's totalitarian elitism – 'the completest system of spiritual and temporal despotism which had ever yet emanated from a human brain'. [134] Indeed Comte promised to rival Bentham as a promoter of social uniformity. Mill's response was to stress individual liberty as a good in itself, and to rely increasingly on politics as an instrument to attain this end. [135] However internally inconsistent this position, it had attractions for academics reared to evangelical individualism, concerned about the future of their universities and their own role in the politics of a changing society. [136]

Comte's appeal was more enhanced by the publicity the positive philosophy received in Mill's *Logic* than damaged by his criticisms. [137] The Comtist contribution to academic liberal thought tended subsequently to be undervalued, largely by being identified only with the small but talented group who embraced religious positivism. Frederic Harrison, Edward Spencer Beesly and John Henry Bridges were introduced to positivism by Richard Congreve, Arnold's best pupil during his time at Rugby, while he was tutor at Wadham during the early 1850s. [138] Wadham was an Evangelical college; Congreve's acolytes were from Evangelical homes, so it is not surprising that on the whole they concentrated on the religious and propagandist aspects of Comte's system, rather than on his sociology. [139] Their conversion to religious positivism was gradual, however, and during the 1850s and 1860s they collaborated closely with academics of other persuasions, as well as with working-class organizations. The positivist church movement of the 1870s was essentially a withdrawal from politics which made them seem, in retrospect, more exclusive than they in fact were. [140] During the 1850s and 1860s numerous academics – Henry Sidgwick, Leslie Stephen, Goldwin Smith, Edward Caird among them – studied Comte seriously and with effect. 'I consider myself to have learnt very much from Comte,' Leslie Stephen wrote in 1882 to Henry Sidgwick, [141]

and I have a higher estimate of him than most people do, especially the scientific people who object to his religion. I only think that evolutionists have made his theory workable and have brought it into a quasi-scientific state more thoroughly than he could do. But I agree that most of my morality is contained in his.

And the Bostonian William Everett, regarded as a 'heretic or Socinian' Unitarian when he matriculated at Cambridge in 1859, found that the opinion of his contemporaries advanced so rapidly along 'positive – anti-religious – Spencerian Comtist' lines that 'they thought me antiquated in 1865 and a hopeless old tory in 1869'. [142] Comtism, however, could not totally satisfy the Evangelical conscience, either as historical explanation or as ethical precept. The concept of a 'science of ethics' – Leslie Stephen's title for the work defended in his letter to Sidgwick was itself significant enough – militated against the whole idea of morality, as Noel Annan has pointed out: [143]

Why should a man feel under a moral obligation when Nature is doing the job for him? Conscience in Stephen's ethics has become 'the utterance of the public spirit of the race, ordering us to obey the primary conditions of its welfare'. The law Do This has become Be This. Directly one substitutes the phrase You Must Do This for You Ought to Do This, ethics ceases to be ethics.

Goldwin Smith was less convinced; in his first lectures as Regius

Professor of History at Oxford he attacked the Comtist denial of free will, and the claim to assimilate the moral with the physical sciences. He argued that to deny the first, and admit that individuals make conscious choices about their conduct, implied denying the second. [144] Henry Sidgwick, a more orthodox utilitarian, later reached a similar position when he argued that 'rational self-interest', the basis of scientific utilitarianism, provided an imperfect guide to individual conduct. A dichotomy existed between 'the natural end of action – private happiness, and the end of duty – general happiness'; man was not obliged to serve society by serving himself, but could choose or ignore the obligations of a dutiful citizen. [145] This restitution of free will made social progress contingent upon such obligations being met, and deprived it of any claim to obey rigid laws. It became the task of the philosopher to determine the limits of common-sense morality, the point at which decisions had to be taken with reference to their consequences for a changing society. 'Impartial reflection on current opinion', social forecasting based on probabilities suggested by the observation of past and present social behaviour, were the preoccupations of moralist and historian alike. [146] 'History', according to Smith, [147]

can never be a science. It is, however, fast becoming a philosophy, having for its basis the tendencies of our social nature, and for the objects of its research the correlation of events, the march of human progress in the race and in the separate nations, and the effects, good or evil, of all the various influences which from age to age have been brought to bear on the character, mind and condition of man.

Goldwin Smith was not a profound thinker – 'The last of our great pamphleteers' A.V. Dicey called him [148] – and his younger contemporaries took the value of historical studies more seriously, yet he resembled them in combining a belief in free will with a conviction that the study of history was an essential guide to practical statecraft. [149] If they rejected its ideology, they accepted the scope and methods of positivist inquiry, and emphasized the 'understanding' gained through accumulating facts and generalizing systematically from them.

In this situation they required a guide to practical research, and found him in Alexis de Tocqueville. In 1861 Henry Sidgwick cited, with approval, de Tocqueville's description of his method: [150]

I investigate, I experimentalise: I try to grasp facts more closely than has yet been attempted, and to wring out of them the general truths which they contain ... I make the utmost efforts to ascertain from contemporary evidence what really happened; and often to

43

spend great labour in discovering what was ready to my hand. When I have gathered in this toilsome harvest, I retire, as it were, into myself: I examine with extreme care, collate and correct the notions which I have acquired, and simply give the result.

This was typical enough of the approach of Sidgwick's own generation, of Bryce, Dicey, J.R.Green, George Otto Trevelyan and John Morley in their scholarly work, and of British historians of the late nineteenth century in general. It was consummated in the programme of the *English Historical Review* (1886) – 'the object of history is to discover and set forth facts' [151] – and the *Cambridge Modern History* (1899). Lord Acton, its editor, conceived 'ultimate history' simply as an extension of 'conventional history', and concluded that 'all information is within reach, and every problem has become capable of solution'. [152] Acton had little time for Goldwin Smith, but this ambition differed little from the 'philosophy of history' Smith had visualized in 1859 as evolving from the analyses of differing schools. [153] The 'metaphysical school of Hegel' and the 'positive school of Comte' could alike contribute. [154]

... though they may be often, though they may hitherto always have been under the perverse guidance of theories more or less one-sided, crude or fantastic, [they] are yet finding a chemistry through their alchemy, and bringing out with their heap of dross grain after grain of sterling gold.

VII

Historical studies were increasingly regarded as an appropriate vocational training for future politicians and administrators; philosophy was more controversial. [155] But by the 1860s dons were, as a rule, indifferent to the religious questions agitated by their predecessors. Dicey and Fawcett remained nominal Christians but cared little for dogma. [156] H.A.L.Fisher found Bryce 'curiously exempt from metaphysical doubts and scruples'. Leslie Stephen and Thorold Rogers promoted the Clerical Disabilities Act of 1871, which allowed clergymen to resign their orders. [157] They were not the only university men to take advantage of it: others included J.R.Green and Arthur Acland at Oxford, John Venn, Edward Carpenter and Charles Kegan Paul at Cambridge. [158] Younger men, like F.H.Bradley and Bernard Bosanquet, who had matriculated in the 1860s with the intention of becoming clergymen, did not proceed to ordination. [159] Partly this was because of the increasing secularization of colleges: the more liberals there were among the seniors, the further the statutes would be stretched to accommodate potential lay fellows, but generally it indicated the decline of philosophies rooted in transcendental values. Although J.A.Symonds wrote that at Oxford in the early 1860s theology cropped up 'at Breakfast parties and at wine parties, out riding and walking, in college gardens, on the river, whenever young men and their elders met together', [160] what he in fact meant was religious politics. The subjects which James Bryce recollected as occupying his mind during his student days were nearly all to do with religion, but one of them – 'the deliverance of the university from clericalism and its popularisation' – pretty adequately describes the rest. [161]

But a religious problem remained. In 1865 Henry Nettleship wrote to Bryce, analysing to destruction the various church factions – biblical critics, 'reasonable' apologists for religion as social discipline, Evangelicals. None seemed to measure up to J.H.Newman's definition of an authority: [162]

Once allow that a thing can be a matter of discussion, and it ceases, from physical or psychological causes, to be an authority. With good cause do the Catholics sneer at the human reason. When once a man is engaged in honest discussion he has admitted the possibility that he may himself be wrong: he has already assumed an authority to which that which he is endeavouring to prove must be subordinate.

He ended: 'I think a kind of poetical materialism, a sort of moral and spiritual Darwinism, might be very interesting to go in for.' His tone was flippant, but his concern serious: 'For something I must have which must speak to me and my age.'

Charles Darwin and Alfred Russel Wallace published their evolutionary studies in 1859, and the battle between religious orthodoxy and free inquiry was joined. The influence of this struggle was important in two respects: it demonstrated that the opponents of university reform would also oppose, and would use traditional privilege to suppress, scientific advance when its conclusions did not concur with dogma. Secondly, by polarizing the debate, it diminished the power of 'reasonable' reformers, and so ensured that the university liberalism of the 1860s supplemented its scientific methods with a political programme.

Science and clericalism collided at the 1860 meeting of the British Association at Oxford. Samuel Wilberforce, Bishop of Oxford, a popular and not wholly illiberal clergyman and favourite of Gladstone, attacked the evolutionary theory in knockabout Union style. He was magisterially rebuked by T.H.Huxley, before an audience which included a number of young university men, T.H. and J.R.Green and Henry Fawcett among them. Robinson Ellis, the future Professor of Latin, wrote to Bryce: [163]

I thought his speech exceedingly effective. It was the triumph of reason against Rhetoric – not so much that the Bp of Oxford had confined himself to Rhetoric, as that he is by nature a Rhetorician and cannot get out of that style. The Bp again replied and was again answered – and altogether got the worst of it. I came away with a strong impression in favour of the Darwin theory.

To Ellis the theory of evolution was not the main issue – Darwin himself was, at that stage, more applauded than understood by many academics [164] – but rather the principle of free inquiry, defended only a year earlier by Mill in his *Liberty*. The Wilberforce – Huxley confrontation merely personalized a conflict which had been intensifying within the universities themselves.

Reacting against the reforms of the commissions, in the later 1850s the clerical party, Evangelical and Tractarian, formed a defensive alliance, 'an ecclesiastical Ring' as Mark Pattison was – in the slang of American politics – to christen it. [165] The resolution of liberal church-men was correspondingly stiffened. They became, in Jowett's words, [166]

determined not to submit to this abominable system of terrorism, which prevents the statement of the plainest facts, and makes true theology or theological education impossible.

The clericals, ably led by H.L.Mansel, used the Church's remaining prerogatives against the liberals: Convocation refused for ten years to pay Jowett his stipend as Professor of Greek; the great German philologist Max Müller was rejected for the Sanskrit chair, and a safe Evangelical appointed. [167] 'The effervescence of their spirituality has passed away,' wrote Stanley, 'and cunning, and activity, and political tactics, have filled up the vacuum.' [168]

The liberal counter-attack took the form of *Essays and Reviews*, published in 1860, a deliberate provocation to the clerical party. The seven contributors more or less restated the Liberal anglican world-view, that a rational study of the Bible would reveal the divine purpose at work in the history of the Jews. 'It is to be interpreted', Jowett explained, [169]

like other books, with attention to the character of its authors, and the prevailing stage of civilisation and knowledge, and with allowance for peculiarities of style and language, and modes of thought and figures of speech. Yet not without a sense that as we read there grows upon us the witness of God in the world, anticipating in a rude and primitive age the truth that was to be ...

This programme required the liberation of scholarship from the dominion of High Church interpretations of the fathers, and the Evangelical insistence on the literal interpretation of scripture. But it assumed that a national church could still play a leading role in the universities, provided that its more flexible doctrines could attract a greater breadth of opinion within its ranks. It was essentially from this standpoint that the Broad Churchmen saw university reform.

Essays and Reviews appeared in February, was reprinted in the summer, but aroused little attention. [170] In October, however, the second edition was reviewed in the *Westminster* in an article entitled 'Neo-Christianity'. Its anonymous author, 'a very clever man, but not one much known', [171] proved to be Frederic Harrison, then twenty-nine and a fellow of Wadham. His criticisms excited 'the entire sympathy and concurrence' of Huxley, and brought on the essayists the outrage of the clergy. [172]

Harrison attacked from a Comtist position, but his arguments would have been shared by most of his contemporaries. He was almost straightforwardly Evangelical: grafting rationalism on to popular Christianity would not enhance it, but simply repel the public by qualification, confusion and indecisiveness, when it wanted certainty of belief and hard-and-fast rules of conduct. [173] A religion deprived of all authority save what it had in common with secular philosophy had no greater validity than its rival. [174] Further, using the Bible as an example of the divine will embodied in history adopted 'the positivist conception of mankind as a colossal man possessing life, and growth, and mind', but rejected universal history for a narrow and arbitrary selection of the Hebrews, Rome, Greece and Asia (Babylonia and Assyria) as 'the four great educators of the human race'. [175] Liberal Anglicanism therefore turned out to be neither rational nor religious.

In the short term Harrison's article propelled the clerical party, led by Bishop Wilberforce, to hound the contributors for heresy: Jowett, Bristow Wilson and Rowland Williams suffering prosecution. [176] But, more significantly, the fact that the Broad Churchmen had to be rescued by the younger men, like Fitzjames Stephen and Harrison himself, who gave 'time, money and every assistance ...to resist the odious persecution', meant that the leadership of the party of free inquiry passed out of their hands. [177] The defence of the essayists led directly to the campaign to abolish the Tests, and the leadership in both cases came from young, secular liberals (See chapter 4). The 'reasonable' containment of speculation within a 'broad' national church and its universities was supplanted by the ideal of the universities as lay seminaries and centres of social inquiry.

'Reasonable' religion as a means of social control maintained, however, a ghostly existence as a pessimistic alternative to democratic politics. Henry Sidgwick, who had justified religion in 1864 as 'the only real elevator ... of the sensual herd', [178] restated the argument in 1886 – a significant enough date: [179]

I find that I grow more and more, on the one hand, to regard Christianity as indispensable and irreplaceable – looking at it from a sociological point of view – and on the other hand to find it more and more incomprehensible how anyone whom I feel to be really akin to myself in intellectual habits and culture can possibly find his religion in this singular.

Fitzjames Stephen's attitude to religion was roughly similar, and his determination to persist in its forms more resolute. [180] But, even when its ideology was under threat, the generation of the 1860s found it difficult to argue in other than political terms. For the last thirty years of their lives James Bryce and A. V. Dicey expressed increasing disquiet about the tendencies of democratic government, but their remedies remained political; they never invoked religious authority. (Indeed, they tended to link religious revival with the spread of socialist ideas.) [181] There can be no greater tribute to the tenacity of their convictions.

VIII

The intellectual character of academic liberalism in the 1860s – the emphasis on individual conviction and responsibility, the concern to project these values into society, to further its moral health – derived from the evangelical impulse of family and home. It developed through interaction with the university and with external social and intellectual change. The Oxford Movement, which institutionalized this concern, also liberated academic thought from party control, in a conservative synthesis of university and society. When this collapsed, liberalism inevitably benefited. Initially concerned to revise religious doctrine, liberalism rapidly assimilated influential secular explanations of social change, and commited itself to incorporating these within the teaching and research of the universities.

In a speech on America delivered in 1864 Richard Cobden condemned the classical bias of university study. [182] To Matthew Arnold this demonstrated the antipathy of radicals for liberal culture. [183] But Cobden was in fact endorsing what Goldwin smith had said in his Inaugural: more utilitarianism, more relevance was needed in university teaching, otherwise [184]

... the great places of national education may avoid Utilitarianism till Government is in the hands of ambitious ignorance, till the Bench of Justice is filled with pettifoggers, till coarse cupidity and ignorance stand beside the sick-bed, till all the great levers of opinion are in low, uneducated hands.

Not Culture but Anarchy, in other words, would follow. Cobden recognized that radicalism would gain by a regenerated university. His peroration was a ringing endorsement: [185]

... and I say, where you can find men who, like Professor Goldwin Smith or Professor Rogers of Oxford, have a vast knowledge of modern affairs, and who, as well as scholars, are at the same time thinkers, these are men I acknowledge to have a vast superiority over me.

The leader of radicalism had admitted the claim of the university liberals to mediate between culture and the forces of social change. From this really dates the self-consciousness and selfconfidence of the university liberal movement.

[3]

THE
UNIVERSITY
CONTEXT

There is little I need ask about Oxford
and its little systems of luminaries.

Frederic Harrison J.H.Bridges, 11 November 1855

Ideology cannot be separated from environment: mid-century academic liberalism was not simply a projection of political and educational concepts but the product of a distinctive university tradition. Reform altered, but did not destroy, this institutional context. In turn, its influence persisted: [1]

Most of the great names usually associated with nineteenth-century university reform are those of men who had trod the traditional upper-class pathway through public school and wealthy residential college, and who, despite their discontent with the existing state of things, were so conditioned as to be incapable of a completely fresh outlook.

Bagehot noticed this in the 1850s; [2] half a century later James Bryce demonstrated it. Theoretically committed to a flexible, comprehensive system of higher education after the Scottish pattern, his deepest loyalties lay with Oxford, with his contemporaries 'who came from the English Universities into public life and infused into it the spirit of the high standard they owned'. [3]

If Oxford impressed itself so strongly on the product of a different and equally distinguished tradition, it is not surprising that Bryce's contemporaries lived in the psychological shadow, if not in the actual neighbourhood, of the two old universities. Condemning his friend Fawcett's academic conservatism and the enervation of Cambridge, [4] Leslie Stephen broke away to the literary society of London, but in his old age he looked back with affection. [5] Henry Sidgwick fretted in Cambridge in the late 1880s, continually talked of leaving, but he stayed. [6] To the end the liberals remained in the ambit of their colleges, their academic dining clubs, their university friends, the academic politics of the day. Their loyalty transcended any educational programme and after 1886 any political differences. As octogenarians Bryce and Dicey, who had been politically opposed for upwards of thirty years, would still make demanding journeys to the Ad Eundem club dinners, [7] and Sir Maurice Bowra recollected the appearance of the ninety-two-year-old Frederic Harrison at the first Wadham feast he attended as a fellow. [8] When Swinburne died in 1909 Bryce wrote to Dicey that [9]

on the whole there doesn't seem to have been any period at Oxford that produced quite so many singular figures who have been heard of as that which began about 1850 and lasted for some ten years or so.

The correspondence which passed between them during the remainder of their lives is in some ways a sustained valediction on this generation.

II

The explanation of this loyalty is surely that Oxford and Cambridge, unlike other British universities, were total experiences. Both towns had no existence apart from the universities. Only St Andrews was similarly placed, but it was tiny and declining. [10] The university at Edinburgh was simply part of a complex civic life of literary and scientific associations, publishers, legal and religious institutions: [11] Oxford and Cambridge were their universities and no more. If a gifted scholar, or at any rate someone who wasn't prepared to idle away three years in 'a pleasant hotel by the banks of the Cam' [12] (or the Thames) wanted to benefit from either place, he had to exploit the university and its residents or go elsewhere. Given the low level of studies prevalent in the eighteenth century he probably would, like Johnson or Gibbon, do just that. But with the higher standards of the later nineteenth century, Oxford and Cambridge, with their hierarchies of scholarships, Fellowships, lectureships and professorships, could keep him there for life. Even if he did move, he could still retain links through a Fellowship or an Honorary Fellowship.

The liberals' attachment was scarcely the aesthetic one of Morris and later Manley Hopkins, as witness the hideous villas of North Oxford and the Madingley Road, nor did they share Gladstone's religious devotion to 'the God-fearing, God-sustaining university of Oxford'. [13] Their reasons were more tangible. The university conferred substantial benefits on professional men. George Brodrick, defending prize-Fellowships from the attack of Pattison and his colleagues in the 1870s argued that most non-resident fellows were [14]

earnestly and honourably employed, being very often indebted to their fellowships alone for the means of subsistence during the earlier stages of their professional careers.

But status as well as money was conferred. The men of whom Brodrick wrote, 'drawn from the hard-working professional class' were seldom 'in possession of or heir to a considerable fortune'. [15] Even if successful in public life, they had to live modestly: a small house or flat in central London, an Oxford monster, a suburban villa like Bryce's at Forest Row; these were possible, a country estate was not. A Fellowship supplied not only an additional social centre, in the college, but an acceptable register of status in the eyes of respectable society; hospitality could be reciprocated, patronage could be avoided. The liberal academics balanced delicately between the great salons of the political aristocracy and the fellowship of the goosequill, between Trollope's Pallisers and Thackeray's Pendennis. They were neither political partisans or Grub Street roués. They could participate in politics, law and literature; they were not dominated by them. For their chosen work, they had the capacity and application this flexibility offered. Whether it helped them to understand the average elector's perception of the political problems they pronounced on is another and more debatable matter. [16]

III

Consciousness of generation was apparent, in almost harrowing terms, in the later years of Dicey, Bryce, Henry Jackson and George Otto Trevelyan, but it was not simply a function of ageing. [17] It had been explicit enough in the 1860s, in what Sidgwick, borrowing Cicero's description of the Indian summer of republican Rome, called 'the consulship of Plancus'. [18] All but three of the fifteen academic writers of the 1867 reform essays were born between 1828 and 1838, and the provisional committee which supervised the Tests agitation were their direct contemporaries (see appendix 2). The leader of the latter group, Charles Roundell, had to work hard in 1865 to convince Gladstone of the existence of a liberal generation 'in possession of the colleges through the Fellowships', but he did not have to be convinced himself. [19]

With the Tractarian generation the younger liberals had, in fact, few contacts. They even tended to regard older liberals with some suspicion, unless, like Goldwin Smith, Jowett and John Conington, they set out to cultivate the younger men. Arnold's 'kid-gloved' dandyism, Pattison's cynicism, Freeman's idiosyncratic High Church radicalism, kept them apart from their juniors. [20] Freeman himself had little time for the aggressive secularism of 'the young monkeys at Balliol': 'their liberalism consists in expecting everybody to think as they do theologically'.[21] To him liberalism was an endorsement of pluralism, to them a scientific ideology, a total view of the relationship of political, ethical and religious thought. They found it difficult to appreciate logically untenable positions. Hence their respect for J.H.Newman, because he epitomized his genera- tion's response to the university problem, and their neglect of his radical brother Franncis – admittedly a crotchety character, but the same could be said of many of them – largely because his views were, for their time, anachronistic. [22] The younger men saw their generation as the product of definite philosophical and institutional advances. On the whole they did not want to attach themselves to a teacher – even to Mill – and they remained suspicious of liberals who reached their position by a different route.

Their connections with their juniors were closer. F.W.Maitland was Leslie Stephen's biographer, his brother-in-law, H.A.L.Fisher, wrote Bryce's life and men from different generations collaborated fairly closely in various academic and political projects towards the end of the century. [23] The Ad Eundem Club (of which more later) included some of the younger men like G.M.Trevelyan, Fisher and R.R.Marrett the anthropologist (although not enough to prevent it from folding when the older men died off). [24] But they tended still to stand *in statu pupillari*. There was a distinct hiatus between the generation of the 1860s, born between 1825 and 1845, and the generation of G.M.Trevelyan, G.E.Moore, Gilbert Murray, Michael Sadler, Bertrand Russell and H.A.L.Fisher, born between 1860 and 1880. The intervening period was not devoid of able men – Bernard Bosanquet, Arnold Toynbee and Maitland were born around 1850 – but they were never a large or self-conscious group.

The liberal generation was extensive in a lateral, geographical sense; it linked both universities and extended to the capital. Before 1850 a don occupying a law Fellowship could live off his endow- ment in London; the reforming commissions greatly increased the number of foundation fellows who could do this, and for a couple of decades the lay fellow was a common feature of the metropolitan political and literary world. When Edward Spencer Beesly consi- dered founding a radical dining club – ultimately the Century – in London in 1865, he wrote to Henry Crompton that its members 'seem likely to be almost entirely university men such as Brodrick, Bowen and the Lushingtons, etc., but Huxley, H.Spencer, Lewes and such men might be induced to join'. [25] Brodrick himself believed that the non-resident Fellow elevated professional life in England to a status far superior to its American equivalent. He was certainly the most energetic element in the liberal alliance of the 1860s, the fulcrum on which its political and academic campaigns turned.

This preliminary survey raises further questions. How did the academic environment come to leave its imprint? Why in the first place was it chosen at all? Why the distinctive generation consciousness? Why the end of the universities' isolation from metropolitan culture? Examination of these problems should deepen our understanding of the mechanics of intellectual change, and focus the relationships, social and institutional, which constituted the matrix of academic liberalism.

IV

In the forties we are aware of a new type issuing from the universities and the public schools, somewhat arrogant and somewhat shy, very conscious of their standing as gentlemen but very conscious of their duties too, men in tweeds who smoke in the streets, disciples of Maurice, willing hearers of Carlyle, passionate for drains and co-operative societies, disposed to bring everything in the state of England to the test of Isaiah and Thucydides, and to find the source of all its defects in what, with youthful violence, they would call the disgusting vice of shopkeeping. These are the Arnoldians.

G.M.Young's sketch was not far from the mark; of academic liberals who attended public schools, Rugbeians were handsomely in the majority. [26] But it would be wrong to see this as a predominant influence in their childhood. Evangelical parents regarded such schools, with reason, as nurseries of vice and violence. [27] Rather fewer of their sons attended, compared with the average university intake of the time; many were educated at home, by relatives or by private tutors. [28] A.V.Dicey brooded on this towards the end of his life. He concluded that 'boys who were detached to a great extent from the influence of training in a public school came to share the political and moral discussion and thoughts which prevailed at home.' [29] Political convictions owed as much to family background as to schooling; especially since family preference governed the choice of school. Yet such pious and conscientious parents then sent their sons to institutions where undergraduate liberty agreeably coexisted with a low level of scholarship. Despite his low opinion of Cambridge, Sir James

Stephen sent both his sons there, when he had earlier removed them from Eton. [30] Why?

The explanation lay in the assumptions of the Evangelical revival. Upper-class Evangelicals wanted to promote moral reformation within the existing social structure; the universities were one of its central components. Even at the nadir of their reputation they brought young men of the ruling classes under a common if loose discipline at the most impressionable stage of their lives, an activity which the reforming commissions of the 1850s applauded: [31]

undergraduates belonging to the superior ranks of society are entrusted to instructors of real knowledge and tried principles; they mix with a number of young men of their own age but from different ranks, and by this freedom of intercourse acquire both larger ideas and kindlier feelings; they are taught to appreciate, and so to cherish, the institutions of their country, while yet they claim for themselves, and learn to concede to others, that liberty and latitude of opinion without which neither truth can be elicited nor improvement forwarded.

Although Evangelicals would wince at 'liberty and latitude of opinion', they valued the universities as fertile grounds for proselytism among the future leaders of society, as well as an essential preliminary to taking orders. [32] Hence the activities of Simeon and his followers at Cambridge and young John Henry Newman's hopes for the conversion of Oxford. By the next generation proselytism was being replaced by reformism. Some very devout parents, like the fathers of Beesly and J.H.Bridges, sent their sons to an impeccably Evangelical college, like Warden Symons's Wadham, but the majority wanted assurances of sound teaching and discipline. [33]

They had to be discriminating. Goldwin Smith, who matriculated at Christ Church in 1841, found that at Oxford the power of the colleges was unchecked, fellowships 'were saddled with all the preferences for birthplace, place of education, kinship or poverty, in which the partiality of a founder, in an age little regardful of differences of intellect, had thought it harmless to indulge'. Discipline was imperfectly maintained by old statutes, the professoriate was almost dead. 'Worst of all ... the University, instead of being as it had once been, a place of general learning, science and education, had become the citadel of ecclesiasticism and the arena of ecclesiastical dispute.' [34] Isolated, conservative, introverted: on the whole, Smith's contemporaries shared his opinion of the place. But his own experience was of two colleges – Christ Church and Magdalen – whose predicament was extreme; [35] elsewhere the local enlightenment of college and tutor benefited many. The liberal cause progressed by the interlinking of such developments. Until the mid-century, reform at the universities was neither general nor uniform, but this cellular growth at least provided it with a tolerable environment.

Goldwin Smith's Oxford was at least an improvement on the university as Sir William Hamilton had found it, when he migrated from Glasgow to Balliol in 1807. His assault, in the *Edinburgh Review* in 1831, Newman termed 'the storm from the North', the intellectual equivalent of the Whigs' attack on the Church. [36] Smith only repeated the indictment in a muted form, but he, and Stanley and Jowett, attacked from within. In the 1800s even a reformer like Provost Coplestone of Oriel had defended Oxford against the *Edinburgh Review*; [37] institutional patriotism had stimulated Whewell and Sedgwick's defence of Cambridge against Hamilton in the 1830s. [38] But a decade later the most sustained criticism was coming from the old universities themselves, as fellows and tutors of reform-minded colleges reconsidered their functions.

At the end of the eighteenth century there had been stirrings. Written degree examinations replaced archaic verbal 'disputations'. Some colleges independently reformed their scholarship and Fellowship regulations: Balliol and Oriel at Oxford, and Trinity at Cambridge, replaced local and institutional preferences by open competition. The principle of examination was, and remained, controversial; it could lead to mindless cramming, and was later the subject of fierce debate among academic liberals. [39] Fellowship reform could, by itself, end simply by endowing London professional men and Oxbridge coaches. But such reforms gave the more able graduates reason to maintain links with the universities. For Newman the Oriel dons – Noetic and Tractarian – made possible the defence of the university against Hamilton's attack. For the Tractarian that might have been sufficient – Newman had no wish to liberalize the university – but his own efforts scarcely won the praise of the old 'high and dry' party. Whately once invited him to a party made up exclusively of dense, drunken dons. These, he pointed out, were what Newman was defending. [40] The party of movement was still distinct from the party of torpor, which didn't want intellectual conservatism, and destroyed Newman and his friends when they tried to make it into an ideology. Newman had some illusions about the capacity of the mass of clerical graduates; his liberal successors had not. They detested the clerical majority in Convocation – 'they think that education is a bad thing, but that justice is worse' Charles Bowen told Grant Duff. [41] This animus was one of liberalism's less attractive characteristics: looking back on the heresy-hunting of the early sixties, Frederick Harrison and Leslie Stephen allowed that the clergy were entitled to react the way they did. [42] But the distinction between liberal elite and pollmen was important, and originated in the essentially collegiate nature of the reform movement prior to the 1850s.

Both universities had 'liberal' and 'conservative' colleges: university election pollbooks enable the strength of the parties at each foundation to be quantified. There were significant differences between Cambridge and Oxford. Until the reforms of 1882 Cambridge colleges usually elected their Fellows only from their own graduates, while Oxford colleges, with the exception of Corpus Christi, were free to elect whom they pleased. [43] This was because Oxford colleges were all roughly the same size, with the exception of Christ Church, whose government was unique, while at Cambridge Trinity and St John's, by far the most radical colleges, were also extremely large. Other foundations feared the possibility of a takeover. In post-1854 Oxford the more radical colleges, like Balliol, used competitive fellowship examinations to colonize other foundations; [44] at Cambridge exclusiveness was maintained. [45] In Oxford liberalism gradually pervaded even the most backward colleges, like Magdalen and St John's, but at Cambridge, even in the early 1880s, there was an enormous difference between Trinity, where the liberals had a 2:1 majority, and Corpus Christi, with only one liberal fellow among ten. [46] Cambridge liberalism depended on action within the colleges, at Oxford the battlefield was university-wide. The reforms of the 1850s at Cambridge guaranteed a partition between liberals and conservatives, with the latter retreating into the colleges they could still hold. At Oxford this security was denied them, and their reaction was predictably desperate.

Such differences were complemented by the gulf between 'reading men' and 'pollmen', between those who wanted to derive educational benefits from the university, and those to whom the university was simply a social experience. There was little contact between the two groups. James Bryce, 'a Trinity scholar and in addition a member of the intellectual Balliol set', had not, according to H.A.L.Fisher 'a very large or diversified circle of acquaintance in the undergraduate world'.[47] Scholarships were important in this. Two thirds of the liberals who attended the Freemasons' Tavern meeting in 1864 had held them (see appendix 2). [48] In a backward college, where local or institutional preferences still held, scholars were little different from ordinary undergraduates, but in, say, post-1800 Balliol they enjoyed almost the prestige of Fellows, being similarly selected by open competition. [49] This identification was important: the scholars and the younger dons would go on reading parties together, the dons took private pupils, still spoke at Union debates and took part in undergraduate societies and dining clubs. Organized sport, which led to the growth of 'undergraduate consciousness', had yet to become obsessive. The concept of 'godliness and good learning' fostered by Thomas Arnold and his disciples, positing an intellectual and moral elitism, was still important. [50] Things were different at Cambridge; Trinity and St John's were so large that the younger dons had enough contemporaries to make them independent of their juniors. Leslie Stephen, in his incarnation as the 'rowing rough' of Trinity Hall, bawling at his crews from the towpath, was to some extent an exception to this rule, but he had failed to be accepted by the 'Trinity set' and the all-important Apostles. [51] His Trinity brother Fitzjames, however, managed to be not only an Apostle but a member of the Oxford Tugendbund as well. [52] The organizations of the reading men overcame not only collegiate but university boundaries.

Charles Henry Pearson, a pretty corrosive critic of Victorian education, thought 'the only real advantage of Oxford ... was in the opportunities it gave for social intercourse'. [53] Yet even he admitted that the reform of the tutorial system, notably at Balliol, was having a beneficial effect on men who might otherwise have fallen victim to intellectual inertia. [54] Parents whose sons experienced the rigours of a home education or the Arnoldian revolution in public-school attitudes to responsibility and discipline, saw the college tutor as a less formal equivalent to the public-school master. *In loco parentis* was a position that the tutor of the 'reformed' colleges was prepared to occupy. The revival of studies in Greek ethics further endowed him with the personality of the Socratic teacher, surrounded by his students, debating with and counselling them. [55] For the retreat from dogma implied no easy-going tolerance where undergraduate discipline and work were concerned. Jowett's admonitions to his young men were famous, but not unique. [56] Discussing college reform in the 1850s both Frederic Harrison at Oxford and Henry Jackson at Cambridge put their faith 'in the effect of a character for careful superintendence and strict moral discipline and diligence'.[57]

Finally, Oxford and Cambridge offered parents the prospect of endowment for their sons' careers. In the 1860s academic liberals made much of the fact that nonconformist graduates, however brilliant, forfeited these 'rewards of scholarship'; [58] this doubtless influenced their parents to send them to the old universities rather than to London, Edinburgh or abroad, provided adequate standards of examination, tuition and discipline were available. The bribe of endowment was probably by itself insufficient – although status through scholarship was a difficult proposition to refuse – but in conjunction with the other requirements it must have been infallibly persuasive.

V

Academic liberals knew each other as friends and contemporaries. But they were also bound together by a network of relationships complex enough to endure for decades, which became a dominant influence in their lives outside the universities. Personality and habit were important, but these existed within the matrix formed by the central problem of the universities, progress and society – the common consciousness of university liberalism, which other relationships could enhance and define, but never by themselves replace. Although family and school were important, their influence was limited: William Wilberforce's Evangelicalism did not prevent some of his children seceding to Rome; Thomas Arnold's injunctions did not inoculate Arthur Hugh Clough against the contagion of the Oxford Movement.

The intermarriage of families in one generation will produce subsequent generations of children who will find themselves roughly of an age with each other. The intermarriage of the 'Clapham Sect' and its friends at the end of the eighteenth century produced the remarkable ramifications of the 'Intellectual Aristocracy' whose generations broke like waves on the nineteenth century. [59] Stephens, Venns, Macaulays, Butlers, Trevelyans – the families extended their social coverage and intensified their internal relationships, decade by decade. This process in a sense paralleled the 'nationalizing' of the universities, in homogenizing Quakers, Evangelicals, Unitarians into a national intellectual class, secure enough by the 1860s for one of its members, Francis Galton, to examine it with scientific detatchment. His eugenic theories might not generally be shared, but such family alliances served the unity of the university liberals. The Diceys were by no means untypical. Thomas Edward Dicey, proprietor of the *Northampton Mercury*, descended from a pedlar of patent medicines, married to a Stephen, sent one son, Edward, born in 1832, to Trinity, Cambridge, and the other, Albert Venn, born in

1835, to Balliol. Edward was a contemporary of his cousin Leslie Stephen, then at Trinity Hall, whose brother Fitzjames had just left Trinity; another cousin, John Venn, would shortly matriculate at Caius. Somewhat older was Henry Smith at Balliol, a relative by marriage. Through his father, Fitzjames came to know Henry Cunningham, the son of the Rev. John Cunningham, proprietor of the Evangelical paper the *Christian Observer*. He married Cunningham's sister. Cunningham was a member of the Oxford Essay Society, along with Brodrick, Arthur Butler, Goschen, Charles Stuart Parker, Pearson, W.L.Newman, Frederic Harrison and Godfrey Lushington, most of whom could claim Evangelical if not Clapham forebears. Along with Goschen, Grant Duff, Pearson and Parker, Stephen was a member of the earlier Oxford Tugend- bund. [60] A stranger from a different environment, James Bryce for instance, could, simply through his friendship with Albert Dicey, gain access to this cousinhood; several such friendships created an elaborate mesh of family connections which enveloped both univer- sities. Two family connections were particularly important: Henry and Arthur Sidgwick went to Trinity, Cambridge, their elder brother William to Merton, Oxford. In 1864 the three brothers were instrumental in founding the Ad Eundem Club to unite the liberals of both universities, [61] and later William and Henry were founder- members of the Radical Club, aimed at uniting university liberals with parliamentary radicals. (see p. 187). Vernon Lushington, the twin brother of Godfrey, went to Trinity, Cambridge, and adopted Comtism also. [62] He too was an early member of the Ad Eundem, and was probably responsible for relaying to Cambridge much of the positivist doctrine which Everett found pervaded the place in the 1860s. [63]

Being educated at a wider range of institutions than their contemporaries, school acquaintanceships were less important for them. 'Arnoldian' influence ensured a certain ideological identity, but this should not be overvalued: several old Rugbeians – Henry Sidgwick, Charles Pearson and T.H.Green – disliked the place and were suspicious of the Arnoldian ethos. [64] But they had gained the friendship of other serious young men, and avoided the brutality of the unreformed schools. Rugby provided important groups of future liberals: between 1845 and 1850 Pearson, Goschen, Godfrey Lushington, J.H.Bridges, Franck Bright and T.W.Jex-Blake; between 1850 and 1855 Henry Sidgwick, Green, Charles Bowen, Rutson and Robinson Ellis. [65] Harrow also contributed in a smaller way: Montague Butler, G.O.Trevelyan, Henry Yates Thompson,

Lionel Tollemache and John Addington Symonds were contemporaries there. [66] Even Eton, which contributed least, produced, between 1845 and 1855, G.C.Brodrick, C.S.Parker, W.H.Fremantle, J.D.Coleridge, Swinburne and Sir George Young. [67] The secondary education of many future academic liberals was not, however, confined to school or home instruction: before they matriculated many spent a year or so at King's College, London. The Anglican component of the university, King's nonetheless provided, in the 1840s and early 1850s, much of the urban liveliness of a Scottish or continental university: Henry Fawcett, the Stephens, Pearson, Thorold Rogers, Edward Bowen, Frederic Harrison and the Diceys went from there to the universities with their expectations of higher education significantly enhanced. [68]

The university career of many liberals was thus predetermined by institutional reform, family connection and school acquaintanceship. Formal academic sanctions could interfere little with this situation. The honours candidate was still restricted to one subject, which meant that the disciplinary divisions which propel contemporary students into disparate intellectual environments, and present them with a fresh set of acquaintances, were absent. The university merely expanded a pattern of relationships family and school had created.

For Charles Pearson Oxford social life had to compensate for Oxford studies. In a strictly educational sense this was close to the truth: inadequacies of instruction had to be made good by the undergraduates themselves, by an elaborate informal system of supplementary tuition. Private tutors, reading parties, discussion groups, the Unions – these were an essential part of the education of the conscientious undergraduate. They also became part of the tissue of the liberal movement as, being informal, they attracted men of similar intellectual tendencies.

The private tutor was educationally ambiguous: in the 1870s Mark Pattison lashed him as a sort of academic racehorse trainer for the examination stakes: [69]

What the aspirant for honours requires is a repetiteur, who knows 'the schools' and who will look over essays for him, teaching him how to collect telling language, and arrange it in a form adequate to the expected question. It soon becomes indifferent to the teacher on what subject he lectures. The process of training for the race is the commanding interest. Training, be it observed, not intellectual discipline, not training in investigation, in research, in scientific procedure, but in the art of producing a clever answer to a question on a subject of which you have no real knowledge.

By then the Oxford private tutor had in fact declined somewhat in importance, and was more likely to be a young fellow, or a recent graduate waiting for a Fellowship, often a personal friend of his pupils. [70] But at Cambridge private tuition had become an industry, where some dons, like Thomas Hopkins and Richard Shilleto, ran virtual wrangler factories. According to Sheldon Rothblatt, this was probably the central cause of the teaching reforms introduced by Henry Sidgwick, Henry Jackson, Oscar Browning and their contemporaries in the 1860s and 1870s, protesting, in a less extreme manner than Pattison, that coaching ate into the very heart of liberal education. [71] Not all coaches were crammers: private tutoring brought young dons into contact with their more promising juniors, in an informal atmosphere where they could discuss politics and philosophy as well as prescribed work. But the threat concentrated their minds on the need for wide-ranging institutional and curricular reform. In the 1860s the former Oxford coach Robert Lowe represented to them not simply the embodiment of political expediency but the cash nexus in academic life.

The reading party was a development of the private tutorial at its informal best, and reflected the increased assiduity and independence of the undergraduates. Vacation tuition had formerly consisted of a few dull weeks cramming in a country rectory; by the fifties, however, most reading men had replaced this with more casual, enjoyable and stimulating arrangements. Undergraduates would club together for a month in the Highlands, the West Country, even Germany, sometimes taking a congenial don along with them. Or dons, holidaying together, would bring along two or three of their favourite pupils. [72] Horizons widened with the growth of railway and steamer routes. On one level, reading parties tested university friendships, and if they stood up to the test, cemented them for life. In the summer of 1863 three reading parties joined up at Heidelberg. They included Bryce, Henry Nettleship, A.V.Dicey, Green, Rutson and Henry Sidgwick. Dicey jotted down little character sketches of the main participants which show the sort of understanding this could lead to. On Bryce, for example: [73]

Bryce is the life of our party. The real strength of his character lies, I think, in the happy combination of various qualities, each of which may be found separately as fully developed in other persons. Most successful at the University, he does not seem to possess extraordinary, so much as admirably balanced, talents. His papers, of which I have seen many, were not perhaps startlingly original, but they were always good and clear, and what was required for the occasion. He has, I fancy, great capacity for development. His most agreeable, and I truly believe his most valuable, quality is his childlike 'life' and go. His kindness and friendship is beyond praise. He stirs us all up, rushes about like a shepherd's dog, collects his friends, makes us meet, leads us into plans and adventures and keeps everything going. His life will, I predict, be one of great and deserved success. Most of the Oxford men of ability are deficient in spirits. Bryce, who has talents and spirits, will go much further than many of his contemporaries, even though as able as himself.

This was the Arcadia of the 'long vacation pastoral', of Clough's *Bothie of Tober-na-Vuolich*. Walking, climbing, flirting with local girls, arguing over religion, poetry and high politics in Highland inns. The reading parties organized by the dons were more formal, intellectually more rigorous and had about them a faint odour of homosexual infatuation on the part of the seniors. John Conington, Professor of Latin at Oxford, was an adept at organizing such excursions; and numbers of future liberals, including Brodrick, Rutson, Charles Puller and John Addington Symonds, were involved in them. T.H.Green went on five, to Keswick, Freshwater, Bideford, Coniston and Ilkley. [74] He met Tennyson at Freshwater, and F.D.Maurice at Ilkley (demonstrating one advantage reading parties run by dons had over those run by undergraduates). On the other hand the obsessive, though apparently innocent, interest taken by Conington in his charges did Rutson and Symonds little good. On one reading party at Whitby Symonds told Conington about the homosexual behaviour of C.J.Vaughan, headmaster of Harrow. Conington, with an alacrity which, bearing in mind his own tendencies, arouses some suspicion, set in motion the campaign which ended in Vaughan's enforced resignation and the destruction of his career. The effect of this on Symonds was to intensify his own sexual problems and banish for a long time any chance he had of coming to terms with them. [75] But not all reading parties had the hothouse atmosphere of Conington's, and their effect generally was to strengthen links between students and dons, and through the dons with notabilities of literature, religion and politics outside the university.

Undergraduate discussion groups had been a feature of university life since Tennyson's time at Trinity: [76]

> Where once we held debate, a band
> Of youthful friends, on mind, and art,
> And labour, and the changing mart,
> And all the framework of the land.

Leslie Stephen was less than reverent when he recollected 'the knot of youthful philosophers who met on Saturday evenings to discuss all problems in heaven or earth ... and indeed talked incredible nonsense on all those subjects'. But he thought that they benefited the undergraduate: [77]

> He learnt to use the tools of his trade, and if his youthful confidence led him to solve a good many problems incapable of solution, it stimulated his powers and prepared them for maturer struggles.

And, on his deathbed, Henry Sidgwick's thoughts still ran back to the meetings of the Apostles: 'the tie of attachment to the society is the strongest corporate bond which I have known in life'. [78]

The Cambridge Conversazione Society was founded in 1830 by Tennyson, Arthur Hallam, Monckton Milnes and John Sterling. Its membership was secret, its politics were radical, but most important its agenda was without restriction. 'Absolute candour', according to Sidgwick, 'was the only duty that the tradition of the Society enforced'. [79] The Apostles responded to a contemporary Cambridge predicament: Connop Thirlwall had recently been persecuted for his religious opinions, the Union was still restricted in the subjects it debated. [80] There had been undergraduate clubs and societies before, but these were mostly convivial or party political. The Apostles had the self-confident earnestness of the German Burschenschaften that Carlyle captured in his life of Sterling (see p. 34). The earliest and most distinguished group, it was not, however, a seminal influence. Discussion groups were a spontaneous development. They germinated in the mental temper of the undergraduates, the desire of young men from an evangelical background to 'go further' (see p. 24); they also supplemented university studies, especially in politics, philosophy and literature.

At Cambridge other more or less ephemeral societies flourished and faded in the less privileged colleges. At Oxford, however, these tended to be university-wide and, usually before one society vanished altogether, some offshoot would blossom out under a new name. There were two reasons for this. Oxford was still in the lassitude which succeeded the Movement, [81] which, anyway, had little truck with Apostolic 'free thinking and plain speaking'; this tended to impede institutional continuity. Further, the Oxford Union had been allowed more rope, and by the forties was much stronger than its Cambridge counterpart. [82] in the fifties it became the focus of undergraduate dialectic and liberal politics. The 'Decade' of the 1840s – Matthew Arnold, Clough, Tait, Jowett, Stanley, Church and other young Fellows of Balliol and Oriel [83] – gave way to the 'Essay' around 1850; [84] by 1856 this was being supplanted by the 'Old Mortality' of John Nichol and G.R.Luke. [85] Between them they managed to include most of the liberal activists of the 1860s (see appendix 4).

The Essay Society developed out of the 'Tungendbund' or 'League of Virtue' – the name, significantly, came from the famous German liberal student group of the 1810s – founded by Charles Pearson during his time at Exeter. Its members set out their aims in detail. The document is so typical of the cast of the young liberal mind that it is worth quoting *in extenso*:

As members of a Society, we are anxious to put on record the reasons which have induced us to unite together, the obligations to which we have pledged ourselves, and our general principles of action. Our object is to impress ourselves more effectually with a sense of the duties entailed upon the educated classes by the present state of society in this country and by every means in our power to prepare ourselves for combined action, wherever it may seem likely to have any useful result. We feel that in a transitional period like the present, intermediate between an old order and a new the formation of such a society may be of the greatest use to ourselves and to those whom we may induce to join us, if it led us to increased thought on the questions of the day, a keener sense of our own duties, and larger and more active sympathies with the interests which surround us. Especially we believe in the possibility of in this turning to good account much of that irresolute energy, and sincere though indefinite desire to do good, which no one connected with the Universities can fail to recognise as characteristic of many of our contemporaries there.

And so on. A rather priggish outpouring of immature self-confidence, possibly, but from its ten members came two Cabinet Ministers, two professors, a Governor of Madras, four M.P.s, two Deans, a Legal Member of the Indian Council and an Assistant Secretary at the Education Department. [87]

The educational function of the societies evolved because, although the Oxford honours course was still formally classical, and Cambridge mathematical, the best tutors demanded of their pupils a knowledge of modern political and economic theory, philosophy and literature. Mill as logician, moralist and economist was important in Schools and Triposes alike, as no post-classical philosopher had ever been (see p. 38). T.H.Green, for example, was expected to write essays on economics, politics, literary criticism and comparative religion; only a relatively small number were on classical topics. [88] Where could he master such knowledge except by his own reading and discussions with his friends? So the Old Mortality set out to study modern literature and philosophy quite methodically. Each week in term there was a meeting, which began with the chairman (the chair rotated alphabetically) reading a passage from a writer of his choice, or delivering a paper of his own. The offering was then discussed. The chairmen in 1855 included Swinburne on Shelley's 'Ode to Liberty', Dicey on 'The Aim of Punishment' – which he found, to the gathering's satisfaction, to be 'the general utility of Society' – Bryce, appropriately enough, on Gibbon and Swinburne again on 'Violenzia'. [89]

The educational element was also important in the Unions. Although in the debates of the 1850s and 1860s the Union rank and file maintained a reputation for reaction, the leadership was on the whole liberal. Motions execrating the French Revolution, denying civil rights to minorities and supporting Church and Queen won easy victories – John Morley lost, 47-3, a motion approving the execution of Charles I as 'a necessary step for the preservation of liberty' [90] – yet between 1850 and 1865 over half the Oxford presidents were 'liberals of the Goldwin Smith type'. [91] The conservative F.H.Jeune regretted the dominance of Pearson, Brodrick, Dicey, Rutson, Green, Bryce and their friends, but he could do little about it: the reading men had a practical interest in the Union absent in their opponents. Banned from the Bodleian and lacking efficient college libraries, they found its library indispensable. [92] A tail of scholar–radicals wagged a Tory dog. Significantly, two attempts by Tories to gain control, by Edward Knatchbull-Huguessen in the late 1840s and by Auberon Herbert in the early 1860s, ended with the conversion of the leaders to liberalism. [93] Only when the liberals split in the 1880s were the Tories able to take over, and a period of partisan mediocrity followed. [94]

One of Auberon Herbert's ploys in his attempt was the founding of the Canning Club to organize the Tory undergraduates in 1861. The Club was premature, but it indicated the way things were moving; in 1877 the liberal undergraduates created the Palmerston Club, a name which must have been less than welcome to the seniors who became its patrons. [95] The informal clubs of the 1850s, combining undergraduates and dons, gave way to stratified groups. In a way this could not be avoided. Matriculations at both universities went up to 50 per cent, from around 400 to 600 during the 1860s, and to 800 by 1880 (see appendix 1). Dons had more to do; more undergraduates posed problems of discipline which they met by inculcating a specifically undergraduate sense of responsibility analagous to that dinned into pupils at the public schools. [96] Team spirit and the cult of *mens sana in corpore sano* replaced the conscientious individualism of the forties and fifties, which linked discontented dons and eager acolytes. [97]

The early 1860s were the watershed. In 1861 the Oxford Political Economy Club was formed. Although it included some pretty odd economists, like Mark Pattison and John Conington, it broke with the open agenda of earlier groups. [98] In 1864, however, the tradition of the Cambridge Apostles and the various Oxford organizations fused in the creation of the Ad Eundem dining club.

The Ad Eundem had its first dinner at Oxford in February 1865, [99] although there seems to have been at least one 'dining club dinner' at Oxford in the preceding year, [100] probably in preparation for the Freemasons' Tavern meeting in June. Although it arose out of the informal contacts which had steadily increased over the years, and specifically owed its creation to the Sidgwick brothers, [101] it was consciously planned as an exercise in interuniversity cooperation. The club dined once a term, alternately at each university. [102] Its membership of twenty was made up of ten from Oxford, ten from Cambridge, (five resident, five non-resident). [103] Writing in 1907 to Henry Jackson about the election of the Cambridge Public Orator, W.G.Clark, George Young recollected that: [104]

The purpose of him first, then of Munro, and then of Thompson [respectively Senior Tutor and Master of Trinity] by Sidgwick marks the distinct carrying out of his policy, that the Club should become a representation of *Cambridge as it was*, and the rejection, by degrees, of what I was inclined, then, to favour, viz., that it should draw on all the nicest people who had been up *with me* (not that I ever *went for* this and I merely had it in my mind).

On the Oxford side too some of the familiar names of Old Mortality and Essay Society days dropped out, to be replaced by senior liberals like Professors Goldwin and Henry Smith. But the core remained, dedicated to its 'inter-University alliance in the cause of academic reform'. [105] Without this concern it would merely have been an agreeable diversion: shared political or philosophical views could have been aired in London or separately at either university; there was no need to convene meetings to discuss them. But, just as politics and philosophy were linked to the cause of academic reform, the Ad Eundem formalized the discussion groups of both universities. A.V.Dicey, an early member, saw it as the logical successor of the Cambridge Apostles and the Oxford Essayists, a product of the period when 'everyone roughly knew what a "Liberal" meant'. [106] Liberalism did not imply party membership but the system of values he and his contemporaries had evolved for themselves at university and were to hold throughout their lives. The Ad Eundem was proof of the common commitment.

VII

By distinguishing between residents and non-residents it also recognized the unique importance of the London academics. A decade earlier the non-resident did not count for much; likewise a decade later, when reforms had fixed time limits to Fellowships. But in the 1850s and 1860s he was, like the private tutor, at once a tactical benefit to the liberals and a comment on the magnitude of the university problem.

The non-resident Fellow was a product of the semi-reformed university. While foundations were, apart from lawyers, exclusively clerical, fellows were usually resident, and stayed for a relatively short time. Clergymen waiting for a living could afford to occupy a few years with whist and port and a little college business, like Parson Woodforde, who was Fellow and steward of New College between 1763 and his presentation to Weston Longueville in 1776. [107] The lawyers construed their Fellowships as subsidies to their London practices, and were only seen in college at feasts or when litigation impended. [108] It is doubtful which group was more (or less) useful. The reforms of the 1850s brought matters to a crisis. Able men could now get Fellowships, but they could not keep them. Many still necessitated ordination, all required celibacy. The year after he resigned his Trinity Hall Fellowship, Leslie Stephen energetically indicted this system: [109]

It would be impossible to devise a scheme of pensioning more injurious to the university; a wise system of pensions is designed to encourage a man to devote his best energies to his work: this is strictly adapted to make a man's stay unsettled and precarious, and to prevent him from devoting his mind to the real work of the place …

This was even apparent to Whewell, who complained in the 1850s that 'all the best men run away from us to study law or to teach schools so that it is difficult to get persons duly qualified to stay here and do the work of the colleges'. [110] Stephen allowed that 'a few persons of special love for study may continue their stay at university' but thought that 'with the increasing temptations to active life, their number tends to diminish'.[111]

Henry Sidgwick stayed. Although he had already begun the studies in philosophy, politics and economics which were to occupy the rest of his life, the debate on his future in the early 1860s was a close-run thing: [112]

The only choice with me is between the Bar in London and study in Cambridge. For the Bar there are: (1) The prospect, very problematical, of attaining the position of a very practical politician (for which I doubt my fitness). (2) The certainty of the precious (to me) stimulus of intellectual society. (3) The conviction that the work of that profession is vastly more improving than tuition. Against it is: (1) The chance of failure, involving the renunciation of domesticity and the adoption, weary and baffled, of the career (of literary action) which I now renounce. (2) The certainty of neglecting in professional and political engagements the deeper problems which now interest me, especially the great one of reconciling my religious instinct with my growing conviction that both individual and social morality ought to be placed on an inductive basis ... (3) I ought perhaps to have mentioned a repugnance, perhaps unreasonable, to advocacy as practised in England.

Sidgwick was exceptional. Of the thirteen academic contributors to the 1867 reform essays [113] – that is, those who held Fellowships – only two, W. L. Newman and Thorold Rogers, were still in residence. Of the remaining eleven, eight had been, or were about to be, called to the bar, although of them only three, Godfrey Lushington, Frederic Harrison and A. V. Dicey, were at that time making anything of it. Harrison and Dicey probably made more money from journalism and this was true to a much greater extent of Bryce and Rutson. Brodrick, who had been called in 1859, had been a full-time leader-writer on *The Times* since 1860. Goldwin Smith was between his professorships at Oxford and Cornell, and had just inherited £30,000; George Young had inherited his baronetcy and estate at Cookham even earlier. Of those who had not this nominal legal association, Charles Pearson had given up his chair at King's College, London, travelled in Australia, and was lecturing part-time in Liverpool to women students; Leslie Stephen was virtually full-time as a journalist with the *Pall Mall Gazette* and *Cornhill*; and Charles Stuart Parker had just ceased to be private secretary to his relative, Edward Cardwell. Some – Smith, Stephen, Parker and to a lesser extent Harrison and Rutson – had taken a part in the running of university or college; others – Brodrick, Bryce, Dicey, Pearson, Young and Lushington – collected their Fellowships and left for London. This did not imply a crude desire to 'eat their cake and have it', as some more conservative academics were to allege; [114] the energy devoted to university reform by the non-residents implicitly denies this: of the last six, four subsequently returned to university life – Brodrick as Warden of Merton, Dicey and Bryce as Law professors at Oxford, and Pearson as a Fellow and lecturer of Trinity,

Cambridge. [115] They had left because they could not anticipate a university career and, not being well-off, could not hope to get a foothold in professional life without their Fellowships. [116]

Even here their course was neither straightforward nor easy. The bar was a necessary preliminary to a political or administrative career unless, like Parker or George Otto Trevelyan or Lord Edmond Fitzmaurice, some relationship within the governing class could be invoked. Secular occupations were more or less limited to schoolteaching and possibly a chair at a Scottish university; [117] a medical career required a lot of application as instruction at both universities was casual in the extreme; [118] for the same reason careers in technology were practically ruled out; in fact a university graduate would start off with a grave disadvantage in a profession where the norm was an early apprenticeship. [119] Once reconciled to the bar, however, the going did not get any easier. 'Oxford training seems to clog me as much as it helps,' complained Bryce: [120]

It is all very well to talk of high (sic) education and very true in its way. But the man with an attorney's intellect is the man for the Bar of England while the law remains as it is.

And the situation was not made any better by having as rivals the pick of one's ablest contemporaries. Even future leaders of the Bar like Fitzjames Stephen and Charles Bowen had lean years to begin with. [121] They had to go into journalism to enhance their income, and most of their contemporaries did likewise. Leslie Stephen has described the academic journalists of the fifties and sixties: [122]

... men, still young enough to be radiant with the halo of brilliant achievements at the University – and therefore, as we confidently believed, about to astonish the universe at large ... could turn an honest penny and raise the general standard of enlightenment, though shining under a bushel in the anonymous state.

In part they were a product of the upsurge in periodical literature in these decades, partly they contributed to it.

This development was oddly similar to the rise of discussion groups of the 'open agenda' sort at the universities (the personnel were frequently the same, anyway). The old publications, the *Edinburgh, Blackwood's,* the *Quarterly,* the *Westminster,* had been founded on *a priori* party-political conviction. Their new rivals owed their inception to its overthrow. Out of the attempt by Peelite journalists to rescue the *Morning Chronicle* came the *Saturday Review,* and, thanks to gifted editing and contributions of a very high standard, the *Saturday* was an impressive success, substantially because the editor had full control, and the proprietor took a back seat. The proprietor was an earnest High Church Tory, Beresford Hope, the editor an uncouth Scotsman, John Douglas Cook. The *Saturday's* politics, however, were not strictly speaking Tory, or rather they were not of very much importance: it was the magazine's tone which Cook made count. [124] Cook took advantage of the convention of anonymous journalism to allow free rein to able young unknowns who were flocking up from the universities. The *Saturday's* tone was bold, cynical, irreverent, but still reassuringly conservative. Leslie Stephen thought the best example of it was Robert Lowe in action against the Reform Bill of 1867, [125] a shrewd enough judgement since much of the political content of the magazine has now been seen to have come from Lowe's most convinced ally, Lord Robert Cecil, Beresford Hope's nephew. [126] The university men were slotted in to write the less political parts, frivolous 'middles' and reviews. [127] Detest the *Saturday's* politics though they might, most of the London academics contributed to it at one time or another. [128] By the end of the fifties, however, more opportunities were available, as more publications, following the *Saturday's* lead of rejecting overt political commitment for an 'attitude of mind' which might not be political at all, came out, notably *Macmillan's*, the *Cornhill* and the *Contemporary*; and in the first half of the following decade came the *Spectator* of Hutton and Townsend, the *London Review* and the *Fortnightly*. [129] Connections were made between the editorial staffs and contributors, and between the contributors themselves in some of the journals, notably *Macmillan's*, the *Specatator* and the *Fortnightly*. But this was not uniform. [130] Delane, at *The Times*, 'kept his beasts in separate cages' and Brodrick, Lowe and Leonard Courtney, who were all leader-writers at the same time, knew each other only distantly, [131] and no one seems to have struck up any intimate friendship with Cecil at the *Saturday* office, where Leslie Stephen saw him seated grimly at his desk. [132] University connections were thus not countered to any great extent by journalist relationships: indeed they were enhanced by Alexander Macmillan's acquaintanceship with both universities as their official publisher, Morley of the *Fortnightly's* Oxford past and Hutton's London professorship. [133]

This was tested when the *Saturday's* line in the intellectual controversies of 1860 and 1861 brought to a head the differences between the two generations of journalists who worked for it. Of the older men Goldwin Smith observed, [134]

It was said of us that whereas with the generation of the Reform Bill, everything had been new, everything had been true, and everything had been of the highest importance, with us nothing was new, nothing was true, and nothing was of any importance.

This was the judgement of a contemporary, though a critical one. The younger men were harsher. Charles Bowen attacked [135] 'that dry polish of literary refinement which innate Tories put on and call it Liberalism', and James Bryce said of one of the *Saturday*'s leading writers, George Stovin Venables, that he [136] 'belonged to that kind of Londoner which called itself Liberal and was Conservative, disliked sentiment, and detested Gladstone'.

The break came when the *Saturday* pitched into the liberal clergy in general and A.P.Stanley in particular over *Essays and Reviews* in 1861. To a generation which took the debate on rationalism and religion seriously and regarded the Liberal Anglicans with sympathy if not with enthusiastic conviction this was the last straw. Six of the ablest university men who contributed – Grant Duff, Henry Cunningham, Fitzjames Stephen, Charles Bowen, George Brodrick and Charles Pearson – seceded. [137] They determined on publication of a liberal alternative, and Bowen wrote to Jowett about it. Jowett replied: [138]

It should be Liberal in politics, yet with the aim of making liberality palatable to the educated and aristocratic; it should be liberal in religion (not in the sense of the *Westminster*); it should have a distinct object (like the *Edinburgh* in old days) which could, in fact, be the politics of ten years hence. It should attach itself to some leading politicians, Lord John, Gladstone, Sir G.Lewis, Lord Stanley.

... It should not fanatically abuse the Emperor Napoleon, John Bright, or competitive examinations, or the Evangelical clergy. It should include High Churchmen and make religion one of its leading topics; it should have no 'isms', no pretensions of superhuman virtue. Above all, it should be amusing ...

The real reconcilement of classes in the world and parties in the church; the balance of foreign and English interests in Europe; the working out and application of political economy to the interests of the lower classes, are fields in which a new review might hope to do some service.

There is little in this that Bowen's friends did not allude to in the reform essays they were to collaborate on six years later. Yet Jowett certainly did not consider himself in the least a radical, merely an academic prudently concerned with the future role of his kind in society: [139]

... is it at all probable that we shall be allowed to remain as we are for twenty years longer, the one solitary, exclusive, unnatural

Corporation ... our enormous wealth without any manifest utilitarian purpose?

His letter indicates the common denominator of agreement which united the academic liberals, resident and non-resident, and which formed the basis of the campaign of the sixties to complete the process of university reform, a campaign in which the cooperation of liberal residents with politically active London-based graduates was to be of central importance. [140] But, as Bowen's companions in the secession from the *Saturday* bore a remarkable resemblance to the personnel of the Oxford Essay Society, it was not unusual that they should seek the advice of the leader of the Oxford reform movement. The university not only created a self-conscious community among its ablest men but, by its very inadequacies, thrust that community into the literary and political life of the capital. University intellectuals had acquired an ideology: they now created a structure of relationships which both enabled and required that ideology to be activated.

[4]

THE
TESTS
AGITATION

Liberalise the national legislature
and the national legislature will liberalise Oxford.

Goldwin Smith – James Bryce, 7 July 1869

The religious Tests which restricted the posts and emoluments
offered by the universities of Oxford and Cambridge to their
Anglican graduates were abolished by Parliament in June 1871
after a campaign which had lasted nine years. The reaction of Pusey
– 'Oxford lost to the Church of England'[1] – typified the dismay of
the traditionalists: the response of Nonconformity and academic
liberalism was correspondingly enthusiastic. Even after a couple of
decades had passed, the *Jubilee Retrospect* of the Liberation Society
could find 'no department of work on which Liberationists can look
back with greater pleasure'.[2] To the younger academic liberals
'leagued to open the universities to all, irrespective of religion', the
Tests struggle was a major preoccupation. G.M.Trevelyan later
claimed that 'perhaps no more important legislative change has been
made in English institutions since the first Reform Bill',[3] yet, on the
face of it, the Tests agitation was concerned with a much narrower
issue than those at stake in the controversies of the 1850s: it did not
affect the curriculum or modes of teaching, the examination system or
the right of government to intervene in university affairs, nor had it
much to do with the major controversy of the 1870s, the battle between
teaching and scholarship. But it was important: the act of 1871 is the
pivot of Lewis Campbell's classic account, and no study of academic
politics or intellectual life in mid-Victorian England can hope to
recreate the liberalism of the time without reference to it. Its neglect
both by political historians and by historians of education stems
doubtless from the reason that it seems, in the context of both
disciplines, relatively unimportant.[4] Yet to the men whose concerns

bridged university affairs and national politics, the course of the controversy was of continuous significance, as it both necessitated an appeal to national politics, and reinforced an alignment with Nonconformist radicalism: for nine years it linked the universities, Liberal politics, Nonconformity and the intellectual world of London.

Although Tests abolition had been the original motive of James Heywood's motion on university reform of 23 April 1850, which led to the government's announcement of the royal commissions,[5] liberal academics were then prepared to acquiesce in a settlement which accepted the continued exclusion of Nonconformists from the university. The abolition of Tests at matriculation and before graduation as Bachelor of Arts was only gained after a bitter attack on the Oxford Bill of 1854 by Heywood and John Bright,[6] and, ironically, the rediscovery of the provisions within the statutes of university and colleges which barred Nonconformists from the higher offices was the work of Goldwin Smith (then secretary to the commission empowered to alter the Oxford Statutes).[7]

Several factors could account for this conservatism: university liberalism was still dominated by Maurice and the Broad-Churchmen who believed that, if Anglican formulas could be interpreted in a liberal spirit,[8] the Establishment had worthwhile spiritual and social advantages.[9] The politics of the leading university reformers were themselves of a moderate, Whig–Peelite inclination.[10] In 1861 Cambridge, traditionally placid, elected as Chancellor the Whig Duke of Devonshire to succeed the moderate, conscientious, Prince Consort; and the difference anyway between a Cambridge liberal like Adam Sedgwick and a Cambridge conservative like William Whewell was one of degree rather than basic attitude.[11] Even at Oxford, where partisan feeling ran higher, liberals like Goldwin Smith were still willing to collaborate with Gladstone – a Tractarian and a Peelite – largely on grounds of political agreement.[12] The work of the Statutory Commission of 1854-9 was a testament to this collaboration. And although the academics had tactical contacts with Nonconformity, their knowledge of its organization and consciousness was still limited.[13]

The reforms of the 1850s were similar at both universities, as were certain of their consequences, although there were also significant differences which affected the course of the subsequent liberal campaign. But the crucial common factor was the breakdown of the Broad Church compromise under the pressure of its own inconsistencies and the growth of utilitarian rationalism. This destroyed the premises on which some of the younger dons had assented to Anglican formulas on taking up their fellowships: for some these had become meaningless, for others, like Henry Sidgwick and Leslie Stephen, a matter for moral disquiet. [14]

The political compromise, too, was breaking up under the pressure of ideological change, sympathy with foreign liberal movements and, most significantly, the impact of the American Civil War on British politics. Influential university reformers, rejecting the values which had sanctioned the earlier reforms, had therefore to determine a new social alignment for the universities. These changes both brought about greater contact with Nonconformist leaders and convinced the academics of their anomalous position. They also provided new allies to remedy it.

Institutional pressures supplemented ideology: clerical restrictions on fellowships – 130 at Oxford and thirty at Cambridge still carried an obligation to proceed to orders [15] – the requirement of celibacy, the absence of academic career structures and opportunities which would keep a fellow at Oxford or Cambridge. These, however, remained peripheral: celibacy was early on a contention at Cambridge, but then dropped into the background; [16] the government successfully resisted an attack on clerical fellowships in 1871. [17] New thinking on the means and ends of academic life paralleled rather than preceded the Tests agitation.

The working out of the changes imposed by the commissions did not sustain the campaign, but it brought matters to a head. The crisis took a different form in each university. In Cambridge the consequence of admitting Nonconformists to degrees but not to the emoluments of university and colleges became apparent when, in 1860 and 1861, a Nonconformist was Senior Wrangler. Neither graduate could proceed to a Fellowship, yet the situation, far from being exceptional, looked as if it might become the rule. Nonconformist undergraduates tended to come up the hard way, by open scholarships (the work of the reforms of the 1850s) from the grammar schools, a process which weeded out all but the very best. [18] (In the next thirty years they were to produce eighteen Senior Wranglers.) [19] Not only did this situation seem patently unfair to the Nonconformists themselves, it also produced intense heart-searching among fellows like Henry Sidgwick who had made the necessary declarations in obedience to religious principles which they felt they could no longer hold.

To this was added growing tension within the colleges, as abler Fellows, elected under the new statutes, chafed at the slowness of reform. At Trinity, the centre of liberal activity, the college meeting at which Statutes could be altered took place only once a year. A motion for alteration had to be tabled a year in advance, at the previous meeting. [21] Success was problematic, and failure could be dispiriting, so, if opportunities arose in the interval, reform-minded fellows were tempted to throw their hand in and get out. Leslie Stephen, whose religious doubts drove him from Cambridge in 1865 and from his Fellowship at Trinity Hall in 1867, found little cause for hope in the progress of internal reform at Cambridge. [22] And, gloomy though his tone was, none of his contemporaries disagreed with him. [23]

College reform was also under way at Oxford, although it was less significant than at Cambridge because all the colleges were small and the overall gain from the reform of a single college that much less. However, because of the 'open' nature of the Fellowship competitions, graduates from the 'reformed' colleges, notably Balliol, were gradually taking over the conservative ones. [24] In the revision of its statutes, All Souls stood out for a time against the Statutory Commission's injunction to elect on intellectual quality alone. It was taken to court by three of its younger, liberal-minded fellows – W.H.Fremantle, A.G.Watson and Godfrey Lushington – and lost in 1864. [25] The Cathedral Canons of Christ Church, too, fought hard to retain the power of 'the most conservative governing body in Oxford' [26] – after 1855 against their own Dean, A.G.Liddell, an appointee of the Whig government – but eventually, in 1867, they succumbed as well.

However this process of reform took place against, and was frequently frustrated by, violent politico-religious controversy. Henry Sidgwick found it (at first glance, and from the safety of Cambridge) appealing: [27]

I wish I was at Oxford, they are always having exciting controversies which keep them alive. Nothing is so fertile as a good semi-theological row. Just now Jowett and his foes divide the attention of the common rooms with Mansel and Goldwin Smith.

In the aftermath of the Movement, Oxford nurtured intense theological animosities: *Essays and Reviews* provoked from conservative academics not theological outrage alone but the ferocity of men desperately and sincerely fighting to retain a confessional ideal of education against liberal tendencies, steadily gaining ground through the government's sponsorship of reform. [28] But, if patronage favoured the academic liberals, their position was vulnerable in several respects, and the conservatives did not hesitate to take advantage of these.

While the Tests were enforced, liberal dons at Oxford were subject to the same moral qualms as their Cambridge colleagues, with the significant difference that, while in Cambridge 'a man may on the whole speak the thing he will', [29] in Oxford the conservative party was prepared to make free with the charge of heresy or at least bad faith. This view was shared by some who were in other respects close to the younger men. John Conington, whose idosyncratic reversion to Evangelicalism earned him the hatred of Mark Pattison, [30] wrote to Henry Sidgwick on the latter's resignation of his Trinity fellowship: [31]

> I do not know anything which more alienated me from the University Liberals than their determination to 'eat their cake and have it', to combine the advantages of an orthodox profession with those of free thought and speech.

And James Bryce's Ulster Presbyterian uncle, Reuben John Bryce, was similarly severe on his nephew's associates: [32]

> I know it's very hard to denounce publicly the errors of those we have a personal regard for. Yet in fact these men are the supports of the system. If a score of men, instead of only one man, are about to give up their fellowships rather than sign a lie, the system would immediately fall. Every man who refuses to be a martyr is a traitor, but it is very hard to say so or think so of a good-natured, warm-hearted, genial fellow whose conversation over a glass or wine or a cup of coffee one enjoys immensely, and who, in every other department of his life, seems an honourable and high-principled man.

While the Tests, and the religious situation they represented, remained, the academic liberals' situation could never be a logically tenable or an honourable one.

Further, the conservatives realized, after the setbacks of the 1850s, that the new compromise gave them ample opportunity to counter-attack. As far as the government of the university was concerned, the Oxford Act of 1854 (the equivalent Cambridge measure came two years later) replaced the Heads of Houses as the controlling body of the university by a Council consisting of the Chancellor, Vice-Chancellor, two Proctors, the Pro-Vice-Chancellor, eighteen members of Congregation, six professors and six members of Convocation. [33] Although the Liberals had only the slimmest of chances of getting a majority on this body, through the Congregation and professorial members, they believed that the creation of Congregation – a body composed of resident M.A.s which could vet the decisions of Council – might produce a liberal majority. [34] However, it soon became apparent that Congregation was not a liberal body. During the parliamentary debates on the Oxford Bill its composition had been expanded, at Gladstone's insistence, from being purely composed of university men to include M.A.s resident in the town. [35] With the growth of clerical support for the High Church the number of such clergy increased, [36] and their support went, for the most part, to the conservative party,[37] 'labouring, under perfect discipline, and with fell unity of purpose, to hold the University in subjection, and fill her government with its nominees'. From about 1859 the clerical conservatives began to organize themselves on explicitly political lines,[38] putting up a 'slate' of candidates for election to Council, for all of whom the conservative M.A. was supposed to vote.[39] These measures took effect rapidly. In 1860 the liberals lost badly in the elections for Council, which defied Congregation by taking decisions on university policy without consultation.[40] Congregation itself became more conservative. Although in 1864 it passed new examination statutes which *The Times* saw as 'the triumph of radical liberalism',[41] the liberals were thereafter weak in it.[42] Convocation never figured much in the liberals' calculations, despite its ultimate authority in matters of finance and legislation.[43] They had always been swamped by the country clergy, and were now placed at an added disadvantage since more of them could be brought up to Oxford by train to vote down liberal measures.[44]

The academic liberals, in desperation, turned from this situation to external political agitation. They wanted a measure which by abolishing the religious Tests would effectively secularize the university. Behind the declarations of solidarity between Oxford and Manchester there was always a strong element of academic calculation. At Cambridge the initial impulse may have been more disinterested, but as time went on concern with the effect of the Tests on Nonconformist consciences was replaced by the business of harnessing Nonconformity to the flagging cause of university reform. But the alliance could not have been purely tactical, as it endured amicably for eight difficult years. It united two disparate groups and maintained this unity against several powerful challenges, demonstrating identities of interest which existed on more than one level.

IV

The parliamentary campaign began when Edward Pleydell-Bouverie, Liberal M.P. for Kilmarnock, presented on 13 June 1862 a petition signed by seventy-four resident fellows and tutors at Cambridge praying for the abolition of the assent to the Act of Uniformity on election to a Fellowship,[45] a Test unique to Cambridge (at Oxford all Fellows save one had to be M.A.s and, as such, subscribed to the Thirty-Nine Articles – see appendix 3). The petition was the work of Henry Fawcett, who was to become one of the most energetic of the Cambridge campaigners; four years earlier he had first raised the celibacy question.[46] The following session, on 5 May

1863, Bouverie introduced a Bill to carry out the terms of the petition. [47] He withdrew it on 24 June because of the lateness of the session, but promised to reintroduce it in 1864. [48]

Although the Cambridge Senate petitioned against it, the debates on the Bill were favourable (it was carried, on introduction, by 157-135). [49] Rather belatedly a petition in its favour from the Oxford liberals also turned up, [50] and in the next session John George Dodson, Liberal M.P. for East Sussex, introduced a Bill to repeal the Test governing the Oxford M.A. degree. [51] The measure was aimed at the university rather than the colleges, but it opened all Fellowships which were restricted *only* by the obligation to proceed to M.A., (but not those covered by declarations authorized by college statutes). Dodson's Bill was introduced on 12 February, given its second reading on 16 March [52] and sent to Committee on 1 May. [53] On 8 May Bouverie was given leave to re-introduce his Bill, [54] and measures to abolish Tests in both universities lay before the House, as they were to do, in various shapes and combinations, for the next seven years.

Certain critical factors influenced the course of the campaign while it remained a parliamentary 'hardy annual'. These altered marginally, but remained important throughout. The first and most obvious requirement was a majority in the Commons. [55] Even so, this by itself was not sufficient. Majorities had to be large and sustained to take the Bill through its four Commons stages – Introduction, Second Reading, Committee and Third Reading. The House had to be sufficiently emphatic to ensure that the Committee reflected its opinion, and sufficiently enthusiastic to advance it to the head of its business, so that, at a time when the parliamentary session lasted only from February to early August, it would not fail through lack of time. Finally, it had to be strong enough to withstand amendments from the House of Lords. In fact, unless a Bill were reasonably non-controversial – which most humanitarian measures of the sort successfully then carried by private members were – it had little chance of success unless it became a government measure. [56] And although Tests abolition managed to get majorities in its favour, these were by no means convincing ones.

The opposition to Dodson's Bill was more than 95 per cent Conservative. [57] Some Tory churchmen, like J.W.Henley, the member for Oxfordshire, Charles Newdegate, the member for North Warwickshire, and the university burgesses, were dedicated guardians of 'the Church in Danger', [58] and their energetic whipping-up narrowly defeated its third reading in 1864. [59] But the party leadership was not prepared to make an issue of the matter and throw the rank and file regularly against it, reckoning, doubtless, that the measure was embarrassing enough to the Liberals without any help from them. [60] Even the attitude of their most vehement partisan, Lord Robert Cecil, was dictated by calculation. Cecil's own intellectual position was not totally at variance with the academics': in his *Saturday Review* articles he had attacked the clerical persecutors of Colenso, [61] but he was prepared to embarrass the Liberals for as long as he could. His speech on the introduction of Bouverie's bill in 1863 demonstrates both his technique and a plausible reason why no liberal academic would dare flirt with political Conservatism: [62]

Fellowships really gave those who held them the power of regulating the studies of the Universities, and therefore the measure was practically a measure for transferring the control over the studies and religious education of the Church of England to the Nonconformists.

But the difficulty was that, unfortunately, the people of England were not as enlightened as the noble lord and the rt. hon. gentleman. What he was afraid of was that if there was a Unitarian or a Jew Vice-Chancellor, or if there was any distinguished teacher in the University who occupied the position of the celebrated Professor at Leyden, the fathers of families throughout the United Kingdom would as soon cut off their right hands as send their children to the Universities. If it was intended to pass a measure which would prevent the Universities from being, what they had heretofore been, the favourite resorts of the upper and middle classes of England, justice required that they should heed the Universities themselves.

Conservative tactics became relevant when associated with the Liberal governments of the period. For in 1864 Lord Palmerston was still premier, and his spirit still permeated the administration. 'We are in the midst of a conservative reaction,' wrote Goldwin Smith, [63]

... The popular party in this country is at the present moment under the guidance of an isolated group of aristocratic leaders ... whose objects and convictions were, in most cases, exhausted when they had carried the Reform Bill, and put an end to their own exclusion from power.

Palmerston had backed the reforms of the 1850s, [64] and in 1863 voted for the introduction of Bouverie's Bill, though without committing himself to vote for it at any later stage. [65] Many members of the Cabinet took a more positive line, notably Lord John Russell, the Foreign Secretary. But university policy was the preserve of the Chancellor of the Exchequer, W.E.Gladstone, who, as sitting member for Oxford University and repository of the trust of the High Church party, could not be expected to be sympathetic. [66] In the debates of 1864 he was arbiter of the situation.

V

Gladstone got wind of the Oxford petition in 1863 in a letter from his friend Henry Wentworth Acland, Professor of Medicine, who had himself refused to sign. [67] Gladstone replied, commending his decision [68] and censuring 'the gross impolicy of such a demand' apparently emanating from 'the friends of Mr Jowett'. However, he was far from complacent: [69]

> As to the general gloominess of the situation for the Church of England and for Oxford its eldest daughter, I think it is too soon to determine whether the very menacing symptoms of the present day and the rapid march on the citadel are transitory phenomena, analogous to what have before appeared, of the signs of a change profound and permanent, or in what degree they are part of either character. I am most alarmed at the weakness of what ought to be the defending force: the general want of study and learning, with few exceptions in the Church.

And his final position, if ambiguous, was by no means hostile to change: [70]

> This would, with me, depend very much 1. upon what was to be substituted. 2. upon the likelihood of a conciliatory effect at the time. 3. upon the prospect of getting a firmer or more shifting standing ground.
> I do not think with respect to this question of Tests in the University that the prospect of ulterior dangers is conclusive against concession of any kind. But I am sure that it is right not to move except to what may reasonably be judged an improved position.

Gladstone's need to be convinced that the liberals represented 'a change profound and permanent', and his search for 'a firmer standing ground', were to affect powerfully the course of the campaign. The debates of 1864 showed the concessions he was initially willing to make. He was prepared to endorse a measure which would open Oxford further to dissenters while retaining its Anglican foundation, and it seems that he arranged for Dodson's Oxford Bill to be tabled early in the session to allow concessions to be implemented which would place Oxford on a par with Cambridge, offering dissenters the M.A. without access to Convocation or to Fellowships. [71] This 'final' concession made, the Cambridge measure could then be rejected.

The academics seem to have calculated on freeing the Oxford M.A. and then, during the debates, trying to get the further concessions of membership of Convocation and the freeing of Fellowships. If they managed this, they hoped to secure an easier passage for Bouverie's Cambridge measure. So the introduction of Bouverie's measure was apparently delayed until the fate of the Oxford Bill was settled.

But, by the time Bouverie introduced his Bill on 8 May, [72] the Oxford Bill was doomed. At the second reading, on 16 March, when it was sent into committee, Gladstone produced his concessions: he was prepared to allow the M.A. and no more. [73] Dodson grudgingly accepted this as a basis for discussion, [74] but found his university backers and their Nonconformist allies unyielding. Goldwin Smith wrote to him: [75]

... unless people are assured that there is no fear of your Bill passing with an amendment excluding Nonconformists from Convocation you are likely to find a part of the support, not only among the Nonconformists but here, turned into indifference and perhaps into positive opposition at the next stage of the discussion.

So Dodson rejected Gladstone's amendment, and his Bill was lost at third reading, after a tied vote, on 1 July. [76]

From memoranda in the Gladstone papers it is apparent that, had the liberals accepted the M.A. as a final settlement, Gladstone was prepared to make concessions which might have set university reform off on an entirely different course. In a memorandum on Oxford reform of 6 July 1863 [77] (another exists dated November 1867, which shows that his position had altered little after four years of liberal agitation) [78] he suggested a completely new type of university organization. Dissenters would be given degrees but no voice in the running of the university or colleges, while Council would be allowed to exempt from Tests all professors (except in Divinity). His last paragraphs were the most remarkable: [79]

Why should there not be at Oxford Houses or establishments extraneous to the University (?)

Of which Heads or Masters should give security to the University by conforming to certain rules (on pain of discommunicating) for the care and discipline of their inmates.

These heads or masters to teach the youth in their own fashion.

Such youth to matriculate, and receive instruction, and take degrees in the university:

Instruction, i.e. from Professors – or from Private Tutors or within Colleges at College lectures so far as Colleges might think fit to arrange.

Some analogy would be found between establishments of this kind and the Halls contemplated in Sir R.Peel's Irish Colleges Act of 1845.

Certain anomalies remained: although the university could appoint Nonconformists to professorships, its government would remain wholly Anglican, and this was bound, from the start, to cause friction. Nor did he attempt to work out how the Anglican university and colleges were to coexist with the new Nonconformist halls. These give the impression that he was not wholly serious about his scheme, and indeed he made no references to it in any of the subsequent debates on university reform.

Gladstone's scheme was in dramatic opposition to the academic liberals' university ideal, but it catered for the reformers who wanted to see the authority of the university and the professoriate enhanced, and it drew to Oxford the same social groups the liberals wanted to reach. Free inquiry and secular university organization were lacking, yet Nonconformists would have lost little by accepting such proposals. Education at independent halls would have been much cheaper than at 'liberated' colleges, and their numbers would have increased more rapidly, with little risk of 'contamination' by Anglican or secularist ideas.

This aspect of Gladstone's thinking on university matters was lost on the liberals, who saw him at best as a wayward but redeemable soul, [80] and at worst as a bigoted obstructive. [81] But it's not possible to speculate on their response, to proposals which were never made public. Presumably Gladstone was deterred by the solidarity in 1864 between academics and Nonconformists: letters insisting on a settlement which gave them a voice in university government came not only from Nonconformist spokesmen [82] but from Oxford teachers. [83] And on 10 June a remarkable demonstration of support for both Bills was held at the Freemason's Tavern, London, at which speeches in their favour were delivered by, among others, Goldwin Smith, Jowett, T.H.Huxley and John Bright (see appendix 2). [84]

VI

The university liberals made much of their alliance with Nonconformity. In 1867 G.C.Brodrick preached the cause at the opening meeting of the Manchester Reform Club, and concluded fulsomely: [85]

All these objects, he believed, they would accomplish with the aid of that motive power which Lancashire, above all places, he believed, could supply: and so great was his faith in that motive power, that he almost ventured to differ from Mr Goldwin Smith, and believe that from an unreformed parliament they might be able to attain some results.

Two years later Goldwin Smith, who had also been present on that
occasion, wrote to James Bryce in similar terms: [86]

However, I have always thought that the hope of the Oxford
Liberals lay not in any contest in Oxford itself – a narrow arena,
where the enemy has long been, and still is, entrenched in
overwhelming strength, but in victory in an ampler field. Liberalise
the national legislature and the national legislature will liberalise
Oxford at one stroke without waste of lives and end this chronic
bitterness. Our alliance with Manchester, which made our cause
that of a party in the nation, has done more for us than all our
fighting with Puseyism in Convocation.

The alliance appeared to fuse provincial social and moral robustness
– the 'plain people' T.H.Green revered – to the 'masculine'
university intellect, an analogue of the union of 'brains and
numbers' [87] the academics envisaged in politics.

In fact it turned out satisfactory to both. The Nonconformists
could credit themselves with liberal, patriotic and far-sighted
conduct, rather than sectionally interested tactical manoeuvre. They
left the management of the campaign to the university men, and
accepted a 'nationalized' university rather than a complex of
confessional colleges. In a bravura speech on Dodson's Bill
E.A.Leatham, Radical M.P. for Huddersfield, stated that Nonconformity, not the Church, would fear its passage; nine out of ten
young Nonconformists would swing over to the Establishment once
they got to Oxford. But 'the great and cardinal principle that the
consciences of men are free' was more important than the health of
Nonconformity. [88] For their part the academics regarded their allies
less as a convenient interest to live off than as men whose
educational and social needs had to be cultivated and assisted.

For Nonconformity, like the Established Church, was experiencing
a crisis of belief. In a *Fortnightly Review* article P.W.Clayden, a
Congregationalist minister and radical journalist who frequented
the same London liberal circles as many of the academics, [89]
described the decline in Evangelical sectarian fervour. The tradition
of a 'democratic' recruitment of leadership: [90]

which has conferred spiritual office, not on social superiority, but on
spiritual ability ... has often sacrificed social advantages and seemed
to make a vulgar choice, but has gained in spiritual efficiency and
popular power ...

was fading and producing in the Nonconformist community a
structure, both of belief and of social order, closer to that of the rest
of society: its leadership tended to be wealthier, and more flexible in

its doctrine. [91] this inevitably created discontent with he existing provincial culture. In 1865 James Bryce, inspecting schools for the Taunton commission, contacted R.D.Darbishire, a leading Manchester Unitarian, to organize support for the Tests campaign in the north. Although Darbishire could write that he felt sure of 'the true response of such a question of the best Manchester public', [92] he regretted that Manchester politics were 'singularly devoid of intelligence and cultivation. Our political intelligence is at the lowest stage.' He went on:

We want sadly a knot of scholarly-minded speakers here. The League, that ought to have died when the Corn Laws finally gave way, trained economical speakers of some ability; but we have no other prominent leaders of thought.

Bryce himself responded to Lancashire with mixed feelings. He wrote to Freeman in May 1865: [93]

Manchester is a much more agreeable place than I had supposed: not so dirty as London: the people rough, but straightforward and hearty: society over-ridden it is true by wealth, but that wealth employed in a bold generous way.

Later, in February 1866, he was less enthusiastic: [94]

People sick of a southern squirearchy admire far off these Lancashire politicians. Near at hand the roughness and the dirt are seen.

Bryce's educational work introduced him to 'a state of society and a framework of notions so unlike what we have in the South of England'. [95] Despite the hostility he frequently encountered, 'as a Government emissary of tyrannical centralisation and an Oxford scholar who can't possibly know anything but Latin verse, [96] he found among the provincial intelligentsia a discontent with existing provisions and a willingness to consider new departures, understandable in a society which has just suffered the material and psychological disruption of the cotton famine during the American Civil War [97].

The closest cooperation came from the elite of Nonconformity. Christie, who moved for an inquiry into the universities in 1845, and Heywood, who was successful in 1850, were both Unitarians, as were Darbishire and James Martineau, two of the academics' closest allies in the 1860s. They were scarcely representative of the mass of chapel-goers, but were well placed during a period when Nonconformity was highly organized, its power concentrated centrally and hierarchically, and when there was a great deal of cooperation between the various sects in agitating causes like the Burials Bill and the abolition of Church Rates. [98] Centralized collaboration was not only possible, but tended to be with the most outward-looking elements in Nonconformity.

The alliance had to be durable, as in 1864 a successful outcome to the Tests campaign was still improbable and the Nonconformist interest at Westminster was still impotent without the backing of the rest of the Liberal party. [99] But Nonconformists and academics were aware that they were in a similar situation. From the minutes of the principal Nonconformist activist body the Society for the Liberation of Religion from State Patronage and Control – the Liberation Society – which collaborated closely with the academics throughout, it is evident that the Nonconformist cause too was suffering from [100] 'that reaction in public sentiment which has encouraged the House of Commons to reject almost every measure of reform lately submitted to it'. In late 1863 it decided to abandon its own parliamentary programme because of this unfavourable climate. [101] At the same time it took a greater interest in the Tests campaign. [102] Evidently, if neither body could succeed on its own, combination might give them a better chance, while, in the long term, both stood to gain by changes in the parliamentary balance of power.

It is impossible, however, to overestimate the importance of one external factor: the relationships and political principles involved in the support of the North during the American Civil War. The contacts politicians like Cobden and Bright made with leaders of university liberalism like Goldwin Smith and Thorold Rogers, the mutual respect of academic and Nonconformist, the common interest in the promotion of popular government and political reform, all effectively underwrote the Tests campaign.

These were supplemented by individual relationships: George Osborne Morgan for instance, although the son of a Welsh vicar, threw in his lot with the Liberation Society in the late 1850s and became a prominent spokesman for Nonconformist causes. [103] Henry Arthur Morgan, his brother, was a fellow of Jesus College, Cambridge, a reformer and friend of Leslie Stephen and Henry Fawcett. Fawcett himself assiduously cultivated Nonconformist radicals and invited many to Trinity Hall to meet his liberal colleagues. [104] At Oxford Thorold Rogers was related to Cobden and, after he became Drummond Professor of Political Economy in 1862, his house became a port of call for radical politicians. [105] Bright was so moved by his sympathetic reception in 'the home of dead languages and undying prejudices' to wish that he had gone there himself. [106] A year later T.H.Green was, like James Bryce, inspecting schools for the Taunton commission, and making contact with leading Nonconformists and educational reformers in the Birmingham area. [107] And Goldwin Smith, whose first contact with organized Nonconformity appears to have been his collaboration with Edward Miall on the Newcastle commission on Popular Education, 1858, had become a fixture on its platforms by the mid 1860s. [108]

The seal of the alliance was set at the Freemasons' Tavern meeting. Following this, a committee of five was set up to draft an Oxford Bill for the next session. It included Roundell, Frederic Harrison, Charles Bowen and Grant Duff. Edward Miall of the Liberation society attended as adviser. [109] Throughout, dissenting involvement seems to have been more with Oxford than with Cambridge, doubtless reflecting more the acerbity of Oxford politics than the needs of the dissenters. Indeed the link with the 'extremist' Liberation Society – whose programme ultimately envisaged the abolition of the State Church – may to some extent have embarrassed the cause. Unquestionably Miall had a reputation as a firebrand and was thus a possible liability, [110] yet from its papers it is quite evident that the Society realized the sensitivity of the question and exerted its influence within nonconformity as diplomatically as possible, leaving the process of parliamentary liaison to the academics. [111]

VII

In 1865 and 1866 both Bills were introduced and passed second reading, but national politics – in the shape of the dissolution and general election of 1865, and the fall of the Liberal ministry on the Reform Bill in 1866 – came between the academics and success in the Commons. The majorities for both Bills were somewhat greater in the new House of 1866, as it contained a greater Nonconformist representation, [112] and the liberal academics themselves were now represented in parliament by George Otto Trevelyan, sitting for Tynemouth, and Henry Fawcett, for Brighton. Another sympathizer, Goschen, was now in the cabinet.

On 6 April 1866 the alliance was further reinforced by a demonstration in the Free Trade Hall, Manchester. The organization of this was largely the work of James Bryce and R.D.Darbishire. During the election of 1865 Bryce tried to get Manchester candidates to commit themselves on Goschen's Bill; Darbishire advised a more elaborate campaign,[113] to bring the weight of 'a Manchester audience of the most respectable character' to bear, expecting that 'the report of a well-arranged occasion of this kind would itself affect public opinion elsewhere'. There had been public meetings about university Tests before; the Liberation Society held several at the time of the Oxford act of 1854, to support Heywood's amendment[114] – but these had been expressions of Nonconformist opinion. Bryce and Darbishire wanted a bipartisan rally. Darbishire suggested that Nonconformist speakers[115] should 'keep to the intrinsic principles of the movement, and avoid the more sectarian [manner] in which it easily presents itself to and through non-university men'. He had hoped for a meeting in November, but, presumably in order to coincide with the passage of the Bill, it was postponed until the April of the following year. Resolutions in support of Coleridge and Bouverie's Bills were moved by Nonconformists supported by academics and vice versa. George Brodrick, Frederick Temple, now Headmaster of Rugby, and William Sidgwick spoke for the academic liberals, William Graham, M.P. for Glasgow, Thomas Bazley, M.P. for Manchester, and several northern ministers and teachers for the Nonconformists. The academics must have appreciated Jacob Bright's conclusion:

It does not appear that Nonconformists are endeavouring to find their way into the universities so much as that members of the universities are trying to take hold of England.

Then, energetically scrambling his metaphors:

If Oxford and Cambridge stretch out the hand for help to Manchester, I do not believe that Manchester will turn a deaf ear to those universities.

Messages of support were read out from Fitzjames Stephen, Coleridge and Bouverie, Goldwin Smith, Fawcett, Freeman and Thorold Rogers;[116] the resolutions were carried with little dissension and the proceedings of the meeting were edited and published with an introduction by Brodrick.

The academic liberals employed their close connections with London journalism, to publicize the cause in the newspaper and periodical press. Hardly a year went by in which one of the monthlies or quarterlies – *Fraser's, Macmillan's,* the *Contemporary,* the *Fortnightly* – did not carry an article on the issue, and mentions were correspondingly more frequent in the weeklies and the dailies; even *The Times* – whose leaders on university matters were written by George Brodrick – came round to their side.[117] Articles were supplemented by pamphlets and books, like Goldwin Smith's *A Plea for the Abolition of Tests*, 1864, Sir George Young's *University Tests: An Apology for their Assailants*, 1868 and Lyulph Stanley's *Oxford University Reform*, which themselves stimulated review articles.

Gladstone, however, still held out against concession. C.S. Roundell saw him just after the Oxford Bill had passed its second reading on 14 June 1865 and strenuously attempted to win him for the liberal cause: [118]

> I appealed to his noble nature and his large sympathies – opened the fire with the growing largesse of the College revenues, and that we must prepare to justify the possession of them before the public – I spoke of the splendour of our opportunities – of the growing necessity of people outside to look up to the Universities with veneration – pointed to the Universities as the true corrective to the materialistic tendencies of the age, in the present development of wealth and commerce.

Gladstone was plainly impressed with Roundell, who, in 1866 was appointed secretary to the commission of inquiry into the response of Governor Eyre to the revolt in Jamaica, [119] and subsequently did much work for the Liberal leader as unpaid private secretary, [120] but he wasn't prepared to budge: [121]

> To all this he warmly responded – assured me that there was nothing he had more at heart, but hitherto, when he had spoken to his Oxford friends on these subjects he had found no response but obstructiveness – that it was quite new to him to hear of the Liberal spirit amongst the young men – and that if he were free-er, he would do anything to work in that direction.

The liberals knew only too well who Gladstone's Oxford friends were. Although, in the general election which followed shortly, he lost his Oxford seat, Roundell's assumption that 'from Oxford to South Lancashire is clear gain' [122] was not borne out by events. The result simply broke the last tenuous links which had connected liberal and Tractarian in Oxford, in joint service on Gladstone's committee. [123] Goldwin Smith assured Gladstone that, 'with a single exception all the young liberals voted for you at last,' [124] but Gladstone was still so far from reciprocating their goodwill that he could write to a dissenter [125] in 1865 that, although, in the reform of Oxford,

the change in the balance of parties effected by the elections will cast upon the liberal majority a serious responsibility ... I would rather see Oxford level with the ground, than its religion regulated in the manner which would please Bishop Colenso.

1867, with the debates on the Conservatives' Reform Bill, was a difficult year, but in the hands of J.D.Coleridge and Grant Duff [126] the Oxford Bill made good progress, reaching the Lords, who threw it out on 25 July. [127] Bouverie's measure – the Uniformity Act Amendment Bill – was introduced on 7 March, passed through its second reading and committee stages, but was lost by a snap division moved by the Conservatives at third reading on 7 August. [128] However, on the introduction of the Oxford Bill, Bouverie's co-sponsor, Henry Fawcett, announced that he would move for the provisions of the Oxford Bill to be made applicable to Cambridge. [129] He apparently did so without consultation, and without the approval of the Oxford liberals, but his motion was accepted at committee stage. A significant step had been taken to amalgamate the two Bills. [130]

This was not achieved without a struggle. The Oxford liberals still wanted a Bill specifically tailored to their requirements and, according to Goldwin Smith, they considered that Coleridge's Bill, after Fawcett's amendment, 'advanced beyond the scope of our deliberations'. [131] While the Bill was still before the Lords (but doomed by their hostility and the lateness of the session), they held a conference at the Ship Hotel [132] to frame 'a measure which ... may lead to a complete and permanent settlement', dealing with matters of internal reform as well. But for Oxford only. Cambridge would be left to fend for itself.

When the Oxford Bill, drafted by Roundell and Bryce over the Christmas vacation of 1867-8, appeared, Cambridge men were dismayed: Henry Fawcett called the draft 'an extraordinary jumble of discordant elements', and pressed for a simple joint measure rather than two separate ones concerned with internal reform. [133] Henry Sidgwick strengthened this case with a memorandum which indicated his inability to sustain for much longer a position he felt to be intellectually dishonest. [134] The decision rested with a joint meeting in January of Oxford and Cambridge reformers convened at Horace Davey's chambers, where the decision to proceed with a joint Bill was carried by the casting vote of James Bryce. [135]

The Oxford and Cambridge Universities Bill was brought in by Coleridge, Bouverie and Grant Duff on 18 February, 1868. [136] Its second reading opened on 13 May and on 1 July it was carried, 198-140, [137] but on 22 July in view of the approaching dissolution it was withdrawn. [138] By now, however, some sort of concession was likely: Gladstone, his eye on the Irish Church, became cautiously sympathetic. Late in February he met Goldwin Smith, proposed several detailed modifications [139] and hinted that he might go further to secure a settlement than they had ever imagined. His search for a 'firmer standing ground' had ultimately led him to take the academic liberal position.

The prospect of a settlement, and of a general election in the near future, brought the clergy out for the first time since 1864 against the Bill. Bishop Wilberforce addressed a protest meeting at Buckingham on 18 April, and on 9 May the Cambridge Senate petitioned both the Archbishop of Canterbury and parliament against it. [140] But the High Church was already moving rapidly towards concession. The *Guardian* now supported abolition, [141] and both Liddon and Pusey attempted to sell Gladstone and the Nonconformists a fifty-fifty share in Oxford provided it remained a religious institution. [142]

Gladstone won the elections in November with a decisive majority and a mandate to disestablish the Irish Church. Tests abolition had figured as one of the subsidiary issues. According to Coleridge, [143] 'there was scarcely an address issued by a Liberal Candidate which did not pledge the candidate to the support of it'. He exaggerated. The academics who participated in the elections found that Gladstone's personality and the character of constituency politics played the critical roles. But their enthusiasm for the reform was sustained. In December Coleridge, now Solicitor-General, asked Gladstone to take over the Bill. In support of his case he cited seven factors: the unity of the party on the issue; the pledges given at the elections; the desires of Nonconformity; the necessity of giving the impression of energetic legislation at the beginning of the ministry; the use of the measure to bind the party together when the Irish issue might tend to divide it; the ease of timetabling its progress through the House; and the disappointment that the Bill's numerous partisans would feel were it to fail yet again. [144] But Gladstone refused to commit the government, and, although the 1869 Bill received the support of individual ministers, this did not prevent the Lords from rejecting it on 19 July. [145]

During the year, however, the university men increased their demands. Henry Sidgwick's decision in June to resign his Trinity fellowship on grounds of conscience quickened activity at Cambridge. [146] There the liberals, despairing of the willingness of colleges to alter their statutes voluntarily – the Bill was simply permissive – pressed for compulsion. [147] After consultation, Roundell asked Gladstone to take over the measure, thus amended. [148] Gladstone replied that the time factor was critical: a 'permissive' Bill would probably pass the Commons rapidly and survive the Lords; he could not guarantee this for the Bill now proposed. [149] Despite further resolutions from Oxford and Cambridge and a deputation of influential Nonconformists which he received at Downing Street on 15 December, he still refused to accept it. [150]

Gladstone's warning to Roundell [151] was proved by the events of 1870. Because of the lengthy and acrimonious debates on the Education Bill, the university measure was not introduced until 25 April. [152] It passed its Commons stages rapidly enough, and went to the Lords on 5 July. There Lord Robert Cecil, now the Marquess of Salisbury, and, since 26 June, Chancellor of Oxford, lay in wait. Salisbury's tactic was not to move outright rejection – the use of the Lords as a Conservative long-stop was a consequence of later party strife – but to set up, by a vote of 95-97, a select committee of the House to inquire into the safeguarding of religious instruction at the universities. [153] After submitting a first report, the committee voted, against Liberal opposition, to adjourn till the next session, which deprived the Bill of its chance of passing in 1870. [154]

The select committee interviewed several representative liberal and clerical dons and produced a report advocating that tutors declare against teaching doctrine hostile to the Church of England. [155] (The conservative attitude had altered somewhat: the threat to the Church was replaced by concern at the propagation of atheistical and radical opinions). It was probably instrumental in retaining clerical Fellowships, [156] but otherwise its conclusions mattered little. Liberal opinion at the universities rejected them out of hand, [157] and, at the beginning of the 1871 session, as he re-introduced the Bill, Gladstone, too, turned them down. [158] The Tory peers and the bishops who had won the select committee the previous session decided not to press the issue, and on 16 June the Bill received the royal assent. [159]

VII

Before the parliament had done with the Tests Bill, Gladstone set in motion another instalment of university reform, a commission to inquire into the income of both universities and their colleges. Roundell, who was charged with drafting its remit, expected [160] the task to take weeks, but the inquiry, under the Duke of Cleveland, was more elaborate, and did not report until the autumn of 1874, by which time Gladstone's government had fallen. [161]

The announcement of the commission did not meet with unqualified approval. In December 1871 Gladstone received a critical memorial from Cambridge dons – inspired, apparently, by Henry Fawcett [162] – questioning the need for a purely financial inquiry, and calling for a second executive Commission. [163] The position of the university liberals was in fact less straightforward, for by 1871 they were dividing on the future educational role of the universities. Hitherto religious and political elements had been dominant; the discussion of educational objectives came late on the scene, and probably some of the acrimony which marked it arose from the slow progresss in parliament.

The most significant contribution towards the defining of these objectives, and the reopening of the controversies of the 1850s, was Mark Pattison's *Suggestions on Academical Organisation,* published late in 1867. The book originated from discussions on the Tests and university reform at Osborne Morgan's chambers in May 1866. [164] 'It is the clearest, finest thing any of us people had put forth,' wrote James Bryce to Henry Sidgwick in January 1868: [165] 'But all the regular liberals call out that it is utopian: some that it is self-interested.' Pattison envisaged a radical expansion of the teaching and research role of the university, the annexation of fellowships to research in specific disciplines, the reduction of the colleges to the position of halls of residence and a drastic cheapening of the costs of a university education, on the pattern of Scotland or Germany. [166] As Bryce indicated, it immediately became a subject of violent controversy.

The movement for university reform associated with Pattison's proposals began energetically enough with the publication, in October 1869, of the first numbers of the *Academy*, edited by Pattison's acolyte Charles Appleton, which was supposed to publicize the cause, the founding of the 'Association for the Organisation of Academical Study' on 16 November 1872 [167] and the production of a volume, *Essays on the Endowment of Research*, in 1876. A good number of the liberals supported it, including Bryce and Sidgwick, Leslie Stephen, the Nettleship brothers and T.H.Green, [168] but it was as vehemently opposed by others, notably by Henry Fawcett at Cambridge and G.C.Brodrick at Oxford. Fawcett and Brodrick, both politically ambitious, saw the existing Fellowship system as a means of easing the transit of young men from the universities into the professions and public life, and suspected the movement to endow research as an attempt to move the universities away from this, towards subsidized pedantry. [169]

This reaction underlay Fawcett's move against the financial inquiry: he hoped for limited reforms which would protect the old collegiate structure, and feared a larger, university-orientated, reform. And by 1875 Brodrick was urging the government 'to aid the spontaneous efforts of corporations on the whole liberal, public-spirited, and progressive', and not to dissipate 'resources already so well employed'. [170]

After the report of the Cleveland commission, Salisbury issued executive commissions to redraft the statutes of both universities and their colleges. From 1877 to 1882 the remaining 'clerical' restrictions – the obligation to proceed to orders and the insistence on celibacy – were quietly repealed. [171] But the general tendency of the institutional reforms, aimed at enhancing the university *vis-à-vis* the colleges, was not universally welcomed. Brodrick thought it a political move aimed at the more radical colleges and at college fellows who went into politics, [172] while liberal heads of colleges – like Jowett, since 1871 Master of Balliol – had already revivified the collegiate ethos to an extent which seemed to make the proposals of the commissions, undertaken as they were against a background of falling college rents, almost irrelevant. [173]

IX

The acrimonious debate in the early 1870s about the nature of university education disposes of the view that the liberal academics were trying in the Tests campaign to create a system of higher education for a democratic England. The question was never absent from their minds, but it was only articulated coherently when repeal was almost certain, and produced no unanimity of approach. Rather the campaign was a functional success: an integration of several areas of concern which met the political needs of academics placed in an uncomfortable position morally and professionally. As radical politicians they found being the pensioners of conservative and socially exclusive institutions uncomfortable, unless they promised to reform them. Even if, as Goldwin Smith claimed, university reform needed political reform, radical academics had still to pledge themselves to it. The attack on the Tests was an essential prerequisite for their entry into the political arena, breaking down the alienation of their own institution in favour of a 'national' commitment.

The cause of Tests repeal was important less for what actually happened than for the way in which the academic liberals interpreted it. In the political theories they were concurrently evolving they were not concerned with the alteration of society through 'positive' acts of intervention by the state, but with the removal of impediments to individual effort and the efforts of individuals working in voluntary collaboration. The Tests campaign fitted smoothly into this theory of the nature of 'progressive' reform. It was, moreover, a campaign in which the demarcation line between enlightenment and reaction seemed to them firmly drawn, where they were fighting for liberal intellectual and educational values against the tyranny of traditional authority and vested interest. The same thing could be said of the debate on the American Civil War and on franchise reform, but this was the cause which came closest to their own situation, and their certainty in this case of where right lay influenced their attitude to the wider field of 'secular' politics. The difficulty was that, in the wider field, the questions that confronted them were more ambiguous, the remedies less straightforward.

And how crucial was the academics' campaign, anyway, in determining the nature of the final reform? Most of them came away from the fray with their opinion of Gladstone little enhanced, yet Gladstone throughout seems to have been the arbiter of the situation. In his *Studies in Contemporary Biography,* James Bryce observed his chief's tendency to absorb arguments about an issue while apparently remaining immovable, then, once his mind was made up, to act rapidly and decisively. [174] His behaviour in the case of the Tests seems to confirm this: in 1863 he realized that some sort of reform was necessary; in 1864 he tentatively moved, and then withdrew, his own scheme; after 1868, seeing that the tide was generally setting against established religion, he adopted and extended the liberal academics' measures. With Gladstone against them, they might have won a 'permissive' bill; after he had determined to move 'to a firmer standing ground' they won a compulsory measure.

For nine years the Tests agitation provided in a changing political situation a constant point of reference, a solid linkage with practical politics. Moreover, being concerned with specific objectives, rather than with a long term scheme of reform, it minimized areas of disagreement and promoted unity. Without its influence, the tendency for university men in journalism, in politics or in residence at Oxford or Cambridge to succumb to the life-style of the situations in which they found themselves would probably have been irresistible, and their distinctive group-consciousness would have been dissipated.

[5]

UNIVERSITY MEN
AND
FOREIGN POLITICS

Take, since you bade it should bear,
These, the seed of your sowing,
Blossom or berry or weed.
Sweet though they be not, or fair,
That the dew of your word kept growing,
Sweet at least was the seed.

Algernon Charles Swinburne 'To Joseph Mazzini'

In an otherwise favourable review of *Essays on Reform*, J.R.Green observed that the contributors seemed 'to feel more at home among the institutions of Switzerland and America than among those of England'. [1] His purpose was to emphasize the alienation of intellectual and working man alike from the political society of the time, but the comment was, in itself, valid enough. Fifty years later A.V.Dicey, writing to James Bryce, remembered that T.H.Green was not [2]

as keenly interested in foreign nationalist movements as I think most of the Old Mortality were. I think he had a far keener interest in social movements at home, and probably somewhat more knowledge than I or perhaps most of us had.

Bryce himself had, four years earlier, put 'the subject nationalities, and especially Italy' at the head of the list of subjects which he recollected 'as chiefly occupying our thoughts and talk' [3] in the 1860s. This was not surprising; since academics came from social and geographical environments far different from the mass of the population, their identification with working-class politics was necessarily indirect. But interest in foreign politics did not imply escapism; it had intellectual validity and ultimately it played an important part in allying the academics with British radicals in and out of parliament during the political crisis of 1866-7. Their preoccupation with Italian unification – despite its overtones of 'romantic radicalism' – helped create the conception of 'moral' nationality which underlay their prescriptions for British political problems; their support for the North in the American Civil War, by forcing them to break with their own social order and cooperate with radical groups, strengthened their democratic convictions and their practical interest in reform.

II

University men had been involved in foreign politics before. The radical sympathies of Wordsworth and Coleridge, Landor and Southey, were kindled at Oxford and Cambridge at the time of the French Revolution; Byron and Shelley flourished a generation later. In 1830 Tennyson, John Sterling and Richard Chenevix-Trench, of the Aspostles, planned an expedition over the Pyrenees to assist a liberal rising, and were lucky to escape with their lives when most of the Spaniards and one young Irish sympathizer were rounded up and shot. [4]

Such involvement has continued to the present day, notably in the 1930s. Although influenced by the course of foreign affairs, social and institutional factors also encouraged it. Since the universities catered until comparatively recently for the wealthier classes, their students were both remote from British radicalism and able to have close contact with foreign politics. Did this reflect a dissociation of political enthusiasm from personal interest, which avoided the charge that its consequences might practically destroy one's own order? In view of the later conservatism of many participants, this argument makes sense; in the 1860s Swinburne and John Nichol recommended violence to Italian radicals; they later condemned it in Ireland. [5] But, unstable though this vicarious radicalism could be, it became one of the bases of political involvement in the 1850s and 1860s.

It was reinforced by two factors: the improvement of communications and the traditional sympathies of the academics' families. Between 1840 and 1850 London, Paris, Berlin, Munich, Vienna and Trieste became connected by rail and steamer. Travel between them became rapid and, at least for the middle classes, cheap. The second factor was less straightforward but no less significant. The academics could draw on family attitudes which, while unsympathetic to the idea of political revolution as such, [6] were critical of the continental autocracies. The fact that the most notorious Western European rulers were Catholics – the Emperor of Austria, the Pope, after 1852 Napoleon III, not to speak of the kings of Spain and Portugal and the Italian rulers – meant that Evangelical England had little time for them. Cavour noted in 1856 that 'the Protestant zealots headed by Lord Shaftesbury' were 'the most enthusiastic' [7] for the Italian Cause; Edmund Gosse described his fundamentalist father's enthusiasm every time trouble broke out in the Papal dominions. [8] While this link was stronger in their fathers' generation than in theirs, enthusiasm for movements against continental repression was firmly implanted in their minds, especially during the traumatic year of 1848.

Seventy years later A.V.Dicey could still recall the impression the events of the year made on a thirteen year old: [9]

It so happened that being brought up at home, and hearing the conversation of parents infinitely nobler and wiser than myself and also of their friends, I entered, not from any precocity, for I was very backward in learning, but from the influence of what I heard, into the events of '48. This really turned the whole intellectual interest of my mind towards political and constitutional controversies, under the sanest and most just of Whig teachers ... in many ways I woke up to conscious existence in 1848.

James Bryce, to whom he wrote, was only ten at the time, but, like Dicey, was taken by his father to hear Kossuth on his British tour in 1851. [10] In Scotland the Hungarian patriot stayed with Professor John Pringle Nichol, father of the founder of the Old Mortality, [11] and was entertained by James Stuart's father at Cupar in Fife. [12] Nor was enthusiasm absent among older university liberals. Jowett and Stanley went to Paris and ended up marching with a revolutionary column around the Place de la Concorde, [13] and Arthur Hugh Clough witnessed at first hand the struggle and collapse of the Roman Republic. [14] Its fall prompted both the detached observation of *'Amours de Voyage'* and the fervour of 'Say not the struggle nought availeth' which passed into anthologies and was sung in public-school chapels. In it Clough implied that the fight, continued on a broader front, would ultimately be successful, and in his last stanza

And not by eastern windows only,
　When daylight comes, comes in the light;
In front the sun climbs slow, how slowly,
　But westward look, the land is bright!

seemed to indicate that the real success of liberalism would come first in the west, in the United States.

In the meantime, however, academic contacts with continental radicals were increased by the flight into Britain of the leaders of the abortive revolutions. Herzen, Mazzini, Saffi, Louis Blanc, Pulszky, Kossuth, came to frequent the same London world, on the fringes of politics and journalism, that drew to it young men from the universities. [15] It was not a particularly tranquil exile community: personal, strategic and national animosities abounded, but it impressed on them the character and aims of radicalism in Europe.

III

This situation had three main consequences for university men: they became involved in the welfare of national minorities within multi-national empires; they interested themselves in the comparative study of national governments; and they concentrated their attention on Italy as the prospective nation whose liberal movement crystallized the positive values of nationality.

The first was relatively straightforward. James Bryce's interest in minority rights stemmed from his reaction to the Austrian Empire's suppression of its dissident nationals after 1848. [16] Subsequently he took up the cause of the Armenians in the Turkish Empire. [17] This reflected a widespread division of labour; Freeman took in hand the cause of the Eastern Christians, [18] Westlake the Finns, [19] Dicey the Russian Jews, [20] Fawcett the Indians, [21] Charles Pearson the Poles and so on. [22] Despite subsequent breaches on domestic politics, they retained this concern to the end.

The 'comparative method' too remained. In his last book, *Modern Democracies*, James Bryce devoted a chapter to it, which repays detailed study, as on its simple axioms the social studies of the academics were based. More or less it ran thus: Human society obeys discoverable laws. [23] Human nature is by and large similar throughout the world. [24] Societies differ through the way in which these laws are adapted to the physical nature of a particular country or its state of historical development. Bryce claimed the method as scientific because: [25]

it reaches general conclusions by tracing similar results to similar causes, eliminating those disturbing influences which, present in one country and absent in another, make the results in the examined cases different in some parts while similar in others.

The parallel with de Tocqueville is obvious enough: social laws were discovered by accumulating facts about political institutions and the like, community by community, and shaking them down into common and comparable categories.

The 'comparative method' was crude. Its notion of human nature in politics was unrealistically rational and disinterested. [26] Further, the rise of industrial society, and its confrontation or interaction with traditional societies, deprived comparisons between communities of much of their validity. However, at that time crude comparisons, using national stereotypes for purposes of political debate, were the rule. De Tocqueville was quoted out of context to condemn democratic government, [27] when the academics felt that his methods could, by examining systems of government in their national and historical contexts, show their true relevance to contemporary British problems. In the European upheavals after 1848, and through their acquaintance with continental liberals, they had an exceptionally fertile field of study.

The physical focus of the academics' attentions was Italy. Why Italy? Evangelical protestantism made its contribution, along with classical learning [28] and enthusiasm for the consciously Anglophile liberalism of Piedmont. [29] But while British enthusiasm generally was diffuse and moderate, favouring simply 'local freedom and reform in the several states', [30] academic sympathies were with the left extremists: the terrorist Mazzini stood as high in their eyes as the prudent liberal Cavour.

'Do you ever hear anything of Mazzini?' wrote Jowett to one of his lady correspondents in August 1861, [31]

He seems to be more abused than any other man in this world. I think he must be a great man, though a visionary and perhaps dangerous. The present state of Italy is greatly due to him. His defence of Rome raised the Italian character.

That this tribute should come from an older and decidedly less 'enthusiastic' liberal is significant enough. The younger men – Bryce, Dicey, Sidgwick, Green – admired him with less reservation. Sidgwick wrote of him in 1868 to J.A.Symonds: [32]

he is a fine arguer, like an eager torrent, at the same time subtle and clear ... I talked politics to him: I determined to put boldly all the commonplaces about assassination, etc. (as far as I believed them) and see what he said: he was wonderfully fair, calm and impressive.

And John Morley considered that he spoke for his generation [33] when he wrote that [34]

Of all the democratic gospellers of that epoch between 1848 and 1870 ... it was Mazzini who went nearest to the heart and true significance of democracy. He had a moral glow, and the light of large historic and literary comprehension, that stretched it into the

101

minds of men with social imagination enough to look for new ideals, and courage enough to resist the sluggard's dread of new illusions.

Mazzini's reputation has not fared well in the twentieth century. To a radical historian of the present day, E.J.Hobsbawm, his personal ineffectuality [35] symbolized 'the disintegration of the European revolutionary movement into national segments'. [36] Mazzini's 'deficiency in affairs' [37] was evident enough to his younger British contemporaries, and ultimately led to their acceptance of Piedmontese dominance in Italy; [38] but to see his national consciousness as ultimately a conservative tendency, as Hobsbawm appears to do, is to misjudge his moral and political impact on them. His influence cannot, anyway, be estimated apart from the manner of its transmission to the British universities. Circumstances combined to force Mazzini and his ideas on the notice of university men, while the latter's cast of mind was adapted to respond enthusiastically to them.

In the liberal London society of the 1850s and 1860s [39] Italian refugees played an important part, from the former Carbonarist Panizzi at the British Museum, through Gabriele Rossetti, father of the poet, to numerous literary men reduced to language teaching, [40] prepared to suffer what Mazzini called 'the Hell of Exile' [41] rather than compromise with monarchy for the relative security of Genoa or Turin. Republicanism even penetrated Oxford when Aurelio Saffi came there as a language teacher in 1853 – and was given a university appointment in 1856. Saffi had been triumvir with his friend Mazzini and Armellini of the Roman Republic. He put Frederic Harrison in touch with many Italian republican leaders, and arranged for him to make several trips to Italy. [43] Subsequently, in 1858, he tried to persuade Beesly to become secretary of a society to agitate for British intervention on the side of continental liberals, but Beesly demurred on the grounds that he was 'too much a follower of Bright to accept their offer'. [44] Brightist 'non-intervention' appealed to some of the university men – usually those with a livelier interest in domestic reform – and detracted from their involvement in Italian affairs. The Old Mortality for instance, was divided by the Crimean War: T.H.Green condemned it on non-interventionist grounds, but John Nichol and A.V.Dicey approved it as a crusade against continental reactionaries. [45] On the whole their attitudes prevailed, but for most of them to learn Italian from Saffi [46] 'became part of the ritual of cultured Liberalism in Oxford and an initiation into the spirit of the Risorgimento'.

James Bryce's action in volunteering (unsuccessfully) in 1860 to serve with the Thousand gave proof of the power of Italian sympathies, for Garibaldi seemed Mazzinian nationalism incarnate.[47] In 1864 Bryce, who would fifty years later claim him and Lincoln, as the only heroes of his age,[48] wrote reverently of him, during his triumphal progress through London: 'a face the sweetest and gentlest I have ever seen'.[49] Bryce's letters give a vivid insight into his social and political views at the time, and help explain where the Italian patriot fitted into them. He wrote to his sister of the procession which accompanied Garibaldi:[50]

a string of dirty and unshaven men carrying the flags and tawdry decorations of their trades unions and friendly societies; many temperance associations among them, Bands of Hope and so forth, shuffling queerly along with a mixture of conscious sense of dirt and self-importance in forming such a ceremony.

And later to Freeman:[51]

We have had great excitement à propos of Garibaldi; the reception was the most wonderful outburst of popular enthusiasm ever seen in London: no greetings of victorious Wellingtons or pseudo-Danish damsels at all comparable to it. Now he is gone, not without rage on the part of the people, especially of the North, who, when Gladstone and Clarendon had denied Lewis' interference, attributed it to the queen.

Taken together, these demonstrate both intellectual republicanism and sympathy for democracy, but they also show the academics' remoteness from domestic politics. Bryce may have been more fastidious than most, but, according to Royden Harrison, even the Positivists at their most radical could condescend.[52] Plainly the academics would find it difficult to make common cause with the masses through the intimacy of shared perceptions and sympathies. But in a roundabout way contact could be made, by shared enthusiasms and enmities in foreign politics, at a time when working-class absorption in foreign-policy questions was at its most intense.[53]

This unity became particularly significant during the American Civil War. But Italian liberalism still had a direct influence on the content of academic radicalism, which strengthened it for that bitter contest. 'The ritual of cultivated liberalism' contained a positive programme. Mazzini's ideology was scarcely lucid or cohesive, but in two significant ways he was influential: he demanded a devotion to the ideal of democratic nationalism which was religious rather than calculating;[54] he argued that politics was a moral rather than a functional activity.[55] The university men, re-interpreting the evangelical tradition on similar lines, welcomed the sanction of a man honoured by a movement to which they were anyway sympathetic.

Mazzini's philosophy was idealist and rejected utilitarianism. Not surprisingly he was venerated most by T.H.Green and his disciples at Oxford. [56] However, the central moral problem he stated – the incompatibility between the utilitarian's call for individuals to will the greatest happiness of the greatest number and his use of the 'self-regarding' individual as the unit from which society was constructed – was common to utilitarians like Sidgwick as well. [57] This dilemma was stated in quite explicit terms in the context of a nationality struggling for freedom. Would that struggle get anywhere at all if there was no loyalty greater than that of the individual's self-interest?

Mazzini's response to this was to advocate loyalty to the nation, an ideal conceived not in racial, linguistic or geographical terms, but as a moral entity. [58] Although he was vague about what precisely this meant, and in practice liberal nationalism boiled down to a reassertion of more primitive loyalties, the concept made sense to the academics. The ideal of citizens making sacrifices for the benefit of the 'nation' gave the moral basis for an ideology of cooperation rather than class-struggle within society. Discussing democracy in 1867 Bryce's arguments were decidedly Mazzinian: [59]

It is undeniable that democracy – the participation of the whole nation in the direction of its own affairs – has a stimulating power such as belongs to no other form of government. By giving the sense of a common interest and purpose it gives unity and strength to the whole State; it rouses the rich and powerful by obliging them to retain their influence not by privilege so much as by energy and intellectual eminence; it elevates the humbler classes by enlarging their sense of vision and their sense of responsibility.

The academics did not derive their conception of nationality from Mazzini and the Italian experience; but these reinforced certain pre-existing tendencies, especially the 'ritual' nature of democratic commitment. The ruling social ideal of Evangelicalism, the notion that rich and poor were at one before omnipotent God, became in the liberalism of the 1860s a commitment to civil and legal equality within the moral framework of the nation: both succeeded by rejecting the premises of utilitarian individualism. It could be argued that in both cases the unstated motive for this was a fear that utilitarian rationality on the part of the deprived would enhance their consciousness of social inequality. But religious commitments are not reinforced by underlining the calculation behind them; Evangelical and academic liberal alike came to their faith through a process which was a response to other, explicitly moral and intellectual, pressures: liberal leanings brought about Italian sympathies, which led to identification with popular support for Italy in Britain. Absence of direct sympathy with popular politics in England remained: the academics were never able to overcome the alienation of two distinct life-styles. But a further crisis in foreign politics, the American Civil War, was to reinforce the identification and ultimately lead to a direct alliance.

IV

As the sentiments of the British government and upper classes were vaguely pro-Italian anyway, the academics' Italian enthusiasm did not provoke confrontation. It might have done so had they continued to sympathize with the republicans, but during the crisis of 1859-60 the majority, albeit with reluctance, accepted the dominance of Piedmont and its liberal monarchy. [60] Over the American Civil War, however, the nation was divided, and the academics found themselves at odds with most of their own class.

The war began on 12 April 1861. At first the attitude of the academics, in fact of English radicals in general, was ambiguous: if a detestation for slavery and a sympathy for democratic ideals led them to sympathize with the Federal side, a suspicion of the protectionist policies of the North, its reluctance to proscribe slavery, and a traditional enthusiasm for minority rights, held them in check. Goldwin Smith adduced these as reasons for his own initial impulse to sanction secession, as did Richard Cobden, but both soon swung round to the support of the North. [61]

Liberal beliefs were compatible with support for the secession of the South: this line was taken throughout the war by Acton and Gladstone. [62] At Cambridge John Jermyn Cowell energetically preached the Southern cause to his friends Henry Sidgwick and George Otto Trevelyan: [63]

We were liberals – we execrated those who presumed anywhere to abuse or maltreat under the pretence of respect for 'religion' or order, people who only wished to be alone and be happy in their own way ... I condemn this war, of course, as an inhuman aggression – but – to my indescribable confusion and disappointment, this crucial test divides us and you admire what I execrate.

Cowell's pro-secession arguments had a certain amount of success. By November 1863 Sidgwick's ardour for the North had cooled, [64] and for much of the war Trevelyan was sympathetic to the South. [65] Both, however, were untypical of their generation, and by the end of the war had come back firmly to the Northern side. [66] Cowell's arguments had been countered by a powerful antithesis which convinced partly by its domestic relevance, and partly by the sheer strength of the moral conception of politics inherited from the evangelical tradition.

Hatred of slavery and the slave trade had been an article of the Evangelical faith, and it was this inherited conviction (rather than any idea that the negroes were being deprived of *political* equality, as by and large they thought them, as a 'backward' race, unfitted for it) [67] that framed their perceptions. The war was, to T.H.Green, the responsibility of 'a slave-holding, slave-breeding and slave-burning oligarchy, on which the curse of God and humanity rests'. [68] John Morley, attempting to explain Gladstone's attitude, attributed it to [69]

the error that lay at the root of our English misconception of the struggle ... We applied ordinary political maxims to what was not merely a political contest, but a social revolution ... The significances of the American war was its relation to slavery.

Leslie Stephen's philippic *'The Times' and the American War*, which he published in 1865, was concerned with the moral gymnastics *The Times* performed in attempting to prove that, while slavery was detestable, the war was not being fought to abolish it, therefore the South was in the right; or if it was being fought to abolish it, the North was condoning the likely barbarities of a servile war, and was therefore in the wrong, and so on. [70] Stephen started from the opinion that slavery was wrong, that, however diplomatically the North had at first masked this, it was fighting to destroy it. [71] Morality stood on one side, infamy on the other. *The Times* failed to accept this; thus its attitude was not governed by morality but by political strategy. As an allegedly liberal paper, it did not state explicitly what to it was 'the true cause of the war', but adopted sly formulations. 'Far be it from us', it pronounced on 18 October 1861, [72]

to dogmatise about democracy, or to attribute the Civil War to representative institutions. The secession of the South is certainly not a necessary consequence of any form of government. Yet it is not too much to say that the form which democracy has taken for the last thirty years, or since the Presidency of Jackson, was likely to lead to such a result.

'In other words,' concluded Stephen, 'we won't distinctly say it, but we will hint it.'

Conservative forces in Britain had therefore imported the argument about democracy. As Goldwin Smith wrote, they used the slavery issue before the war to belabour the American democracy, and ignored it, or obfuscated it, during the war in order to continue the beating. [73] Democracy was to them, Bryce wrote later, [74]

a monster like the Chimaera of the Iliad, terrible in every part, 'a lion in front and a dragon behind, breathing forth the dreadful might of quenchless fire.'

The Times appropriated the war as a suitable environment for the beast, and the bulk of the British press followed its lead. They described a Union driven by the mania of Lincoln, variously presented as 'a Moloch of slaughter and devastation' [75] or the puppet of his military chiefs, [76] the power of both wrenched from corrupt assemblies, after these had bankrupted the state with borrowing, inflated the currency with paper money and thrown up tariff walls to destroy free trade. [77] While at the front the incompetence and venality of the 'democratic' federal administration decimated its 'citizen' armies, and then flung Irish and German mercenaries, specially imported, into the breach, [78] the South, with its plantation aristocracy, its military abilities, its natural preference for free trade, remained 'stable' and recognizably 'English'. [79]

Leslie Stephen set out to destroy this caricature, and prefaced his pamphlet with an anecdote which set *The Times's* activities in their British context. [80] A former editor of *The Times*, he wrote, used to keep a shrewd, idle, clergyman simply to hang about the clubs and pick up, from gossip, the prevailing opinion of respectable society. Printing House Square gave this a leavening of 'scholarship', then retailed it back to the public in the leaders. The anecdote was more than an embellishment; it identified the enemy of 'sober truthspeaking' and progressive politics as respectable society itself.

'Respectable society' had no doubt where blame for the war lay. Robert Lowe, as a *Times* leader-writer responsible for that newspaper's attitude, later wrote that [81]

the political evils of America [can] be traced to that which to common sense would seem their natural fountain, the form of its government.

This was a debater's argument. Thoughtful conservatives less well placed than Lowe to project their ideas, like Sir Edward Bulwer

Lytton and Charles Adderley, came about the same time to the opposite conclusion, that the checks and balances of the Federal Constitution were a bridle on popular recklessness. [82] But the upper classes had made up their minds about the menace of popular democracy, and exploited the war as ample illustration of this: [83]

... the problem of blockade rights, of British maritime interests, of free trade and the supplies of cotton for the Lancashire mills, largely lost their relevance and became subordinate to the main debate on the merits and defects of a democratic system.

Dr Henry Pelling's judgement was reflected at the time by James Bryce, writing in February 1863 to Edward Freeman: [84]

... the prospects of anything being done for ourselves in England seem so much connected with the progress of more democratic republicanism against oligarchy that we feel less disposed to acquiesce in secession.

V

In 1861 university liberals inclined to a stance in politics which was only mildly left of centre. Goldwin Smith, who was to become their leader, had most of his political connections with Whigs or Peelites, the latter predominating. [85] Academics who admitted to radicalism of the school of Cobden and Bright – T.H.Green and, for a time, the Oxford Positivists – were in a small minority. [86] The course of the war, and the reactions to it of the various sections of British society, alienated them from old allies and gave them new ones. Three main factors influenced this transition: direct contact with pro-Federal American intellectuals, identification with 'honest' reporting of the war, and admiration for the line taken by working people and their leaders during it.

The moral issue of slavery, and the effect of the Federal blockade on the cotton industry, meant that the war was followed with interest in Britain and, after over twenty-five years of steam navigation on the Atlantic, America could be easily reached by those who wanted to find out for themselves what was going on. [87] In the case of those university men who made the journey – Edward Dicey, Leslie Stephen, Lord Houghton, Goldwin Smith and Henry Yates Thompson had done so before the war ended – the result was a powerful reinforcement of their initial sympathies. [88]

This was substantially due to the fact that they discovered in America – especially around Boston – a comparable intellectual group, men like J.R.Lowell, C.E.Norton, the Adams family,

E.L.Godkin and the Wendell Holmeses. [89] Although they made contacts throughout American political life – Goldwin Smith met Emerson, the historian Bancroft, Secretary of the Treasury Chase, Secretary of State Seward, General Butler and Lincoln himself – their closest links thereafter were with the Unitarian 'Brahmans' of Boston. [90] Their very existence was significant, as it defied conservative arguments that democracy was bound to bring about the extinction of cultivated and educated society. [91] Since they were militantly in favour of the Union and opposed to the Southern ethos on political and moral grounds, the inference their English visitors drew was that, if liberal-minded men who had experienced democratic institutions at work had no time for an undemocratic society, then there was even less justification for pro-Southern sympathies in Britain.

Visits to America were also supplemented by contacts with pro-Federal Americans resident in Britain. Young Henry Adams came over in 1861 as private secretary to his father, Charles Francis Adams, the American minister, and, as a sort of public relations officer for the embassy, found himself dealing with a public opinion which was largely hostile. [92] Although he classed the universities along with *The Times*, the Church and most of the aristocracy as pillars of that 'ideal eccentricity' [93] whose heart went out to the rebel South, he found congenial society which 'affected his whole life' in friendship with Charles Milnes Gaskell of Trinity College, Cambridge, and his undergraduate colleagues. [94] Adams was introduced to Cambridge society by his cousin, William Everett, who was also a Trinity undergraduate. [95] Everett, the son of the Boston Unitarian preacher and statesman, had matriculated in 1859, and between then and 1863 became an Apostle, President of the Union and a close friend of younger Cambridge academics like Henry Sidgwick and Henry Jackson. [96] When Cowell complained to Sidgwick of what he considered the latter's irrational pro-Northern bias, he specifically blamed this on Everett's proselytizing. [97]

Such contacts not only strengthened pro-Northern sentiment in the Universities, but provided a standard of personal observation and experience against which to judge the way the press reacted to the war. Press bias, moreover posed the immediate problem of getting publicity for pro-Northern views. Few newspapers were 'sound'; in 1864 Goldwin Smith complained to Alexander Macmillan, who was publishing his *Letter to a Whig Member of the Southern Independence Association* – at the Professor's own expense – that his views made him 'an unmarketable article on this side of the Atlantic'. [98] Two years earlier Macmillan had written. [99]

our *Magazine (Macmillan's Magazine)* has stood almost exclusively among the magazines, and stands with few public prints of any kind in advocating the cause of the North.

Henry Adams could count only the *Daily News* (which had the Anglo-Irish E.L.Godkin as its New York correspondent), [100] the ailing *Morning Star* and the *Spectator* as publications at all sympathetic to the Federal side. [101]

But unpopularity stimulated rather than cowed the academics. Leslie Stephen recollected that, at Cambridge, [102]

the sense that we were in a minority in our own class gave a special zest to our advocacy. Many a college feast was resolved into a vehement debating society, and passions ran higher than has ever since been the case, unless during the Eastern Question of 1877, and the recent Boer War.

At Oxford T.H.Green, a convinced and almost reckless pro-Federal, found 'more people sound' on the war in Oxford 'than among the same number anywhere else in England'.

After all, in spite of our Toryism here, I believe there are more people sound on that point in Oxford than are to be found among the same number anywhere else in England.

After Green's death James Bryce wrote, corroborating his evidence, [103] that there was 'no place in England ... in which so large a proportion of the educated class sympathized with the cause of the North'.

The degree to which this confrontation allied them with the newspapers and publishing houses which supported the North is demonstrated by the reform essays of 1867. Their publisher was Alexander Macmillan. A former Christian Socialist, he had moved towards more orthodox liberalism, becoming in 1863 chairman of Henry Fawcett's committee at the Cambridge borough election, [104] and as publisher to both universities he was in contact with the younger dons, publishing work by Leslie Stephen, James Bryce and Sir George Young. In 1863 he published Edward Dicey's sympathetic *Six Months in the Federal States* and a year later, by publishing his *Letter to a Whig Member*, began a close connection with Goldwin Smith. [105] Macmillan cultivated close relations with his authors and drew the younger men into the society of Thomas Hughes and John Malcolm Ludlow, friends from the beginning of his business life, whom John Stuart Mill saw as the North's foremost defenders. [106]

Ludlow contributed an essay to *Questions for a Reformed Parliament* (Hughes intended to, but eventually didn't); two other notable Northern partisans, Richard Holt Hutton and Meredith White Townsend of the *Spectator*, were also among the reform essayists. [107] They had taken over the ailing weekly in 1861, and boldly set it on a pro-Federal course, thus attracting to it academic journalists like A.V.Dicey and Charles Henry Pearson. [108] Moreover, their war coverage was of a high standard. Their military correspondent, George Hooper, who wrote on 'Army Reform' in *Questions for a Reformed Parliament*, was, according to the *Dictionary of National Biography*, alone in perceiving the significance of Sherman's controversial 'wasting' of Georgia as the critical move which would shorten the war. [109]

Another pro-Northern editor was Frank Harrison Hill, between 1861 and 1865 on the *Northern Whig* in Belfast, a Unitarian protégé of Hutton who had studied under James Martineau and had been tutor to the Darbishire family [110] in Manchester: 'Alone of Irish journalists he supported the North in the American struggle, and he risked temporary unpopularity in the cause.' In 1865 he became the assistant editor of the *Daily News*, where he joined the Scotsman John Boyd Kinnear, a fervent Italian partisan and leader-writer on the paper. [111] Both contributed to the 1867 essays.

Besides journalists, the academics moved closer to the few politicians who took the Northern side. Before the war Goldwin Smith had been considered a Peelite, largely through his close working relationship with Gladstone in the reform of Oxford. [112] He was sufficiently moderate to be appointed to the Regius Chair by Lord Derby in 1858, and his Inaugural Lecture could still be construed as a plea for conservative reform. [113] The reaction of propertied society to the war destroyed this hope of its magnanimity. In 1864 he was writing to Macmillan that [114] national policy was 'the balanced selfishness of the landowners and the commercial capitalists'. And in 1867 Acton, reviewing Smith's *Lectures on Three English Statesmen*, commented that he reserved his especial venom for aristocracy, [115] as 'a foreign substance that preys on confiscated rights and properties'.

Smith's disgust drove him to identify with the resolute opponents of the South, whom he styled 'the Manchester School'. [116] What he understood by that term was something different from the men of 1846. Although accepting market economics, [117] he recognized that the moral qualities he associated with them were no longer displayed by successful North-Country cotton-spinners. They were as partisan for the South as clubland Tories. [118] He meant instead John Bright, Richard Cobden and half a dozen sympathetic Northern manufacturers headed by Thomas Bayley Potter, whom he took as remaining faithful to the full social and moral implications of the Free Trade Movement.

Unrepresentative of North-Country middle-class opinion though Smith's contacts were – James Bryce wrote to Freeman in 1865 that Potter was 'unpopular, save for a small set' [119] – the energy with which he leaped into political action brought vividly to the public mind a new image of the university man, and seemed to open to university men a new political option, the 'alliance with Manchester'. [120] Recollecting the period thirty-odd years later, the Irish journalist Justin McCarthy wrote: [121]

> As a rule the followers of Cobden and Bright had not until that epoch found themselves much in companionship with leading representatives of University culture in these countries. The University Don kept himself for the most part away from popular organisations and there was a sort of vague impression permeating society that culture and scholarship could not give much countenance to the popular doctrines about the equality of classes, the civic rights of man, and the rights of labour which were advocated from what was called the Manchester platform. I can well remember the delight not unmingled with surprise felt by Cobden and Bright when they found University scholars and magnates like Goldwin Smith presenting themselves at public meetings as champions of these popular but not socially recognised doctrines.

Cobden and Bright responded to Goldwin Smith's overtures. The professor first appeared in public at a meeting of Potter's Manchester Union and Emancipation Society, called on 6 April 1863 to protest against the building of warships for the Confederacy in British shipyards. [122] Further lectures and pamphlets followed until, according to McCarthy, [123] 'we read in every day's newspapers the account of the part he had played in some great controversy then occupying public attention'. 1864 seemed to see the consummation of the relationship, with Bright's visit to Oxford. Goldwin Smith breakfasted on 15 May; Bright reported: [124]'Greatly pleased with him; calm, thoughtful, conscientious and profoundly instructed he seems to me. It is a pleasure to listen to him.' On the next day he left, suitably impressed: [125] 'My little visit to Oxford has been an unmixed pleasure to me. Everything was beautiful – the buildings, the gardens, the weather, the season; and the society was most cultivated and liberal.' Just a month later he graced the academics' Tests Abolition meeting at the Freemasons' Tavern.

While Bright was at Oxford, T.H.Green called to worship: [126]

I was in his company for a couple of hours. To my great enjoyment. I can best describe him as a great brick. He is simple as a boy, full of fun, with a pleasant flow of conversation and lots of good stories. He does not seem to mind what he says to anybody, but though he is sufficiently brusque, his good humour saves him from seeming rude. There is nothing declamatory or pretentious about his talk; indeed, though very pleasant, it would not be very striking but for the strong feeling it sometimes shows – I was pleased by his recalling as soon as I was introduced to him a letter which I wrote to him more than three years ago.

By and large the younger men, with their radical enthusiasms generated by 'positive' commitments like that to Italian unification, were more straightforward in their adoption of the Northern cause, less embittered than Goldwin Smith by the attitude of respectable society because they had been less committed to it. Their American friends marvelled at their enthusiasm. Mrs Adams, the wife of the Federal minister, told Bright of Lyulph Stanley: [127]

His talk rapid and earnest 'would talk the hair off my head'. Knows every minute detail of U.S. affairs. 'Knows more than Mr Adams a pile.' (i.e. a heap or great quantity, more than Mr Adams) of details of geography, etc.

Her son found Stanley's partisanship almost embarrassing: [128]

Stanley has the merit of being 'plus royaliste que le roi'; at least when he has his aristocratic friends here to argue with ... but his tendencies are certainly very strong towards democracy, or human equality, as he would rather call it; and he upholds our cause hotly on this side, even in his own family, where he meets an energetic opposition. I dare not always say yes to his doctrines myself.

Finally, although their interpretation of it was inaccurate, the academics believed organized labour to be the defender of the North. They accepted Bright's view of a Lancashire working class menaced by the Federals' blockade of cotton yet self-sacrificial in its support of Lincoln, drawing from him in January 1863, a famous tribute to their 'sublime Christian heroism'. [129] Oxford gave generously to the funds for the alleviation of distress in the stricken areas. In 1864 T.H.Green noted that £5,000 had been collected in the university – £400 of that at Balliol. [130] A year earlier he had travelled to London to be among the audience – which also included Henry Adams and Karl Marx – at the great Trades Union demonstration in favour of the Emancipation Proclamation at St James's Hall on 26 March 1863. [131]

The working-class attitude convinced the academics that it was prepared to take the moral view of politics, abnegating class interests, their concept of the 'nation' or 'commonwealth' required. Arguing from the Civil War experience, Richard Holt Hutton wrote in *Essays on Reform* that [132]

the working class, though they had a far deeper *interest* in the matter than the professional classes, and that an interest opposed to the line of policy they adopted, saw but one great idea involved in that struggle – that of freedom contending with slavery: and this decided them ... they saw the one great issue, and left out of consideration all the comparatively unimportant issues, to which our professional classes attached such undue weight.

This solid conviction would provide a reformed parliament with the sort of moral ballast which would secure sensible policies, an argument also echoed by Henry Fawcett in the debates in 1866 on Gladstone's Reform Bill. [133]

Workmen on the other hand interpreted reactions to the war less in moral terms than as a projection of upper-class hostility to their own organizations. E.S.Beesly's blunt statement at the St James's Hall meeting was exceptional among the academics: [134]

They (the upper classes) assign openly as their reason for supporting the South, that the slave-owners are gentlemen. They are passing the word round to stand by their order. Well, you stand by yours.

Despite their enthusiasm, indeed their fitness for the role, the academics played little part in coordinating the various pro-Federal groups in Britain. This consisted of three major components. First, there was the movement among radicals and trade unionists, whose efforts rose to a climax in 1863, despite the hostility to the Federals of its own press, largely run by former Chartists whose hatred of the 'wage-slavery' of Bright and the middle-class rule he represented was greater than their distaste for slavery. [135] Second, there was the campaign, in and out of parliament, of the politicians – Bright, Cobden, Forster, Potter – who were sympathetic to the North, which itself became more and more identified with the working-class movement. [136] Third, there was the press and publicity campaign in which the academics were most involved, revolving round sympathetic journals, and the few social figures – Lord Houghton and the Duke of Argyll – bold enough to support the North, which existed more to assure the North that it had some support in Britain than to do anything else. [137]

Certain connections subsisted between these: the press linked the academics with the politicians; public meetings and demonstrations linked the politicians and the working-class agitation; relief work, and the particular involvement of the Positivists in the labour agitation in London, connected the academics and the working class. But the figure which really linked all three was Bright, and Bright, however sympathetically regarded by the academics, was not an effective coordinator. His leadership was improvisatory, his political analysis minimal; though he welcomed support from the universities, he was incapable of adapting his campaign to give the university men a role in it, and they were too unfamiliar with popular politics to create a role for themselves. Under pressure their political views became radical, but they were not projected at a democratic audience. They might praise the working classes' fidelity to the moral conception of politics, but they still directed their literature at the 'educated class' although they knew it would not be read. They were better known, and made closer alliances, in Boston than in Bolton.

J.R. Green wrote of the reform essays: [138]

They set before us with remarkable force ... the strength of a demand for reform which knits together two classes at first sight so unlike, and yet between which there is so much similarity, as the artisan and intellectual classes, and which springs out of the alienation of both from the present state of English politics.

This shared sense of alienation, dramatically demonstrated by the American Civil War, rather than any shared analysis of society or political programme, was to draw working man and university liberal together in the struggle for political reform.

This much, however, must also be said. The 'alliance with Manchester' was not wholly an illusion. The options on university reform open to the dissenters and their representatives in 1864 were not confined to those proposed by the academics. Other schemes – ranging from universities partitioned on confessional lines to a wholesale dispersal of endowments – might have carried the day. That they did not, that the academics sold the dissenters their philosophy of university reform, was substantially due to the meeting of minds on the issue of the American Civil War.

[6]

THE
UNIVERSITY LIBERALS
AND THE
REFORM AGITATION

Of books some great adventures ... a volume called
Essays on Reform (1867) issued in reply to the
Cassandra prophecies of Robert Lowe by Dicey, Bryce,
Goldwin Smith, Harrison, Leslie Stephen *et al.*
Leslie Stephen particularly good and the whole
thing a singularly arresting performance as stating
with singular insight the particular difficulties of
our own time.

Harold Laski to Justice Oliver Wendell Holmes,
18 September 1920 [1]

The publication of *Essays on Reform* and *Questions for a Reformed
Parliament* marked the climax of the university liberals' political
involvement. Publicists and politicians took note of the new
intellectual group, and in later life the contributors themselves
tended to refer back to the essays as a political datum. They have
since been commended by political scientists as well as historians as
a major contribution to the study of democratic politics. But were
the essays less of a judicious assessment of a political situation than
an urgent response to it? Not an authoritative part of the wider
reform movement but the only weapon the academics had to hand?

This issue focuses attention on the environment of the intellectual
response to reform in the mid-1860s. Hitherto this has been largely
interpreted as literary history, with attention centred on the far from
representative views of Carlyle, Arnold and George Eliot, or as
abstract political analysis, which pays rather too much attention to
Mill and Bagehot. Even when the reform essays themselves have
been the subject of academic comment, this has not always been
illuminating. [2] H.L.Beales's 'Centenary Tribute to an Appeal for
Modernization' in *Essays on Reform, 1967* accepts them as 'the voice
of the university mind in anxious thought about the political needs

116

of the day', putting forward a programme of institutional reform, drafted by 'experts through study', similar to other mid-nineteenth-century organizations like the Financial Reform Association. [3] But, as there is no evidence of any connection between such bodies and the essayists, this approach scarcely illuminates the distinctive nature of the academic attitude. To determine the outlook of such a group by reference to present-day concerns – like 'modernization', a vogue word of the mid-1960s – is dangerous; to relate political programmes to one another simply by comparing theory, neglecting the evidence of personal relationships and particular historial situations, is little better. But the attempt to combine a study of the writing of the essays with an analysis of their political content is necessarily complex, so while this chapter is concerned with the actions and relationships of the academics during the reform crisis the next will deal with their analysis of the situation.

The political options open to the academics between 1859 and 1866 were limited. Like the forces of political reform, they were isolated and weak. Why then did the situation in 1866 make action imperative, and what circumstances influenced the course of action eventually taken? What was its political effect?

II

University men wrote little about political reform before the mid-1860s, although what they did publish shows that they were moving towards the diagnosis of the reform essays. In 1855 George Brodrick won the Arnold history prize at Oxford with an essay on popular government; read out at the Encaenia of 1855 before an audience which included Derby, Gladstone and Montalembert, it was a forceful argument for democratic institutions. [4] Its basic premises endured: political institutions must approximate to social situations; politics was morality rather than expediency. [5] True government, Brodrick contended, was 'a means of moral training, not less valuable than the immediate results to be produced by it'. This being so, participation ought ultimately to be extended to all the adult male population. [6]

The younger liberals who took part in Oxford Union debates during the 1850s and early 1860s generally shared this position, but they qualified proposals for suffrage extension with fairly stringent safeguards. For example, T.H.Green and John Nichol moved, on 15 May 1856, [7]

That it is the undoubted right of every Englishman to possess the suffrage, and that, as the time has not yet arrived to carry this principle into effect without serious danger, every means should be taken, by liberal development of education, to bring it about.

The university liberals always distinguished between 'right' and 'occasion'; even in 1867 they were far from unanimous about the actual reform which should be enacted. But the tone of their argument changed. '(The educated classes) have been alarmed by the demonstrations. But we shall have to alarm them a little more before we get what we want.' Green told the Oxford Reform League in March 1867: [8]

We are the last people to threaten physical force. But if we took our opponents, the 'philosophical liberals', at their word, we should have to resort to it, for they tell us it is absurd to claim representation as a right; but if the plea of right is not listened to, the plea of force alone remains.

Much the same could be said of Cambridge, although Cambridge liberals were more sympathetic to Mill and his views on franchise reform, which reflected the influence of Thomas Hare's two tracts on proportional representation – *The Machinery of Representation* of 1857 and the *Treatise on the Election of Representatives* of 1859. These seemed to him to provide a way of representing minorities while securing equality of political rights, which he publicized in his *Considerations on Representative Government* of 1861. [9] Mill's enthusiasm was taken up at Cambridge by Leonard Courtney, Henry Fawcett and John Westlake, although Courtney, to the end of his days an enthusiast for the Hare scheme, distrusted Fawcett, who kept ideology on a lighter rein. [10] Certainly, in the early 1860s, Fawcett's political career showed some violent ideological oscillations: in 1859 he suggested a very conservative reform scheme, proposing to enfranchise only those who had saved more than sixty pounds; [11] in November 1860, as radical candidate for Southwark, he advocated not only household but lodger suffrage. [12] Between 1860 and 1864, however, he also paid homage to Mill's principles and doubts: 'We can never do enough', Mill wrote to him in 1860,[13]

in pressing abroad Mr Hare's plan, which, in my deliberate belief, contains the true solution of the political difficulties of the future. It is an uphill race, and a race against time, for if the American form of democracy overtakes us first, the majority will no more relax their despotism than a single despot would. But our only chance is to come forward as Liberals, carrying out the democratic idea, not as Conservatives, resisting it.

This meeting of minds was undoubtedly convenient for Fawcett, as Mill's wholehearted support of him for the Chair of Political Economy at Cambridge in 1863 showed. [14] But the closer the disciple got to active politics, the less reliable he became. Following defeat at the Cambridge borough election in 1863, and a good showing at Brighton in 1864, [15] he began to cultivate the constituency and echo his supporters' demands. This worried Mill: [16]

What I could have wished otherwise was not the omission to speak more definitely respecting Hare's plan, but the employment of an argument which tells against the need of such a plan, and which I think unsound, namely, that the working classes are greatly divided in opinion. Like other classes, they are divided in points not involving the class interests or prejudices, but not therefore less likely to be united on those which do.

Mill's trepidation was shared by many radicals, even those pledged to reform, and it was reflected at Cambridge. [17] George Otto Trevelyan – after 1867 the consistent advocate of the enfranchisement of the country labourer – was still a Whig. [18] Henry Sidgwick was still preoccupied with his religious doubts. [19] Leslie Stephen had helped Fawcett in his election contests, scorned proportional representation as needless jugglery, but even he commented little on politics before 1866. [20] Lord Houghton, visiting Cambridge in that year to speak at the opening of the new Union, had to admit that the political studies increasingly pursued at the university seemed to have reinforced its indifference to reform. [21]

III

But, between 1860 and 1865, the cause of reform made little progress in the country either. John Bright had revived the cry in 1858 and 1859, only to have it stifled by the failure of the government reform bill in 1860. At the time, the universities had shown some interest. Frederic Harrison, in London since 1856, wrote to Beesly about getting a group of university men together to cooperate with Bright, aiming at [22] 'some answer to *The Times* and the *Saturday Review*, addressed to their readers and written at any rate from the same educational level'. Harrison realized that they could not get far by themselves; but his political contacts were tenuous:

It is possible that [Bright's] party already have some organisation at work of the kind and they might be on the lookout for literary cooperation. I cannot doubt that the reform agitation is organised.

Not surprisingly, nothing came of this. Although Harrison's initiative anticipated the reform essays – and in 1862 Cobden asked Thorold Rogers to canvass academic support for a bill [23] – academics did not again consider intervention for a further six years.

There seem to be four main reasons for this abstention. First, intellectual life in the early 1860s was dominated by conflicts over Darwin and *Essays and Reviews* which, while ultimately promoting political activity, initially concentrated attention on the Tests campaign. Second, academic political contacts, slight anyway, were, until 1864 biased towards the whigs and Peelites, who were lukewarm about reform. Foreign politics, again, tended only indirectly to interest academics in domestic politics: Brightist 'non-intervention' was unpalatable while Italy had to be united and Poland set free. Finally, distance barred them from radicalism's northern base. Before 1865, when the Reform League was formed, there was no national radical organization. With their London, home-counties and rural backgrounds, the academics had little in common with the society Cobden and Bright represented; they had to make a conscious effort to share its politics.

In 1862 Goldwin Smith wrote to Cobden: [24]

No one can be more sensible than I am of the risks and evils attending a great and sudden transfer of political power; and yet I see the absolute necessity of struggling for a great measure of Parliamentary reform, as the indispensable condition of every other measure of improvement and justice ...

The American War and the Tests issue were creating a dialogue, but they also limited the options open to academic and radical alike. The politicians best placed to deliver reform – Gladstone and Russell – disgraced themselves by their sympathy for the South. [25] Gladstone's freedom as M.P. for Oxford was always circumscribed by his high-church allies. By the time he had become acceptable he was M.P. no longer. [26] Russell's position on university reform was more favourable, but age and Whig exclusiveness ruled him out. [27] And on 4 April 1865 Cobden died. The intellectual part of the great partnership, he was possibly the leader the academics needed and lacked. In the early 1860s he made contact with Smith, Rogers, Harrison and Fawcett;[28] when he touched on university matters his views were close to theirs, where Bright simply proffered compliments. [29] His death was probably a greater blow than any of them realized, then or subsequently.

Cobden was soon followed by the great obstructive himself. On 18

October 1865 Palmerston died. 'He was becoming, if he had not rather already become, a power for evil and not for good,' Grant Duff later told his Scottish constitutents. [30] Few of his academic friends would have disagreed. But although they expected Russell to bring in a Reform Bill, they were not optimistic about its prospects. In May 1865 Bryce had noticed scant enthusiasm for reform in Lancashire. Little had changed by February 1866: only 'among the poorer electors' was there much support for reform; the non-electors were apathetic, the rich hostile. [31] The newly founded Reform League found the same situation; parliamentarians desisted from attempts at mass agitation, even when the government introduced its Bill in March. [32] But both academics and popular organizations were to be given their chance by the circumstances which surrounded its rejection in June.

IV

The academics' close involvement in the reform issue was due more than anything else to the activity of the Bill's most notorious opponent – Robert Lowe. Thirty-five years later Bryce reckoned that 'the moderate bill of 1866' would, if passed, have put reform to sleep for thirty years. In the circumstances 'Robert Lowe, as much as Disraeli and Gladstone, may in a sense be called an author of the tremendous change which has passed upon the British Constitution since 1866, and the extent of which was not for a long time realised'. [33] Lowe's role in the reform imbroglio appears less significant in parliament than out of it. The publicist rather than the leader of the Adullamites, themselves more a collection of political eccentrics than a whig secession, he was allowed to preach against concession to demonstrate the strength, or lack of it, of the anti-reformers, and was then ruthlessly discarded by his putative Tory allies. Gladstone and Disraeli moved towards concession, Lowe was left isolated. [35] But the academic liberals did not see him from the angle of party politicians with their eyes on the opportunities of mass politics: Lowe posed a direct threat to their politics and their own credibility. For not only did he oppose any and every attempt to reduce the franchise, surpassing even Lord Cranborne in his obduracy, [36] but he set himself up as the spokesman for intellect.

Lowe was no conservative but a utilitarian radical of rather an extreme sort. Asa Briggs's description of him as 'an intellectual pleading for government by the educated against government by the masses' is misleading. [37] He had no sympathy with traditional culture, which he derided as 'an absurd and effete scheme of

121

education'. [38] Bryce, who had collaborated with him on university reform, found his ideas

crude and barren, limited, indeed, to the substitution of what the Germans call 'bread studies' for mental cultivation, and to the extension of the plan for competitive examinations.

Lowe might have agreed with Matthew Arnold in wanting to flog the Hyde Park rioters and fling their leaders from rocks, but he would never have shared Arnold's motives. He cared nothing for Mill's concern to delineate individual liberties and collective opportunities. The case for efficient government in the interests of property was being made out more adequately by Bagehot in the *Fortnightly*. [39] But Lowe's ascendancy was a matter of personality and milieu: his ideas were secondary, his ability – and his sense of it – enormous. Goldwin Smith and Bryce bore witness to this. [40] To Jowett he was 'the quickest, the clearest, the ablest, and one of the most public-spirited men (really) whom I have ever known.' But, he added, 'he wants to do everything by force ... when he came to have a whole profession against him ... he would be likely to sink under the load of unpopularity.' [41] Politically as well as physically myopic, Lowe walked into trouble. At the Education Office between 1860 and 1864 his reputation stood high as a departmental minister – some put him before Forster [42] – but the enforcement of his innovations, the system of payment by results and supervision by examination, attracted bitter opposition, not least from Matthew Arnold himself. [43] In 1864 an all-party assault, headed by Lord Robert Cecil, secured his resignation after he had been accused of tampering with his inspectors' reports. [44]

Nevertheless, a year later Lord Robert was applauding, from the anonymity of his *Saturday* column, Lowe's first assault on reform, in the shape of Edward Baines's Borough Franchise Bill. [45] Experiences in Australia and travels in America had given Lowe a profound distaste for democratic societies, [46] which he blended with a dogmatic and confident interpretation of utilitarian social thought. Lowe believed wholeheartedly in the civic virtue of the market: contemporaries like Cairnes thought his economics primitive, [47] but they pervaded his minimalist conception of government, as he demonstrated, reproving the backsliding Mill in 1866: [48]

We are here to legislate for this country and if we look after our executive government pretty sharply – if we take care of our finance, and if we watch the Foreign Office, we shall be doing better than we should do by converting this House into an Academy for the instruction of the elite of the working classes.

The test of good government was the promotion of economic liberty, and this was best left in the hands of those whose interests were directly affected: [49]

Persons also who have something to lose are less anxious to lose it than those who have little at stake, even though these last may by the loss be reduced to absolute poverty.

The working class should let well alone.

John Austin had voiced, and Bagehot was voicing, similar views, but neither had Lowe's debating skill and parliamentary position. [50] Goldwin Smith called him 'the most naturally and spontaneously brilliant talker that I ever knew', and he made full use of his gifts on the tractable material of the House of Commons and the 'educated classes'. Bryce attributed Lowe's impact to his 'remarkable rhetorical and dialectical power': this activated the broad range of his knowledge, while his doctrinaire utilitarianism fitted a mental template over his facts and arranged them as cogent argument. Further, he spoke against his own party, and was given credit for the 'conscientious conviction' which made him isolate himself: 'No position gives a debater in the House of Commons such a vantage ground for securing attention.' [51] Lowe found a receptive audience among 'nominal Liberals', merchant and banking magnates and whigs. These, according to Bryce, [52]

were already beginning to pass into habits of thought which were practically Tory. They did not know how far they had gone till Lowe's speeches told them, and they welcomed his ideas as justifying their own tendencies.

He was also clasped to the bosom of Henry Adams's 'sacred eccentrics', the literary allies of the late Confederacy, [53] and the university liberals became increasingly perturbed that his most vocal supporters – publicists of the vintage of Delane and Reeve – claimed to represent education and intellect. Bryce recollected G.S. Venables of the *Saturday* delivering [54]

amid general applause, the opinion that Lowe was an intellectual giant compared to Mr Gladstone, and that the reputation of the latter had been extinguished for ever.

The academics' reaction was twofold: they recognized that Lowe's arguments, published as *Speeches and Letters on Reform* in February 1867, were effective enough, and merited reply. In fact they were much more respectful towards him than he was to them. To Frederic Harrison they were 'the only thing on Reform worth reading': [55] George Brodrick found them a triumphant application of Benthamism. [56] Both were agreed that Lowe's standard – good government as the test of reform – had to be abided by, or at least re-interpreted to sanction suffrage extension. 'We cannot afford', wrote Brodrick, 'to leave so redoubtable a fortress, untaken, in our rear.' [57] Especially when the fortress menaced their own credibility.

The appeal to good government could be used against Lowe. The academics could claim that, far from the body politic being healthy, parliamentary exclusiveness inhibited necessary reforms, and might produce a menacing situation. The Positivists, while applauding Lowe's assaults on parliamentary democracy, were more alert than the others to this. Frederic Harrison wrote in March 1867: [58]

Our people are ignorant below the standard of any civilised race north of the Alps. Our pauperism is the most colossal and corroding. Our public administration and our legal machinery the most chaotic; our municipal and sanitary system the most cumbrous; the state of our great cities and our labourers' homes the most utterly heartrending; the state of Ireland the despair of our policy.

But a similar indictment was made out by Albert Rutson, the editor of the reform essays: [59]

When we remember that, notwithstanding all our extraordinary advantages, it is only in the South and Centre of Italy, in parts of the Austrian dominion, in Spain and in Russia, that we can find anything worse, and in no other European country anything so bad, we are compelled to ask how it is that so little has been accomplished.

John Vincent has attacked the liberal intellectuals of the 1860s for [60]

crying over the unspilt milk of the future exhausting on apprehension energies needed for investigation, producing in the end an intelligentsia unpolitical apparently through disinterestedness, but actually made so because of its lack of relevant social information.

To a certain extent this view is tenable. There was much social investigation in the reform essays, but not all of it was written by academics, and much of what they did write was 'mugged up' rather than researched. But in their own field – the reform of higher education – they had enough experience of the obstructive power of an unreformed parliament to enable them to visualize its consequences elsewhere.

But the nature and tone of Lowe's assault also demanded a reply which dissociated them from the 'educated class' he claimed to represent. Lowe was not content with theory: if he had been, his audience would certainly have been smaller. He was violently hostile to the supporters of reform, and the working classes in particular: [61]

If you want venality, if you want ignorance, if you want drunkenness and facility for being intimidated, or if, on the other hand, you want impulsive and violent people, where do you look for them in the constituencies? Do you go to the top or the bottom?

He seized on and publicized the most lurid accounts of working-class behaviour, and endowed the prospective electorate with every conceivable economic delusion. Once enfranchised, it would 'launch itself' as a 'compact mass' on British institutions, subverting them in its own interests. [62] All to great effect. Before Lowe the anti-reform forces were, according to Harrison, 'inorganic'. His speeches gave them direction, 'roused the upper classes to resistance, terrified the middle classes into hesitation, and stung the working classes into action'. [63] Bright and Beales clambered on to their platforms, and in their turn the academics had to stand up and be counted, or risk being classed with the bitter enemies of the disenfranchised.

V

Yet their response was still distinctive. They took no action for five months after the failure of the government Bill; their intervention, when it came, was not directly political but literary. How, then, did they relate to political agitation between June and November 1866, and to what extent did this determine their subsequent action?

The Adullamite success aroused reform opinion at last. The Reform League, predominantly working class and based in London, and the middle-class National Reform Union, built on the remains of the Anti-Corn-Law League and centred in Manchester, rapidly expanded their activities. [64] Popular agitation showed its mettle at Hyde Park on 23 July and thereafter, powerfully reinforced by Bright, went on from strength to strength. [65] In October Leslie Stephen summed up for the benefit of his American readers: the Reform Bill which, without Lowe, 'would have fallen altogether dead', had been impressively revived: [66]

A much wider measure must be proposed by the leaders of the Conservative party next session, if they are to carry the popular feeling with them.

Goldwin Smith later paid tribute, in an open letter to Howell, to the public agitation, and the League in particular, as [67]

the main instrument in turning the present holders of power from

125

the opponents of the limited Reform Bill of last session into the advocates of household suffrage.

But even Smith, who, practically alone of the academics, knew the leaders of both the League and the Union, and spoke frequently on behalf of both, had otherwise no close connection with either body. The League's contacts with intellectual radicals were peripheral; they gave donations, made speeches; some were among its hundred or so vice-presidents, but they played no part in its administration. [68] Even in the university towns there was relatively little involvement. Thorold Rogers helped set up an Oxford branch of the League in April 1866. He became its chairman and moving force, but he was the only academic on its committee, although Goldwin Smith, T.H.Green and R.S.Wright addressed meetings from time to time. [69] At Cambridge even less happened. The local liberal weekly, the *Cambridge Independent Press* mentioned no significant reform agitation – save a contested borough election in April 1866 – or academic involvement apart from a couple of speeches by Fawcett and Abdy, the Regius Professor of Civil Law. [70]

Why this limited collaboration with popular organizations? In a sense, Lowe's challenge made this unlikely, as academics felt that they had to appeal to those of their own class who opposed reform. [71] This imposed its own pattern of action: parliament and the courts rose in July; political society adjourned until the autumn, or even later, as Gladstone and several of his colleagues remained in Italy until the end of January. [72] The academics wanted change, but not in their own life-style. For Leslie Stephen the agitation resumed when his friends returned 'from Continental rambles, from Alpine climbs, from Norway salmon rivers and from Scotch moors'. [73] He had been climbing with Bryce in the Carpathians, Charles Bowen was in Norway, Frederic Harrison in Venice, while Bright addressed demonstrations a hundred thousand strong in northern cities. [74]

Even when in town, there were other political causes to be fought for. In January 1866 a commission had been sent to Jamaica to investigate allegations of brutality, illegality and judicial murder in Governor Eyre's suppression of a native revolt in October 1865. Charles Roundell was its secretary, and its report, published on 9 April, censured Eyre on the last charge, and condemned as barbarous reprisals ordered by two of his subordinates, Colonel Nelson and Lieutenant Brand. On 27 July a group headed by Mill, Huxley, Herbert Spencer, Goldwin Smith and Thomas Hughes resolved to prosecute Eyre, Nelson and Brand. [75] It constituted itself the Jamaica Committee and by the end of the year had gained considerable support from radicals in and out of parliament, including a large number of university men. [76]

Like the American War, the Jamaica Committee 'united the Liberal intelligentsia with the Nonconformist conscience'. [77] Both causes were interpreted in the same way: the favour shown Eyre by British reactionaries was as good a reason for prosecuting him as his actual behaviour. Roundell, debarred from the Jamaica Committee by his position, was quite explicit about this when he addressed the Social Science Congress at Manchester in October 1866: [78]

... the ultimate appeal in this great national inquest lies, not to a few literary cynics, but to the warm heart and rough but true instincts of the mass of the people. If I do not read the national verdict amiss, I read in it a record of burning indignation, and shame unutterable ...

The Committee had a much higher proportion of university men than any of the political reform organizations. In the long term it served the same ends but, with its distinctive moral and legal implications, and its challenge to the 'literary cynics' – Carlyle, Ruskin, Tennyson and the other members of the Eyre Committee [79] – it was particularly attractive to the academics. Possibly too attractive, too well adapted to the academic situation: to choose it, rather than a direct identification with reform, was to choose the line of least resistance.

With the progress of the Tests Bills made even more complex by the reform upheavals, university politics continued to be absorbing. The change of government killed both abolition measures; public agitation was blighted by reform demonstrations; [80] Oxford was plunged into intrigues by the clerical party's management of the Hebdomadal Council elections, and by the appointment of a new Regius Professor of Modern History to succeed Goldwin Smith, who had resigned at the beginning of 1866. [81] The liberals were divided. Bryce and Freeman feared governmental insensitivity: Russell might appoint Froude, or, under radical pressure, Thorold Rogers; the Tories might elevate Montague Burrows, their local party boss. [82] In the event Derby appointed William Stubbs in September. Though a Tory, Stubbs was a historian, not a theological partisan, and Freeman at least breathed a sigh of relief. [83]

Meanwhile theological controversy had migrated to Cambridge. F.D.Maurice's election to the Moral Philosophy chair in November 1866 provoked Evangelical disquiet, and Henry Sidgwick feared that 'the peaceful times are passing away ... we shall presently be steeped in polemics to the same extent as Oxford'. [84] *Ecce Homo*, J.R.Seeley's naturalistic account of Christ's life and teach ing, had, a year earlier, been described by Lord Shaftesbury as 'a book vomited from the jaws of Hell'. [85] Maurice proved a spent force, and *Ecce Homo*, by stressing political and national rather than transcendental values in religion, had more significance as an anticipation of its author's liberal imperialism, [86] but the debates surrounding both underlined the resilience of old preoccu- pations.

The academic liberal group was itself changing. Goldwin Smith, hitherto its leading light, was in the midst of the personal crisis whose consequences clouded his later career. His father, injured in a railway accident, became depressive and suicidal. Smith had to resign his chair, sell his Oxford house, and move back to the family estate near Reading. [87] Although he continued to appear on radical platforms, he was no longer securely at the head of the Oxford liberals. His abdication possibly furthered the establishment of more formal academic bodies at Oxford, Cambridge and London. The Ad Eundem was joined in 1866 by the Century Club in London. The idea had been suggested by Beesly and Harrison in 1864, [88] and Harrison was one of a group, including Lyulph Stanley, Yates Thompson and Roundell, who got the project going in the spring of 1866. The Century's members – a predictable enough group – met after dinner twice a week, at first in the Inns of Court, later at the Alpine Club, 'to smoke, talk and organise'. [89] According to Harri- son: [90]

> It was to uphold definite and very strict principles of political and religious liberalism. It was to help fight the battles which Gladstone and Bright, Mill and Spencer, were fighting in Parliament and public opinion. It was to have, not a social character, but a political and intellectual character. It was to consist not of celebrities, or of pleasant fellows, but of keen workers in the cause of thought and popular progress.

The Century included London and provincial politicians, fathered the Radical Club in 1870 and ultimately expanded into the National Liberal Club in 1882. [91] But it was also the successor of the debating and discussion groups of the universities, and was inevita- bly identified with the Tests struggle and the writing of the reform essays. [92] Its very existence implied that the academics had made the transition from the universities to the metropolis which made such projects possible.

VI

Essays on Reform was published on 16 March 1867, and *Questions for a Reformed Parliament* on 27 April: [93] the fruit of a project set on foot in the autumn of 1866, after the drift back from the long vacation. By 29 November planning had reached a firm stage. 'Macmillan talked to me yesterday,' Roundell wrote to Bryce at Oxford: [94]

I will see Goldwin Smith. I most heartily approve.
I wish to see you. My spirit is stirred within me by what I conceive to be the essential unsoundness and reaction of 'Society'. In very truth, I think the times are ripe for an Isaiah and a Juvenal.

Preliminary discussions were probably held at the Century, and early on contact was made with Alexander Macmillan. As well as being an enthusiastic Liberal, Macmillan had done well by promoting young writers from the universities. [95] Two similar symposia on institutional reform – *Essays on a Liberal Education* and *Essays on Church Policy* – were to be published by him in the next two years. The idea of a series which would further liberalism, the careers of his friends and the prestige of his imprint had obvious attractions.

Albert Rutson, Bryce and Charles Bowen were apparently active from the first. Bryce probably provided the connection with Macmillan: his *Holy Roman Empire* has been a major success for the firm, and was now in a second edition. [96] Bowen had been attempting to give the younger liberals a public voice since the *Saturday Review* split in 1861, in the intervals of an untypically successful legal career. [97] Rutson, who had overall editorial responsibility, was more representative in being a briefless barrister. A Rugby friend of Henry Sidgwick and T.H.Green, he had been since 1860 a non-resident Fellow of Magdalen. He settled in London with John Addington Symonds, contributed to the *Saturday Review* and embroiled himself in Symonds's tangled private life. Their relationship was not homosexual, but Rutson's behaviour was embarrassingly emotional. [98] He fell in love with Symonds's sister, Charlotte (who later married T.H.Green) and then with Catherine North (who later married Symonds); both suits were checked by the disclosure that there was a history of insanity in his family. [99] Rutson was certainly highly strung and argumentative; he later wrote to Lord Houghton that he found it difficult to concentrate, to formulate ideas logically and get them down on paper. [100] (Certainly, apart from the *Saturday Review* work, the reform essays and a few articles, he published little; but he remained active in politics as a member of the London School Board, Alderman of the North Riding County Council and Liberal candidate in the 1880 and 1886 elections. He died in 1890.) [101]

In 1866 Rutson's relationship with Symonds came to a crisis. The pair broke off contact and did not resume their friendship for over a decade. [102] Already, with another Oxford liberal, Christopher Puller, Rutson was trying to lose himself working as a voluntary almoner in the East End, so the prospect of editing the essays must have come as a welcome relief. [103] The nephew of William Ewart M.P., the humanitarian reformer, and the neighbour of the Earls of Ripon, Rutson was well placed politically, and flung himself into his task with energy. [104]

Editing the essays meant drawing on the connections between the universities and London journalistic and radical life built up over the preceding decade. The group at the centre drafted a general plan of contents and set about matching men and subjects. Initially they approached their university friends, [105] but, when in January 1867 Rutson wrote to invite Lord Houghton, he mentioned that they hoped to bring in Frederick Temple, then headmaster of Rugby, Jowett, Forster, Mill and Stansfeld; 'big' names which he hoped would appeal to 'Dicky Milnes'' taste for the company of the notable. The trouble with the academics and journalists to hand was that [106]

it may be said (not truly, or really to the point – if the essays have merit – but still so as to damage the book) 'These writers are all mere mouthpieces of Mr Goldwin Smith and the *Spectator*.'

But the initiative remained with the academics. Goldwin Smith and Bryce brought Macmillan up to Oxford for a 'council of war' early in December, making contact with W.L.Newman, fellow of Balliol, whom Harrison had hoped to involve in his 1859 project, and T.H.Green, whom Rutson hoped would write on bribery. [107] Bryce selected his own subject, the history of democratic institutions. Some contributors proved difficult to manage. Bryce noted in pencil on Rutson's letter, 'I hope Green will not fail us. Newman will take Land Laws and Pauperism – if materials provided and lawyer will criticise.' [108] Green was notoriously lazy. [109] Rutson gave 'Bribery' to Thorold Rogers [110] and transferred him to 'Opportunities and Shortcomings of Government in England'. [111] To no avail. Eventually he had to write it himself. Newman exemplified another problem: lack of expertise. Experts had therefore to be brought in: Goschen helped his secretary Bernard Cracroft write 'The Analysis of the House of Commons', Freeman helped Bryce, and Godfrey Lushington, starting out as an adviser to Thomas Hughes on 'Workmen and Trade Unions', ultimately took the essay over. [112]

Rutson's letters to Houghton give useful descriptions of work in progress. The first, sent via Lord de Grey (not himself greatly sympathetic to reform), ‡[13] sketched briefly the aims and general arrangement of the book. [114] Goldwin Smith was to contribute a preface. He would not specify particular schemes for the franchise and redistribution (Lowe's intransigence gave the academics valuable freedom of manoeuvre) but he would cite past Liberal Reform Bills 'as indicating the policy the essays are intended to support'. As to contributors: Houghton would, at present, know few, possibly only Charles Pearson, for his book *The Early Ages of English History*, and Thomas Hughes. Rutson then went on to suggest possible subjects, but, because the plan he enclosed has not survived, the references to them, by letter and number, are difficult to identify. Four groups, A,B,C and D, can be reconstructed, but appear to have been purely arbitrary. However, if the ultimate form reflected the original intention, five main groupings expressed the intentions of the essayists.

When *Essays on Reform* came out, the *Daily News* reviewer (who must have known about the project, because of the involvement of the paper's editorial staff (see p. 134) gave the book a fourfold purpose: to examine the theory of the franchise; to examine its working in contemporary Britain; to compare the British situation with that in other nations; to estimate the overall effect of reform on government machinery. In order of reading, three essays fell into the first category, three into the second, three into the third, and the last two into the fourth. [115] At the time Rutson wrote to Houghton only one volume was contemplated; by itself *Questions for a Reformed Parliament* constituted a fifth category in the original scheme.

Rutson's second letter, on 17 January, indicated that practically all the essays later included in *Questions for a Reformed Parliament* had been allocated. There were subsequent changes: Hughes and Bowen dropped out in February; after a disagreement, Trevelyan withdrew his essay on education in March. Harrison replaced Bowen on 'Foreign Policy' and Charles Stuart Parker replaced Trevelyan. [116] But if the *second* volume was almost complete, why had Rutson details of barely half the contributors to the first? The project must have been changed, early in February, from one volume dealing mainly with institutional reform, to two: the first, now the more important, dealing at greater length with constitutional issues.

Opportunity and resources alike contributed. In parliament the cabinet moved tentatively towards legislation, introducing resolutions on reform on 11 February; then, on his own initiative, Disraeli promised a bill. [117] Timetabling and content were patently indeterminate: the options were open. Shortly afterwards Lowe's *Speeches* appeared, to rally the men of no compromise. At this stage the academics must have taken their decision. More essays could now be accommodated: A.V.Dicey and Leslie Stephen seem to have been recruited at this time, [118] to combat 'the view that prevails, that intelligence and all good influence are to be obscured and made powerless by numbers'. This meant the delay of the 'institutional' section, and the advancing of the publication date for *Essays on Reform* from the end of March to 9 March. [119]

The production of an original work, 600 pages long, in five months would be remarkable today. Nothing similar was attempted at the time: Lowe simply republished his speeches; Bagehot's *English Constitution* had been serialized. This success was due as much to close links between the contributors as to Rutson's abilities as editor or Macmillan's as publisher. Fifteen out of the twenty-two had attended the older universities, eleven going to Oxford, four to Cambridge, and of these, eleven belonged to three or more of the five groups in appendix 8. The sort of relationships indicated will be clear from preceding chapters. Although connections with 'non-academic' contributors did not fall into the same pattern, they too were close.

The professional journalists represented an intelligentsia of their own: Nonconformist, frequently university-educated but, lacking Fellowships, forced to settle for remunerative work at an earlier age. Hutton and Hill, for instance, both took first-class honours from London, and studied under James Martineau at the Unitarian Manchester New College. Kinnear, a graduate of Edinburgh and St Andrews, had been political secretary to the Lord Advocate from 1852 to 1856, and was now a colleague of Hill's. They also had commercial links: Hutton was Townsend's partner on the *Spectator*, Hooper their military correspondent (see p. 111).

The journalists' links with the university men were many. A.V.Dicey and his brother Edward had contributed to the *Spectator* since 1861. [120] C.H.Pearson had been co-editor with Hutton and Bagehot of the Unitarian *National Review* as well as a regular contributor to the *Spectator*. [121] Goldwin Smith had contributed his letters on 'The Empire' to the *Daily News* in 1862 and 1863, [122] and Frederic Harrison his letters on 'Martial Law' (anent the Eyre case) in 1866. [123] Leslie Stephen and John Boyd Kinnear both wrote for the *Pall Mall Gazette*. Relationships had matured for several years; again, the alignment on the American Civil War was critical.

VII

Ten days after the publication of *Essays on Reform*, priced at 10s. 6d., Disraeli introduced his second Reform Bill of the session. [124] His first, the 'Ten Minute' Bill, had been brought in on 25 February. Subject to the scrutiny of Cranborne and the cabinet ultras, it was moderate – the vote came with a six-pound rate in the boroughs and a twenty-pound rate in the counties, subject to all manner of 'fancy franchises' aimed at preserving a 'balance of classes' in the House. The House scorned it, and it was withdrawn the following day. His second, still retaining 'fancy franchises', promised the vote to all borough householders personally paying rates (the qualification was important and provided the subject for many a weary hour's debate) and county householders rated at fifteen pounds. A battle started which was to last four months and ultimately produce a reform more extensive than most M.P.s had imagined possible, or indeed wished. The essayists had intervened at a propitious time.

But what sort of impact did they actually have? From various letters written after publication, the academics appear to have been reasonably satisfied with their reception. But were they influential, in the way present-day commentators have assumed? [125] Did they contribute to the direction legislation took? Did they, in Rutson's words, [126] 'meet the objections to reform and the alarm about reform current among educated men'?

As far as parliament was concerned, the influence of the essayists was negligible. The debates on the Bill were, as Bagehot wrote in 1872, 'taken up with technicalities as to the ratepayers and the compound householder. Nobody in the country knew what was being done.' [127] Theoretical arguments were rarely heard – virtually only when Lowe or some ultra cited an unflattering American or continental precedent, thus proving their ignorance of Bryce or Goldwin Smith. M.P.s brandished statistics about bribery, interest and the imbalance of constituencies, as Thorold Rogers, Cracroft and Kinnear had done, but this sort of thing had always come naturally to members with access to blue-books, newspapers and *Dod*, who were unlikely to heed outsiders' contributions.

The only sustained debate which raised issues of political theory was on 5 July, when Lowe moved a clause giving the voter in a multi-member country the right to 'plump' for one candidate, and thereby guarantee a form of minority representation. Several associates of the academics backed the clause: Hughes, Fawcett, Walter Morrison and Mill, naturally praising Hare's scheme; but others, including Goschen and Trevelyan, opposed it. Only the Conservatives Cranborne, Newdegate and Hicks-Beach addressed themselves to the concerns of the essayists and, of course, came to entirely different conclusions. The clause was lost, and Bright's comment seemed to typify the attitude of parliamentary radicals to the whole debate: [128]

I thought it exactly that sort of subject that one would hear discussed at University College Debating Society, or which would probably be discussed in the debating clubs of Oxford and Cambridge, but which has not sufficient claim to be discussed in parliament.

Outside parliament the campaign continued, broadcast by daily and weekly papers in London and the provinces which carried detailed – frequently verbatim – reports of speeches at meetings, demonstrations and dinners. Yet only the *Daily News*, of the London papers, noticed *Essays on Reform* when it appeared: [129]

The volume ought to be, and doubtless soon will be, in the hands of all who are interested in the subject of reform, whether friends or opponents. It is fitted powerfully to influence opinion on the special requirements of the present crisis, and on those deeper problems of government of which the questions of the hour are merely applications.

This enthusiasm was predictable, given its editorial connection with the projects. Such contact was important to ensure that a book would be reviewed: in the case of the essays this was less successful than it ought to have been. Leslie Stephen, who worked for the evening *Pall Mall Gazette*, failed to get them featured there, [130] and, despite Brodrick, *The Times* did not mention them until 3 May, when its American correspondent denounced Goldwin Smith's 'Experience of the American Commonwealth'. [131] The essays were no better served in the provinces, where the papers were usually dependent on the London dailies for reviews. The *Manchester Examiner*, on 23 March, was enthusiastic, but this seems to have been because of Bryce's and Goldwin Smith's close connections with the paper. [132] Reports on the reform debates tended to exclude other topics, in national and provincial papers alike; even the Liberal *Oxford Chronicle,* sympathetic to reform and reform-minded dons, and Dicey's own *Northampton Mercury,* carried no reference to the essays. The working-class press was no better. The essays were not intended anyway for working men – price and style were proof enough of that, but although some contributors like Frederic

Harrison had contact with *Reynolds' Newspaper* and the *Bee-hive*, these carried no mention of them. The working class had made up its mind on reform; the national campaign was more relevant to it than theoretical discussion.

The same applied to the public speeches of parliamentarians and reform agitators. There were few enough, anyway, by politicians of the first rank: Gladstone spoke only twice in public – once in Paris – between January and June 1867. [133] Though Bright was regularly on the stump – to considerable effect – he extemporized on current themes, and set out no logical strategy to which theoreticians could contribute. [134] The parliamentary situation gave other M.P.s ample scope, without having to bring theory in at all. The Reform League and the Reform Union were content to draw on their own speakers. The League held regular demonstrations in London and the provinces; its branch meets were addressed by paid lecturers as well as by its own leaders, [135] but their speeches were influenced little by political theory, let alone by the reform essays. Even the speeches delivered in Hyde Park during the great demonstration of 6 May – a major victory for reform agitators over the government [136] – were no exception. The League's chairman, Edmond Beales, and its vice-chairman, Colonel Dickson, dealt solely with the government's failure to ban the meeting or produce an adequate bill. Charles Bradlaugh had more ambitious aims, but confined himself to praising working-class organization, attacking the whigs and then giving a history of reform since the reign of Elizabeth, more inspirational than analytical in style. [137] For the stump orator of the day this sort of thing, suitably adapted in points of local or topical detail, usually sufficed. It was no vehicle for discussions of political theory in the manner of Bryce or Brodrick.

Even when they were, as in 1867, determined to intervene, the academics had still to find a way to connect with working-class politics. Although the reform essays were not intended to do this, their failure to influence the arguments laid before the prospective electorate during the crisis was not a good omen for the future. The only one who really got across was Thorold Rogers. Coarse-grained he may have been, but he could talk the language of working men and gain their trust. [138] He was a moderate by Reform League standards, [139] but the Oxford branch had enough confidence in him to put him up for parliament, orders and all. [140] His speeches, broad, homely, combative, created a sense of shared involvement with his audience: he mastered political language, while Goldwin Smith never learned the distinction between style and intent. What was for Rogers a rhetorical flourish became with the more moderate Smith an apparently logical extremism: [141] he attempted to connect with his audience by elaborating some part of his argument to accord with what he thought its views were. A tap-room threat became a calculated challenge. He, and many of his friends, risked political isolation, becoming too extreme for their own class, yet were unable to establish any real rapport with the working class. This was to be made explicit in their public activity during and after 1868.

University liberalism was, however, established in the conscious-ness of the 'educated classes'. The passing of the Reform Bill weakened the old 'pseudo-liberal' oracles; the optimism of the essays, and the credentials of their writers, were on the whole endorsed, even by Robert Lowe: [142]

... we owe some respect to the writers who have endeavoured to put into a permanent form the principles of the new order of things, and we take leave of them with the frank admission that though we cannot accept them for our teachers, they are undoubtedly our masters.

At the other extreme of the Liberal party, John Morley rejoiced: [143]

It is impossible to study a volume like the one under notice, with knowledge of the kind of men who have written it and of all they represent, without seeing that though the obstructionists in Church and State may have their little day, we others have the future.

The essays generally got a good press. The *Saturday Review, Spectator* and *Guardian* were enthusiastic, the *Athenaeum* hostile. The *Spectator's* attitude was predictable, but the *Guardian* was High Church and the *Saturday* the sworn enemy of reform. In both cases the personality of the reviewer probably counted; the *Guardian* reviewer remains a mystery, but Freeman wrote regularly for the paper, and may have helped get a favourable review (though he did not write it himself). [144] He was certainly responsible for introducing J. R. Green to the *Saturday*, and *Essays on Reform* was one of Green's first review assignments. [145]

Both periodicals welcomed the project and paid particular attention to the role of the academics. Although the *Guardian* reviewer had doubts about the speed at which the reform fence was being taken, he concluded: [146]

It is desirable that the movement, of which perhaps we now see only the beginning, should be essentially an intelligent movement ... there should be always at hand men at once of enlarged hearts and cultivated minds, ready to comprehend the position, and, if possible, to control it.

These sentiments were echoed more enthusiastically by J.R.Green and by Morley. In fact the tone of the reviews was generally determined by opinions on the issue of intellectuals in politics. Hostile reviews in the *Athenaeum, Contemporary* and *Quarterly* were prefaced by denials that universities could possibly contribute anything to politics. 'Ex-M.P.', the *Contemporary*'s reviewer wrote scornfully: [147]

When we read this volume, its abstractions, predictions, demonstrations and conclusions, it seems to us that we pass from the facts of history and life to the cloudy land of dreams ... If these writers – eight of whom, out of twelve, are Fellows of Oxford or Cambridge – fairly represent the intellectual tone of the coming agitation, and are soon to form our statesmen, we confess that we shall look with even increased anxiety to the coming destiny of the English government.

This could be countered by a debating argument brisk enough for Lowe (which probably explains why he didn't court it): if reform extinguished intellect in politics, why did the cream of the universities believe in it? Lowe, however, did his best, arguing that the classical education offered at the universities militated against political understanding: [148]

The writers seem almost all to have received a good classical education; none of them display any considerable knowledge of English history or constitutional principles; all are fervent advocates of democratic change, and none, so far as we are able to gather, possess any practical experience of the manner in which public business is carried on, or any very clear views as to the limits of legislation or of the action of government.

Lowe might have had a case here, but, tired and embittered, he did not develop it. Most of his review was ill-tempered abuse: [149]

We are in good health, let us take poison; we have knowledge, let us subordinate it to ignorance; we have peace, let us seek for war; we have directed our affairs on the basis of individual liberty, let us change it for a deference for authority, organisation, and such words of evil omen; we have prospered under the principles of Adam Smith, let us, for a little variety, try Owen and Saint-Simon ...

The essayists had approached these risks with their eyes open. Such petulance did not seriously challenge their position. It fell to J.R.Green to express, obliquely, reservations about their political role and the perceptions they derived from it.

Green approved the intervention, but thought that, while the shared alienation from politics of academic and artisan could create a sufficiently strong combination to destroy false political prescriptions and to initiate specific reforms, weaknesses would arise from the lack of any interpenetration of ideals. [150] Academics may have become radicals, but did they understand the realities of political life, working-class life in particular? Did they realize that its internal complexity – especially the alienation of the unskilled from the 'labour aristocracy' – posed possibly a greater threat to their conception of democracy than did the 'compact mass' they had worked so hard to disperse? [151]

As some of their more perceptive critics pointed out, the academics were radical because their opponents – like Lowe – were extremely conservative: 'the Reform Bills of Liberal Governments since 1852' were quite different from the measure which had evolved by the late spring of 1867. [152] But, in general, opinions about the fitness or otherwise of academics in politics determined the tone of the reviews.

Different essays, too, attracted different criticisms. Brodrick was well received, even by Lowe (he received seven favorable notices, while one was hostile); Dicey (4:1) and Stephen (5:1) were thought able but aggressive and found favour mainly with Liberal reviewers, while Hutton (3:3) and Goldwin Smith (2:5) provoked predictable reactions – *The Times* and the *Economist* concentrating their attack on Smith's essay. Cracroft, Mr Beales's 'father of psephology', came in for a lot of criticism (2:5) – the *Athenaeum* discovered that he had based his estimate of aristocratic influence on *Dod's Electoral Facts*, published in 1853, and tore much of his case to shreds. [153] His reply in the *Daily News* did not convince, [154] and subsequent reviewers, friendly as well as hostile to the essays in general, found little good to say of his essay. Houghton, Kinnear, Pearson, Bryce, Rutson and Young got reasonably respectful notices from the two or three reviewers who mentioned their essays.

Essays on Reform was, on the whole, fortunate. *Questions for a Reformed Parliament* came late, and in the mounting excitement over the parliamentary contest relatively little notice was taken of it. By this time too the unity of the contributors was being put under stress by the rapidity of the drive towards democracy. By the end of March discipline among the Liberals had broken down. Gladstone, trying to hold the party to a ratepaying franchise of five pounds in the boroughs, was opposed by right and left in the 'tea-room' revolt. His amendment at second reading on 13 April failed, and he virtually abdicated from the leadership. [155] The academics were divided: the 'tea-room' threat was 'horrible news' to Bryce; [156] Rutson wrote to the *Daily News*, warning against household suffrage without redistribution as a blow against artisans and in favour of 'the ignorant and subservient householders of the market towns and the decaying boroughs'. Instead he backed Gladstone's proposal as an interim measure, to ensure that a Liberal house was returned pledged to destroy or group the smaller boroughs. [157] His vehemence was greater than his perspicacity: there was no guarantee that redistribution would aid the Liberals, and small boroughs tended, anyway, to be more Liberal than Tory. [158] But he was not alone in trying to put the brakes on. A few days earlier in Manchester Goldwin Smith had called for the raising of the voting age from twenty-one to twenty-five, the imposition of an educational test and the replacement of the House of Lords by a senate of nominated life peers, as 'securities for reform'. [159]

Disquiet was not, however, general. Fawcett's earlier conservatism was succeeded by a single-minded effort to secure the widest measure possible. [160] Leslie Stephen agreed; he had developed a theory of his own, which in fact brought him close to Mr Beales's model of the 'modernizer'. He believed that the victory of Prussia over Austria in the Seven Weeks' War dramatically exposed the inadequacies of British institutions, destroying Lowe's Panglossian optimism and turning the attention of the British governing classes 'rather against established institutions than against reforms'. Reform had to be settled both to accelerate 'modernization' and simply to free parliament for positive legislation. [161] His line was interesting but unique; the other contributors usually sympathized with Germany for cultural rather than administrative reasons, and, although armaments and military organization occupied many column inches in the newspapers after Königgratz, they played no part in the parliamentary debates. [162]

Others viewed household suffrage with equanimity: Dicey's essay argued for equality of political rights; [163] Rogers continued to advocate full manhood suffrage; [164] likewise Lushington and Harrison. [165] A successful Lords amendment which ensured minority representation in three-member constituencies by giving each elector only two votes (said to be the result of Leonard Courtney's advocacy in *The Times*) [166] partially mollified the doubtful, and, as an incidental reinforcement of arguments for reform, in April wealthy British juries acquitted Lieutenant Brand and Colonel, by then General, Nelson, having refused to indict Governor Eyre himself in March.

VIII

The reform essays were not an intervention by experts in politics but the distinctive reaction of the university liberals to the circumstances in which the reform debate was conducted. They supported reform because they had defended the theory of popular government, espcially during the American War, and because during the struggle for university reform they had experienced the inertia of British institutions. These concerns, however, had only indirect connections with popular reform movements. What really activated them to intervene was Lowe's anti-reform polemic and his influence among the 'educated classes'.

Their chosen response – the symposium – was suited to group production, and met their need to identify themselves. Here lay its success, for the essays otherwise made little contribution to the reform agitation. Despite mixed feelings about the Act, the academics could maintain their corporate political identity in preparing for the elections on the new franchise. Leslie Stephen summed up their feelings in June 1868: [167]

English politics just now are in a most befuddled condition. Parliament wrangles and disputes and does nothing. There are no leaders and no policy and no common sense. The Reform Bill will change all this and we will shoot Niagara. I am very glad of it, for we are terribly in want of an earthquake.

[7]

THE
SCIENCE AND ART
OF POLITICS

> ... the demand for a more national Parliament is
> not a mere cry to which it would be folly and weak-
> ness to give way, or the expedient of a party anx-
> ious to attain power by the aid of popular agitat-
> ion, but a conviction seriously entertained and
> capable of being supported by arguments worthy
> of the attention of those who wish to legislate deliber-
> ately and in an impartial spirit for the good of the
> whole people.

from the preface to *Essays on Reform*, 1867

During the 1860s university liberals came to share a number of
perceptions about the nature of British society and politics. Taken
together these constituted an ideology, a philosophical framework
which facilitated cohesion and political intervention by defining an
overall scheme of values into which particular situations could be
fitted. The solidarity produced by specific predicaments and
campaigns – the Tests agitation, the American War – could be
carried into other issues only if it became a rationalization profound
and resilient enough to require only detailed adaptation to cope
with them.

The ideology required was functional: concerned with the general
problems of the group and the period. It had to unite men whose
fundamental ethical approaches, professional concerns and political
preoccupations could differ considerably: to link the idealist
T.H.Green with the utilitarian Henry Sidgwick, the historian Bryce
with the economist Fawcett, the land expert Brodrick with the critic
Leslie Stephen. It was successful in that, despite intellectual and
political disagreements, the men of the 1860s retained, in most cases
as long as they lived, a common vocabulary and a common political
agenda.

141

How did this differ from other liberal interpretations of the politics of the 1860s? In some ways the critical issues were not the obvious ones. The role of the universities as political seminaries for a governing elite – identified as significant by some commentators at the time, and by more since [1] – was not, in itself, a major concern, being contingent on a distinctive reading of politics which substantially excluded both the machinery of government and the manipulative role of the elite. Not by accident: for the concern of the academics was not about individuals manipulating institutions, but about the degree to which their behaviour was conditioned by them. Accustomed to dealing with the affairs of universities and colleges, they were acutely aware of the tensions which existed between their responsibilities and opportunities as individuals and as members of corporations or professions; intellectual and social change within the universities had impelled them into external activity. Both factors influenced their approach to the agenda of national politics. Ethically they had to justify being liberals in a confessional community, possessing the endowments and privileges of the professions in a changing society, a problem rendered more acute by the imperatives they had inherited from Evangelicalism. A laxer age, less concerned to equate individual and social morality, might have accepted the situation. They could not. [2] The political commonwealth had to occupy in their minds the place that salvation had occupied in their fathers' and grandfathers': like them, they worked to bring their institutions into harmony with this cause. They may have found it difficult to establish a definite role for the universities, but the task had to be attempted. Hence the Tests agitation, a campaign which grew in strength as political goals replaced academic ones. It also demonstrated what Leslie Stephen called 'the occult and unacknowledged forces' within British institutions, which made them resistant to even the most powerful social pressures. [3] Their experience led to a healthy disregard of the gloomy forecasts of those liberals who expected franchise reform unaccompanied by complicated safeguards to produce an unbridled radicalism.

II

It is a reflection of the limitations of academic liberalism that it failed to analyse the theory and practice of political leadership. The study of political elites entered the curriculum of British universities from the Continent after the First World War. The native tradition, descriptive, biographical, autobiographical and mainly the work of non-academics, continued, and only in the last few years has there been any attempt to combine the two, not always with success. The political and social divisions of the traditionalists may have been loose and unscientific, yet the contemporary social scientist may find his more precise categories quite inappropriate to a society whose framework differs radically from his own. Theories of elites, applied to the 1860s, exemplify this difficulty. The academic liberals were unquestionably a privileged group, endowed, partly through intellectual ability, with power over the most opulent and influential part of the educational system. Yet their educational programme neither asserted the privileges of an *ancien régime*, nor did it attempt modernization in the interests of a meritocracy. Their politics were participatory rather than manipulative.

The classic texts of elite sociology are unhelpful largely because of their relevance to the twentieth century. Mosca and Pareto, Weber [4] and Wright Mills analysed situations where a relatively homogeneous elite depended on the concentration of decision-making in government and agencies closely related to it: pre-fascist Italy, Wilhelmine Germany and 1950s America were quite different from the unfocused, plural society of 1860s Britain. The academics were less concerned to wield political power than to preserve society from forces which threatened to pull it apart. Group interest was not absent, but it was not the prime motive of their political intervention and, as we have seen, this intervention did not have the effectiveness expected of an elite. In other words, to be at all useful, elite theory has to be stood on its head: the academics needed democracy in order to survive.

In mid-nineteenth-century Britain few political thinkers believed that an elite could manipulate mass democracy. Class was the reality which prompted Mill to construct his minority representation machines, which set Disraeli to redistribute seats in the Tories' favour, which in 1867 terrified hitherto confident defenders of the Palmerstonian constitution, like Lowe and Bagehot. Since the Positivists were, despite their left-wing politics, the only confident elitists, and, since their academic colleagues had several of the characteristics of an elite, it is only too easy to assume that they accepted the Positivist interpretation, minus the liturgical bits, and prospered because of it. A continuum of conscious political elitism at Oxford and Cambridge seems self-evident.

However, the approach of university liberals to the education of political leaders shows that this was far from being the case. Although the theme of using the universities as seminaries for politicians recurred during the 1860s, no agreed programme with this end in mind materialized. And discussions of this problem usually tended to bring into focus other, more absorbing preoccupations, which turned on the maladies affecting society in general.

III

The ambivalence of the academics towards political elites and their education was eloquently stated by Leslie Stephen in his reform essay 'On the choice of representatives by popular constituencies' where he concerned himself with the 'supposed tendency towards a deterioration of public men' in democracies. [5] Stephen admitted the importance of M.P.s being 'drawn from our most highly educated classes' and the desirability of their being 'men of trained intellect ... familiar with such thought as at present passes for political science'. [6] He could see no reason, given traditional British deference, for an exodus from government of statesmanship and intellect, but in the last analysis if the standard of members deteriorated, 'it would be a cheap price to pay for filling up the existing social gulf'. [7] This position was not, apparently, shared by the history professors. Goldwin Smith at Oxford in 1859 and J.R.Seeley at Cambridge a decade later both stressed in their inaugural lectures the importance of the universities as political seminaries. [8] But on closer inspection their positions were less straightforward and emphasized the academics' inability to theorize coherently about elite education in a period of social and intellectual uncertainty.

Despite his celebration of the republican virtues, Goldwin Smith did not address the middle class. University extension he considered valuable, but the university's 'proper charge' remained the education of the 'mental aristocracy of the country': the traditional intelligentsia of the territorial aristocracy and the old professions. [9] Even within this limited social context, which he acknowledged was contingent on the distribution of political power, his bold proposals for curricular reform were qualified. History was most valuable to the passman, the future J.P.; a true liberal education still required classics and geometry: Smith's evidence to the Taunton Commission in 1866 implicitly admitted that no relevant alternative to the old system had yet been worked out. [10] By this time, moreover, his own Oxford projects had collapsed, his disillusion with the traditional intelligentsia was complete, and he was about to exchange Oxford for the 'working man's university' of Cornell in America – about as complete a rejection of the elitist ideal as was possible. [11]

Seeley was more explicit and intially more successful: he wanted the university to instil, through the teaching of contemporary history, 'a solid knowledge of political and social wellbeing in its nature and its causes' and managed to arrange the history syllabus to include inductive politics and economics. [12] But in practice the arrangement neither challenged the supremacy of mathematics and classics nor won the support of Cambridge's abler historians, like F.W.Maitland and William Cunningham. Lacking conceptual depth, it remained an undemanding passman's option, and expired after 1886 when its two principal sponsors, Seeley and Oscar Browning, disagreed over Home Rule, which Seeley believed showed the futility of expecting politicians to learn from history. [13]

The experience of Smith and Seeley shows the difficulty of linking theories of elite education to proposals for political change. As Stephen implied, curricular reform was more important in exposing the inadequacies of elite politics: the classical curriculum reflected the failure of the traditional elite to respond to social change, allowing a false political consciousness to emerge among the masses which ultimately endangered national institutions, including the universities. This situation could only be remedied by extending citizenship to the classes at present excluded from the national legislature as well as from the universities. T.H.Green, in an Oxford essay written about 1858, stated the problem in terms which were politically imprecise but intellectually stimulating: the university ought to bring 'all branches of political talent and learning ... under the sway of the highest methodising intellect', but, to be socially effective, to allow 'the highest philosophy' to prevail over 'the transient will of the majority', it had to be open to 'all ranks and degrees of men'. [14]

The lucidity and force of this youthful manifesto, oddly neglected by Green's biographers, testify to the moral influence his contemporaries recognized, despite philosophical differences, and the relevance of his educational preoccupations. Nor was there much his political idols, Cobden and Bright, could object to. Indulgent towards the leaders of Oxford Reform, Cobden probably credited Goldwin Smith with being rather more radical than he was (see p. 49); but in his contribution to F.W.Farrar's *Essays on a Liberal Education*, which Macmillan published in 1867, uniform with the reform essays, Green's tutor Charles Stuart Parker went far to endorse the Radicals' criticisms of the curriculum, while restating the need for social and educational incorporation. Unless the classical curriculum, preserved by inertia, were discarded, the mercantile and manufacturing communities would lose liberal education altogether. The universities,

Parker concluded, 'must open their eyes to see the true dimensions of a nation'. [15]

This perception was critical, both in itself and as an analogue of the national predicament. The academics were struck by the failure of a national institution to be truly national and the dimensions of the cultural problems thus disclosed. Despite the 'alliance with Manchester' – possibly because of it – the industrial north, in particular, appeared alien. In a *Times* [16] leader of 1862 George Brodrick noted 'the strange isolation of Lancashire from the rest of England', and London society's ignorance of that opulent province. Given this, was it surprising that the northern magnate stayed put?

He rarely aspires to a seat in Parliament, or sends his sons to the University, or migrates southward to find an opening into the ranks of the landed aristocracy.

James Bryce confirmed these observations. School-inspecting in Lancashire, he found a society quite different from that in London, which regarded the accomplishments of Oxford as worse than useless, where 'scientific' – in effect vocational – ideals dominated education. Yet it was also a society whose culture was in steady decline. [17]

By examining the function of the university in society, the academics saw how theoretically national institutions had been perverted to cater for a single class, which showed little interest in them, while commerce and manufacture remained isolated from the cultural and political life of the nation, 'forced', as Rutson wrote in his own essay, 'into an extreme isolation and an exaggerated self-reliance' both by this and by the pressures inherent in these activities. [18] Given the weakness of nationality, was it surprising that, in their turn, working men were driven back on their own resources? If social change continued, unaccompanied by political adjustment, 'national' institutions would atrophy altogether and a philistine plutocracy 'hitherto left to find a mean and narrow education' would rule, all the time observed by a working class which owed neither it nor the nation any loyalty. [19]

But the significance of institutions in politics did not stop there. If universities were not 'seminaries for statesmen' they were where the academics got their practical political training. Along with the Church and the aristocracy they were tangible realities, not the abstractions of reformers tied, like Mill, to theories centred on individual political behaviour. In Leslie Stephen's view Mill exaggerated the power of individuals and of conscious legislation,

146

but neglected 'the forces intellectual and moral, which must always lie behind institutions'. [20] Mill's institutions – even universities – were purely functional bodies; needs were felt, the appropriate signals made and institutions created. The problem was to ensure that the right signals were made, after due consideration by all concerned, through legislative machinery specially adapted to the purpose. Given this conviction, Mill not surprisingly regarded the onset of democracy with mixed feelings. Hence his canvassing of balanced legislatures attained through proportional representation. Academics, on the other hand, with ample experience of institutional inertia, could see that the sort of institution the British universities represented was an inbuilt safeguard against precipitate political action by democratic assemblies. [21]

IV

The academics had enough first-hand knowledge of the aristocracy and the commercial and manufacturing class to persuade themselves that neither – assuming that it had the will – could create a national politics. It followed that such impetus must come from the working classes, particularly from the artisans. But with them their relations were distant, despite the confidence they had in working-class morality as applied to foreign policy. Contact through the social work of the Charity Organisation Society (not always an organization which aroused friendly feelings) and the university settlements did not begin until the 1870s and 1880s (see p. 195). Academic liberal religion, such as it was, tended towards the Broad Church or more rationalistic bodies like the Unitarians, which commanded no real popular following. Even teaching at F.D.Maurice's Working Men's College in London and its Oxford and Cambridge counterparts, scarcely brought them into contact with representative workmen (they were not, on the whole, very able teachers), and their contacts with the Reform League and its branches had been limited. [22]

For their picture of the working class the academics depended on second-hand knowledge, on colleagues whose more intense political convictions made them collaborate with working men. Significantly the reform essays which dealt with working-class concerns – Hutton on 'The Political Character of the Working Classes' in *Essays on Reform*, Godfrey Lushington on trade unions, Townsend on the poor, Ludlow and Lloyd Jones on 'The Progress of the Working Classes' in *Questions for a Reformed Parliament* – were written by men closely connected with the Christian Socialists (Hutton, Townsend, Ludlow and Lloyd Jones, while Lushington was a Positivist). [23] Both groups

were involved deeply in cooperation and trade unionism respectively. Their views of the likely future of the working classes differed
radically, but they contained arguments which favoured the sort of
reforms the academics wanted.

To a Positivist like Frederic Harrison the working class could
become the motor of reform without wanting to get into the driving
seat: [24]

> Governing is one thing; but electors of any class cannot, or ought
> not, to govern. Electing, or giving an indirect approval of Govern-
> ment, is another thing, and demands wholly different qualities.
> These are moral, not intellectual, practical, not special gifts; gifts of
> a very plain and almost universal order. Such are – firstly, social
> sympathies and sense of justice; then openness and plainness of
> character; lastly, habits of action, and a practical knowledge of
> social misery. These are the qualities which fit men to be the
> arbiters, or ultimate source (though certainly not the instruments) of
> political power. These qualities the best working men possess in a far
> higher degree than any other portion of the community.

This attitude was incorporated, minus the elitism, more or less
directly into the thought of the liberals. Rutson wrote in *Essays on
Reform*: [25]

> The working class possesses, far more completely than any other
> class, that strong desire for a better future, without which social
> progress is a matter of chance and accident ... the working man,
> especially in large towns, is constantly reminded that he is one of a
> great multitude, whose prosperity or adversity he must share. The
> consciousness of mutual dependence makes the working class
> generous; while the sense of untrained powers and undeveloped
> facilities gives them aspirations, which are not the least powerful of
> the social forces to be made available for the national service by a
> Parliamentary government.
> For working men the need of social progress is a matter of every
> day's experience. They could not be largely represented in the
> House of Commons, without the statesmen in it feeling that a new
> force had arisen which would support them in difficult undertak-
> ings: that a demand had been created for exertions on their part in
> paths almost untrodden before.

Both Positivists and liberals saw the working class as a force for
more active government; they differed, however, in their concepts
both of government and class. To the Positivists government was an
expert science, Parliament humbug. Their ideal was presidential: an
enlightened executive commissioned by a sovereign people to
undertake a programme of wide-ranging reform. Reform undertaken by the elite in the interests of the majority would *ipso facto*

benefit the working class. [26] Being parliamentarians, the academic liberals regarded the reform campaign as aiming at the participation of the working class in existing institutions, using its numerical force to secure an open society in which class feelings would ultimately be dissipated. Both were united, however, in the belief that the common sense of working men would gain immediate and necessary reforms in central government.

If Positivism to this extent validated the 'incorporation' of the working class, the Christian Socialist contribution, though different in content, complemented it. Christian Socialists generally distrusted government intervention and advocated and assisted 'mutual aid' by working men. Ludlow and Edward Vansittart Neale played a major part in directing consumers' cooperatives, while Tom Hughes was similarly employed with the trade unions. Townsend and Hutton were connected with them through Maurice and the *Spectator*. They reported the efforts made by working men, with or without the aid of enabling legislation, to raise themselves and their class by cooperation, temperance societies, trade unions and the like. But, while they stressed that the working classes were materially approximating towards the rest of society, they also insisted that enfranchisement would lead to them learning, [27]

from political responsibility and intercourse with statesmen, to take a larger view of the interests of their own class, as inseparable from the interests of the nation.

Underlying their present situation, argued Hutton, lay 'great, if misdirected, class patriotism'. He quoted Tom Hughes: [28]

... the artisans have many of them so high a conception of the obligation of the individual working man to remain in his class and raise its level, rather than to rise out of it into the richer class above, that they regard a working man who so uses his liberty as to prove that he cares more for his own fortunes than for those of his class.

The moral of this was obvious: if the working man was not 'incorporated' he would further entrench himself in his own institutions, with ominous consequences for the nation. Echoing this from a more orthodox liberal position, Leslie Stephen warned: [29]

Does not the fact of excluding them (the working classes) from legislative influence, teach them to look to other means, and weaken Parliament quite as much as it weakens the Democracy?

From the Positivists and the Christian Socialists the academics drew the same lesson as they drew from their dealings with the urban middle class: the governing class's neglect of reform was leading to the alienation of the other classes from the nation and its institutions. In the case of the urban middle classes a continuation of this tendency promised the emergence of plutocracy; in the case of the working classes the result in the long term might be far worse. Combining historical analogy with a study of the contemporary situation, James Bryce wrote: [30]

If the history of Greece and Rome teaches anything, it teaches us that it is not democracy but the interested government of an upper class which naturally and inevitably produces the worst type of demagogue. This being, who is painted in such dark colours as the destroyer of national peace, is not a wanton manifestation of human wickedness; he is the legitimate consequence of a system which abandons the idea of an undivided Commonwealth, in whose prosperity all citizens are to share, and which substitutes for this conception that of a State composed of different classes with discordant interests, in which whatever is given to one must be taken from some other, and where the most that can be hoped for is a sort of armed neutrality of mutually hostile powers.

Arguing now from the conclusions of de Tocqueville, Bryce went on: [31]

Those things which are the bases of political power – knowledge, self-respect and the capacity for combined action – having formerly been possessed by the few only, are now possessed by the many, and among them by persons who do not enjoy civil privileges, though they feel themselves in every other respect the equals of those who do. Or, in other words, the social progress of democracy has outrun its political progress. This is dangerous, because it makes the organs of our political life no longer an adequate expression of the national will; and because there is nothing more dangerous than a democratic society without democratic institutions.

This was obviously a shrewd inference from the evidence to hand: the working classes had the moral and material qualifications to participate in the Commonwealth, but if 'unincorporated' they might exalt over it a sense of class solidarity, and so destroy it. 'The real danger to England', Bryce concluded, [32] 'is not from the working class, for no working class in any country was ever more peaceably disposed than ours is, but from the isolation of classes'.

V

The academics analysed British politics in terms of the health of the 'Nation', the 'Commonwealth' or the 'Democracy' and the threats to it, a concept which, during this critical period, they fused to the ruling utilitarianism of mid-Victorian liberalism. They did not consider this a contribution to political philosophy; once the crisis had passed, and they were at liberty to speculate in more abstract fashion, their political perceptions again became disparate, and the more logical constructs of contemporaries – like Bagehot – ignored at the time, were revalued. But as an expedient, intended to make sense of a particular situation, their modification of utilitarianism worked more or less satisfactorily.

Academic liberalism was deeply committed to utilitarianism, and Mill was reverenced not simply for his writings but for his personal radicalism and political courage. [33] Reference to him was necessary for those who accepted the social analysis of Benthamism, 'just as lunar observations are requisite to correct the errors of chronometers and dead reckoning'. [34] Even idealists like T.H.Green accepted his moral authority: the shared political perceptions which held utilitarian and idealist together were, in the 1860s, more important than their divergent philosophies. [35] But both believed that the prevalent popular conception of utilitarianism had to be revised, for two main reasons: one moral and one prudential. Morally, was a philosophy adequate if it sanctioned the action which propertied society in Britain – the great beneficiary of practical utilitarianism – had taken during the American War, when self-interest overrode justice? [36] And, in prudence, could 'good government' exclude notions of 'right' and 'justice' and still inculcate a sense of responsibility into the mass of the community? [37]

Lowe, for the utilitarians of the right, identified 'good government' with the *status quo*: a propertied elite superintending a free-enterprise economy, allowing its efficient operation to maximize material prosperity. Criticizing this in *Essays on Reform*, Brodrick argued that a purely material definition of wellbeing did not merely diminish the moral purpose of government, but put at risk the whole principle of representation: [38]

'The happiness of the people at large' is the familiar watchword of despotism ... The vice of despotic government, and that which renders it as ruinous economically as it is morally degrading, consists not in its wilful neglect of popular interests, but in its contempt for popular opinions, in treating the people as passive materials for benevolent superintendence: and this vice must attach, more or less, to every government constituted with reference to the happiness only, and without reference to the voice, of the governed.

Such a government faced a threefold peril: unrepresentative *in fact*, it might become unrepresentative in theory as well, and operate as an administrative bureaucracy;[39] lacking information which came from a 'national' representation, its legislation would be neither expedient nor efficient;[40] and to the working classes it would be an interest to be coerced and exploited – probably to their material benefit – rather than an institution to respect. 'Men who are denied the privileges, are apt to forget the duties of citizenship,' he concluded. [41]

The prescriptions of Mill, for the utilitarians of the left, were also greeted sceptically. Between 1859 and 1862 he had written to sanction representative assemblies as appropriate agencies for supervising government; but they were to be concerned only with vetting measures drafted by a salaried commission. [42] Parliament's function was to express opinion about legislation, its composition so adjusted by proportional representation that such opinion reflected divisions within the country.

The academics respected Mill's integrity but were not prepared to accept him as an infallible political guide. In his 1859 review of the *Principles of Parliamentary Reform*, Brodrick credited him with 'shrewd observation and a knowledge of the external conditions of politics', but observed that 'his way of dealing with society as a whole is that of the political economist rather than the statesman'. [43] Mill was a 'doctrinaire', who preferred abstract theory to the study of real political situations. Thus he produced proposals – the enfranchisement of women and the conferring of plural votes on educated persons – which may have been consistent with his overall view of human nature, but in the context of actual political behaviour seemed crotchety and pedantic. [44] Underlying this Brodrick, like Leslie Stephen, found an exaggerated emphasis of the impact of government on society, which Mill apparently felt had to be mitigated by such schemes. [45] Brodrick on the whole reflected the views of his colleagues when he wrote that [46]

representative machinery, if it is to fulfil its purpose, must work in subordination to the habits and associations which operate not only at contested elections, but in the daily intercourse of the market place and the family, and which lie deeper than any positive institutions.

National politics ought to reflect such realities, without any need for electoral machinery to protect wealth and intellect; the habitual and fairly amicable relationship these had with the community would see to that [47] But when parliament was alienated from the rest of society its educational function atrophied; it could neither carry out sound policy, nor instruct the populace about its nature. [48]

The academics respected parliament because it was a participatory institution, not merely a representative element in a complex constitutional mechanism. Leslie Stephen accepted conservative allegations about the low quality of American Congressmen because, he argued, the restricted powers of Congress made this inevitable. [49] In Britain, by contrast, [50]

Parliamentary power is now so all-pervading, it reaches every man in so many different relations of life, and it daily grows so much in importance, that it is not likely to lose its charms for our ablest men.

For Rutson the uniqueness of the British parliamentary tradition was a major advantage for a country contemplating the transition to democracy: [51]

Englishmen regard Parliamentary Government with an admiration that is merited. They justly observe that it produces or encourages among the enfranchised classes an excellent understanding of each other, common sympathies, a habit of cooperation, and mutual confidence; and that, by means of it, such expression is given to the public opinion of those classes that, as a general rule, all their well-considered wishes and plans speedily become laws.

And the essential of parliamentary government was that [52]

The House of Commons does not merely accept or reject the proposals of the Minister, it practically determines what the character of those proposals must be.

In this situation it was therefore essential that the character of the House be one with which the nation as a whole could identify.

In modifying utilitarianism in ways which he found morally and intellectually more satisfying, Mill was aware that he was detracting from its force as a creed. [53] Finding that the calculus of unregenerate Benthamism put at risk the values he had come to accept, he tried to create a political balance between the representative and the cultivated by 'rigging' the representative element and restricting its function. But the Mill the academics understood was the Mill of the *Logic* and the early editions of the *Political Economy* – the declaratory, straightforward Mill who could be cited in favour of sound economics, freedom of thought and civil equality. They were puzzled by his later, more complex, politics and economics, which seemed to vitiate his force. [54] Such modifications, they argued, would not help the new democracy: the creed ought to be kept simple, and the masses educated in it by being admitted into existing institutions, whose intrinsic conservatism would restrain

153

them from rash initiatives. The distinction the Evangelicals made between rational and vital religion reappeared: the rationalist, like Mill, tended to see the disadvantages of democracy, as he conceived society as an aggregate of self-interested social atoms, and democracy as the tyranny of 51 per cent of the atoms over the rest. The Evangelical academics saw, on the other hand, individuals with a capacity for altruistic behaviour spontaneously committing themselves to institutions and adapting them to direct and instruct popular sentiments.

The critical example was the national community. National consciousness had not been on Bentham's agenda. A rationalist of the Enlightenment, he presumed, on the basis of associationist psychology, an identical causality of social relationships throughout mankind. The Benthamite method was manifest in James Mill's *History of India* (1818): Indian institutions and society were judged and graded by the standards of British utility. [55] John Stuart Mill knew European liberals and European liberalism, but as an internationalist ideologue rather than a sympathizer with specific nationalist movements. These did not deeply concern him; for a good part of each year he lived contentedly under the rule of Napoleon III at Avignon, something which would have been unthinkable to many of the academics, who loathed the Emperor with almost irrational intensity. [56] In his *Autobiography* there is no mention of Italy, or indeed of European nationalism, save a brief, gloomy reference to 'the European reaction after 1848 (which) put an end, as it seemed, to all present hope of freedom or social improvement in France and the Continent'. [57] His heartiest sympathies went to foreign causes like the North in the American War, and the Eyre case, which implied radical criticism of the ruling class at home. If nationality had little reality to the philosophic utilitarian, neither had domestic institutions whose function could not be explained wholly in terms of utility, like the universities, to which the academics were bound by loyalties founded on something more than calculation. Such institutional loyalty, on the other hand, reinforced their enthusiasm for the national principle abroad, and made them aware of its possible role in domestic politics.

Through historical study the university liberals could comprehend the political environment of other nations: Rutson opened his essay by stressing not their uniformity but their variety, and the exceptionally advantageous bequest of the English tradition, not only parliamentarianism but [58] the no less peculiar and no less momentous advantage of being able to look back upon an unbroken history. The greatest revolutions in political and religious ideas have been effected in England without any social convulsion. Our annals record no abrupt changes, no long period of unnatural repression ending in anarchy. There has been a continuous growth and a steady development. Misgovernment, such as has frequently existed for generations in all continental countries, has in England been always unknown. Not only the prolonged dominion of foreigners, but temporary conquest, and even the presence on our soil of a foreign army, has for six centuries been equally unknown. Far different has been the fortune of other countries.

Despite its Whig tones, this was a more valid interpretation of British politics than Mill's. Noel Annan has pointed out that the liberal morality of *On Liberty*, which purported to have a universal validity, could only work in a pacific and prosperous nation. [59] The liberal academics accepted Mill's ethics, but they were aware more than he was, or admitted he was, that they were more likely to be realized in Britain than elsewhere. The history of other nations showed, they argued, not that popular institutions became corrupt but that their effectiveness depended on their relationships with the different political, diplomatic, social and psychological pressures which had formed national character. [60] Despite all this some democratic nations – notably the United States – had succeeded in coping with considerable problems. [61] If they could overcome such disadvantages, Britain, in her position, must submit to a more severe analysis. [62]

The academic liberal view of nationality was the outcome of a dialogue between Millite utilitarianism and the historical or comparative method practised at the universities. It owed much to their intellectual traditions. In classics the study of the politics of the Greek city-states – where citizens' rights were co-terminous with the boundaries of the 'polis', where the political debate was couched in terms of 'civic virtue', where, even in a restricted area and over a relatively short time span, the traditions of individual cities and their governments varied widely – could scarcely stimulate a belief in the uniformity of political motivation or a disregard of the mechanism of existing institutions. [63] Liberal Anglicanism, still with some residual influence in the universities, had incorporated from Germany a theory of history predominantly national in orientation. Thomas Arnold and F.D.Maurice saw the alienation of classes threatening English civilization, and redemption resting with the cooperation of intellect and labour, the programme of the Christian

Socialists. [64] Though they might reject its theological and philo-sophical basis, the university liberals retained, in their association of patriotism and class cooperation, elements of its political programme. On a less sophisticated level other Oxford historians – Freeman, J.R.Green and, less stridently, Bryce – elaborated a quasi-anthropological nationalism which stressed an Anglo-Saxon aptitude for liberty and cooperation inherited from 'the free forests of Germany' which, to some extent, accorded with the folk-memory of 'the Norman yoke' that radical orators still invoked. [65]

Italian nationalism further demonstrated what could be achieved by subordinating individual ends to a common national goal. Old Italy had been aristocratic, clerical, divided and misgoverned; it was now united, liberal and attempting to remove the abuses of the past. This was, according to Frederic Harrison, the triumph of the spirit of Mazzini, the arms of Garibaldi and the statesmanship of Cavour. [66] The feuds of the various sections of Italian nationalism were forgotten: altruism prevailed. Mazzini's self-sacrifice, his lifetime in exile, the Lion's return as a peasant to Caprera, Cavour dying in harness – all this for the nation Mazzini conceived as a moral rather than a political unity. His nation was threefold: liberator, cooperative commonwealth, moral educator. [67] Neither a monolith of institutional conservatism, where established groups counted for all and the individual for nought, nor a Benthamite machine, subject to the will of a captious majority, it embodied the highest aims of politics, self-evidently more important than the interests of classes or groups. The Italian experience convinced the academics that such a conception could command the support of men of all ranks if the right appeal were made, by a truly national legislature which had the confidence of the people through its awareness of their needs.

Finally, the academics' support for the North in the American War involved not only a political realignment but an increased awareness of the theories of de Tocqueville, whom they had come to venerate. [68] The anti-democratic arguments of Lowe and his friends were illustrated by selective quotation from Henry Reeve's biased translation of *Democracy in America*, highlighting the decline in leadership, public life, the spread of corruption and so forth. Their own reading of de Tocqueville, along with first-hand information from the United States, enabled them to counter-attack. But they did more than vindicate American society: they recognized de Tocqueville's masterpiece for what it really was, a comprehensive and on the whole sympathetic study of the tendency towards democratic politics, [70] whose implications were self-evident: [71]

The tendency of the last seven centuries of European history has been to an equalization of the conditions of men – an equalization not so much (in England at least) of wealth as of physical force, of manners, and of intelligence. The feeling of subordination – that reverence of the lower classes for the upper, which was once the cause and the justification of the feudal policy – has disappeared; political equality has become a passion in some countries, legal or civil equality is admitted to be necessary in all (speaking, of course, of civilised communities only). Exclusive systems of government are therefore out of date.

Because of their confidence in the stimulating power of nationality and the moderating influence of institutions, the university liberals ought not to be seen as 'crying over the unspilt milk of the future, exhausting on apprehension energies needed for investigation': [72] John Vincent's strictures may be true in some respects of Mill, but to extend the condemnation to Leslie Stephen and talk of the 'posture of apprehension' of university men is unfair. Take Stephen himself: [73]

... the influences of rank, and wealth, and education, are not limited by the recognition given to them in the Constitution; protected or unprotected, they will produce an effect which no legislation can take from them ... I do not believe that in a normal state of things there is any class of English society in which money and social position do not produce a great effect; hence I do not believe that any complete transfer of power is possible, if desirable; the effect of natural social forces cannot be eliminated by any legislative artifice.

Whatever this was, it was not the talk of someone intellectually immobilized by the spectre of mass democracy.

In his review of the *Principles of Parliamentary Reform* Brodrick summed up a critical aspect of the academics' divergence from Mill: [74]

All that a lucid exposition of principles could do he has done. If he has failed in the task of construction, he has but shared the fate of all who have attempted in this subject to combine the 'luciferous' and the 'fructiferous' in a single process. The science and art of politics cannot be cultivated together, they must proceed by contrary methods, and are best intrusted to minds of different orders. He who deals with the wills of his fellow men must often be satisfied with that philosophical abomination, a compromise, or rather a perpetual series of compromises.

In books like *Essays on Reform* the academics vindicated compromise: so expertly did they juggle with aspirations and principles and realities and instutions that none of these got out of hand. Democracy would not lead to attempts at socialist utopias and the repudiation of the National Debt, because of the power of wealthy and traditional institutions. On the other hand the latter were inhibiting progress and would have to be shaken up. Hence democracy. Given 'political artistry' it would all balance out, whatever the 'scientist' thought.

But 'political artistry' of course implied certain assumptions about the nature of political life in Britain and the direction reform ought to pursue. Professor Vincent has further indicted the intellectuals of the 1860s with being indifferent to 'urgent social matters of a less hypothetical nature' – slums, the impact of transport schemes, the plight of agricultural labour – which demanded government intervention. [75] If Stephen and his colleagues can be absolved from charges of defensive apprehension, they still have to face this accusation, for the ideology of the reform essays was as far from being, in Mr W.L.Guttsman's words, 'a forerunner to the Fabian Essays' as it was from Professor Vincent's stereotype. Which raises the question: what in fact did the academics mean by social reform, and how did this relate to their ideal of social progress?

In 'The Opportunities and Shortcomings of Government in England' Rutson wrote: [76]

For two or three generations the recognition of the duty of social progress, and of the possibility of furthering it by legislation, has been the basis of politics.

But seven years earlier Brodrick, commenting on Mill, had berated 'the error of attempting by political machinery to accelerate social progress'. [77] This apparent contradiction can be interpreted in various ways. Did the academics disagree about the role of government in society? Did their political thought – and on most issues Rutson's opinions were much the same as Brodrick's – move towards collective action between 1859 and 1867? Or, analysing their language, is there in fact a difference between 'social progress' and 'the duty of social progress', which discloses the logic underlying their social thought?

The academics related 'social progress' to representative government in much the same way as Goldwin Smith, in his Inaugural Lecture, distinguished between the 'social sciences' and history – the former being concerned with normative elements in human behaviour, the latter with distinctive national and institutional developments – and Brodrick separated 'political science' from 'the art of politics'. [78] When Brodrick described Mill as more of an economist than a politician, he did not deny the importance of economics, but insisted that the political community was something more than an economic relationship, and that its study implied an awareness of the role of custom and obligation. [79]

Goldwin Smith included in his Inaugural Lecture an elaborate paean to economics: [80]

... the most beautiful and wonderful of the natural laws of God, through their beauty and their wonderful wisdom they, like the other laws of nature which science explores, are not without a poetry of their own. Silently, surely, without any man's taking thought, if human folly will only refrain from hindering them, they gather, store, dispense, husband, if need be, against scarcity, the wealth of the great community of nations ...

Though Smith's language is extravagant, he typified the academics' implicit acceptance of 'classical' economics as the basis of social life. 'We all assumed individualism as obviously and absolutely right', Bryce wrote to Dicey fifty years later, [81]

We were not indifferent to the misfortunes of the poor, but looked on them as inevitable, and did not feel the restless anxiety to remove them, even in defiance of economic laws, which burns in the breasts of modern youth.

The attitudes of Henry Fawcett, Leslie Stephen, Brodrick and Sidgwick were similar. [82] But the function of government was not limited to safeguarding economic laws. When Brodrick distinguished between expedient and good government, he defined the latter in terms which most of his contemporaries accepted: [83]

The other system considers the process of government, as a means of moral training, not less valuable than the immediate results to be produced by it. It denies the title of 'good government' to policies in which the noblest faculties of the citizens are left unemployed. All free opinions it accepts as contributions to the public treasury of wisdom. It places no bound to the aspirations of political society, except where the rights of individuals, or of other societies, would be infringed. It regards the individual members of a state as moral beings, engaged in a common search for their highest attainable condition, and the national assembly as the place in which the various results of the enquiry are compared ... 'The dignity of government depends on the dignity of the governed' is a sentiment worthy of its author; and of this dignity, whether it consist in character or in mental cultivation, mere possession of property is no fit criterion. Well would it be for the happiness of mankind, if more thought was bestowed on those upon whom the fabric of society ultimately rests, if the language of politics were borrowed from the moral rather than from the economical world, and if the interests of citizens in the common weal were measured less by their financial investments – for who can stake more than his all – and more by their appreciation of the grand and enduring benefits conferred by a wise government on an intelligent people.

Linked to this was the principle that political institutions were a projection of the social realities of the time. In Bryce's words: [84] 'a political system or form of government by itself is nothing, and acquires a meaning only when it is regarded as the result and efflux of national life'.

The academics did not regard government as a promoter of social welfare. 'The result and efflux of national life' meant a general tendency towards material, mental and moral progress, which government – recognizing 'the duty of social progress' – ought to accord with. Reform only became necessary when this did not happen, and a brisk but temporary campaign of institutional reform, like that undertaken after 1830, became necessary. Since then 'improvement' had been accepted 'as the general law in public affairs', [85] but the time was now ripe for a further accommodation, and a further campaign. [86] Danger threatened when the social groups the last settlement had represented in government, their power set at risk by the march of progress, attempted to use the institutions of government in their own interest.

Brodrick and Leslie Stephen noted in particular the power of the aristocracy in British society, a power statistically demonstrated by Boyd Kinnear's essay on 'The Redistribution of Seats' and Bernard Cracroft's on 'The Analysis of the House of Commons, or Indirect Representation', Cracroft concluded that [87]

not less than five hundred Members in the House of Commons are either County Members or, if representing boroughs, either peers or relatives of peers, or landowners or under landowners' influence, constituting ... one vast cousinhood.

Such an unbalanced representation could only distort legislature and legislation. Rutson, writing to Lord Houghton to solicit his support, argued that 'the shortcomings of our Legislation and Government' stemmed from the constitution of the House [88]

representing only *a part of the nation*, and that part from its own circumstances the most contented with things as they are, and the least sensible of the need for change in matters affecting the mass of the people – from the predominance in it of *prejudices* or of *interested motives* such as obstruct legislation on Education, the Universities, the Army &c., from *want of public spirit and of a sense of responsibility* owing to the circumstances of so many members, either representing boroughs where there is no real opinion upon, or interest in, the national policy, or having got into parliament by means of bought votes.

Sir George Young saw this as the result of the ebbing of the political momentum of the early 1830s, and drew the fairly obvious moral that inertia, rather than headlong change, was to be feared after reform. [89] After 1832 this had been partly due to failure to utilize and extend the machinery of government – to tackle electoral corruption and redistribute seats – even to accord with contemporary realities of power. But more fundamental was the rigidity of the 1832 settlement. While admitting the principle of representation, it conciliated the groups then in the ascendant: land by the enfranchisement of tenants-at-will and the retention of the small boroughs; urban property by the ten pound franchise. [90] This may have balanced out in 1832; it certainly did so no longer. Should the attempt at 'balance' be revived? The answer of the academics was firmly negative. Dismissing Mill's argument for a cumulative vote on an educational basis, Brodrick in 1859 insisted that [91]

the natural inequality of members of the same body should not be directly recognised but left to the unseen operation of laws presupposed by all political systems ... Nothing should be made the subject of a give-and-take compromise that can be equitably adjusted through the medium of a comprehensive principle.

Dicey went even further and argued that any attempt to 'mirror' classes – to give the working classes representation without influence – would be worse than no reform at all, since their representatives would become the narrowest type of class tribune. (As examples he cited the leaders of the parish clergy in Convocation and, ominously, the leaders of the Irish party.) [92] The only real alternative was 'the free representation in Parliament of different portions of society'. 'We need', wrote Brodrick, [93]

no 'concordat' between classes, as such, to define the disputed frontier of their relative power. It is better that it should remain unsettled: and it is their own fault if the advantage does not remain with those whose superior wealth, leisure, and education must give them something like a monopoly of political action, if not of political privileges, and among whose claims to supremacy one only, that founded on class interests, excites suspicion and mistrust.

A franchise reduction, redistribution and effective action against corrupt practices would be sufficient to harness working-class common sense to the legislature and enable it to clear up the backlog of reform inherited from the old regime.

VI

In terms of the welfare politics which until recently provided the criteria for most academic studies of Victorian society, academic attitudes to state intervention were far from straightforward, at once apparently sanctioning and prohibiting it. Comprehension was not helped by their own retrospection, conveyed with force in Dicey's *Law and Public Opinion*. Revising his 1898 lectures for publication, Dicey confessed himself puzzled by the move towards collectivism which was apparently under way in the 1860s, 'when individualism was supreme, and, as my own memory can unfortunately tell me, Socialism or Collectivism was generally discredited among sensible people'. [94] Although he cited franchise extension as a factor contributing towards collectivism, it was not critical. He suspected that trade unionists who supported democratic agitation in the 1860s were more socialistically inclined, despite their political moderation, than the Chartists had been; but democracy itself, exemplified in Chartism and American politics, was inherently individualist in tendency. [95] The other four of his five conditions were already in existence by 1867: 'Tory Philanthropy and the Factory Movement – the Changed Attitude after 1848 of the Working Classes – the Modification of Economic Beliefs – the Characteristics of Modern Commerce. [96] Why did he and his colleagues not recognize them?

Dicey's rigid categories and important omissions have given rise to much subsequent academic controversy, but the fact that it took him until the 1890s to realize the significance of at least some of the tendencies he had ignored during the 1860s illustrates how distinctive the academic outlook was at the time, and how closely tied to this were the prescriptions put forward. What he did not realize in retrospect was that these prescriptions were less vulnerable to antithetical ideologies – like 'collectivism' – than to social changes which destroyed the environment in which they had been formulated.

The academics' priorities for 'positive' government legislation embraced the three related fields of land, law and education. This may seem a strange agenda in an age which had urban, sanitary and labour problems in abundance and yet, given their perception of society, there was logic in it. The dynamic elements in mid-Victorian Britain – industrialization and urbanization – have

162

perhaps been overstressed by modern social historians. Although
more than half of the population lived in towns by 1851, and half of
these in cities of more than 100,000 people, in 1861 over 60 per cent
still lived in the countryside or in towns smaller than Oxford or
Cambridge (both at that time around the 30,000 mark): in the sort
of society, in other words, that most of the academics had been
raised in and were most familiar with. [97] The horror and exhilara-
tion of industry and city life impinged on sensitive and eloquent
social groups – churchmen, administrators, medical men and
publicists – sometimes more vividly as metaphor than as fact, but
the stability of the old order still pervaded the political life which
preoccupied the academics. With reason: centralization and bureaucracy had suffered setbacks in the 1850s, and the popular forces
making for participatory government, especially the artisans, were
still, in John Vincent's words, 'employed in the immemorial crafts of
old Europe'. [98] There was plenty of room for politics which accepted
urban and industrial problems as important, but believed that the
social tendencies which created them could be checked by modifications to traditional society.

Their attitude to large towns exemplifies this. In the 1860s these
were seen as providing political opportunities as well as social
problems. In *Essays on Reform* Stephen and Rutson contrasted their
tendency to return members of high calibre with the behaviour of
the small boroughs. [99] Later, as urban growth continued, and their
own political and social initiatives foundered, their reaction was
pessimistic. Charles Pearson's gloom, in *National Life and Character*,
was extreme but not unique: [100]

Is it not unavoidable that the city type should become more and
more pronounced? Is it not probable that the type elaborated will
not be so much that of the mobile, critical, imaginative Athenian,
who was practically an aristocrat among slaves, as of the Manchester and Bellevue operative, with an inheritance of premature
decrepitude, with a horizon narrowed to parochial limits, with no
interests except those of the factory or the Trades-Union; with the
faith of the Salvation Army, that finds expression in antics and
buffoonery, or with that even more lamentable scepticism to which
the bestial element in man is the only reality?

In the 1860s J.R.Green, as an East End clergyman struggling with
pauperism and his own declining faith, wrote in rather similar
terms, [101] but this was still a time when the situation he had to cope
with could be put down to non-urban factors. To W.L.Newman,
writing on 'The Land Laws' in *Questions for a Reformed Parliament*,

urban dangers were a function of distinct, and preventable, rural inequities: [102]

> The very misery of agriculture has intensified the flight from the country to the towns, and given a wild energy to manufacturing progress. A gigantic wages-receiving class fills the cities, and stands against an equally powerful organisation of capitalists ... We stand in danger, in one respect, of the fate of the ancient Greek States, where the antagonism of rich and poor made all excellence of political constitution fruitless and nugatory; where the social weakness overpowered and neutralized the political advance.

Despite a commitment to liberal individualism, this implied a distrust of capitalist industry itself. The academics shared Mill's doubts about whether mechanization had raised the living standards of working people, and few of them managed to follow him in escaping from wages-fund theories which asserted that 'it was physically impossible that any permanent rise in wages should take place without a corresponding diminution of profit' and consequently in investment, employment and ultimately wages. [103]

Out of this squirrel-cage there appeared to be only one route – to educate the working class in habits of prudence, forethought and cooperation. 'The crucial test of the value of all the agencies which are brought into operation to improve the condition of the labouring poor is this: Do they exert a direct tendency to make the labourer rely on self-help?' Thus Fawcett. [104] Remedies like cooperative production and distribution appealed to the academics as they did to Mill. Involvement in the management of industry, like admission to parliamentary politics, educated the worker in the laws of social progress. Fawcett and Sidgwick were as enthusiastic in supporting producers' and consumers' cooperatives as they were in policing the Poor Law – the Achilles' heel of Victorian individualism. The same could be said of many of their colleagues. [105]

The academics did not look complacently on the growth of industry. Goldwin Smith's energetic and successful campaign of 1865 against the plan of the Great Western Railway to build its carriage works at Oxford – 'the greatest fight of my life' – was not opposed by any of his liberal friends who wanted to see the working class at closer range. [106] More seriously, the controversy about the decline of Britain's coal reserves started by W.S. Jevons's *The Coal Question* in 1865 made them conscious of the insecure nature of the country's economic growth. Leonard Courtney, another authoritative classical voice, was far from optimistic: [107]

> The real danger to British industry arises from much deeper

causes ... he (Courtney) warns his readers of the possible shrinkage of our natural resources, and bids them prepare for recurring depressions and growing emigration. The population that can be sustained at any given time is limited by a variety of causes, some of which are wholly or partially beyond our control ... 'Much yet remains to be done to improve the condition of the people by the reform of our laws, above all those relating to land; but if all that could be suggested were accomplished, it would still remain with the people themselves to determine their own condition.'

Existing land law distorted the free working of the economy, and the ability of working men to shift for themselves in it. The misery of a still 'feudalized' agricultural population affected the process of urbanization. Aristocratic privileges, chiefly those governing bequest and entail, by inhibiting the 'free sale' of land, prevented its efficient exploitation and equitable distribution. The indictment, summed up by T.H.Green in 1879, had been familiar enough to his colleagues for a couple of decades: [108]

The whole history of the ownership of land in Europe has been of a kind to lead to the agglomeration of a proletariate neither holding nor seeking property, wherever a sudden demand has arisen for labour in mines or manufactures. This at any rate was the case down to the epoch of the French Revolution; and this, which brought to other countries deliverance from feudalism, left England, where feudalism had previously passed into unrestrained landlord-ism, almost untouched. And while those influences of feudalism and landlordism which tend to throw a shiftless population upon the centres of industry have been left unchecked, nothing till quite lately was done to give such a population a chance of bettering itself, when it had been brought together. Their health, housing, and schooling were unprovided for. They were left to be freely victimised by deleterious employments, foul air, and consequent craving for deleterious drinks. When we consider all this, we shall see the unfairness of laying on capitalism or the free development of individual wealth the blame which is really due to the arbitrary and violent manner in which rights over land have been acquired and exercised, and the failure of the state to fulfil those functions which under a system of unlimited private ownership are necessary to maintain the conditions of a free life.

The academics saw in the privileges of landed society the bane of a potentially sound market system. The free market in American land, and the fact that 'the explosive forces can always find an outlet in emigration to the West', [109] figured much in the debate on Reform. Goldwin Smith argued that the absence of such privileges in the U.S.A. meant that there was greater freedom for individual and cooperative initiatives and so, ultimately, less need for government. [110]

Critics of democracy, like the *Economist*, could argue that the flexibility of American society was distinctive, and its institutions incapable of being transferred into a British context; [111] but they then found the academics entrenched on their second line, arguing that if land were not free in Britain it should be, and that such a situation would contribute to the stability of a reform settlement.

The academics wanted a 'free land' programme – essentially a campaign against the laws permitting primogeniture and entail. They argued that 'free sale' would permit land to play a proper role in the market, allowing the sensible siting of industry and housing and the creation of what Rutson called a 'rural middle class' of peasant proprietors. [112] Fawcett emphasized the value of such a class to the social stability of the nation: [113]

How much more powerfully would prudence be stimulated, if a definite prospect were held out, that a labourer might in the course of time, by means of his saving, secure a small landed property! The value of such an acquisition to the labourer is not to be estimated by the amount of wealth with which it enriches him. It makes him, in fact, a different man; it raises him from the position of a labourer, and calls forth all those active qualities of mind, which are sure to be exerted when a man has the consciousness that he is working on his own account.

His commendation was repeated in political terms by W.L.Newman: [114]

The proprietor, however small, has the conservative interests of a proprietor. His stake in the good order of the country is not, perhaps, greater – it is probably even safer, and less liable to be affected by civil disturbance, than that of the receiver of wages; but it is more tangible. His interest is stronger because it is less mercenary, and more the result of tradition, instinct and habit.

In *Culture and Anarchy* Matthew Arnold attacked radical proposals to limit the freedom of bequest as an instance of the intellectual cowardice of the middle class, its reliance on 'machinery' to attain its ends, its reluctance to expose the inadequacy of its ideology by openly challenging the rule of the 'barbarians'. [115] This charge cannot really be sustained against the academics. They stated explicitly that they wanted to disperse the property of the great landed families, to curb the power derived from it which had been used to impede the 'scientific' functioning of the laws of social progress. Rutson, inferring straightforwardly enough from the economic situation of the time, argued that aristocratic power distorted British conservatism – properly the preserve of industrial wealth. Rational conservatism was weakened by artificial privilege. [116] The charm of land-law reform was that, without suspending any of the principles of classical economics, it would remedy this anomaly.

Land law was also accessible: it allowed university liberals to employ their legal and historical expertise. This also applied to their schemes for the reform of law in general. Behind Dicey's desire to justify the legal profession in a national context, as with the agitation to 'nationalize' the universities, lay an awareness of the consequences of neglect summed up in Macaulay's dictum: 'People crushed by law have no hopes but from power. If laws are their enemies, they will be enemies to laws ...' [117] In a *Fortnightly Review* article 'The Legal Boundaries of Liberty', published in January 1868, Dicey argued that the law regarding associations and freedom of expression was much more restrictive of individual freedom than was generally believed, and, in deference to the conservative sentiments of the governing classes, was being interpreted in an over-severe manner. Unless it were rationally reformed, it would be seen as class law: [118]

... as long as the law is in theory either intolerant or oppressive, our security for the existence of practical freedom depends, not (as it should do) on the maintenance of laws which cannot be changed without due deliberation, but on the permanence of a condition of public sentiment which fluctuates from day to day, which has undergone great changes, and which at any moment may undergo changes still greater.

In other words, unless the law were reformed, the working class might make it as explicit an instrument of class tyranny as the aristocracy had done.

As regards the law dealing with associations, the academics were concerned at the hostility shown by the courts to the trade unions. When they turned to the unions themselves, they recognized a potential divergence between their own economic philosophy and their political position. Given a continuing belief in the wages fund, they could see little economic justification in trade unionism (see p. 164), but the unions were politically moderate and conciliatory, and their patent legal disadvantages militated against the effective incorporation of the working class. Fawcett granted that they tended to make employers aware of changes in the terms of trade which made an increase in wages apposite; [119] and this view was shared by the Positivist Godfrey Lushington in *Questions for a Reformed Parliament*, in an essay which, however, concentrated almost exclusively on the legal issues at stake. [120] The academics saw no equity in the sanction by the courts of associations of professional men – like the legal profession itself – which seemed every bit as much 'in restraint of trade' as the unions, while the latter were subject to criminal prosecution. [121] The 'Master and Servant' laws seemed an apt illustration of Dicey's observation about the general political state of Britain in the mid 1860s, 'John Smith qua John Smith cannot be suppressed, but John Smith qua artisan can'. [122]

Lushington's proposals in his reform essay were moderate by Positivist standards, and would be accepted by the other contributors. Enfranchisement would speed 'the social incorporation of the working classes' and attach the trade unionist to national institutions: [123]

No longer will he see in his master the representative of privilege, he will feel himself secure of equal laws, and of a fair hearing from the legislature and the public.

The law of association ought to be reformed, simplified and made equitable between master and man. Nothing more. When the Trade Disputes Act of 1906 put the unions in what the academics saw as a privileged position, they were among its most severe critics. [124]

Together with their desire to make the law socially equitable went an even stronger desire to make it accessible. 'One grand purpose of all Law Reform', wrote Sir George Young, [125]

is to enable the people, without more specialised training than may be given to every citizen, to understand the law under which they live, and under which their business is transacted. Liberals believe that it is both possible and expedient to do so. Our representatives at all events must know the laws that exist, or at least must be able to understand them when they are read, if they are to do justice to their task.

The law had to be digested, simplified and systematized, in order that the ordinary citizen would be induced to conduct his affairs in accordance with the 'scientific', economic and social laws which it predicated. [126] This ideal could be taken to extremes, as with the Liberal jurist, Lord Bramwell, who, Sidney Webb later alleged, wished to reduce government intervention in the economy to simply ensuring freedom of contract and enforcing the criminal law, [127] but on the whole it complemented the academics' ideal of the educational value of participation in government.

Many academics immersed themselves in law reform and legal education. Possibly the best description of this process and the philosophy behind it is given by Leslie Stephen in his biography of Fitzjames. [128] Although Fitzjames was very much a fringe liberal, his activities in law reform were appreciated. When the Positivists, regarded as extremists, attempted to sell law reform to the Trades Union Congress in the 1870s, they got him to address it; [129] and, if there was cooperation between the extremes, there was plenty of activity in the centre, with Dicey's work on *The Digest of the Law of England*, Kenelm Digby and Sir William Anson as Vinerian readers at Oxford [130] and Bryce's attempt to revive the study of Roman Law there from his Regius Chair. As Fitzjames found, the process of modification, simplification and digestion proved overwhelming, not simply because of the government's lack of enthusiasm, but also because of the very complexity of the task. [131] The lasting moments to the legal projects of the academic liberals were to lie in the foundations of legal studies – particularly legal history – at Oxford and Cambridge, rather than in an efficient code. [132]

Education, secondary education in particular, brought the university liberals back to their point of departure. But it also reopened the debate between elitism and participation: practical decisions on organization and resources had to be taken, whose implications contradicted their political optimism. Their failure to face up to these was to have serious consequences, yet factors in their political thought favoured the sort of conservative educational settlement that was obtained. The role of endowments was critical, and directly linked to their schemes for land and law reform. These institutions had required conservative surgery; only then could they be used to facilitate social progress. This also applied to public endowments. An earlier generation of Benthamites – Lowe, for instance – would have sold them off without compunction: 'Get rid of them. Throw them into the sea!' was his prescription. [133] University liberals – uniquely aware of their value – thought of them as a sort of 'national' capital which could be used, or redistributed, to foster institutions to channel social forces. This influenced their attitude to the retention of land in public hands – they were pioneers of the Commons Preservation Society – and to charity organization, [134] but it was most significant in education, and played an important part in separating their prescriptions for secondary schools from their approach to elementary education.

The academics shared Lowe's opionion that it would be 'absolutely necessary to compel our future masters to learn their letters'. [135] In his essay on 'Popular Education' in *Questions for a Reformed Parliament*, Charles Stuart Parker allowed that [136]

The Lights of Liberalism

... education prepares the way for the franchise, which in prudence must be withheld where gross ignorance prevails. For political power without knowledge, when it means anything, means mischief.

But he went on to argue that only a reformed parliament was likely to extend elementary education on the scale required. [137] The urgency of this argument overrode the sanctity of market economics, and made the academics press for public intervention. Existing bodies would be given a period of grace to meet requirements laid down by a new Minister of Public Instruction, then, if they failed, elected school boards, empowered to rate, would statutorily be set up. [138] Only a literate electorate could appreciate the proper function of representative government; an educational system which continued to rely on local and voluntary organization would remain a prey to the old enemy of clericalism. [139]

Elementary education was directly linked to political reform; secondary-education reform would determine the future role of the universities in society, and the nature of political leadership. Yet, despite the fact that they were peculiarly well qualified to take a leading role in secondary-education reform, they did not do so. Bryce, T.H.Green, R.S.Wright, Lempriere Hammond and James Stuart were Assistant Commisioners on the Taunton Commission on secondary education, 1865-7; Henry Sidgwick's friend H.J.Roby, also a Trinity don, was its secretary; [140] yet Bryce's own Commission, thirty years later, had to admit that only a fraction of the earlier body's recommendations had been carried out, and that much of what had been done had proved inappropriate in the years after 1870. [141] Taunton had recommended the reform and redistribution of endowments, the creation of provincial authorities to control secondary education, and supervision of these and their schools by a central board responsible to the government. [142] Only the endowments were touched; the administrative system was shelved in 1869 and never revived. [143] Despite their involvement, there was no sustained agitation by academics for implementation. Why?

Looking back, Bryce advanced three main reasons: the importance of the endowments question; the absence of a local-government sub-structure; the absence of strong public pressure for reform. [144] His own report showed the decline in importance of the first, the creation of the second through school boards and county councils and the growth of a powerful and autonomous education interest of administrators, teachers and local authorities. [145] But the question remained: what had stopped a group of radically minded, well-informed men from accelerating the evolution of such bodies, even at the moderate pace suggested by Taunton? Several institutional factors retarded innovation: the Education Department was dominated by Oxford and Cambridge men of a somewhat earlier generation, Liberal-voting but educationally even more conservative than Lowe; [146] reliance on examination as a means of central control was beginning to disturb many of the younger academics; [147] the better-run public schools were resisting government intervention; [148] the academics were drawn more to teaching or to direct political participation than to administration. But underlying these was a more significant, if unexpressed, disquiet at the extent to which social calculations about secondary education contradicted their own political ideals.

Parker had commended the Prussian level of elementary education provision as an acceptable target for England: 160 children per 1,000 population attending elementary school. [149] But the highest number Taunton envisaged continuing their education after age twelve was a tenth of that number, of whom rather more than half would simply continue to age fourteen at 'third-grade' schools for the sons of 'small tenant farmers, small tradesmen and superior artisans'. [150] Three to five boys per 1,000 population, the sons of more substantial commercial men, farmers and managers, having received a 'modern' education at a 'second-grade' school (mainly day, but a few boarding), would leave at sixteen. A 'liberal' – still defined as classical – education would require at least six years at a first-grade school (mainly boarding, with a handful of day schools in the biggest towns) and would reach only two to three boys in every 1,000 of the population. Only a fraction of these proceeded to the universities – George Brodrick in 1875 calculated that only one boy per 4,500 population reached Oxford, Cambridge and London. [151] Dicey, in *Essays on Reform*, stated that 'the so-called working class is, like all others, notoriously broken down into divisions ... a free extension of the franchise will, in thirty years, make the artisans ... little distinguishable from the rest of the nation.' [152] Taunton's evidence and proposals must have brought home the uncomfortable truth that British society was more rigidly divided than they had cared to think. Bryce, Green, James Stuart and Lyulph Stanley continued to envisage – with more hope than confidence – the creation of step-ladders extending from elementary schools to university, [153] and the commitment to comprehensive adult education reasserted itself in the university extension movement (see p. 206), but the experience must have emphasized that the 'nationalization'

171

of the universities was politically symbolic rather than practically effective in providing a flexible educational system for the new democracy.

VII

Starting from a concern, however imprecisely articulated, with the predicament of the universities, the academics had arrived back near, if not at, their point of departure. The university was a microcosm of British politics, an institution perverted by internal interests from its true function. Those whom it existed to serve were turning elsewhere: unless it were made relevant, it would be treated as an obstruction and got rid of. Yet the alternative institutions of the new classes, created as a reflex of their exclusion, were defective, lacking tradition and experience. Comparing the potential of a reformed Oxford or Cambridge with the 'bread studies' of some Lancashire 'scientific academy' was, to the academics, like comparing the apparatus of constitutional government with the pretensions of the emergent trade-union and labour movement. [154] The nationalization of the universities would preserve the cultural values the academics believed in; the nationalization of the constitution, and the incorporation of the working classes, would preserve individuality against the otherwise deadly combination of utilitarian mechanics with the grievances of the hitherto unrepresented.

The academics' politics evolved naturally from their social, institutional and political relationships; they were not an intellectual formulation from first principles, but an adequate response to the problems of the time. The claim that their indifference to welfare made them irrelevant cannot be sustained, given the dominant role of market economics in the social thought of the 1860s. Indeed Professor Vincent himself, in *Pollbooks: How Victorians Voted*, has written: [155]

To prefer the criterion of welfare is not only to neglect the extraordinary and lasting nineteenth-century achievement in the deliberate total structural change of the political society, but to foist a modern *Realpolitik* of bread, on men who needed politics chiefly to supply the circuses of their lives.

Though the academics saw politics as education rather than entertainment, the theme of restructuring was cardinal, along with the necessary assumption that there *was* a political structure. They were more realistic than the orthodox utilitarians, whose atomistic conception of society presaged violent changes following on franchise extension. Such a threat appeared improbable to men who had felt at first hand the inertia of an entrenched institution, which had to be overcome before any forward move could be made.

This insistence on the retarding effect of traditional institutions was important in the context of the 1860s, but it had a serious internal inconsistency and, as time proved, only a limited validity. They saw it like the governor on a steam engine, securing a moderate progress towards liberal goals. Liberty, equality and fraternity would impel the working class forward, deference for wealth and education would ensure that its power would be delegated to the upper orders. But what happened if the possessors of intellect or wealth employed their advantages not to educate but to mislead? Brodrick, reviewing his political ideas of the 1860s, wrote in 1900: [156]

I assumed too easily that candidates of the higher class would do their best to educate the new constituencies, and, without rising altogether superior to party bias, would appeal to the better feelings and aspirations of their hearers. Mr Lowe's acquaintance with demagogy in Australia had convinced him of the very reverse. He knew that men of ability and professing high principles would not scruple to flatter the prejudices, pander to the passions, and inflame the class antipathies of voters whom they might have educated, for the sake of winning their support. This is exactly what has occurred ...

This was a post-Home Rule diagnosis by a fervent Unionist, but Brodrick's views would have been the same after the 1868 election, with the Duke of Marlborough in the place of Gladstone (see p. 181). Landed wealth and institutional power had proved not only a barrier against Jacobinism, but an obstacle to rational politics. Yet even this forceful lesson was unhelpful, as, accelerated after 1874 by economic and demographic change, the political balance swung decisively against the territorial aristocracy. Earlier prescriptions became misleading. With their politics – and their internal cohesion – defined by the 1860s situation, the academics found adaptation difficult. They were the last victims of the *ancien régime*; they were also the victims of their own logic.

[8]

PRACTICAL POLITICS, 1868-86

Is this the country that we dreamed in youth
Where wisdom and not numbers should have weight,
Seed-field of simpler manners, proven truth,
Where shams should cease to dominate
In household, church and state?

James Russell Lowell

The reform essays were followed in the autumn of 1868 by a well-publicized descent of university liberals on the hustings. Eighteen years later they appeared to make an equally dramatic exit from Liberal politics over Irish Home Rule. G.M.Trevelyan wrote of his father's milieu: [1]

The intellectual and literary society of London and the Universities in which he had lived and moved all his life had been mainly Liberal; it now became mainly Unionist, nourishing hot detestation of Gladstone and moral reprobation of his followers.

Professor John Roach, in his article 'Liberalism and the Victorian Intelligentsia' has interpreted his secession as a general intellectual rejection of liberal democracy and Gladstone as its leader, [2] in Fitzjames Stephen's words,

... on the high road towards a destruction of nearly everything which I for one and I suppose many thousand others chiefly like and value in English life and society.

Although Fitzjames and Sir Henry Maine, whose opinions Roach relies on, were by the 1870s only on the fringe of Liberalism, the secession of university men was sweeping. Of the twenty contributors to the reform essays still alive in 1886 only seven remained loyal to Gladstone: eleven went Unionist. [3] But was this the result of disillusion with democracy? The next chapter will argue that it was

174

really a political miscalculation which most of them lived to regret. Liberal ways of thought were not discarded but persisted as dogma in a situation which required a heightened awareness both of the problem at issue – Ireland – and of the institutions of mass politics in Britain. In the period between 1868 and 1886 university liberal disillusion was less significant than the breakdown of the dialogue with democratic institutions sustained during the 1860s.

This process was twofold: political institutions altered; so did the academic community. A widened franchise influenced electoral organization and party management; within the Liberal party ideology and leadership changed, in a complicated effort to preserve party cohesion. [4] Further, society as a whole had to respond to new economic pressures which inflicted severe stress on the old governing class, with which the academics were particularly familiar and on whose resilience their political ideas intimately depended. They could not foresee the ease with which the decline of agricultural prices would destroy the power of the landed aristocracy in the late 1870s and 1880s, and, with a side-swipe, damage the university endowments on which institutional reform depended. Yet they might have been expected to cope with the crisis when it came: instead, in a gesture, they relapsed into political impotence. After 1886 the academics did not count in Liberal politics: although the party leadership did not cease to recruit from the universities. The reasons for this development were more complex than the failure to appraise unfamiliar political terrain: they were inherent in the nature of the academic group itself, and were reinforced by the experience of trying to put ideals into practice in the years after 1867 in parliamentary politics, policy-making and political education. Experience in these interrelated fields affected both ideology and group-consciousness, but it did not make the first more sophisticated or the second more effective.

II

The academics placed a high value on the political life. To James Bryce in 1913 it was still 'the finest career to which a man of activity and ambition could devote himself', [5] and he spoke for many of his contemporaries who wanted to put their ideals into practice. Considering that Bernard Cracroft had in 1867 discovered 136 Oxford and 110 Cambridge men in the Commons (most of them admittedly with pass degrees), [6] the number of academic liberal candidates was not large, but it was a respectable proportion of the group. Of the seventy-eight Oxford men at the Freemasons' Tavern

175

meeting in 1864, twenty-four had stood or were to stand for parliament, and, of these, fifteen were associated with the academic liberal group in the sense of being members of it rather than parliamentary allies (see appendix 2). All stood as Liberals, at least until 1886. Twenty-eight Oxford and twenty Cambridge men similarly connected with the teaching bodies of their universities stood between 1868 and 1886.

General Election	Number of candidates			Successful candidates		
	Oxford	Cambridge	Total	Oxford	Cambridge	Total
1868	11	8	19	4	5	9
1874	8	7	15	4	4	8
1880	16	9	25	11	5	16
1885	14	11	25	7	11	18
1886	13	12	25	5	6	11

In 1868 the academics intervened in some strength; in 1874 their number dropped, to rise again in 1880. In the elections of 1885 and 1886 the number standing remained stable, falling off at the later contests of 1892, 1895 and 1900. Their most successful year was 1885, when they won eighteen of the twenty-five seats fought.

Their consciousness as a group was strongest, however, in their first two elections, and was recognized as such especially in the election of 1868. By 1880 not only had this consciousness weakened but Liberal party organization had become more elaborate. Their failure in 1868 highlighted the difficulties the academics had to face in practical politics, and partly explains their inability to penetrate to high office when they finally got into parliament.

The election of 1868, announced on 11 November, was the test of the new electorate; it had been expected ever since the success of Gladstone's resolutions on the disestablishment of the Irish Church at the end of March demonstrated the unity of the Liberal party. [7] Throughout the summer the campaign, businesslike rather than agitated, got under way. [8] Leslie Stephen, writing in July in the *Nation*, echoed John Morley in seeing little change in the constituencies and little hope for radical candidates: [9] 'a new kind of man has hardly a chance of being heard, much less of being pitched upon, as the candidate of the party'. [10] Morley foreboded 'a second impotent and do-less legislature, a worn-out aristocracy, a rich middle class

176

without courage, or true sagacity' as the masters of the new situation. Given another economic breakdown like that of 1866, 'the peaceful and orderly solution to which all good men are looking might be seriously hindered'. [11]

Stephen oscillated between euphoria and depression; only a month before he had been welcoming the explosive possibilities of the Reform Bill (see p.140). Morley's subsequent actions cast doubt on the sincerity of his *Fortnightly* leaders (see p.311). But on the whole the attitude of university men was far different from their mixture of enthusiasm and apprehension a year earlier. Goldwin Smith, in 1867 obsessed with 'constitutional safeguards' (see p.139), campaigned throughout the summer for most of his colleagues who were standing, and left for America on 27 October, before the poll, remarking to Frederic Harrison that the power of wealth in the election seemed greater than it had ever been. [12]

This pessimism arose from the difficulty the academics found in adapting to the mores of the mid-nineteenth-century electoral system. In the first place elections were expensive, especially in the medium-sized and larger towns, the constituencies the academics hoped would be changed in character by an enlarged electorate. [13] Leslie Stephen, who had election experience in Brighton with Fawcett, [14] noted in 1868 a steady increase in the expense of borough contests. [15] Bryce was favourably considered for the nomination at York late in 1867, but, as a friend, Joshua Girling Fitch, pointed out to him, [16]

the candidate should not only be a sound liberal and a good speaker, but should also have money to spend, especially as he may be called on to fight his opponent on an election petition. I said that I feared, though I did not know, that you did not fulfil this last requirement ...

A year later A.O.Rutson was brought forward as a 'purity of election' candidate in the same constituency, but the same pressures, and a quarrel with his backers, the Rowntrees, forced his withdrawal. [17]

The situation in county constituencies was little different. Brodrick, on the look-out for a seat since 1865, [18] found them 'too expensive for candidates of small means but prepared for hard work'. [19] Freeman, Auberon Herbert and Charles Robarts, standing respectively for Mid-Somerset and Berkshire, had to be 'carried' by the other Liberal candidates, a situation they resented but could do little about. [20] In Denbighshire, Osborne Morgan was supported by the Liberation Society, but this implied a commitment to sectarianism which few of his colleagues were prepared to accept. [21]

In the larger boroughs some candidates connected with the university liberals – Goschen in the City, Sir William Harcourt at Oxford and Charles Dilke in Chelsea – were better placed, but Goschen's university connections were weaker than his city links, and Harcourt could scarcely be claimed as an academic liberal. Dilke, hitherto little involved with the academics but an important ally in the future, owed his claim to Chelsea to his father's wealth. [22] Fawcett was the only candidate who tackled an urban constituency on the sort of income available to most of his colleagues. His contest in 1865 had cost £900, nearly all of which was met by the members of his committee. [23] But he was unique, an instinctive politician, capable of a cool realism which obviously jarred on his biographer's sensibilities. [24] Brodrick shrewdly observed that his blindness 'was not an unmixed disadvantage to him'. [25]

Money won elections: a county contest cost £3,011, a borough £988 (*average* direct expenses in 1868); [26] keeping up the register cost from £150 a year in counties to £300 -a year in boroughs; [27] an election petition meant Counsel at 500 guineas plus 100 guineas a day. [28] Electioneering was difficult for a struggling lawyer living on a fellowship of about £300 a year. The fact that a small borough contest only cost £350 was all that could be said in its favour, but it was a compelling argument. [29]

Thus many academics had to contest the very rural boroughs which they had hoped the Reform Act would abolish. Brodrick came forward at the Duke of Marlborough's Woodstock, George Young at Chippenham, Godfrey Lushington at Abingdon, Charles Roundell at Clitheroe and Charles Milnes-Gaskell at Pontefract. Such 'close' boroughs were at least not venal. [30] A contest would be cheap, and the enlarged electorate possibly independent enough to carry a 'purity' candidate. On the other side of this argument George Trevelyan exchanged Tynemouth, where his family had bought an estate to influence its tenantry in 1865, for the solid Liberalism of Hawick and Galashiels [31] and, ironically, Edmond Fitzmaurice simply inherited the Lansdowne seat of Calne from, of all people, Robert Lowe.

Could Reform League assistance not have put more of them in Fawcett's position? Certainly its secretary, George Howell, was eager to please, endorsed Fawcett (not himself a League member) [32] and attempted to get Lyulph Stanley a candidacy, [33] and the Oxford branch wanted to put Thorold Rogers up for the borough. [34]

He was debarred as a clergyman, and, although he wrote an article for *Fraser's* proving to his own satisfaction that clergymen were entitled to sit in the Commons, [35] he had to wait until the passage of the Clerical Disabilities Act to resign orders and stand. But on the whole the academics were in much the same situation as the members of the League – including Howell himself – who stood, and were no more successful.

The campaign was lengthy and energetic: under way by early August, the last results were not in until the first week of December. Throughout the academics fought hard and distinctively. Early in September the *Spectator*, admittedly favourable, contrasted the addresses of Herbert, Brodrick and Leicester Warren, 'the young Whiglings', with Lord Hartington's pedestrian declaration of loyalty to Gladstone: [36]

... these young men are doing a good thing, throwing aside the Whig faith in favour of a newer, more lively and more earnest creed.

Two months later it expanded its list to include Freeman, Roundell and Robarts and, in general, 'the young Radicals from the Universities': [37]

They have appealed to the electors on grounds almost altogether new, and perhaps they represent the nearest approach to a veritable representation of the working-class interest that the election of this year will furnish. They belong, at all events, to a new school, and their recognition of rights in the electors is, apart from the speeches of a very few men like Mr Gladstone, among the clearest and most certain political sounds of the year.

Since lack of cash ruled out the traditional legal methods of electioneering – influencing registration and paid canvassing – they had to rely on other, novel, approaches: personal canvassing, encouraging voluntary political organization, elaborate propaganda. In all of these they involved their university colleagues.

By early August Roundell was canvassing twelve hours a day in his constituency (technically a borough but in fact a substantial tract of northern Lancashire), riding back through the night to breakfast at his home, Gledstone Hall: [38]

... no joke, but amply repaying me in the practical experience which I gain ... everything promises well, the working men are heartily with me, and their wives and children too. In fact I seem to have made friends with the entire *population*, which is a great thing. They are bent on extirpating Toryism and they identify their cause with mine.

In the next few weeks *The Times* reported energetic canvassing at Chippenham and Abingdon. [39] At Woodstock Brodrick spoke in the villages, and at Bladon, hitherto assumed to be totally subservient to Blenheim Palace, his carriage was hauled triumphantly through the streets by the new electors. [40] In Mid-Somerset Freeman was adopted late, on 19 October, but threw himself energetically into the fray. [41] 'Three days glorious stump!' he wrote to Bryce: [42]

I am not sanguine, but I believe we really have a *chance*, which at first I doubted. We shall at least not be beaten ignominiously. The enthusiasm after thirty years bondage is wonderful. The railway people come out to bless us, like Arnold's description of the march of Livius and Nero.

The academic candidates tried to get their constituents organized, both against Tory landlords and against 'the dominion of solicitors' Rutson had fallen foul of at York. [43] The Reform League agents sent out by George Howell on behalf of the Liberal whips reported that at Chippenham [44] Sir George Young's first meeting led to the constituency's first Liberal association; [45] at Woodstock the working men on Brodrick's committee were forming an Agricultural Union. [46] In Mid-Somerset, uncontested for thirty years, Freeman was busy founding branch associations. [47]

Howell's agents reported that the Woodstock voters needed 'political education in simple language'. [48] Brodrick was energetically supplying this. His adoption was proposed on 18 August by Goldwin Smith; on 9 October Henry Fawcett and William Sidgwick spoke for him; 18 October Auberon Herbert; on 23 October Kenelm Digby, R.E.Williams, a Fellow of Merton, T.H.Green and Thorold Rogers; on 28 October William Sidgwick, Charles Roundell and William Harcourt; on 2 November Roundell again; on 6 November Williams and Rutson; and, on 16 November, on the eve of poll, Green, Williams and Rutson. [49] Brodrick's *Times* connection assured him of good coverage, but his experience was far from unique. Sir George Young helped Auberon Herbert in Berkshire; [50] Roundell helped Yates Thompson and Gladstone in South-East Lancashire as well as Brodrick; [51] Bryce and Dicey went to Freeman's help via Abingdon and Chippenham, and ended up speaking from the same platform as Bagehot, the local banker, at Langport [52] – a combination of constitutional theorists never seen, before or since, at a county election. Until his emigration Goldwin Smith was well-nigh ubiquitous [53] and, with a subvention from Samuel Morley, Thorold Rogers flitted from constituency to constituency in the enforced but convenient guise of 'a clergyman speaking in favour of the disestablishment of the Irish Church'. [54]

Bryce and Charles Roundell attempted to broaden this cooperation and tried to draft a representative sample of academic liberals to write a series of 'Electoral Tracts, or Tracts for the People': [55]

We might put Temple to deal with no.1 [the Irish Church]. G.Smith would doubtless help. Could we not get assistance from Dicey, C.Bowen, Davey, Miall, H.Smith, Sir G.Young, Westlake, Dean of Canterbury, Kinneir [sic] Brodrick, Rutson, M.Arnold, Jowett, Berkley, Probyn, Dr. Hook, Courtney? Or some of them?

The 'Tracts' amounted to a simplified version of the reform essays: they were to deal with the Reform Act, Education, Expenditure, Army and Civil Service Reform, the Irish Church,

the measures especially concerning the working classes e.g., Sunday Closing Bill, Permissive Bill, Eight Hours Labour Bill, Artisans in Towns, Dwellings Bill, Poor Law, Pauperism, Trades Unions ...
Need of sending the best men to Parliament – mischief done by the Adullamites ...
What representatives working men should choose – showing the Plutocrats and bad men ...

and much else besides. None of the tracts seems to have been published, but the scheme had the same faith in rational argument as the reform essays. New to campaigning, the academics understandably reached for the weapon which came most easily to hand. But the relevance of such approaches to an inexperienced and barely literate electorate was another matter.

Their problems were real enough. Like most Lancashire Liberals Roundell was under pressure from militant Protestant organizations: 'The Parsons', he wrote, 'are playing the very devil with the women.' [56] This systematic intervention was virtually confined to the north-west, [57] but elsewhere squire and rector increasingly exerted their influence. At Chippenham Young discovered a majority which would vote for him 'if they could', [58] but Howell's agents noted that the landowners were directing their tenants' votes against him. [59] The situation was the same at Woodstock. The villagers were frank about it: they were compelled to vote Tory 'but wished Mr Brodrick to be successful'. [60] These cases prove that the charges of intimidation of voters most of the academics made at the declaration of poll were by and large substantiated. Freeman found rustics voting for 'Farmer Vowles – Farmer Barnard – The Paason', an example which could be multiplied. [61] But he also came across less explicable reactions. At Wedmore he was nearly lynched by a Tory mob which seemed to represent the sense of the whole area: [62]

> The Yellow men may preach,
>   with their gabble and their speech,
> But we know how to answer with a
>   shout of 'Blue, Blue, Blue',
> The Yellow men may reason,
>   but 'tis sadly out of season,
> When our singlesticks can cut them
>   short, with a cry of 'Blue, Blue, Blue!'

'Of my friends who were trying for Parliament', T.H.Green wrote to his sister at the end of November, [63]

(except C.S.P[arker]) all have failed, not because they were philosophers, but because being unknown and without local connections they were trying, on 'purity principles', for boroughs either corrupt or virtually close.

The Times, with evident satisfaction, had earlier recorded that: [64]

The younger members of the Universities, principally of Oxford, who issued forth to take the world by storm, have been defeated without a single exception ... [They] ... have not discovered the secret of winning seats ... The experience of yesterday ... happily discredits those who trusted to turn it [reform] into an instrument of Government through the vices of a residuum and the dreams of a wild democracy.

While Morley allowed himself a long jeremiad on 'The Chamber of Mediocrity', concluding: [65]

At any rate, the composition of the new house will prevent us from resorting to the old taunt against the Americans, that they excluded the best men of the country from Congress.

The consequences of failure were greater than the academics realized, and affected their political consciousness as well as their subsequent careers. Their experiences, however gloomy, were not a valid introduction to the realities of the new democracy; rural boroughs and counties did not represent the new mass urban electorate. Their enemies – the squire and the parson – were traditional and (although they did not look it) facing a speedy decline. Their existing view of politics was confirmed rather than developed. The most interesting statement about the election came not from the contestants but from the East End. J.R.Green had supported Edmond Beales, the Reform League chairman, at Tower Hamlets, and expected him to win. [66] He attributed his defeat to the labour aristocracy's support for Samuda, a right-wing Liberal: three quarters of them, he calculated, would have voted Tory in a straight fight with Beales. [67] This bore out his contention that the 'labour aristocracy' tended to assimilate to the middle classes, neglecting 'mere Demos' and weakening radicalism. [68] This conclusion was debateable, but it was derived from the behaviour of an expanded urban electorate. It was unlikely that such perceptions could be obtained in Abingdon and Woodstock.

Although they could not be expected to know it at the time, the defeat of the academics excluded most of them from parliament until 1880. This meant their entry into active politics was delayed, and their chance of high office proportionately lessened. The average age of Gladstone's cabinet in 1880 was fifty-seven; and ministers had upwards of twenty-five years parliamentary service. When the academics got into parliament most were in their forties. Although, in his later cabinets, Gladstone drew on men with briefer parliamentary careers, length of parliamentary experience was still important in determining selection for high office. By then, middle-aged academics were at a disadvantage compared with wealthy contemporaries like Dilke or Trevelyan, or men like Joseph Chamberlain who could count on a well-organized external pressure-group.

III

However, the election brought some compensations. With Trevelyan, Dilke, Fawcett and Parker returned, the academics had more parliamentary contacts; Auberon Herbert got in at a by-election in 1870. George Young wrote to him: [69] 'You are the first of our lot in parliament: you have fairly earned it, and may you long continue the first, in work, in worth, and in honour.' And James Bryce hoped that [70] 'before long some more of our common friends, members of what we venture to call the party of faith and enlightenment, will follow you into the House'.

For the present they benefited from government patronage: in 1869, besides giving Seeley the Cambridge history chair, Gladstone gave Bryce the Regius Chair of Civil Law at Oxford and appointed Frederic Harrison to the Statute Law Commission. Besides these, Sir George Young served on the British Guiana Emigration Commission, George Brodrick on the Commission into the allegations of ill-treatment made by Fenian prisoners, Charles Bowen and Fitzjames Stephen on the Bribery Commissions and Charles Bowen, Alexander Craig-Sellar and R. S. Wright on the Truck Commission.

Roundell became Gladstone's unpaid private secretary trusted with negotiations on the Irish Church, and in 1871 secretary to the Cleveland Commission on University finances. [71]

Patronage and tests abolition mollified the academics, but by mid-1871 the impetus of reform was running out. The brawling over the Education Act in 1870 was succeeded by even greater disquiet over the Irish Universities Bill of 1873. Like most party activists the university men were increasingly alienated from the government and approached the dissolution which became likely in 1873 with little optimism. [72]

On 23 January 1874 Gladstone, without warning, dissolved parliament. The campaign was brisk and brief, most results were in by 10 February, and the Conservatives gained a majority of fifty seats. [73] Fewer academics fought, with little hope of success, and with little opportunity of developing the tactics of 1868. Brodrick, called back from Evesham to Woodstock by an earlier pledge, [74] fought a dispirited campaign against the full forces of Blenheim arrayed behind Lord Randolph Churchill. [75] His party was disunited. Joseph Arch's Agricultural Labourers' Union threw its weight behind him – he held Arch in high regard as a 'prudent' unionist – but this alienated 'many farmers, small tradespeople, and non-Unionist labourers' [76] from his cause. He was heavily defeated by 160 votes. In 1868 the margin had been twenty-one. [77]

Divisions within the Liberal party which marked the election appeared in three other contests: Thorold Rogers at Scarborough, James Bryce in the Northern Burghs and Leonard Courtney at Liskeard, doubtful about winning Tory seats, took on right-wing Liberals who received implicit Conservative backing. [78] Rogers in a two-member constituency fought a Tory and two local Liberal landowners; [79] Bryce and Courtney undertook straight fights at short notice, although they were familiar with their constituencies. [80] Bryce had considered the Northern Burghs – a 'grouped' consti-tuency of a type peculiar to Scotland, consisting of Dingwall, Tain, Wick, Thurso and Kirkwall – at a by-election in 1872, but withdrew when the industrialist, Samuel Laing, announced that he would stand against another 'money-bag' Liberal, John Pender, an energetic telegraph financier who had lost Totnes when allega-tions of bribery were proved against him. [81] Thereafter Bryce tried various constituencies: Kilmarnock, [82] Glasgow and Aberdeen Universities, [83] even an Irish seat. [84] Again the problem was cash: Kilmarnock was too expensive; [85] even the University seat would cost more than £1,000. [86] Only at the end of 1873 could he afford to gamble. [87] Courtney's decision was even more sudden. On 29 January he learned that the Liskeard radical candidate had been adopted for Leicester; the following day he travelled down to Cornwall and came forward against the old Adullamite Edward Horsman. [88]

Both Bryce and Courtney fought hard against unscrupulous opponents. Of the Northern Burghs Bryce could count on Wick and Thurso; Dingwall, Dornock and Tain were 'bond-slaves of the slaves of the Duke of Sutherland'. [89] The contest pivoted on Kirkwall, where Laing, now M.P. for Orkney, exerted influence. Bryce had the report of the Totnes Bribery Commission reprinted and circulated in the constituency. Pender counter-attacked furiously: Bryce was a Communist, a Republican, a Carpet-Bagger, a Failed Barrister, worst of all a disciple of Goldwin Smith, belonging [90] 'to a small school at Oxford who profess these opinions, and who send out their members on such missions as my opponent is now engaged in'. Bryce cannot have liked making 'indignant denials' of these charges, and they helped little. [91] Laing delivered Pender the Kirkwall vote. He was mobbed by Bryce's supporters when he was tactless enough to take the same coach south as Bryce after the declaration, [92] but by that time Pender had won, 857-730. 'You stood at the end,' Freeman wrote to him in consolation, [93] 'the one coal that was left, and so to be quenched. It is too bad.'

The Liskeard election was no less violent, and the columns of *The Times* carried accusation and counter-accusation by the two candidates for some time after the declaration, when Horsman gained the seat by the narrow margin of five votes. [94] By this time Parker had lost Perthshire and Fawcett Brighton. [95] 'We are in a state of total collapse insofar as politics go,' Bryce wrote to Freeman as he surveyed the wreckage. [96]

Bryce's concern lay with the party programme: 'The fact is we have no policy, and what are Liberals without a policy? We can't exist merely as a party, as the Tories or the two parties in America, nor indeed is it desirable.' But Liberal gains in 1880 owed as much to party organization as to policy. [97] Although a greater number of academics stood – many for urban constituencies – and were successful, there was little joint action: constituency organization, the 'caucus' and the selection mechanism, took the initiative away from the candidate. This divided the academics. Some accepted it, like Bryce and T.H.Green, whose involvement in Liberal party affairs in Oxford increased steadily and was only halted by his early death in March 1882. [98] Others, like Brodrick, while approving the caucus for increasing local interest in politics, deprecated its inroads on the freedom of action of candidates, [99] and attacked the attempt to make the leadership answerable to the caucuses through the National Liberal Federation. [100] In 1878 Bryce tried to take the initiative. With George Howell and Henry Broadhurst he founded the National Liberal League, capitalizing on the anti-imperial enthusiasm which had united working- and middle-class radicals, to promote a coherent programme of reform. Broadhurst became secretary and William Morris treasurer. [101] His initiative, and the support of his Oxford friend Samuel Barnett, radical vicar of St Jude's, Whitechapel, commended him to the Tower Hamlets 'three hundred' who, in March 1879, asked him to stand. [102] The following year he was elected, despite a challenge from Benjamin Lucraft, a former member of the International. [103] The League, however, played little part in securing the sweeping Liberal victory, and went out of existence in 1882, [104] while the split in working-class support shadowed his tenure of the seat. [105] In 1868 the university men were a distinctive group in an otherwise formless situation; by 1880 they had to come to terms, as individuals, with highly organized Liberal bodies, locally and nationally. Although more of them were successful, and those who were elected tried to keep up their university connections, the prospect of a 'party of faith and enlightenment' as an influential component of the House of Commons had gone.

Political contests also created a divergence between those who appreciated 'the charm of politics' and those who did not; the latter tended to stage a 'principled' withdrawal. Leslie Stephen was increasingly distressed by Fawcett's lenience towards 'the ordinary code of political morality'. [106] 'A rather mean pursuit' [107] was how he described politics to his cousin A.V.Dicey. 'I sometimes wonder', the latter observed gloomily, 'whether I ought not to have laid these words more to heart than I have.' Even Bryce, who had defended the caucus in 1882, came to distrust and fear the growing power of party oligarchies. [108]

Organisation and discipline mean the command of leaders, the subordination and obedience of the rank and file; and they mean also the growth of the party spirit which is in itself irrational, impelling men to vote from considerations which have little to do with the love of truth or a sense of justice.

IV

Bryce blamed the Liberals' downfall in 1874 on lack of policy. He was not alone in this, but as a non-parliamentarian his perceptions were different from those of the party leadership: in various ways the problem exercised party magnates who sought after an alternative bond to replace the Whig hegemony which had sufficed in the past, to harness the growing sophistication of party organization to the cause of party unity. [109] Opinions differed as to the role of policy in promoting unity: the fear of sectarianism could lead either to the formulation of comprehensive programmes – as canvassed by Chamberlain, Dilke and Bryce – or to the exploitation of 'great issues', a policy favoured by Gladstone and Morley. As the intention of the reform essays suggested, most academics were programmatic radicals, but their experience in attempting to formulate policy during Gladstone's first government – the Radical Club – was scarcely a dramatic vindication of this approach.

The Radical Club developed from an informal group (which included John Stuart Mill) [110] founded by Fawcett after his election in 1865, the Century, and Howell's unsuccessful 'Adelphi', which catered for working-class radicals. [111] Its inaugural meeting was attended by six M.P.s – Fawcett, Sir David Wedderburn, McCullagh Torrens, Peter Taylor, Walter Morrison and Sir Charles Dilke – and nine 'laymen' – Mill and his proportional representation crony Thomas Hare; Morley, Leslie Stephen, Frank Harrison Hill and Leonard Courtney representing 'enlightened' journalists; William and Henry Sidgwick representing Oxford and Cambridge, and John Elliot Cairnes the Irish universities. [112] Dilke was elected secretary, and a constitution was framed: half the membership was to be drawn from parliament, half from outside. In deference to Mill and Fawcett, women were to be eligible. The Club was to meet each week during the parliamentary session. [113]

Fairly soon there were about forty members; the parliamentarians included Edmond Fitzmaurice, Auberon Herbert and George Otto Trevelyan, the laymen and women T.H.Huxley, F.W.Chesson, who had been secretary of the Jamaica Committee, Mrs Fawcett and Harriet Taylor, Mill's stepdaughter. George Odger, the shoemaker trade unionist who had stood against Dilke at Chelsea in 1868, was also brought in, to represent the unions. The Club met for Sunday evening dinner at an inn in London or along the Thames; a paper was read by a member on a current political topic or likely field of action, and then debated by the members present. [114]

However, the project soon ran into trouble. Its members were wildly heterodox: clashes were frequent. Sir Louis Mallet, formerly Cobden's private secretary and an individualist of the old school found himself, by February 1871 'less and less in harmony with the prevailing opinions of the body ... Torrens, Odger, Fawcett, F.Harrison, are so opposed to my form of radicalism as to make it almost absurd that our names should be on the same list'. [115] Harrison, however, was no happier. Ten days later he wrote to Morley that the Club epitomized 'the inherently metaphysical and impotent nature of modern Radicalism'. Harrison went on to attack Mill and 'the politics of Rights – wrong from top to bottom' and concluded by appealing to Morley to 'come out of that barren and parched wilderness'. [116]

The political events of 1870 and 1871 further divided the membership. The Franco–Prussian War found the Positivists on the side of the French, Mill on the side of the Germans, [117] and the Commune widened this divergence. [118] Forster's Education Act split adherents of the Birmingham-centred National Education League – like Dilke – from more doctrinaire individualists like the Fawcetts. [119] Although many if not most of the Radicals were anti-Monarchists, the controversy of 1871 divided the explicit republicans, like Dilke and Auberon Herbert, who were prepared to put their case in public, from those whose courage failed them, [120] and those, like Fawcett, who disassociated themselves from a flagging cause by attacking its leaders. [121]

Differences in policy were aggravated by difference in life-style. Sundays were convenient for M.P.s, less so for lay members, who might want to be at Oxford or Cambridge or, as they came to marry, with their families. This was Harrison's reason for his resignation in February 1872, but he also observed that the expense of dinner cut the Club off from working men. [122] At £2 per head [123] – a skilled artisan's weekly wage at the time – one wonders how Odger managed to dine at all. Certainly the Club did not sustain for long the comprehensive membership originally envisaged. The Sidgwicks dropped out fairly early, Mill died in November 1873, Leslie Stephen drifted away from politics, and the Club which, according to Roy Jenkins, 'never attained quite the influence which was anticipated by its founders', [124] became a mainly parliamentary organization run by Dilke, Fawcett and Fitzmaurice. [125]

A further reason for its flagging vitality was the arrival of a new and dynamic radical force. Joseph Chamberlain's National Education League signalled the reconstruction of provincial radicalism, with Chamberlain as a new Cobden. Both Chamberlain and the Radical Club agreed on the necessity of a programme, but where the club tried to frame policies in accord with 'sound' liberal philosophy, and in so doing split, Chamberlain used settled policies to cement his radical organization. In 1873 Morley, hitherto the acolyte of Mill and Harrison, met and proclaimed him 'decidedly a leader for an English progressive party',[126] but a meeting with Fawcett, Courtney and Harrison offered little prospect of common action: 'The three differed quite as much from one another as they did from Birmingham.'[127] Morley, however, 'came out of the wilderness'. He had already drifted far from the Positivists when an argument with Harrison in 1875 over the policy of the *Fortnighty* brought about an open breach.[128] A year later he was urging radicals to identify themselves with the 'third party' of Chamberlain,[129] while beginning to formulate his own distinctive and influential view that Liberal policy lay with the exploitation of great issues rather than programmes.

V

Legislative programmes seemed automatically to provoke dissension, education in particular. If academics regarded Gladstone with coolness, their concern was not limited to the Tests Bill: the 1870 Education Act and the Irish Universities Bill of 1873 demonstrated the continuing reality of the sectarian claim on the legislature, which they had hoped the extension of participation in government would lessen, and, moreover, emphasized Gladstone's ambivalence to the sort of rational liberalism they represented. The academics had to re-examine the small print of the political agreement of the 1860s, once the action of governments brought it to the head of the agenda. The results put both their political beliefs and their internal cohesion under strain.

In 1867 the academics saw a reformed parliament quickly solving the education question. Their broad commitment to reform meant that they did not demur at Charles Stuart Parker's proposals in his essay on 'Popular Education' in *Questions for a Reformed Parliament*: although denouncing landlord and clerical obstruction in education,[130] he endorsed the Bill introduced the same year by H.A.Bruce and W.E.Forster which, while proposing free and compulsory education under local control, allowed Church schools to continue as part of the system.[131] This concession provoked Nonconformist hostility and the Bill was thrown out.[132] Plainly the course of any Bill would be determined by religious rather than educational consideration, and behind the immediate controversy would loom the greater problem of the future of the established church.

In 1867 Henry Sidgwick anticipated that a future Liberal government 'will not only settle the Irish Church but dispose of education without particular regard for the ecclesiastical obstacles that are generally in the way'. [133] The establishment itself would inevitably be doomed. However, three years later, when the government was under attack from radicals, including some of his friends, [134] for the concessions to the Church of England involved in Forster's Bill, he came to its defence: [135] 'I believe in Forster's Bill and in administration generally. I don't want the English Revolution and don't believe in it ...' Leslie Stephen, a dedicated opponent of the established Church, considered that speedy and decisive action was more important than satisfying the Nonconformist conscience. [136] From the tone of his despatches to the *Nation* in 1870, the wrangling over the issue depressed him and contributed to his 'growing indifference to wearisome politics'. [137] He admitted that opposing the Bill on secularist grounds made sense; but insisting on 'unsectarian' religious instruction was simply throwing 'a sop to the prejudices of the British public'. Thereafter Nonconformists campaigned against the Act, opposing a clause permitting School Boards to pay the fees of needy pupils attending Church schools (a form of indirect subsidy), which they had allowed to pass in 1870 with little comment. Thus began the process which, by 1880, produced the National Liberal Federation and Chamberlain as a major public figure. [138] To men like Morley the development was important, but other academic liberals, arguing from the agenda of the 1860s, saw Nonconformist rancour as dangerously irrelevant. Rutson, now private secretary to Bruce, the Home Secretary, predicted [139] in 1872 that the Nonconformists would damage the government without delivering working-class votes, and William Berkley, a friend of Bryce and Dicey and a Broad Church vicar, wrote to *The Times* on the eve of the 1874 election to protest against the Nonconformists' aggressiveness, [140] interpreting their actions as an attack on the National Church. Like some of the academics he still wanted a Church whose undogmatic creed embraced the whole nation; [141] at the other extreme Stephen wanted religion out of education altogether; few were attracted by the Nonconformist tendency to put sectarianism above a tolerable system.

Irish university reform demonstrated further the limitations of 'rational' liberalism, and anticipated future conflicts between the academics, Gladstone and Irish Catholicism. In *Questions for a Reformed Parliament* Frank Harrison Hill had argued along 'incorporationist' lines that the Catholics wanted their own educational system because they were excluded from the privileges of the Establishment. Once these had been removed a 'liberal and enlightened laity' would emerge among them, favourable to unsectarian education. [142] However, disestablishment produced no moderating of catholic demands. James Bryce wrote to Freeman in May 1872 after a visit to Ireland that he found [143]

people there very excited and bitter on the Irish Educational question – the Papalini cock-a-hoop, the Protestants cursing Gladstone's supposed willingness to play into Cullen's hands, and evident unwillingness to break with the ultramontane members.

On 20 March 1872 Gladstone spoke against a Bill introduced by Henry Fawcett to abolish Tests at Trinity College, Dublin, promising a more comprehensive settlement of the Irish university question. A year later, on 13 February 1873, he introduced a Bill to provide for a teaching and examining University of Dublin establishment on 'undenominational' lines to which, at the discretion of its Council, denominational colleges could be affiliated. As the Catholics had wanted their own faltering university endowed, and proscribed the 'godless colleges' at Galway and Cork, Gladstone restricted the freedom of the new university: religious controversy was forbidden, in terms akin to Lord Salisbury's 1870 amendment to the Tests Bill; teaching by the university of theology, modern history, mental and moral philosophy was prohibited, although the colleges were free to teach such subjects. [144]

Such 'gagging clauses' inevitably drew the fire of academic liberals. They came, as Morley observed, [145]

at a moment when in spite of the specialisation of research, the deepest questions in the domain of thought and belief ... inevitably thrust themselves forward within common and indivisible precincts.

Henry Fawcett became the Bill's most resolute opponent in the Commons, allying himself with its Irish Catholic opponents. The alliance was purely tactical: the Irish objected to the absence of direct endowment; Fawcett, backed outside the House by Leonard Courtney and John Elliot Cairnes, opposed the gagging clauses. [146] He construed the Bill as a wholesale assault on liberalism in higher education. If studies of contemporary importance were excluded, what would the university teach? If no controversial matters were to be contested, how could students be examined? If Tests on opinion were to be imposed, how could staff be recruited? He ended in defiance: [147]

If the Prime Minister could succeed in introducing these clauses into English Universities he (Fawcett) should feel that he could not conscientiously hold his professorship for a single hour.

The Bill was lost and Gladstone tendered his resignation, but Disraeli refused to form a ministry, and allowed the Liberals to 'stumble out of office', though they took the rest of the year to accomplish this. The failure of the Bill was not the work of Fawcett but of the Irish and the Conservatives. Most British Liberals thought the Bill the best settlement that could be got, although they accepted that it diverged widely from the ideal. [148] For the men who had fought during the 1860s for the cause of free inquiry at the universities and who had in 1867 agreed with Hill's diagnosis of the Irish education problem, it must have seemed a retrograde step which put their loyalty to the Liberal government severely under strain. Fawcett was incapable of any such adjustment; his almost total isolation later in 1873 indicated what being a doctrinaire cost in terms of political advancement. [149]

VI

The period in opposition gave Gladstone the chance to regroup the party around, not a programme, but the 'great issue' of opposition to Conservative foreign policy. Despite their predilection for a radical programme, he was supported in this by many academics. At the climax of the Bulgarian agitation university men, including Trevelyan, Young, Bryce, Freeman, Roundell, Pattison and Fawcett, made up a fifth of the platform party at the great St James's Hall demonstration on the Eastern Question, held on 8 and 9 December 1876. [150] Freeman's propaganda for the eastern Christians made him a national and controversial figure; [151] Bryce and Young became the organizers of the Eastern Question Association, which sustained the agitation and tried to extend it into a critique of Tory foreign policy as a whole. [152] A.J.P. Taylor and R.T. Shannon have seen the agitation as a masterpiece of Gladstonian manoeuvre: [153] the 'agitators' raised the moral head of steam while Gladstone took the train where he wanted to go, back into office with radical support and the freedom to manufacture a Whig cabinet. [154] According to Taylor the academic role was an exercise in *amour propre*: ignorance of Balkan politics was matched by the arrogance of 'secular missionaries' whose faith was under attack. [155] There is truth in the last accusation, but Freeman was not alone in knowing the area well: Bryce and Rutson, who published two of the earliest analyses of the situation in the *Fortnightly* in 1876, [156] had both travelled that year in the Middle East [157] and the academics as a group could count on the expertise of acquaintances whose knowledge of Turkey and the Balkans extended over many years, like Humphry Sandwith, Donald MacKenzie Wallace, Sir George Campbell and 'that amazing creature Burton at Trieste who surely once was a Mussulman and still calls himself a Conservative'. [158] Personal involvement and moral conviction converged, as they had done in the case of Italian unification and the American Civil War: [159] the 'classes' were perverting 'national' institutions to their own ends and the nation had to declare against them. [160]

Nevertheless the academics looked at the relations between democracy and foreign policy with some unease. In the reform essays R.H.Hutton had argued that the working class would judge foreign policy impartially, and 'hold back its sympathy even after we had engaged in a struggle, if the policy of England seemed to be selfish and wrong'. Nevertheless Disraeli's initiative of 1867 upset their forecasts. [161] According to Bryce, Disraeli believed that 1874 was proof that the political power of middle-class Nonconformity had been destroyed, [162] that 'the working classes were ready to follow the lead of the rich ... and that the bulk of the nation would be dazzled by a warlike mien, and an active, even aggressive, foreign policy'. By the agitation the academics were trying to keep the working class 'sound' on this issue. Bryce thought the campaign ultimately successful, [163] but the real victor was a personality, Gladstone, and not a coalition between intellect and labour.

Further, although most academic liberals supported the agitation, there was no unanimity: Positivists and Broad Churchmen generally took the government side. The latter had always disliked the High Churchmen who backed the Eastern (Orthodox) Christians on theological grounds, and were themselves increasingly assuming a 'national' role. [164] Positivist foreign policy had always been distinctive, even in the 1860s, when it exalted Bonapartist France and execrated 'the barbaric legions of Russia'. [165] The general academic solidarity on reform had then maintained unity; when it diminished in importance, disagreements re-emerged.

Just before Disraeli's policy reached its climax at Berlin, Oxford graduates elected a new burgess to succeed Gathorne Hardy, the victor of 1865, who had gone to the Lords. The Liberal residents selected Henry Smith as candidate although he was known to be sympathetic to the government's Eastern policy; [166] but even its convinced opponents, like Gladstone, Bryce and Goldwin Smith rallied to his support. [167] Smith carried the teaching staff and residents 440-259, but was badly beaten by the Tory, J.G.Talbot, 2,687-989. [168] The institutional connection could still survive serious divergences; but many academics must have agreed with Goldwin

Smith that, to maintain unity, too many concessions had been made. [169]

Looking back on the Eastern question, James Bryce saw it as signalling the first substantial defections of property from the Liberal party; [170] Dr Shannon has also detected a withdrawal of university men, citing Benjamin Jowett's 'intellectual conviction of its inadequate conception of the national idea' [171] but does not go so far as Professor Roach in seeing this as an early stage of the general secession of the intellectuals. [172] But neither seems to appreciate the growing tension which existed between two life-styles. The agitation owed a great deal to the information and fervour of the academics, especially those with connections in party Liberalism *and* in the universities: Bryce appreciated it in terms of the political perceptions he retained from the 1860s. But this framework was less apparent to men who had settled into university society: to them the agitation could appear eccentric and irrelevant. To Dilke and Chamberlain, at the other end of the spectrum, it was simply a factor in an internal party conflict, which they supported to advance a radical takeover – with effect, as Gladstone sanctioned their National Liberal Federation in 1877, albeit for his own ends. But as the commitment of the 'political' academics to the agitation, however wholehearted, was compromised by the need to maintain contact with their 'resident' colleagues, their exertions left them weakened and increasingly isolated from the course of Liberal politics. [173]

In each of these conflicts, issues on which unity – or at least a truce – had been enforced by the circumstances of the 1860s became individually contentious, both among the university liberals and between them and the party nationally. Despite this, a continuing group loyalty may have retarded the absorption of the more 'political' into a developing party structure. The 'residents', however, were not necessarily rejecting political involvement but exploring different political relationships, which ultimately became difficult to reconcile with 'party' liberalism.

VII

The failure of the Liberal ministry of 1868-74 to sustain its momentum caused many Liberals to secede to single-issue bodies, like the National Education League or Mrs Josephine Butler's National Association agitating against the Contagious Diseases Acts. [174] In the case of the university liberals this took the form of a heightened civic awareness in the university towns, [175] where residents were coming to occupy professorships and headships, marry and set up house. University men, their wives and sisters, attempted to put liberal principles into practice by supporting cooperative projects (see p. 164), temperance and public health movements; [176] they created organizations for liberal political education [177] and sat on the school boards. [178] In general the effect of their intervention was marginal, but in one important area – poor relief – they were dramatically successful. This, however, created a rift between their political ideas and local Liberalism.

Their commitment to economic liberalism made them enthusiastic supporters of the Charity Organisation Society when it was founded in 1869 to coordinate private alms-giving with the Poor Law and combat the increasing tendency of the latter to give outdoor relief. In the Society's main area of operations, London, this ideal of collaboration was never achieved, [179] but, from 1878 at Oxford under Arnold Toynbee and from 1875 at Cambridge under Henry Sidgwick, charities were regulated, outdoor relief was curtailed and the workhouse test enforced. [180]

This unique effectiveness stemmed from university representation on the local Boards of Guardians granted after the reforms of the 1850s. At Oxford the University Guardians accounted for thirteen members of the Incorporation of thirty-five. [181] The local C.O.S., consisting mainly of members of the universities and Liberal voters, was able to build on this base and capture the Boards when, from the 1870s on, it was supported by university householders. [182] The worsening financial position of the colleges and the rise in the poor rate resulting from the agricultural depression also prompted greater university intervention. And to good effect. At Oxford expenditure on out-relief fell from £2,500 in 1869 to £1,100 in 1880 and £350 in 1900. [183] Over the period 1879-1900 the inmates of the St Aldate's workhouse rose 100 per cent from forty-six to ninety-six in any one week, [184] and the poor rate declined from 2s. 3d. (12p) to 8½d. (4p) between 1870 and 1900. [185]

However, this relief did not help the Liberal party at either town. In 1885 the Liberals lost the Cambridge seat, according to Henry Sidgwick because of working-class hostility caused by the Liberal Guardians' refusal of outdoor relief, [186] and in 1886 the Tory victor at Oxford attributed part of his success to resentment at the severity of 'young and flippant' university Guardians. [187]

University liberals enforced the Poor Law not from any hostility to the working classes but because they saw outdoor relief as a threat to the independence of the individual and a distortion of the working of market economics (see p.164). Active C.O.S. partisans like Henry Sidgwick, Arnold Toynbee and Bernard Bosanquet were in fact more sympathetic to working-class ideals than many of their colleagues, increasingly questioned economic orthodoxy [188] and were respected by younger men of more explicitly radical views. But their activities distanced the academic community from working men. For the unemployed man, who saw the C.O.S. as 'the enemy' in Beatrice Webb's London, its effective rule at Cambridge or Oxford must have seemed [189] much more repellent, and the academics had, in their turn, little confidence that the growing working-class movement would share their 'scientific' approach to the alleviation of poverty. Henry Sidgwick wrote in 1888 that [190]

the increasing power which the growth of democracy places in the hands of manual labourers is not unlikely to be used in the direction of diminishing the deterrent character of our poor law administration.

Three years earlier he had tried in vain to persuade his brother-in-law, Arthur Balfour, to withold the franchise from the recipients of medical relief: [191]

I think this is the kind of question on which Tories – and indeed any sensible ministry – should yield reluctantly, and only the very minimum they are forced to yield, if they yield at all ... Practical philanthropists are against it. They have been trying hard for fifteen years to teach the poor thrift, and now the moral weight of the legislature is to be thrown into the other scale ... Soon all paupers out of the workhouse will be enfranchised in the unseemly competition for popularity.

If there was any one issue which prompted university liberals to have grave doubts about the effect of democratic government on the laws of social progress, it was poor relief. In 1902 Dicey wrote to Bryce after re-reading Thomas Mackay's *History of the English Poor Law*: [192]

The reflections the book causes are mainly sad. We are right in maintaining that there were some tasks for which one needed a reformed or democratic Parliament but most of us forgot that there were tasks for which an unreformed or middle-class parliament was much better suited than a democratic parliament and carrying the reform of the Poor Law to its legitimate and logical results was one of them.

Yet Dicey, too, could state the deeper dilemma behind the academics' attitudes; after reading a novel by George Gissing in 1897 he wrote: [193]

I doubt whether those who have habitually lived among well-to-do people and have only slightly, if at all, felt the dread of poverty can form an idea of what it means ... The conviction is forced upon me that I and people like me do live in great luxury. By luxury ... I do not necessarily mean something blamable. I use it as a word to express a state of ease in money matters.

The same sense of guilt lay behind the activities of men like Sidgwick and Toynbee: they were trapped between their devotion to market economics and their political ideal of common action with working people. For the younger men who went off to Toynbee Hall after 1883, or those involved in national politics, the conflict was muted by other common causes, like education or foreign policy, but in the university towns the tension was patent and must have accelerated the alienation of the residents from national Liberal politics.

VIII

The Liberal government of 1868-74 demonstrated the difficulty of reconciling 'scientific' and popular conceptions of government, and drove many university liberals away from party activity. Leslie Stephen's appetite for reform, according to Noel Annan, was sated by 1874: [194]

He lost interest in politics because he saw that the principles which he had applied with such zeal in the 1860s, had degenerated into formulae and that he lacked the ability to give them meaning. Liberal principles were merely pretexts for acting in a convenient way ...

John Morley had noticed this at the time: [195] 'His philosophy did not harden him, as sensible philosophy should, against the creaking and slow grinding of political machinery.' Neither is altogether fair to Stephen – then grief-stricken by the death of his wife. While the failure of the Liberal administration certainly provoked him to reconsider this position, he didn't lose faith in liberalism, instead he attempted to discover other options for the liberal intellectual, when the directly political field was closed to him.

In 1875 he contributed two essays on politics to Morley's *Fortnightly Review*. While 'Order and Progress' – a review of Frederic Harrison's book – and 'The Use of Political Machinery' both demonstrate his irritation with democratic actuality they also appealed to liberal intellectuals to reconsider their own role in society, restating the political analysis of the 1860s, attacking Mill's theory of representative government, giving qualified endorsement to the Positivist ideal of an enlightened elite and calling on intellectuals to answer the question: [196] 'How can a rational authority be erected on the shifting sands of modern democracy?'

In 1867 the academics saw British social conservatism as a providential brake on democratic change. After 1874 they regarded it as a buffer stop. Stephen asked: what was wrong with radicalism, that made it so easy to check? To the analysis of the 1860s [197] he added two lessons. The second Reform Bill had gone in the right direction, but for the wrong reasons: it had been gained by popular agitation combined with the old-fashioned theory of natural rights. [198] This sort of hybrid, unscientific reform could never weaken the forces of conservatism: [199] there had to be a satisfactory explanation of the way society functioned, and it had to be conveyed to the mass of the electorate: [200]

For a solid reform therefore we must look to the gradual infiltration of sound beliefs though the whole social organism, which must end by bearing the fruit of an intelligent loyalty to trustworthy leaders. The change must be inward before it can be outward; no shuffling of the cards can make them all turn up trumps; it is a new force that is required, not a new machinery; and all constitution-mongering is thrown away till a new spirit has been breathed into the dead bones.

Stephen's analysis predicated three main areas of concern: the provision of educated political leadership, the extension of political education and the necessity of inquiry into the nature of modern society. He concluded: [201]

Philosophic reasoners, freed from the necessity of proposing immediate reforms, may cooperate most usefully by stimulating the growth of sounder opinion. Without their aid the mechanical changes would be mere waste of labour.

Despite his own alienation from university life, [202] Stephen's concerns were shared by many of his contemporaries at Oxford or Cambridge who attempted to further the education of the political leadership, university extension and the inquiry into society.

IX

The academics' ambiguity about the role of universities in the education of the political elite was reflected in their actual achievement. Although the Liberal and Conservative front benches remained, in the early years of the twentieth century, substantially dominated by Oxford and Cambridge graduates, they showed little evidence of having been influenced by academic liberalism, [203] nor did the surviving academics repose much confidence in the younger men, politicians and civil servants alike. Their ideas on social progress were unsound; they were susceptible to external pressure; they were motivated by financial gain. [204] Kenelm Digby, on his death in 1916, was mourned by Bryce as [205]

a fine specimen of a type of public servant less adequately represented now than it was in the generation of Lingen, Jenkyns, Welby, Spencer Walpole, T.H.Farrer, Robert Herbert, Louis Mallet, Pauncefote ...

The unflattering comparison of the politicians and officials associated with the 'new liberalism' with their stern Cobdenite predecessors provides another reason for doubting the academics' influence on the evolution of Liberal policy, although this had owed much to ideology provided by Oxford and Cambridge men, [206] in particular L.T.Hobhouse, J.A.Hobson and C.F.G.Masterman. Plainly the absence, initially, of any elite educational policy in the 1860s accounts at least partially for this. But for the post-1870 period, when academics like Seeley and Oscar Browning in Cambridge and Bryce and T.H.Green in Oxford were creating schemes of more or less explicit political instruction, a more complex explanation is necessary.

Their failure was partly the result of setbacks in university policy and changes in the ideologies that prevailed there, and partly the result of changes in the Liberal party itself. Academics who aspired to political education found it difficult to maintain the undergraduate contacts of the 1860s and before. Fellows were transformed from discontented senior scholars into professional teachers; a 'collegiate ethos' converted their relationships with the scholars into those of masters and pupils. [207] Groups like the Essay Society and the Old Mortality, which united teachers and taught, disappeared as specifically undergraduate political and sporting organizations fostered undergraduate self-consciousness, creating in due course political enthusiasms and ideals which were not shared by the seniors.

The ideal of the university as a teaching body with a modernized curriculum had, of course, appealed during the 1860s. Besides, getting a chair was until 1882 one of the few ways dons could stay on at Oxford or Cambridge and marry. Yet, as the colleges improved, the role of the professors declined in relative importance: college instruction and the traditional curriculum resisted attempts at radical change. This was dramatically exemplified by the contrast between Henry Jackson, from 1866 assistant tutor, and Henry Sidgwick, from 1869 praelector in moral sciences, at Trinity,

Cambridge. Jackson was instrumental in re-invigorating Trinity, but, despite his political radicalism, his reforms were carried out in the interest of college instruction and classical studies. [208] Sidgwick, Knightsbridge Professor of Moral Philosophy from 1883, attempted to foster modern studies and the methodical organization of university teaching through the General Board of Studies, yet, at the end of his career, remained bitterly disappointed with what had been achieved. [209]

Ample illustration of this is provided by the results of the 1880 Triposes. Of the sixty-one first classes awarded, only one was in moral sciences, against thirty-three in mathematics and sixteen in classics. [210] Four years later Alfred Marshall attacked Sidgwick for his lack of success, contrasting his Trinity lecture room containing a 'handful of men', [211]

bolting down what they regard as useful for examination, with that of Green, in which a hundred men, half of them B.A.s – ignoring examinations – were wont to hang on the lips of the man who was sincerely anxious to teach them the truth about the universe and human life.

Angrily Sidgwick appended to his journal a quotation from Walter Bagehot's essay on Arthur Hugh Clough which, he wrote, 'represents my relation to T.H.G. and his work': [212]

He saw what it is considered cynical to see – the absurdities of many persons, the pomposities of many creeds, the splendid zeal with which missionaries rush on to teach what they do not know, the wonderful earnestness with which most incomplete solutions of the universe are thrust upon us as complete and satisfying.

But this picture was already out of date when Green died. James Bryce, whose own chair, despite his efforts, remained decorative, [213] noted that Green as professor, after 1878, was less influential than he had been as a college tutor. [214] When Mrs Humphry Ward's celebration of Oxford virtue, *Robert Elsmere*, appeared in 1888, with Green thinly disguised as the messianic Professor Grey, Sidgwick wrote that it described the Oxford situation of his own generation, not that of the present one. [215]

Into this void came new political and intellectual ideals, and new teachers. In 1869 Ruskin returned to Oxford as Slade Professor of the Fine Arts, to preach his gospel that [216] 'Competition and Anarchy are Laws of Death; Government and Cooperation are Laws of Life'. Dean Kitchin, one of the few sympathetic liberal academics, noted the disapprobation of 'the graver world' of the dons. [217] At best they saw him, in Leslie Stephen's words, as [218] 'a man of genius, placed in a pillory to be pelted by a thick-skinned

200

mob ... urged by a sense of his helplessness to utter the bitterest taunts that he can invent'. At worst he was the reactionary bigot who had supported Governor Eyre, the perverse critic of political economy, the sentimentalist who attacked the appointment of John Burdon-Sanderson, 'the virtual founder of the Oxford medical school' on the grounds that he was a vivisector. [219] Ruskin recognized their hostility: [220]

During seven years I went on appealing to my fellow-scholars, in words clear enough to them, though not to you [the working men], had they chosen to hear; but no one cared nor listened, till that sign sternly given to me that my message to the learned and rich was given and ended.

But on many of the younger men Ruskin had an impact comparable only to that of J.H.Newman two generations before. H.W.Nevinson, who was at Christ Church between 1875 and 1879, remembered [221]

how in that last course he so overwhelmed us with solemn awe, that when he closed his book no one moved or spoke. We sat there absolutely silent. We no more thought of the usual thunder of applause than we should have thought of clapping an angel's song that makes the heavens be mute.

Ruskin did not influence students towards specific doctrines but, like Carlyle with the preceding generation, he produced a general unsettlement of mind (see p.37) Arnold Toynbee, J.A.Hobson the economist, E.T.Cook the editor, Alfred Milner and Michael Sadler the educationalist, as well as Nevinson, were all in varying degrees affected by his appeal 'to bring somewhere the conditions of fine art into existence'. [222] But while Carlyle's assault on accepted values had coincided with the flood-tide of utilitarian liberalism, Ruskin attacked while liberalism was on the ebb in national politics and while industrial and agricultural depression and unrest were demonstrating its limitations. It is a tribute to party Liberalism's resilience at the universities that it incorporated the social concern of the younger men. But they were not as prepared to accept the 'scientific liberalism' of their elders. Ruskin's economics, 'inexplicable perversity' to Leslie Stephen, were, for J.A.Hobson, [223]

the basic thought for my subsequent economic writings, viz., the necessity of going behind the current monetary estimates of wealth, cost and utility to reach the body of human benefits and satisfactions which give them a real meaning.

Not surprisingly he found organizations like the London Ethical

Society, dominated by Stephen and agnostic individualists of his generation, [224]

committed so strongly to the stress upon individual progress as to make it the enemy of that political and economic democracy which I was coming to regard as the chief instrument of social progress and justice.

The Ruskin episode did not imply an overall re-interpretation of politics at the universities – Arnold Toynbee, custodian of the principles of 1834, could still tramp the country before his death to warn artisans against the heresies of Henry George [225] – but it demonstrated the weakening of the identity of science, economy and liberalism the 1860s had sustained. Dicey and Bryce, writing in the New York *Nation* in the early 1880s, observed this dissolution with regret. The propertied classes, whose liberalism had once been instinctual, were deserting it; academic youth seemed impatient of the laws of economics and eager to intervene directly to ameliorate social squalor; 'sentiment' rather than science seemed to have prevailed. [226]

This was only partly due, however, to the political predilections of the new generation. Economics and philosophy as disciplines were themselves evolving away from the unity of the 1860s. In economics there was little sign that many of the academics of the earlier generation appreciated the change, implied in Jevons's and Marshall's substitution of exchange value for labour as the criterion of value, from 'iron laws' towards a recognition of plural social values, as well as towards a more technical, mathematically competent, profession. Bryce could deprecate Fawcett's shellback individualism in his *Nation* obituary, but still regretted the loss of a man who could fuse a political appeal to his economics. [227] From an earlier obituary of Jevons, his colleague at Owen's College, it is evident that the latter's economic innovations were of little interest to him. [228] Even Sidgwick, who persevered with his economic interests, still tended to view the economic future pessimistically as a choice between the market and some sort of collectivism, while increasingly doubting his own competence. [229] Against tendencies which were on the whole towards apolitical professionalism and 'economic chivalry', the other survivors of the 1860s [230] stood out for an economics which remained simple and communicable, and condemned concessions towards 'sentimentality' in social policy. [231]

Likewise with philosophy. Differences of interpretation, submerged in the 1860s for the sake of unity, surfaced in the next decade, as the desire to produce a simple, serviceable ethics slackened, to be replaced by more rigorous intellectual debates about fundamental questions of philosophy. There was more ideological distinction between schools of thought and, within them, greater concern with research and scholarship. Philosophy was maturing as a profession at the universities – henceforth, even when philosophers remained concerned with politics, fundamental postulates about the nature of mind and the analysis of concepts and relationships played a much greater part in forming their ideas: [232] whether one was an idealist, or a utilitarian, affected the ordering of the political agenda. Henry Sidgwick's observations on T.H.Green reflected the degree to which such issues could separate men whose similar predicament in the 1860s had led to close cooperation; [233] a volume like *Essays in Philosophic Criticism* (Murray, 1884), produced in memory of Green and, like him, radical in its politics, was nonetheless distant in manner and approach from the reform essays of 1867. Abstract analysis predominated over predicament. Ultimately, in the case of many of the younger idealists, it triumphed over politics. In the eyes of men like Lewis Farnell, Cook Wilson, F.H.Bradley and William Wallace, revelling in the complexity of Hegelian philosophy, 'Bethnal Green' himself was more philanthropic than professional. [234] Even on the utilitarian side Sidgwick tended to be discounted as a survival from a remote age, troubled by religious doubts which no longer seemed relevant. [235] For the generation of Moore, Whitehead and Russell there were other, more stimulating avenues to be explored. The nature of authority at the universities was changing, in ways which the Home Rule issue confirmed but did not initiate. Politics as a lived experience declined in importance, intellectual values were enhanced. The university was increasingly a separate, internally satisfying world; the need to go beyond it, into the political world, for a life which was meaningful and responsible diminished.

Politics, too, created its own environment. Late in his life James Bryce regretted the passing of ' the "old country gentlemen" who used to form more than half the house of Commons, and from whom many brilliant figures came'. [236] This was not the view he and his friends had taken in the 1860s but reflected his own experience of the parliament of 1880-85, when the aristocratic supremacy of which he had hitherto complained enjoyed a brief parity with the representatives of other classes before the delayed effects of electoral reform and agricultural depression swept it aside. [237] Dicey had cited his election as outweighing 'a hundred lamentations over the alleged incapacity of artisans or shopkeepers to recognize character and integrity, [238] but he admitted that the slackening of aristocratic control had tended to exclude more intellectuals than previously. On the whole he was not alarmed by this: the standard of public opinion was the guarantee of the constitution, and that appeared to have improved. Bryce had to find out for himself the limitations of an ill-attended House, subject to systematic obstruction by the Tory and Irish opposition, dominated by party discipline and government initiatives [239] – scarcely Brodrick's 'national assembly in which the results of the enquiry are compared'. [240] Although he did what he could in his energetic way to mobilize back-bench opinion through bodies like the National Liberal League and the Committee on Irish Affairs, and attempted to prod the government towards an agreed and systematic programme of legislation, his ineffectiveness ultimately led him to an intellectual sympathy for Bagehot's conception of a cabinet elite and towards a practical acquiescence in the acts of the party leadership. [241] In these circumstances the 'brute votes' of the old regime, whom he knew, were better than Birmingham radicals, whom he did not. A life-long adherence to the party leadership, outriding private doubts, was the result. [242] There appeared to be little option for other M.P.s, both those associated with the government and those who left the party over Home Rule. The level of decision-making had risen to the Cabinet, and was increasingly dominated by the immediate circumstances and perceptions of ministers and government, rather than by any reference to 'scientific criteria' (for a fuller discussion see p. 219). The 'fit' that the academics had seen between the situation of the intellectuals, national politics and parliamentary government in the 1860s had been destroyed by the speed of social and political change.

X

During the 1860s university liberals limited themselves to acknowledging, by implication, a hierarchy of higher education which secondary-education reforms merely reinforced, and which conflicted with their democratic ideals. But the extension of higher education could not be pigeon-holed, and the fate of the Liberal government made it more urgent. Papers delivered by liberal academics to the Cambridge Reform Club in late 1872 and early 1873 were preoccupied with supplementing political participation by instruction in the laws of social development: [243] giving the vote without giving such 'primary political education' was, according to John Fletcher Moulton, like teaching students the properties of drugs by letting them loose in a laboratory. [244] It was out of this sort of concern that the university extension movement of the 1870s, in which Cambridge took a leading role, came into existence, to [245] 'afford assistance to the higher education in great towns of those classes who are inevitably debarred from residence at our University'.

In the 1860s Oxford had created university extension committees, but their mandate was to expand the existing university by means of new colleges, halls of residence and non-collegiate students. [246] A committee under Goldwin Smith did go further, and recommended affiliating institutions of higher education like Owen's College, Manchester, but Smith's sights were still fixed at a middle rather than a working-class clientele: [247]

Nobody would wish to throw cold water on any efforts to assist poor men of merit; but it must be borne in mind that the class now knocking for admission to places of liberal education are not objects of charity; they are people well-to-do, though not rich enough to afford the present expenses of Oxford life.

Oxford liberals, moreover, insisted that the Tests issue be cleared up first. They suspected that the clergy's enthusiasm for the education of needy scholars stemmed from a desire for more ordinands, [248] and their suspicions were confirmed by the initiation of the Keble College scheme in 1866 which provided, under an authoritarian constitution, for cheaper board and instruction. [249] Their reply was to encourage undergraduates to live out of college and matriculate as 'non-collegiate' students. [250] Balliol took the initiative and T.H.Green was appointed in 1867 the first warden of Balliol Hall; a year later the university accepted both principles. [251] But this simply brought Oxford level with Cambridge, where student lodgings had long been allowed: [252] an expedient to make the supply of university places match the demand, it enabled little effective reduction in cost. [253] Moreover, especially at Oxford, the claims of university extension clashed with those of research. Balliol, the most 'extension-ist' college, was also the strongest partisan of teaching. [254] Such currents and counter currents held Oxford's hand. At Cambridge, however, a different tradition, catering for a different demand, helped create the extension movement proper which was, by 1889, to be examining 46,000 part-time students. [255]

The first moves came as the result of efforts to secure better education for middle-class women. Anne Jemima Clough, sister of the poet, founded at Liverpool in 1867 the North of England Council for Promoting the Higher Education of Women. This received the support of James Bryce, T.H.Green, Henry Sidgwick, Charles Pearson and James Stuart, who elaborated the courses by introducing examinations, 'syllabuses' (abstracts of lectures, not programmes) and lists of prescribed reading. [256] Stuart also started to lecture to workmen at Crewe and to cooperators at Rochdale, [257] and with Sidgwick in 1871 formally approached the Cambridge Senate with memorials from the Rochdale Pioneers, the Crewe Mechanics' Institute and the Corporation of Leeds which asked for the lectures and associated activities to be made official. [258] A Syndicate was authorized to inquire into the proposal, with Stuart as secretary, and after its favourable report official courses began in Nottingham, Leicester and Derby in the autumn of 1873. [259]

Stuart, in 1867 a twenty-four-year-old Fellow of Trinity, was the son of a linen manufacturer in Fife. [260] He had attended St Andrews, and was there impressed with the democratic intake of the Scottish universities. Many of his fellow students were the sons of artisans or small farmers, who would do manual labour through the summer vacation to sustain themselves during term in lodgings at a cost of under £10 a session. Moreover, many of them came, not from secondary schools, but from village schools where, in the hope of his pupils gaining a bursary to the university, the schoolmaster would also teach elementary Latin and mathematics. The Scottish experience seemed to indicate that a link could be created between the products of the elementary school and the university which by-passed the social gradations imposed by the secondary-school system, an educational parallel to the link liberal academics advocated in politics. [261]

Stuart and the other supporters of the new mode of extension did not want a wholesale reconstruction of the old universities on the ascetic Scots model – although a transformation as drastic was suggested by Pattison in his *Suggestions on Academical Organisation*. [262] But they hoped that, by decentralizing teaching, Oxford and Cambridge would gradually become institutions for research and postgraduate studies. In this way extension would come peacefully to coexist with the endowment of research. [263]

The social groups the extension movement wished to cater for were defined by the Cambridge memorialists as: [264]

1. Ladies and persons at leisure during the day

2. Young men of the middle classes, clerks, and others engaged in business who have only the evenings at their disposal

3. Artisans

It was assumed that the third would present most problems, yet in the eyes of the liberals it was the most important. [265] Progress was initially slow, but there were indications that a demand existed and could be developed. It must have been especially gratifying to the organizers to see Sheffield steel-workers, who only six years before had been linked in the public mind with 'trade union outrages', paying for their apprentices to attend classes in political economy. [266]

The cost of running a course of twelve lectures and associated classes was high, and was expected to be met out of revenue. Stuart realized that this would militate against artisan involvement so he advocated a form of cross-subsidy: local societies would charge what the market would bear for afternoon lectures, chiefly to well-off ladies, and use the profits thus gained to lower the fees for evening lectures. [267] Ingenious though this was, it soon ran into difficulties. A fee of 6s. 0d. (30p) a course was still a difficult lump sum for an artisan to meet out of a weekly wage of not much over £1, and it meant that local organization was in the hands of middle-class people with whom artisans were reluctant to associate, and whose desires were often for courses which had little relevance for a working-class audience. [268] It was only when control of the classes was put in the hands of 'artisan committees' that recruiting among working people was effective. [269] This characterized what the Cambridge extensionists claimed as their greatest success, the spread of interest in higher education among the pitmen of Northumberland and Durham after 1879. By 1881 lectures were being given in five centres to 1,300 pitmen, in English history, geology, mining, chemistry, physiology, physical geography and English literature. [270]

The pitmen's courses grew throughout the early eighties. This was the heyday of 'conciliation' between masters and men on the coalfield, associated with Thomas Burt's leadership of the miners, his election to parliament as Liberal member for Morpeth in 1880 and the agreement to relate wages to coal prices by the 'sliding scale'. [271] Between 1883 and 1886 the extensionists attempted to get the union to take the project under its wing, and employed arguments which derived from this favourable situation: [272]

Should the Trades Unionists decide to support the lectures from their funds the scheme will become a national system of education ... Trade organisations have secured the settlement of trade disputes by conciliatory methods. The energy that used to be spent in industrial quarrels is now free to be spent in educational work. The elementary schools and Science and Art classes are preparing the way for higher education. If the Universities do not supply sound education some other kind will be supplied from another source.

This was, in fact, a development of a scheme proposed by Stuart to the Cooperative Congress in 1879, for a 'Cooperative University' to be financed by diverting a proportion of societies' profits from the dividend. [273]

However, this success was exceptional, and was menaced both by internal university politics and social change. When Stuart got his chair in 1876, the direction of the Cambridge delegacy fell into the hands of the Rev. George Browne, a pugnacious Conservative, who checked its radical impetus and ruthlessly cut back the growth of local centres. That extension survived at all was due to his energetic and underpaid assistant R.D.Roberts, but the damage done was, in the opinion of the Cambridge extension's latest historian, 'little less than tragic'. [274] The appeal to the unions was critical: the pitmen's courses were uneconomic, and were subsidized by the university to the tune of £300 a year. The university sustained this until 1885, and then withdrew the subsidy. Although sympathetic dons collected £150, the pitmen's courses were already declining when in 1887 the Northern coalfield was riven by a strike which lasted four months. [275] The effect was disastrous. Although the number of students increased nationally, such penetration of a working-class community was not achieved for two decades. When Ruskin Hall was founded in Oxford in 1900, its magazine, *Young Oxford*, condemned the extension classes of both universities as genteel recreation for middle-class ladies. [276] Edward Carpenter, Leslie Stephen's successor and Goodbehere Fellow of Trinity Hall, who organized Cambridge extension classes at Leeds, Nottingham and Sheffield between 1873 and 1880, found that this was by and large the case even in the early days. His students were 'mainly of the "young lady" class' with a 'a very small sprinkling of manual workers'. [277]

It would be wrong to see the university extension movement as running into the sands of gentility. One reason for its irregular contact with the larger provincial towns was the fact that the years 1871-84 saw the founding of eleven higher-education institutions throughout the country. [278] The colleges at Nottingham and Sheffield were the direct result of the extension classes. [279] The movement also drew to the provinces many young dons like Michael Sadler and Halford Mackinder who were subsequently to make their careers in the new institutions. [280] Partly this was the result of internal developments at the old universities. Matriculations had doubled since 1860. (They levelled off in the early 1880s as the agricultural depression began to make itself felt in college revenues: see appendix 1) The first generation of non-clerical professional academics were in post with lengthy careers ahead of them. The cash did not exist to fund further posts at Oxford and Cambridge, so the younger men had therefore little alternative but to get out. [281] The extension movement provided a channel by which the old universities were able to service the new.

The provincial colleges came to cater for the vocational and professional studies of middle-class students, the extension classes for middle-class women. In the process, however, the goal of working-class education was lost sight of. Considering that the £300 a year necessary to keep the pitmen's courses going amounted to one thousandth of the annual revenue of the Cambridge colleges in 1886 (the smallest college, Magdalene, had an income of £4,929), [282] the scorn which radicals like William Morris and Thomas Hardy, who had had close relations with academic liberals, directed at the universities in *News from Nowhere* (1890) [283] and *Jude the Obscure* (1895), [284] is understandable.

To Stuart, Sidgwick and many of the younger men who recognized that the extension movement could affect both national politics and the character of the universities, its fate was bound up with the increasing polarization of the positions of university and mass society. [285] Other liberals, like Lewis Campbell and Henry Jackson, were indifferent. [286] Such divergences, in their turn, reflected changes in the nature of university studies which, in some ways, distanced the universities yet further from the community.

XI

Perhaps the most serious condemnation of university liberalism is that it failed to develop its group-consciousness and political experience into an interpretation of its social role, and an analysis of society itself. Echoing Gramsci, a recent Marxist attack on Britain's intellectual isolation, Perry Anderson's 'Components of the National Culture', sees such an inquiry aborted by the desire of the middle class to merge with rather than overthrow the landed aristocracy, [287] which allowed safe and domesticated university intellectuals, personified by 'the grey and ponderous figure of Henry Sidgwick (brother in law, needless to say, of Prime Minister Balfour)' [288] to connive at the wilful neglect in Britain of classical sociology, 'the great intellectual achievement of the European bourgeoisie at the end of the nineteenth and the beginning of the twentieth centuries'. [289]

Anderson's charges, and those of other recent commentators, [290] are, at the level of work actually produced, valid. Although the university liberals of the 1860s wrote much on contemporary society and its problems, and produced monuments of liberal historical scholarship like the *Oxford English Dictionary* (1884-1921), the *Cambridge Modern History* (1901-12) and (substantially) the *Dictionary of National Biography* (1886-1901), neither Oxford nor Cambridge played any substantial role as centres of inquiry into the nature of modern society and its culture until the twentieth century. That task was left to foreign scholars – Ostrogorski, Lowell, Halevy, Mantoux [291] – and the products of other traditions of education within Britain – Charles Booth, the Webbs, Graham Wallas and Patrick Geddes. [292] University men did make pioneering contributions to political studies, social and economic history, like James Bryce's *The American Commonwealth*, A.V.Dicey's *Law and Opinion*, and Thorold Rogers's *History of Agriculture and Prices in England*, but these were individual *tours de force*, admittedly comparable with the achievements of 'lay' scholars, but owing little to the sort of coordinated inquiry to be expected in a university situation.

However the notion of an academic will to accommodate the political establishment overestimates the academics' freedom to make such a choice. Sidgwick himself personified not blind acceptance of an allotted role but the attempt to establish such an inquiry at the universities and its failure. In the late 1860s, prompted by his own crisis of conscience over the tenure of his fellowship, he began to inquire into the social context of moral judgements. He concluded, on reading Aristotle, that [293]

what he gave us was the Common Sense Morality of Greece, reduced to consistency by careful comparison: given not as something external to him but as what 'we' – he and others – think, ascertained by reflection ... Might I not imitate this: do the same for *our* morality here and now, in the same manner of impartial reflection on current opinion?

At the same time T.H.Green began a similar examination in his essay on Popular Philosophy and its Relation to Life.' [294] Sidgwick's end-product, *The Methods of Ethics*, only tentatively modified his acquired utilitarianism; Green deflected his attack from the society which had 'taken sides with wilfulness' in 'the great struggle with social right' across the Atlantic to engage with the 'philosophy based on feeling' which he believed had led it there: [295] both accepted the orthodox framework of philosophical debate. But the circumstances under which they began, and the fact that several of their friends – Leslie Stephen, James Bryce and A.O.Rutson – intended to write treatments of democratic government, [296] suggests that, given favourable circumstances, a general social inquiry might have emerged.

Such an inquiry was not, however, general or coordinated. Academic ideology, in the sanguine 1860s, exerted a countervailing force. The belief that democratic society could be instructed in 'sound doctrines' by participation in politics meant that the academics' role, as political teachers, was essentially one of involvement (see p.153). Even when this prospect had receded, by 1874, the necessity of inquiry into society was implied rather than stated. In Leslie Stephen's 'Order and Progress' essay of 1875 the description of 'the power of the governing classes' which [297]

does not depend on the political machinery alone, or principally, but upon a whole series of social, intellectual and moral conditions, upon prejudices deeply rooted in the mind of the nation, upon the distribution of wealth and education, and a thousand complicating causes

predicates inquiry, but coexists with an insistence that a stock of 'sound philosophy' already exists, which has only to be communicated to the democracy. [298]

Drastic reform of university teaching and studies was an essential prerequisite, but it failed to take effect and the primacy of the traditional curriculum continued (see p. 200). At Balliol, for example, the most radical politically of the Oxford colleges, seven out of the ten Fellows in 1878 were classicists and, later, Jowett demonstrated by his treatment of T.H.Green and A.C.Bradley, who wanted to advance philosophy and English literature, that he was determined to maintain this position. [299] Yet the contributors to *Essays on a Liberal Education* in 1867 had made the dethronement of classics a central issue. Henry Sidgwick, in his essay on 'The Theory of Classical Education', gave his subject no quarter. He traced the shallow, unspecialized and overcompetitive orientation of Cambridge teaching, which J.R.Seeley also censured in the same volume, [300] back to the 'unmeaning linguistic exercises [301] of a classical public-school education. Confining himself to secondary education, Sidgwick agreed with Seeley that it ought to fit the student to study philosophy, conceived in very broad terms as [302]'the sustained effort to frame a complete and reasoned synthesis of

211

the facts of the universe'. He dismissed the claims of classical education to exercise the cognitive faculties and impart literary discrimination; for the first he proposed instead natural science, 'the completest instrument of thought in the world', [303] and for the second modern European literature: [304]

The branch of this study which seems to have the greatest utility, if the space we allot to it is limited, is surely that which explains to us (as far as is possible) the intellectual life of our own age; which teaches us the antecedents of the ideas and feelings among which, and in which, we shall live and move.

These reforms were limited to preliminary measures, and merely emphasized the formidable task of renovating the higher-education curriculum. Classics (mixed with ever greater devotion to games) remained dominant at the public schools for the rest of the century. [305] Although the 'modern side', initiated by Sidgwick's friend Edward Bowen at Harrow in 1869, enhanced the status of 'extra masters' and 'army classes', it was virtually restricted to boys who did not intend to proceed to university; [306] the survival of 'compulsory Greek' at both Oxford and Cambridge ensured this. [307] The frustration of the new professoriate was understandable.

New disciplines required staff, students, scholarships, library facilities, periodicals. The endowment of chairs was not enough. This was especially true of disciplines like history, philosophy and economics, whose secure establishment was a necessary preliminary to any sustained social inquiry. If Green's struggle with Jowett highlighted philosophy's problems, then Thorold Roger's expulsion from his Oxford chair in 1868 by clerical conservatives, [308] and the Cambridge Senate's veto on Henry Yates Thompson's project for a university lectureship in American history, [309] showed that the other disciplines too had to struggle to establish themselves. The position did not greatly improve when direct clerical antagonism died away. William Stubbs, than whom no more orthodox Churchman could be found, could make little of his position as head of the Oxford history department, neither could his friend and successor Freeman, [310] while at Cambridge Seeley's broad historical curriculum floundered, and Sidgwick tried in vain to create a Faculty structure from the system of Boards of Studies established and then neglected by the university. [311]

Progress in 'modernization' was most dramatic where marginal factors – a student body distinct from the ordinary undergraduates, a close connection with an external profession or pressure group – were important. Cunningham and Toynbee, along with Thorold

Rogers (who was also Tooke Professor at King's College, London, 1859-91), the pioneers of the study of economic history, lectured respectively to extension students and Indian civilians. [312] With Dicey, Anson and Holland at Oxford, and Maine, Maitland and Kenny at Cambridge, legal studies – a field in which teaching stimulated research – thrived on the continuance of the London connection, now 'professionalized' and shorn of the insecurities of the 1860s. [313] And in the natural sciences, prompted by German example, the universities proved receptive to the energetic external agitation of men like Huxley and Playfair. [314]

But in the humanities and the nascent social sciences the pressure for modernization was only as strong as the individuals who were prepared to work, and sometimes to pay, for it. Henry Sidgwick compensated for the failure of his university initiatives by financing the University Readership in English Law which brought Maitland back from his conveyancer's desk in London. [315] Maitland's Cambridge career, a triumph for historical research, could be construed as the disassociation of research from contemporary concerns, but in a letter of the same year Sidgwick treated such an ideal with bitter irony: [316]

I believe that the movement for the English school at Athens is still going on. I fear, however, that it will take years to collect the money they want and I do not think that it is very easy just now to collect money for this kind of object. One is apt to judge the world from the part of it one sees: but the impression produced on me is that it is in a rather sternly philanthropic frame of mind, rather socialistic, rather inclined to find culture frivolous, and to busy itself with poverty in the East End of London. However, research must go on, though a third of the families of London live in one room.

The paradox of later-nineteenth-century university reform was that the endowment of research and 'scientific' study could actually reinforce the existing curriculum and abstract it further from modern society. Both the 'school-keeping' of Jowett and the 'scholarship' of Pattison were concerned with governing or understanding the contemporary world. Pattison's devotion to an abstract and uninvolved scholarship [317] was, by his own testimony, governed by his intellectual situation; his great work on Scaliger was to be a study of the tension between the claims of the individual reason and social authority: [318] the seventeenth-century philologer under threat from the Jesuits was a projection of the nineteenth-century academic liberal under threat from the Church. To younger supporters of 'the endowment of research', however, like Ingram Bywater, Henry

213

Nettleship, Lewis Farnell and Henry Pelham, who had been through the 'Greats' school and had settled for a career teaching classics at the university, research had not those connotations. [319] It was to be undertaken for itself, not for any didactic purposes, not to illuminate a contemporary cultural situation.

The same progression applied to historical studies. Sheldon Rothblatt quotes Maitland's reluctance to provide moral messages for the 'muchedumbre' as evidence of an aloofness from public involvement unthinkable in the 1860s. [320] A later generation of medievalists came to venerate him as the personification of pure research. Yet Maitland was a sincere legal reformer and his interest in legal history stemmed naturally from this. [321] His brother-in-law, H.A.L.Fisher, wrote that to him [322]

Law was the product of human life, the expression of human needs, the declaration of the social will; and so a rational view of law would be won only from some height whence it would be possible to survey the great historic prospect which stretches from the Twelve Tables and the Leges Barbarorum to the German Civil Code and the judgements reported in the morning newspaper.

A more recent biographer, C.H.S.Fifoot, has argued that Maitland's scholarship was adversely affected by contemporary influences: [323] the drive to pronounce ethical judgements, to come to terms with theories of evolution and to instruct society. [324] Yet it can be argued that Maitland's respect for contemporary concerns made his work of seminal importance to the study of social history. Fifoot scarcely improves the case for divorcing legal history from such concerns by attacking Karl Marx as another (this time unpresentable) mid-nineteenth-century dogmatist. [325] Marx's inquiry at least had a structure which allocated importance to particular areas of historical activity. To discard such a structure, which Maitland himself did not do, but which many who called themselves his disciples did, was ultimately to make the activity of the historian subordinate to the research predilections of his colleagues and the apparent availability of historical material. Profession and material managed the historian, instead of the other way about. The penalties of this were demonstrated by the great project of the *Victoria History of the Counties of England*, commenced in 1899 with prestigious advisory committees which included Acton, Pollock and Maitland. [326] The precedent existed in the two *Statistical Accounts of Scotland* – parish-by-parish studies of the natural and civil history, society and economy of the country, originated by Sir John Sinclair in the 1790s and repeated in the 1830s – for a sophisticated inquiry into the effect of the social and economic changes of the last century. Since its take-over by the Institute of Historical Research in 1933 the Victoria History has done this, with great success, which only emphasizes the antiquarianism of the earlier volumes, with their concentration on medieval landholding and religious history. 'The object of history', James Bryce had written in the first number of the *English Historical Review* in 1886, 'is to discover and set forth facts'. [327] The *Victoria History,* and the *Review* itself, which published scarcely any articles on nineteenth-century history until the 1930s, demonstrated that this object was conditioned by the nature and aims of professional historians, and that these had drifted far, in practice, from the inquiry into the nature of modern society Bryce and his colleagues had wished to see.

Such an inquiry figured in the objects of the British Academy, established in 1902 largely through the agency of Bryce and Sidgwick [328] to encourage and coordinate inquries into those aspects of the arts and social sciences which could be studied 'scientifically': history and archaeology, philology, jurisprudence and economics. Lord Reay, its President, endorsed the claims of history to be treated as a science, in terms which must have been applauded by Bryce as a stout defender of the 'comparative method', [329] but the Academy demonstrated that research at the universities was diffused into sectors which were only tenuously linked by the principle of 'scientific inquiry'. About half of its membership was concerned with the study of classical and pre-classical cultures. Admittedly the later nineteenth century had seen great advances in this field, associated with the work of Fellows like Arthur Evans and J.G. Frazer, and the institutionalizing of this work was itself valuable, but what connection could it possibly have with the 'questions of housing, old age pensions, children's employment and hours of labour' [330] which the Academy also included within its remit? Only eleven Fellows had contemporary interests: the jurists Anson, Dicey and Pollock, the economists Cunningham and Marshall, the philosopher James Ward, four politicians with scholarly inclinations, Balfour, Bryce, Morley and Rosebery, and Leslie Stephen. The Academy's professed interest in education and politics did not extend to having any Fellows who were educationalists or political scientists (there were no chairs in either subject at Oxford or Cambridge). As far as it re-stated the need for contemporary inquiry, the British Academy dramatized the consciousness of academic liberalism that it was under pressure from new doctrines and new institutions (see p.235). But a rallying of the old academic community could never be an adequate response to the activities of young, energetic and heterodox social scientists at institutions like the London School of Economics, which, although it drew on academics who had been involved in the extension movement, was really the product of a totally different tradition of higher education: that of the Scots and German Universities, and French École Libre des Sciences Politiques. [331]

XII

The academics' political involvement cannot be treated separately from their university situation, as their failure to find a significant role for themselves in post-reform Britain was largely due to the wealth of options – academic and political – available to them in the later 1860s. Then they had lived in an atmosphere of political and institutional crisis, sharpening their awareness of current social problems and stimulating deeper inquiry into the nature of their society. Once the dual crisis was on the way to being resolved, however, the ideal of involvement presented itself as a range of options rather than a single imperative. Academics who failed to enter parliament could attempt to influence party politics, or agitate specific issues, or urge the reform of higher education, or simply integrate themselves into a more professional university milieu. Some confined themselves to one field, others involved themselves in more than one, either concurrently or successively, with the result that their efforts were, during the 1870s, diffused among a wide variety of causes. The integration of the 1860s could no longer be sustained.

The initial casualty was the attempt to develop higher education for a democratic society. It had been the weakest point in the university liberals' social analysis during the reform crisis; now the importance of parliamentary and party strategies diverted attention away from the linked problems of university extension and curricular reform. Although the failure of the Liberal government in 1874 re-emphasized their importance, subsequent developments were weakened by a crystallizing university structure and an academic liberalism increasingly divided in life-style and in educational policies.

The British Academy was a belated attempt at re-integration, but it simply reflected the dispersal of a group which could find unity only in political retrospection. In 1870 an organization of this sort might have provided a means of focusing the academic mind on the study of its social and intellectual environment. The academics'

greatest failure was to neglect to inquire into their own consciousness. Mark Pattison's verdict on the Oxford liberals at the beginning
of the century has an uncanny appositeness here: [332]

A philosophy must be the concentrated expression of the life of a
period. The thinking of these men did not amount to a philosophy,
for they could not grasp in its totality the self-consciousness of their
generation ... They wanted a knowledge of the past, a knowledge of
the present, and of the thread by which the present is tied to the
past. They were imperfectly acquainted with the condition of their
own England.

Failure to understand their time, to rationalize their group-
consciousness save in retrospective terms, was to lead to doctrinal
inflexibility. The effect of this was exemplified in the secession of
1886 which, by further weakening the group, made it regard a
changing society with an increasing sense of alienation and
pessimism.

[9]

1886
AND AFTER

All Souls appears just now to be a living *fons juri
publici* while, thanks to the Warden, Dr Holland,
Professor Dicey and Professor Bryce himself, the Law
Faculty of the University was never so much before
the country or, we believe, so genuinely useful to it
as it is now.

Oxford Magazine, 26 May 1886

We are living in a new world, and strangely enough
the change seems to me to have come almost entirely
in the fifteen years between 1885 and 1900. 'The
foundations are removed and what hath the right-
eous done?'

James Bryce – A.V. Dicey, 14 October 1919

To academics the Home Rule split of 1886 was a 'parting of friends'
as important and poignant as the break-up of the Oxford Movement forty years earlier, and marked the end of the cohesive
liberalism of the universities. During and after the struggle Unionist and Gladstonian dons alike believed that their contribution to
the debate was important, and that there had been a serious
divergence between intellectual opinion and popular liberalism. The
cooperative politics of the 1860s had broken down and, lacking
unity, the academics could no longer hope to reactivate it. The
Unionists did not want to; the Gladstonians no longer represented
the universities.

The role allotted to ideology in the Home Rule crisis by many
historians sustained the academics' assessment. Until recently,
indeed, more seemed to be written about intellectual attitudes to
Home Rule than about the political reasons for it. [1] But if, as the
last chapter has argued, university involvement in politics was
steadily declining before 1886, the interpretation advanced recently

218

by John Vincent and Alastair Cooke – that Home Rule owed much to political manoeuvre and little to ideological conviction – is strengthened, and the role of the academics properly reduced to an amateur sideshow. [2]

Politicians unquestionably acknowledged academic opinion on the issue to a much greater extent than they had done in 1867. Dicey was commended by Gladstone and Hartington in the first reading of the Bill and subsequently became Liberal Unionism's leading constitutionalist. Bryce performed a similar role for the Gladstonians. [3] Several academics spoke in the debates, and were respectfully listened to. Their experience of parliamentary elections and organization was not such as to make them confident about their influence on the House, but in the years before 1886 they had come to believe that the sort of informed opinion they represented had a vital role to play in moulding national attitudes. In an article in the New York *Nation* in 1883 Dicey argued that, with elementary education and franchise extension, political society had been so widened that parliament no longer truly represented it. [4] Although this had ominous implications in the growth of caucuses and the power of the press, it also indicated that the growth of political education outside of electoral politics – exemplified by university extension and projects like Toynbee Hall – could allow academic ideals to irradiate public opinion.

The academics welcomed the crisis of the mid-1880s. Home Rule, as an issue, seemed remarkably well adapted to their own predilections. They were subsequently to realize, however, that their role was only marginal, that the party battle transformed intellectual disagreement into political separation and led to a breakdown in their own cohesion. The more conservative residents also realized that an accommodation with the Unionist alliance would guarantee academic liberalism as an interest group – but no longer a political irritant. The consequence was, in the long run, a weakening of the ties which had bound academics, Unionist and Gladstonian alike, to active politics.

II

July 5, 1886: Unionists gaining slowly but steadily. Dined in Hall, and was surprised to find the great preponderance of Unionist sentiment among the Trinity Fellows, a body always, since I have known Trinity, predominantly Liberal. [5]

Henry Sidgwick, like Dicey and the editor of the *Oxford Magazine*, noted with satisfaction that 'the sentiment prevalent in ... the class of lawyers and university men' was against Gladstone's policy. [6] The *Oxford Magazine* reported on 16 June that 'among the dons the number of Home Rulers is estimated by the sanguine Home Rule whip at seventeen'. This was challenged in the next issue by a letter from an anonymous Home Ruler who claimed forty-three dons as Home Rulers, but admitted that the number was far lower at Cambridge, probably as few as the original seventeen. [7] Considering that 288 dons had voted Liberal in the 1878 Oxford election, the defection was overwhelming. [8] A sample taken from more activist dons is only slightly less daunting: among Oxford residents in 1886, fifteen had attended the Freemason's Tavern meeting on Tests Abolition in June 1864; of these, nine were now Unionist and only four Gladstonian (see appendix 2). Even Bryce and Morley had later to admit that Unionism had become 'the prevailing creed of ... highly educated Englishmen'. [9]

This predominance, however, was peculiarly the outcome of the 1886 situation. Before then it was next to impossible to predict, on previous form, the direction in which individual academics would move, even if, after a quarter of a century's companionship, a civil exchange of opinions was to be expected. One letter sums up the tone of the debate. Just after the failure of Gladstone's Bill Leslie Stephen wrote to Bryce regretting that he might have given his friend to believe that he saw him as 'a mere follower of Gladstone', insincere in his support for Home Rule as a policy. Surprised that Bryce valued 'the opinion of an old hermit like me', he rather touchingly expressed his faith in his integrity. Admitting that he rejected the Bill as 'radically wrong', although he 'had long been for home rule in some shape', he ended:[10]

In truth I perceived in your words a suspicion that an old friend might be judging you harshly and I therefore do not feel easy till I have said in so many words that contrary-wise my opinion of you is what it always has been, that is as high as any one's can be.

Relations throughout the academic community – between Dicey and Bryce, Henry Sidgwick and Trevelyan (whose volte-face cost him many of his political friends), Morley and Leslie Stephen – remained similarly cordial. [11] They had to be, as divisions frequently cut through families, departments and colleges: Henry Sidgwick, for instance, led the Unionists at Cambridge, his brother Arthur led the Gladstonians at Oxford. [12] It was all rather like Walter Raleigh's description of the contest between Faith and Doubt, as refereed by Henry Sidgwick: the combatants spent more time shaking hands, exchanging compliments and costumes, than in actually fighting. Each had more trouble establishing his own identity than hitting his opponent. [13]

Before 1886 academic attitudes to the Home Rule issue were as indeterminate as those of the politicians. Undoubtedly this partly stemmed from the general weakening of the cohesion of the 1860s. Had it persisted, they would probably have been more forthright, and in theory more inclined to Unionism. In *Questions for a Reformed Parliament* Frank Harrison Hill had called for a closer integration of Ireland with the rest of the United Kingdom: the Union 'which was at first political and legal should become one of heart and mind'. [14] None of his co-authors disagreed with him: where the Irish figured in the essays it was as subjects for – or impediments to – good government, not as candidates for self-government. [15] Mill and Mazzini, both of whom proposed drastic remedies for Ireland's ills, deprecated moves towards separatism; those among the academics with Irish connections – almost exclusively with Protestant Ireland – agreed. [16] Where a certain sanction for separatism existed, it was a negative emotion rather than a positive programme, founded on a desire to exclude 'a corrupt element' from a democratic polity: [17] Leslie Stephen, Goldwin Smith and James Bryce, discussing proven instances of corruption in American politics, tended to attribute these to 'an emigration of ignorant [Irish] peasants utterly unaccustomed to any form of self-government', rather than to the political system itself. [18] In the early 1880s, with the Land League and the Irish parliamentary party making their presence felt, this Anglo-Saxon attitude gained strength. [19] Institutional reform, coercion or separatism? Given this mix of opinions on Ireland, it became virtually impossible to predict the options academics would plump for. Other problems of course were present: alarm about the consequences, economic and otherwise, of popular government: concern for the Empire; distrust of Gladstone. But it was very difficult to infer anyone's ultimate position from his opinions in, say, 1883.

Both Bryce and Sidgwick were, for example, deeply concerned about the socialistic implications of the new democracy. Of the two, Bryce was on the whole the more pessimistic, while Sidgwick was reasonably confident that some form of government could be evolved to 'guide modern industrial society successfully towards its socialistic goal'. Yet Sidgwick could condemn Home Rule as 'putting a premium ... on a combination of political and agrarian agitation' with the revolutionary dangers which this foreboded.

Auberon Herbert, now a stalwart of the Liberty and Property Defence League, was much gloomier about socialist encroachments than either of them, but opted for Home Rule, [20] while Dicey, who believed that democracy had no inherently socialistic tendencies, became a fervent Unionist. [21]

If there was no necessary identity between individualism and Unionism, attitudes to Empire were no more reliable as indicators. Seeley, at Cambridge, specifically cited imperial interests as arguments against Home Rule, [22] yet some of Unionism's most vociferous supporters, like Leonard Courtney, Goldwin Smith and Mrs Fawcett, were dedicated 'Little Englanders'. [23] Among Oxford men the arch-imperialist Milner – whose local influence was later to prove important – admitted privately that he didn't care 'two straws for the Union', [24] while James Bryce was a supporter of the Imperial Federation League, on the grounds that a federal settlement with Ireland could lead naturally to federation within the colonies and ultimately (he hoped) to a restoration of links with the United States. [25]

Bryce's imperial sympathies were not shared by his fellow Home Ruler Edward Freeman, who believed, like Goldwin Smith, in the separation of the colonies from the mother-country. [26] Neither did Freeman share Bryce's desire to retain Irish members at Westminster. Although the historian of federal government, he had as little enthusiasm as Dicey for its application to Britain: it was much better to be rid of the Irish altogether. [27] Freeman hated them as intensely as Goldwin Smith. 'This would be a grand land if only every Irishman would kill a negro and be hanged for it!' he had written from America in 1881. [28] Racialism was far from being a reflex of Unionism – or imperialism, for that matter. Dicey, for instance, treated Irish opinion with respect, and admitted that if he were Irish he would be 'an out and out Nationalist'. [29] Even after 1886 he was distressed when Irish Nationalists criticized his books as unfair, and elated when they praised them. [30] The insistent anti-Irish attitudes of the later 1880s – particularly noticeable in Liberal Unionist publications – were the focusing by the Unionists of sentiments which had hitherto been disseminated throughout the Liberal party. The only thorough-going and consistent support for Home Rule which pre-dated 1886 came from the Positivists, who had been sympathetic since the 1860s, and it is indicative of how isolated they were that their opposition to coercion in 1882 was the cause of their final break with the trade union movement, which had little interest in Irish and foreign affairs. [31]

Gladstone was, of course, a contention of long standing. Memories of the American Civil War and the Tests issue still provoked mistrust: Leslie Stephen's 1868 complaint that 'no one can feel quite certain of his principles' was echoed by his cousin Dicey in the early 1880s. [32] Why was Gladstone 'abhorred with an intensity of abhorrence felt towards no other politician'. by the educated class? He adduced four main reasons: he had made political democracy a reality; he was unconnected with traditional Whig-Liberalism; as a Scotsman he appealed, like Carlyle, to the emotions; and he was too much the disciple of Cardinal Newman and Sir Robert Peel: [33]

Neither teacher was exactly the man to foster in a disciple that kind of plain speaking which, often very wrongly, the English public fancy to be the sole and sufficient guarantee of public safety.

Mistrust of Gladstone was widespread, even among personal friends, like Brodrick or Sidgwick, yet such attitudes were unimportant in the pre-1886 context, as the general expectation was that his retirement was imminent. [34] Until late 1885 the character of Gladstone was a less serious matter than the contest for the succession.

Mistrust of Gladstone did not, however, imply confidence in any other Liberal leader. Academics had never had much time for Hartington and the Whigs; they had even less for Chamberlain and the Radicals. [35] Neither did they follow their former allies, Goschen and Forster, in their move to the right. The landed interest and the caucus inspired as much suspicion as the charismatic leader. This was a bequest of the 1860s: leadership was seen as a function of the health of parliament, and until parliament was fully representative inappropriate leaders were inevitable. [36] After the Reform Act of 1884 this changed: the entrenched forces within the Liberal party seemed determined on a showdown. For a party activist like Morley, hitherto identified with Chamberlain, a guarantor of the party's survival in the face of the radical challenge became essential. By late 1885 he was to hand, in the shape of the rejuvenated Gladstone: the politics of the next year concerned his efforts to secure this end, and their substantial success. [37] The initial response of the academics, including parliamentarians, could only be to acquiesce. They could accept or reject Gladstone's proposals; they could not replace him or pre-empt them. Leadership, of a type they had never envisaged, now became of the essence.

This might not have been the case had the academic representatives in parliament proved effective. On the whole they were not, although the sessions of 1880 to 1885, racked by procedural disputes, were scarcely conducive to the rise of independently minded M.P.s from the government back benches. The fact that some were ministers did not assist their functioning as a group; and the indifferent success and general undependability of Trevelyan, Fawcett and Courtney probably put their colleagues at a further disadvantage. Trevelyan was a disaster as Chief Secretary [38] and Fawcett's role as the Liberals' *periculosa hereditas*, ended by his death in November 1884, [39] was diligently inherited by Courtney, who resigned from the government a month later over its failure to make any concessions on proportional representation. [40] Until August 1885 Dilke was well placed; thereafter his involvement in the Crawford divorce damned him in the eyes of most academic liberals. [41]

Things were little better on the back benches. When James Stuart was elected for Hackney in place of Fawcett, Edward Hamilton, Gladstone's private secretary, found him likeable but nursing 'some nasty crotchets', [42] which put him in the same category as a couple of other academic pains-in-the-neck, Thorold Rogers and Lyulph Stanley. [43] Bryce, by contrast, was quiet and diligent, assiduously cultivated the Premier's intellectual preoccupations and limited his crotchets to the Middle East and rights of way. [44] But he was a bad speaker and his academic and journalistic interests meant that he was more often to be found in the Library than in the Chamber. Not being 'a good House of Commons man' probably cost him ministerial office when he was considered for the Under-Secretaryship at the India Office in 1883. [45]

But he had thought long on Ireland. His speech in the Home Rule debate was received with respect; [46] Acton considered him better equipped than Morley for the Chief Secretaryship. [47] Though Morley's observations on his own qualifications had point: he was firm on the issue, he had an eye for party opinion, and he stood well with the Irish. [48] Bryce had doubts about the bill, about the party caucuses and, as an Ulsterman, about the Irish. Unlike Morley he had no rank-and-file support; unhappy (largely because of the Irish) in his London constituency, he had just moved to deferential Aberdeen (which only required his attentions for a week each year); [49] in 1884 he had tried to organize a Committee on Irish Affairs composed of Irish Liberals and English back-benchers, to offer an alternative, reformist focus to the Parnellites. [50] Its secretary, B.F.C.Costelloe, was a young Catholic radical, by Toynbee Hall out of Balliol, who was later to become a leading Progressive on the London County Council. [51] But the Reform Bill doomed the

Committee before it had got properly started. Single-member constituencies and a wider Irish franchise promised the extinction of Irish Liberalism; attention was transferred to proportional representation in Ireland in an attempt to avert this. [52] To no avail: Irish Liberalism was utterly destroyed in the 1885 election by the Tory – Parnellite alliance, but not before it had, in Bryce's eyes, fatally compromised itself by attempts to ally with the Tories. [53] Cooke and Vincent have thought it odd that Bryce did not use his position to represent Scottish and Ulster opinion; but he was only nominally a Scottish M.P. and his Ulster *démarche* had failed. [54] For the middle-of-the-road constitutionalism he believed in, Gladstone alone seemed to offer the prospect of salvation.

The weakness of the parliamentary academics was important, because on the whole they backed Home Rule. Of the eighteen academics who had attended the Freemasons' Tavern and gone on to stand for parliament between 1864 and 1886 eleven continued as Liberals, while only five became Unionists (see appendix 2). But they did not carry authority. Others did: in particular respected university figures like Seeley, Brodrick, Henry Sidgwick and the Oxford lawyers, especially Dicey. Their commitment to Unionism was probably critical in rallying academic support. [55]

Brodrick and Seeley were predictable opponents of Home Rule. Brodrick, who had failed by eight hours to be born an Irish landlord, and had held strongly unionist opinions since his *Times* days, admitted past misgovernment but held that 'a peasantry whose minds have been dwarfed … by the effect of the penal laws' could not govern itself and carry out the programme of land and educational reform necessary to modernize the country. [56] He had, further, long ceased to repose any trust in Gladstone. [57] So too had Seeley; but, where Brodrick stressed the backwardness of Ireland, he ignored altogether national differences within the United Kingdom. Separatism was dismissed as unthinkable, *tout court*. [58] Both were active from the first in the Unionist cause, yet it was the commitment of two hitherto radical and detached figures, Sidgwick and Dicey, which was the more influential in the latter part of 1886; a commitment which did not in fact become definitive until after the defeat of Gladstone's Bill.

Sidgwick's attitudes fluctuated violently between April 1885, when he turned down an offer to stand as Liberal candidate for Cambridgeshire, and December 1886, when he joined the Liberal Unionist party. [59] His growing interest in social policy and his acquaintance with, and admiration for, Sir Henry Maine were

225

causing him, early in 1886, 'to find something wooden and fatuous in the sublime smile of Freedom' and to consider a 'Caesarist' type of government as better adapted for interventionism. [60] Yet when the Home Rule Bill was introduced on 8 April his opposition was tentative. The previous day he had talked with Bryce: [61]

His chief argument is that Democracy will not coerce, and therefore we must come to this in the end: so we had better to be it [sic] at once quickly. I think he is very likely right as to the ultimate result: but I do not think that the H.R. in the bush is sufficiently *more* mischievous than the H.R. in the hand to make it imprudent to figure on a bare chance of staving it off altogether.

By 2 June he concluded that Bryce was right: a rapid settlement would be the best outcome, and he left to holiday in Switzerland. [62] When Gladstone was defeated and dissolved Parliament, however, he reverted to his earlier position, and hurried back to vote for the Conservative candidate at Cambridge. [63]

Despite his involvement in the Liberal Unionist organization – which was sufficiently energetic to detach his wife from the Conservatives – he remained sceptical. [64] On 28 March 1887, not long before he headed the Liberal Unionist deputation to Lord Hartington from the universities, he wrote to Symonds that he found himself substantially in agreement with Bryce over Home Rule, [65] and a visit to his brother-in-law the Chief Secretary in the following year increased his doubts about the Union, [66] though he remained indulgent to the martyrs of Unionist propaganda. 'A set of idle, incompetent, self-indulgent idiots, when they are not worse' was his wife's verdict on the Irish landlords, [67] one that the individualistic Liberal in him could not share. Until his death he believed (a) that Home Rule was inevitable and (b) that it would involve an intolerable diminution of the rights of property: a situation of political paralysis which his 'Tory votes' accompanied by 'Liberal principles' only decorated. [68]

Dicey was a resolute, almost fanatical, Unionist, but his attitudes before June 1886 were no more straightforward. Overall he moved from a position of friendly neutrality towards Irish aspirations in 1882 to outright hostility to the idea of Home Rule in 1886, but he would still have been prepared to acquiesce if Gladstone had carried his Bill. [69] His attitude derived in part from his study of parliamentary sovereignty, published as *The Law and Working of the Constitution* in 1885, yet he recognized that the preservation of a 'flexible constitution' for mainland Britain was still compatible with Irish independence. [70] This made him condone (theoretically) Irish

separatism – then veto it on grounds of national security. [71] Dicey
was not an energetic imperialist – he certainly thought much less about
imperial matters than Bryce – but he had been distressed by the
ineptitude of Gladstone's Egyptian policy, on which subject his brother
Edward was an acknowledged expert, and this heightened his
antipathy for Gladstone's initiative. [72] However, a conservative,
imperially-conscious attitude need not necessarily have led him to
Unionism: as Bryce's position implied, it could embrace a form of
Federalism. In 1885 certain conservative theorists were thinking in such
terms. In a *Nation* article early in 1886 Dicey discussed such a solution,
achieved through adoption of a constitution closer to the Swiss than to
the American pattern and concluded that, although it promised
stability, it would not expedite reform. [73] Such a solution probably
continued to lurk in the back of his mind until the defeat of
Gladstone's Bill. But it was the conservative in Dicey which favoured
it, and radical arguments which regenerated his opposition when the
Bill failed: a unitary parliament alone could achieve the legislative
revolution that Ireland required – the creation of a propertied
peasantry. Only this would bring stability. Home Rule would mean
federal conservatism in Britain, while a semi-independent Ireland
would revenge itself on its landowners. Gladstone's dual settlement
might have prevented this; but with its rejection there was no cause to
repeat the prescription, with the costs it entailed. [74] Conservatism –
with the inference that Home Rule was part of some great radical
conspiracy – was subsequently to pervade Dicey's attitudes, but Bryce's
commendation of his friend's Unionist manifesto, *England's Case against
Home Rule,* was not simply gallantry: Dicey's position in November
1886 was in many ways more radical and more confident of the
capacity of the British democracy to settle the Irish problem.

III

The older academics lent authority and dignity to academic
Unionism, but they were neither ideologically cohesive nor politically active – at least until after Gladstone's Bill was lost. Their
mobilization, which appeared by mid-1887 impressive, required
more application than they were willing to give, or were capable of
giving. It was the work of other hands, chiefly of energetic and
rather unscrupulous young right-wing Liberals, aided by tendencies
within university opinion which had relatively little to do with
national politics: a partial repetition of the 1860s situation, but with
the universities being manipulated by the politicians rather than
spontaneously intervening.

There were differences between the two universities, but a central role was played at each by men, on the whole agnostic about Home Rule as such, whose main loyalties lay with external political groups: at Oxford Milner and Philip Lyttelton Gell, Brodrick's nephew, acted on behalf of Goschen, with his desire for a right-wing 'ralliement', [75] while at Cambridge Alfred Dale, son of the spiritual head of Birmingham Radicalism, the Rev. R.W.Dale, organized the main Unionist initiatives of 1886 and 1887. [76] Gell and Milner – involved from the beginning with Liberal Unionist organization – intervened effectively at Oxford during the election of July 1886, persuading their friend Charles Fyffe to stand down as candidate and dissuading a militantly Gladstonian Liberal association from a contest. [77] They also acted as a clearing-house for academic Unionist speakers, like Brodrick, Thomas Raleigh, Sir William Anson and Goldwin Smith (in fire-eating fettle), whom they despatched around the country. [78] Dale organized, in June 1886, a manifesto of academics pledging themselves to support the Unionist parties. Thereafter he was inactive for the better part of a year – probably while his father was closely identified with attempts at Liberal reunion – but returned to organize the academic Unionist memorial to Lord Hartington in June 1887. [79]

This hiatus was important, and it was not simply due to external political developments – the 'round table' conferences and their failure – but to a changing situation in the universities themselves. Unionism, the academics found, could lead to political isolation: Gell, Brodrick and Raleigh found themselves in a minority of five when they tried to wean the Oxford Liberal 300 away from Gladstone; [80] Sidgwick found the Liberal Unionist conference in December 'more like a regiment of officers without common soldiers, and with little prospect of finding a rank and file'. [81] But, however unrepresentative and heterogeneous, the Liberal Unionist leaders were university men, or were respectful towards university men. Presiding over a party largely run by amateurs, they looked on the universities and their amateur ideologues with sympathy. [82] This sentiment was reciprocated: for the first time academic liberals could gain the support of a congenial political force and through this an enduring recognition. In the mid-1880s this was a necessity: the Act of 1877 had given government increased powers over the universities, through a committee of the Privy Council; rents were falling, impeding the reform programme; the future of the provincial university colleges, and London University, was increasingly being discussed. Yet the dons had no direct political representatives on which they could rely. [83] Their four burgesses were run-of-the-mill Tories, their two chancellors were Salisbury, put into office by the Oxford clerical party in 1869, and at Cambridge the Duke of Devonshire who, although liberal and generous, was reclusive. [84] The break with Liberalism threatened to isolate them further; on the other hand it gave them the chance, for the first time, to secure an armistice from the Tories and direct parliamentary representation. The Unionist activity of mid-1887 makes most sense in this context.

From the beginning of the year the academic Unionists had shown themselves anxious both to secure Liberal Unionist burgesses and to avoid overmuch indebtedness to the Tories. Early in January Tories and Liberal Unionists at Oxford jointly approached Goschen, who had just joined the government as Chancellor of the Exchequer and was in re-election trouble at Liverpool, to stand at Oxford. [85] Goschen lost at Liverpool, but by then, under pressure from town Tories, who disliked the way Liberal political economy was applied to poor relief, and the clergy, personified by Archdeacon Denison, the alliance had broken down. [86] He was elected instead for the safe West End seat of St George's, Hanover Square. By the middle of the year the Cambridge Unionists had their chance. One of the burgesses, Beresford Hope, a die-hard and Salisbury's brother-in-law, became mortally ill and a by-election was expected. This seemed an appropriate time to secure a Liberal Unionist representative, especially as the Gladstonians were starting to rally and organize: and who better to petition than the party's leader and the Chancellor's heir?

The move was well timed as *The Times*'s 'Parnellism and Crime' articles dampened the Gladstonian recovery. The response was enthusiastic – seventy-five academics signed from each university, including the heads of ten Oxford and four Cambridge colleges, fourteen Oxford and ten Cambridge professors – and the tone was resolute. Gladstone and his supporters were represented as 'the English division of the Home Rule party' while Hartington was commended [87]

as the leader of a party rich in Parliamentary distinction and rich in rising talent, a party which may soon come to be recognised as the true representative of the great traditions of English Liberalism.

Hartington's own response was shrewd, dwelling on the contribution of academic liberalism as 'a protest ... against that old and obstructive conservatism with which, formerly, the Universities were supposed to be identified' and only referring to Ireland *en passant.* [88] He was not, however, to be wooed to Cambridge. When Beresford Hope died in October the Tories chose their own candidate, without consulting the Liberal Unionists: he turned out to be Sir George Gabriel Stokes, Lucasian Professor of Natural Philosophy, the first distinguished academic to sit for a university seat. [89] This was at least an indication that the party managers would no longer press home the advantage the clerical vote gave them. By the end of the century both universities had Conservative or Liberal Unionist members who could fairly be said to represent the views of most of the residents – Sir Richard Jebb at Cambridge and Sir William Anson at Oxford. Hartington himself succeeded his father as Chancellor in 1892. [90] A decade later Goschen succeeded Salisbury at Oxford. The old liberals had become the new establishment.

Academic Unionism in 1886-7 was not authoritative, nor was it purely a response to the Irish issue, but it was handled by the various groups involved in such a way that it appeared to be both. University residents, lapsing from politics anyway, became Unionists partly (with some prompting) in protest against Gladstone's policy, partly because Liberal Unionism legitimized a liberalism confined to the universities and freed from troublesome external commitments. But it was more than a simple accommodation: by 1887 it had acquired coherent ideologists and means of publicity. Brodrick, Dicey, Courtney and Goldwin Smith could now sink their differences and participate in a common programme, while St Loe Strachey's *Liberal Unionist* provided them with a platform. [91] Dicey, who considered that his reputation had been made by the coincidence of the crisis with the publication of his *Law and Working of the Constitution*, [92] seemed to personify academic rigour when in many articles and pamphlets, he pronounced on Home Rule in measured, circumspect but ultimately damnatory terms. 'You will say that I have wandered into a kind of religion rather than politics,' he told a Dublin meeting in 1893: [93]

I cannot separate the two. Fervour of feeling is essential to vigour of action. You will never triumph unless you make a kind of religion of your politics, or turn your politics into a kind of religion.

The Evangelical appeal survived, and still retained its relevance. However impractical and extreme Dicey sounded outside, he remained the Mr Standfast of the issue within the universities. His personal sincerity and decency, coupled with the strict logic of his argument, convinced his contemporaries. Bryce, the leading ideologue of Home Rule, did not. Admittedly the strength of his argument was somewhat vitiated by the closeness of his personal friendship with Dicey, but he did not attempt to challenge Dicey's logic. He only offered the unhelpful political observation that the alternative to Home Rule would be coercion, and that a democracy was unlikely to have sufficient fixity of purpose to enforce it over the necessary period. [94] The longer the Tories remained in power, the less plausible this appeared. Besides, to the academic mind practical appraisal of the inclinations of groups of voters was less attractive than comprehending, rationalizing and simplifying the legislative process itself. Ironically Dicey's continuing theoretical confidence in democracy led him to the right, while Bryce's pessimism kept him to the left.

The contest between academic Unionism and its well-mannered opponents was, however, of limited interest, and in due course this became apparent even to the participants. The 'social movement' Bryce and Dicey had anxiously observed before 1886 continued to expand. Toynbee Hall, which drew support from both universities, the revival of the High Church in a socially committed role, the formation of societies for educational and social reform, the revival of extension teaching at Oxford, all assumed, in the eyes of the younger dons and undergraduates, a greater importance than the constitutional niceties of the Irish question. [95] The radicalism of the younger men was more 'sentimental' than 'scientific', a mixture of logically incompatible ingredients like imperialism, Hegelianism, socialism and religion, which contained the germ both of Milnerite state-socialism and its quasi-Marxist critique. In 1895 the 'Six Oxford Men' who wrote *Essays in Liberalism* considered that they had to refine a pure doctrine from its muddy stream. [96] Bryce and Dicey would have approved, but the 'sentimentalists' had at least kept in touch with popular politics. The Unionists had not. Leonard Courtney wrote to Mrs Fawcett during the general election of 1886 that, however much his own attacks on Home Rule convinced them, his working-class electors retained their faith in Gladstone. However radical they claimed to be, Unionists were kept in their seats by Tory votes. They had broken off contact with the intelligent working men and small farmers whom they liked to think constituted the Liberal electorate – or would constitute it if their reforms were carried out. Only in Birmingham was Liberal Unionism a popular movement, and there the mixture of caucus management and municipal socialism (with imperialism in the offing) was toxic.

With the dissolution of the matrix of the 1860s, academics had for some time found it difficult to relate to a changing political scene. Unionism at least gave a new 'fix' for most of them. But it left no opening to the future. And enough of the matrix – relationships, concerns, language – remained to tie their Gladstonian colleagues to them, and to the old politics.

The advantage of the academic Unionists soon diminished. In 1888, as Brodrick and Dicey promoted the alliance with the Conservatives as 'the birth of a great national party', on the grounds that with the triumph of democracy 'old lines of demarcation' had been effaced, the Gladstonians recovered. [97] Organized by the Shakespearian scholar E.K.Chambers, Fellow of Corpus Christi, an Oxford Home Rule Association was formed, [98] which by February 1888 had equalled the Unionist manifesto of the previous year, with a memorial to Gladstone signed by seventy-five dons, mainly historians and philologers. Gladstone, in interesting, and infuriating, contrast to Hartington, praised their conservatism. [99] The Unionists retaliated with more meetings, but at one of them Brodrick spoke of the Irish party in such terms that he was haled before the Parnell Commission for contempt. [100] Thereafter Oxford Unionism was subdued, but worse was to come. In December 1891 Hartington succeeded to his Dukedom and Chamberlain took over the effective leadership of the Liberal Unionists. After the Gladstonian victory in July 1892 Goschen formally joined the Tories. The character of the party rapidly changed from being a tent of Whigs and discontented intellectuals to become an extension of the Birmingham caucus. [101] The *Liberal Unionist* was closed down. There was now little room for the amateurs and their 'old liberalism'.

Trevelyan and Morley returned to office. Bryce at last entered the Cabinet – which also included university men of a younger generation, Asquith and Arthur Acland. But, despite this intellectual strength, new initiatives were not taken; after the defeat in the Lords of the second Home Rule Bill the government, lacking policies and confidence and plagued by internal dissensions, willingly surrendered office in June 1895. [102] The failure was as shattering as that of 1874, but Bryce and his generation, now in positions of much greater influence, no longer called for new policies. The debate on the future of Liberalism was to be carried on by younger men.

IV

The extent of academic liberal unease about the course of modern politics – and more significantly the paralysis of the intellect which accompanied it – was demonstrated by the impact of Charles Pearson's *National Life and Character*. Pearson had emigrated to Victoria in 1871, where he took an active part in radical politics, becoming a Liberal M.P. in 1878 and Minister of Education in 1886. He set about creating a Taunton-style system of secondary education – separating it from the primary schools, providing scholarships, widening the curriculum and abolishing payment by results – but his efforts were frustrated by the fall of the government in 1890, brought on by the bankruptcy of the Government Railways and a general strike. [103] He returned to England that year as Agent-General – he had always kept up a close correspondence with his university friends Bryce, Sidgwick, Goschen, Dilke, Brodrick and Harrison – and began work on a forecast of future social development. On the recommendation of Bryce, *National Life and Character* was published by Macmillan in 1893. [104]

Its last paragraph captures the tone of this remarkable book: [105]

Summing up, then, we seem to find that we are slowly but demonstrably approaching what we may regard as the age of reason or of a sublimated humanity; and that this will give us a great deal that we are expecting from it – well-ordered polities, security to labour, education, freedom from gross superstitions, improved health and longer life, the destruction of privilege in society and of caprice in family life, better guarantees for the peace of the world, and enforced regard for life and property when war unfortunately breaks out. It is possible to conceive the administration of the most advanced states so equitable and efficient that no-one will even desire seriously to disturb it. On the other hand, it seems reasonable to assume that religion will gradually pass into a recognition of ethical precepts and a graceful habit of morality; that the mind will occupy itself less and less with works of genius, and more and more with trivial results and ephemeral discussions; that husband and wife, parents and children, will come to mean less to one another; that romantic feeling will die out in consequence; that the old will increase on the young; that two great incentives to effort, the desire to use power for noble ends, and the desire to be highly esteemed, will come to promise less to capable men as the field of human energy is crowded; and generally that the world will be left without deep convictions or enthusiasm, without the regenerating influence of the ardour for political reform and the fervour of pious faith which have quickened men for centuries past as nothing else has quickened them, with a passion purifying the soul ... The decline of the higher classes as an influence in society, the organisation of the inferior races throughout the tropical zone, are the natural result of principles that we cannot disown if we would ... even now no practical statesman could dream of arresting Chinese power or Hindoo or negro expansion by wholesale massacres. The world is

233

becoming too fibreless, too weak, too good to contemplate or to carry out great changes which imply lamentable suffering. It trusts more and more to experience, less and less to insight and will ... Yet there seems no reason why men of this kind should not perpetuate the race, increasing and multiplying till every rod of earth maintains its man, and the savour of vacant lives will go up to God from every home.

Pearson's achievement was considerable if ambiguous: his anticipation of a welfare-state England conceding its imperial acquisitions to races better adapted by tradition to cope with mass society has turned out nearer the truth than the aggressive Anglo-Saxonism of the 1890s; less happily, his persistent re-statement of the inferiority of the coloured races did much to stimulate 'yellow peril' agitation and 'white Australia' policies. [106] As a convinced and hard-working radical, his assessment of the tendencies making for collectivism was shrewd and not unsympathetic; but the book was penetrated by searing, pessimistic judgements about the consequences for human personality of such developments. In part this was a re-statement of the criticisms of industrial society made by Victorian thinkers like Carlyle and the Tennyson of *Locksley Hall*, in part it reflected the anti-materialist tendencies of European social thought associated with Nietzche and the older Ibsen – whom Pearson admired – writers who feared for the individual imagination in the mass age. [107] But it was also a lament for the politics of the 1860s: no longer a secular religion, it had merely become the means of social reconstruction, while the economic machine now seemed to exalt pliability and sociability over excellence and integrity. [108]

It is possible to see *National Life and Character* as the morbid product of political rejection and ill health (Pearson was ill with tuberculosis when he wrote it and died not long after it was published), [109] or as a new departure in political theorizing. In the main, however, Pearson's friends and contemporaries saw it as a sort of burial office for the 'Evangelical politics' they had believed in. Bryce wrote to him: 'The epitome has interested me extremely. Gloomy your forecast certainly is: but I know of nothing in Europe and not very much even in America to make me think it too despondent.' [110] Somewhat more detached, Henry Sidgwick criticized the methodology of Pearson's forecasting. Given that he was extrapolating from existing trends, what he said made sense; but could the future combination of such trends not produce a catalytic situation out of which some dominant economic or technological factor, hitherto unpredicted, might emerge? Could the impact of the railway have been predicted by extrapolating the technological, social and economic trends present in 1820? [111] Apart from this, he thought it 'the most impressive book of a prophetic nature which has appeared in England for many years'. [112] Pearson found that few of his contemporaries disagreed with him: only the Christian Socialists and to a lesser extent the Positivists, who felt they could still re-animate religion as the implement of elite rule. [113] Never elitist, academic liberals lacked that consolation, while their political weakness and intellectual rigidity inhibited them from using Pearson's perceptions to frame a social philosophy which would avoid the situation he forecast. Henceforth their politics involved excluding the unacceptable, not combating it.

The rise of the new trade unionism and the socialist movement brought them no comfort. In 1888 Henry Sidgwick, who had been reading the proofs of *The American Commonwealth*, wrote to Bryce: [114]

No sign of class hatred. But the formidable class hatred of the present and future is that between labour and capital: and is not the development of boycotting in the United States and the action of the Knights of Labour something of a sign of this?

Without disagreeing with what is said on p. 882, I should myself lay more stress on the general movement towards Socialism in the modern civilised community.

His own attitude was ambivalent; Bryce, Dicey and most of their friends were hostile. Few of them would have disagreed with Brodrick in finding socialism 'the most pernicious, while it is the most demonstratively false, delusion of our age': its redistributive programme aimed like a lance at the heart of sound economics. [115] (see p. 164) And trade unionism, its ally, had changed for the worse since the 1860s, promising now 'government of the people, by a class for a class'. [116] Even its strongest partisans, the Positivists, now turned against it. [117]

In this, however, they were not followed by the younger men, the generation who grew up along with Ruskin's lectures and Toynbee Hall. They were no less concerned about the alienation of the working class, about the urban violence to which commercial depression gave rise, but their more flexible politics and economics sanctioned attempts at 'socialization' through trade unions and political organizations. Both the neo-classical economist, whose concepts of 'economic chivalry' integrated trade unionism with economic rationality, and the idealist, who believed that politics could only be established around the primacy of catering for the needs of the human personality, could combine in causes like the dock strike of 1889 and the unionization of agricultural labour in the 1890s. [118] Idealism in particular, in the hands of Edward Caird, R.B.Haldane, Arthur Acland and Sidney Ball, explicitly reversed the priority the liberals of the 1860s had given to the 'scientific' functioning of classical economics. [119] The consequences, to the older men, were ominous.

In particular, it enabled the Church to counter-attack. John Morley wrote in 1891: [120]

T.Fowler of Corpus and I dined at Club together. Very interesting talk about the current drift of things in Oxford. How the Anglicans were trying to capture science, criticism, philosophy, and the new social spirit. Told me about *Lux Mundi* – the famous attempt to reconcile Anglicanism *alias* Catholicism with the most advanced Biblical criticism ... Fowler assigns the beginning of this movement to T.H.Green, and the revival in his teaching of Transcendental Philosophy.

To his contemporaries the catholic revival within the Church of England both threatened to destroy the true spirit of intellectual inquiry at the universities and, through 'the sinister alliance of Ritualism and Socialism', to foster political delusions among the working class. When academics like Mark Pattison, George Brodrick and Lewis Campbell talked, in the last two decades of the century, about the anti-liberal reaction at the universities, this was what they meant. [121]

V

As in the 1860s, however, the role of ideology still depended on the situation of the group. However pessimistic they were in theory, they had in the main achieved professional success and this mitigated their political disappointments. Honorary degrees and fellowships, knighthoods, chairs and decorations; more poignantly, creditable obituaries: these set the seal of recognition on their efforts. For academics in late middle age, installed in college or married and settled in London, the 1890s was a good time to live in. The men who had in the 1850s roamed over Europe on foot and by the first steamers and trains now found the world opened to them in the heyday of the liner and the Pullman car: technology in a sense renewed their youth. They could climb in new and remote mountain ranges; they could overcome pessimism about domestic politics by preoccupying themselves with the politics of other countries. Bryce remained a cheerful American radical, Dicey a liberal French Republican, devoted to the vindication of Dreyfus and the destruction of clericalism. [122] Dicey, however, was still capable of disturbing his own certainties with flashes of insight. Supposing, he would ask himself from time to time, the Irish were right to be nationalist, the poor were right to be socialist, just as he, in his privileged situation, thought it right to protect the *status quo*? [123] He found it difficult to credit his opponents with mass delusions, yet he did not want to admit that his own position might be a false one. He continued to agitate for his causes in a manner which reflected the conviction of the 1860s, but this merely emphasized the fact that others had the future.

However, politics did not follow in the wake of the ideological developments that they feared. Tory policy at the turn of the century rallied them again in defence of the old ideals of national liberty and freedom of trade. On his deathbed Henry Sidgwick condemned the Boer War: [124]

Our peculiar national stupidity has never been so strongly shown as in the manner in which we have broken the policy of the century and dropt our traditional sympathy with nationalities struggling for freedom – without apparently being aware of this violent change of attitude.

His sentiments were echoed by other unionists, Leslie Stephen, Leonard Courtney, Frederic Maitland and Goldwin Smith. [125] James Bryce wrote to Smith, mingling denunciation with hope: [126]

You would be astonished, remembering the England of forty years ago, to see the England of today, intoxicated with militarism, blinded by arrogance, indifferent to truth and justice. This is what England seems to be: yet is not really, for a noisy mob has succeeded for a time in frightening most of the sober sense of the nation into silence, some from timidity, some because they think they must wait for Philip to sleep off the fumes of victory before they address his reason. And in excuse for the mob even it must be pleaded that the press has kept them so ignorant of the true facts of the case that their errors are half excusable. We have had a formidable lesson of the power which the press and financial groups can exert.

Dislike of imperialism and imperialists – 'England has been ruled by bad men before now, but never before by a cad,' Goldwin Smith wrote of Chamberlain [127] led to the resolving of old quarrels. Smith wrote to Bryce that if Home Rule was the only way of stopping Jingoism he would support it. [128] Eventually he did, at least to the extent of supporting the Liberals in 1906. [129] Courtney returned, and went to the Lords as a Liberal peer in 1906. Lyulph Stanley, Sir Frederick Pollock and Maitland reconciled themselves. [130] The move back was swollen by the flirtation of the Conservatives and

Unionists with Chamberlain's protectionist Programme. [131] By 1906, of the academics who still participated in politics, the Unionists were now a dwindling minority. Dicey could still work himself up into legalistic tantrums about the Liberals' defiance of the law of the land, [132] but he was increasingly conscious that his opinion counted for little among the politicians. [133]

The Liberal government did not, however, satisfy them for long; On the strength of his vast range of information about foreign politics, and a firm friendship with Henry Campbell-Bannerman, Bryce had hoped for the Foreign Office, and was bitterly disappointed when the most he could expect turned out to be the troublesome Irish Secretaryship. [134] Fitzmaurice, another of the little band which survived from the 1860s, returned as Under-Secretary for Foreign Affairs; he had wanted Education and a seat in the Cabinet. [135] Their presence in the government was only an acknowledgement of long and faithful service: unlike Morley, who went to the India Office, they had no pull in the higher echelons of politics, now dominated by men up to twenty years their junior. Bryce, 'too gentle and scholarly', was not a success in Ireland, and threatened to become a menace in the cabinet: [136]

He knew every place, how to get there, how long it took you to get to the railhead, and how long to cross the desert by camel, and the rest of it.

The chance of sending him to Washington as Ambassador in 1907 was obviously a heaven-sent opportunity to promote out of the way a decent, hard-working, kindly and pedantic old man who was patently unfitted for high politics. As the Permanent Under-Secretary, Sir Charles Hardinge, wrote at the time: [137]

I realised that he would be greatly appreciated in America as knowing more of the history and constitution of America than most Americans. He had also the quality of liking to make long and rather dull speeches on commonplace subjects which I knew to be a trait that would be popular with the American masses. He had also a charming and agreeable wife.

On 13 February 1907 Bryce sailed for the United States in the *Oceanic*, to remain there for five years on a mission which consolidated the Anglo–American entente. A personality with whom the American public could identify was needed as British envoy at this stage, rather than a professional diplomat and, as Hardinge expected, Bryce fulfilled this role with great success. [138] He enjoyed being in America; he did not regret leaving British politics. He had little sympathy with what the government had done while he was in office, and even less for what it was about to do. [139] The crystal doctrines of his youth were being disregarded. But what else could be expected from the coalition the Liberal party had now become? The Trades Disputes Act, the granting of Old Age Pensions, the People's Budget and the Parliament Act, all were gloomily analysed in the letters he exchanged with Dicey, Goldwin Smith and his old American friends: [140]

I am not hopeful about the present state of our country. The time-honoured constitutional system seems in danger of breaking down under the strain of three or four parties instead of two parties only. The emergence of industrial and labour issues, which are class issues and pocket issues, has given a new and disagreeable turn to democracy. The reckless extravagance of popular governments is a feature which none of the older school of hostile critics seems to have expected.

But there were fewer friends to write to. The generation of the 1860s was now dwindling rapidly. Of the twenty-two writers of the reform essays fourteen survived in 1900, twelve in 1906, only six in 1914. Of the seventy-eight Oxford men at the Freemasons' Tavern in 1864, only nineteen remained in that year. Henry Sidgwick had died of cancer late in 1900; George Brodrick died in 1903. Leslie Stephen died, also of cancer, in 1904; Grant Duff and Roundell in 1906; Lushington, Maitland and Horace Davey in 1907; Caird in 1908; Goldwin Smith in 1910. 'No new light seemed to break on him,' wrote Bryce of Smith: 'Everything was judged by the old doctrines and condemned by the old phrases.' [141] The same could, however, be said of Bryce and the handful of his friends – Jackson, Dicey, Harrison, Trevelyan and Young – who remained. But old doctrines and phrases still had a part to play.

When war broke out in August 1914, it was not immediately apparent how the surviving academics would respond. Morley resigned from the Cabinet over the decision to assist France; Bryce was sympathetic to his position. In September he could still view the conflict with detachment, mingled with some regret, [142] but in that month he was asked by the British government to chair a committee – three of whose six members were close personal friends – to inquire into allegations of German atrocities in Belgium. [143] The role of the Bryce Committee remains controversial: unquestionably it achieved what the government desired, in the picture it drew of a small country subjected to rapine, slaughter and vandalism by its invader. Among neutral and neutralist opinion it served the allied cause well, particularly in view of its chairman's reputation for high-minded dissent on foreign policy and his considerable popularity in the largest neutral country, the United States. But the atrocities, though exaggerated by the allied propaganda machine, were not all invented. Remembering the savagery of the latter part of the Franco–Prussian war, when the French people had risen against them, the Germans had responded with ferocity to nominal Belgian provocation, hoping to cow the population into acquiescence. [144] To a man who still remembered with affection the Germany of the 1860s and had rejoiced in its victory in 1870, the revelations were appalling. In 1916 Bryce had to intersperse his morose commentary on the extinction of liberalism in Britain with saving clauses like 'Better anything than the destruction of morality which has come in Germany'. [145] Inevitably his contemporaries adopted his views: Henry Jackson, whom Sir George Otto Trevelyan found still a Germanophile 'of the old school' in September 1914, [146] became a fire-eating warrior, and had Bertrand Russell removed from Trinity for his pacifist views. [147] Frederic Harrison, who admittedly had been advocating rearmament in 1909 on his usual pro-French and anti-German platform, rejoiced that the war had confirmed his antipathies. [148] Dicey applauded the rekindling of a national and patriotic spirit. [149]

Behind this enthusiasm lay not merely anger at German barbarism or any delight in war itself, but the sense that party and class differences had been subordinated to the claims of the nation. As with Italy and the North in their respective struggles, a unity, a commonwealth, seemed to have been achieved. [150] But this euphoria was short-lived, and gave way in its turn to an even deeper pessimism: the war implied state intervention in the economy to a greater extent than even Pearson had feared in the 1890s; [151] at home organized labour grew in strength and aggressiveness; [152] abroad the Communists seized power in Russia: [153] in each case the old men interpreted these disturbing developments with antique vigour. Could not undergraduates from Jesus College be sent to South Wales to talk the miners out of a strike? [154] Was Goldwin Smith not right after all in his approval of the Russian pogroms, since so many Jews seemed to be leading the Communists? [155] Could the rise of the Labour party have been prevented if the second Reform Bill had not been enacted in 1867? [156]

Their isolation increased, not least from younger men from the same environment. An exception proves the rule: stern old-fashioned individualist though he was, Leonard Courtney resolutely opposed the war in concert with socialists in the Union of Democratic Control and attempted to get justice for conscientious objectors. When he died in 1918, Charles Roden Buxton, a young former Liberal M.P. and a relative of one of the Liberal M.P.s who had supported the abolition of Tests in 1864, wrote to his widow: [157]

What you say about Lord Courtney's feeling of indebtedness to the younger men is very striking. It gives one something new and rather surprising to think about. I have an instinctive respect for the old, I think, and the attitude taken up in this war by old men whom one had believed in – e.g. Lord Bryce – was to me something shocking. I should have become quite outrageously cynical about old age, if it had not been for Lord Courtney. There were one or two others, of course – a very few – but he was head and shoulders above them.

Shortly afterwards Buxton joined the Labour party. Sir George Otto Trevelyan suffered the defection of two of his sons. Yates Thompson found him 'naturally somewhat silent about Charles and Robert – as to whom no sign of a quarrel, but evidently a certain sadness'. [158] Sir George Young's eldest son, who had been one of Bryce's aides at Washington, went over too. [159]

VI

Mr Dear Dicey,

Have you had, among the youth who come to see you, any of the young Oxford Socialists, Christian or Pagan? Nothing strikes me more than the way in which a wave of opinion seems to sweep over the youth of a country, just like Influenza. Though I cannot catch it, I am trying hard to understand it, and even to sympathise; but I am astonished that their zeal for the end – viz. the bettering of the condition of the mass, seems to make them ignore the difficulties which the means present. They seem to think human nature perfectible, just as the men of 1789 did. Perhaps it is well that mankind should never shake itself free from this illusion. The same notion seems to be at the bottom of this passion for women's suffrage. People fancy that the more voters you have, the more wisdom you have at the service of the state. Did we think so when we wrote the essays on Reform just fifty years ago?

This is Bryce [160] at his best, with his pessimism punctuated by shafts of self-awareness – even although the self of which he was aware lived in the England of Gladstone and Lowe. Every so often, after he, Jackson, Trevelyan and Dicey had indulged themselves with fears about the menace of the trade unions [161] and the revolutionary nature of the Labour Party [162] – a morbid pessimism excusable enough in the tiny handful of survivors of a once powerful and confident, and still cohesive, group – the light of liberal rationality would break in and they would agree that things could be worse. [163] In the case of Bryce, when he managed to tear himself away from his contemporaries, the transformation was quite dramatic. Arnold J.Toynbee and H.A.L.Fisher found an enthusiastic and hard-working Liberal, eager to mitigate the severities of Versailles, help with propagandist work for the League of Nations, chair a conference on the future of the House of Lords, and, as a farewell to that House, move, with John Morley, the motion which ratified the treaty setting up the Irish Free State. [164]

That was in December 1921. In January Bryce went on holiday to Sidmouth, an active holiday spent walking and preparing his articles on foreign travel for reprinting. On 22 January he was found dead in bed; he had died, painlessly of heart failure, in his sleep. [165] Two months later Dicey died at Oxford. Trevelyan survived for five years longer, in seclusion at Wallington. [166]

Sir George Young was the last to go. An active county councillor in Berkshire until earlier the same year, he died at the age of ninety-three on 4 July 1930, at his home, Formosa Fishery at Cookham, whence his Evangelical grandfather had gone to hunt down slavers and establish Sierra Leone. The concluding sentences of *The Times* obituary could serve as an epitaph to his generation: [167]

Tall, bearded, and of impressive appearance; of a somewhat formidable manner, tempered by humour and an old world courtesy; liberal and just in sentiment, but remote from the currents and changing interest of ordinary life, and yet none the less absolute in his judgements upon them; and retaining into extreme age all his youthful vigour of outlook, his powers of dramatic reading and speaking, of infallible quotation and opinion, and an inflexible self-control and individualism, he lived to be venerated, even by those who did not know the gentleness and generosity of character which his discipline of life concealed, as a last and distinguished representative of a bygone tradition.

And ye, red-lipped and smooth-browed; list, Gentlemen;
Much there is waits you we have missed;
Much lore we leave you worth the knowing,
Much, much has lain outside our ken:
Nay, rush not: time serves: we are going, Gentlemen.

Thomas Hardy 'An Ancient to Ancients'

APPENDICES

Appendix 1

The table opposite shows Matriculations at Oxford and Cambridge, 1800-1890

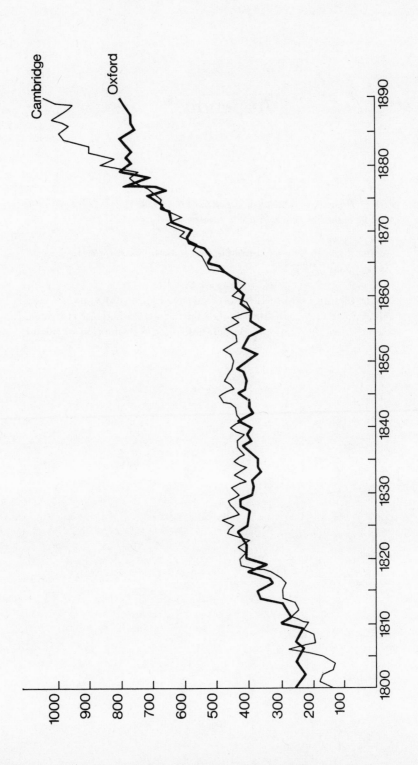

Appendix 2

List of Persons whose Names are Recorded as having been Present at the Meeting in the Freemasons' Tavern, London, on 10 June 1864

(Appendix C in Lewis Campbell, *The Nationalisation of the Old English Universities*, pp. 284-93.)

I print the original list. It is accurate save for one entry, no. 63, who was not the G. W. Hastings noted, but George Woodyatt Hastings, Secretary of the National Association for the Promotion of Social Science.

Names as Written Down	Names in Full	In 1864	Subsequently
1. *Mr Humphreys*	Arthur Charles Humphreys-Owen	B.A. of Trinity Coll., Cambridge	Barrister; M.P. for Mont-gomeryshire
2. *Mr Jebb*	Richard Claverhouse Jebb	Fellow and Lecturer Trinity Coll. Cambridge	Knight; Litt. D.; Regius Professor of Greek, Cambridge; M.P. for Cambridge University.
3. *George Rolleston*	George Rolleston	Professor of Physiology, Oxford	Died 1881.
4. *Philip Lutley Sclater*	Philip Lutley Sclater	Fell. of Corpus Christi Coll., Oxford	Secretary of Zoological Society, London.
5. *Arthur Milman*	Arthur Milman	M.A. of Christ Church, Oxford	Registrar of the University of London; Biographer of Dean Milman.
6. *Francis Otter*	Francis Otter	Fellow of C.C.C., Oxford	M.P. for South division of Lincolnshire. Died 1895.
7. *W.H. Flower*	William Henry Flower	Conservator of Museum of Royal College of Surgeons	K.C.B.; F.R.S.; Director of Natural History Museum, South Kensington. Died 1899.
8. *John Westlake*	John Westlake	Late Fellow of Trinity Coll., Cambridge	Q.C.; Professor of International Law, Cambridge; M.P. for Romford.
9. *James Martineau*	James Martineau	Prof. of Philosophy, Manchester New College	Principal of Manchester New College. Died 1900.
10. *B.C. Brodie*	Benjamin Collins Brodie	Baronet; B.A. of Balliol College, Oxford	Waynflete Professor of Chemistry, Oxford. Died 1880.

Names as Written Down	Names in Full	In 1864	Subsequently
11. *Albert Rutson*	Albert Osliff Rutson	Fellow of Magdalen Coll., Oxford; Barrister	Died 1890.
12. *Vincent Scully*	Vincent Scully	Ch. Ch., Oxford	
13. *Edward Poste*	Edward Poste	Fellow of Oriel College, Oxford; Barrister	Director of Civil Service Examinations.
14. *A.P. Whateley*	Arthur Pepys Whateley	M.A. of Ch. Ch., Oxford	Barrister and Journalist.
15. *George Young*	Sir George Young, Bart	Fellow of Trinity Coll., Cambridge	Charity Commissioner.
16. *W. Morrison*, M.P.	Walter Morrison	M.A. of Balliol College, Oxford; M.P. for Plymouth	M.P. for Skipton, Yorks.
17. *Charles Bowen*	Charles Synge Bowen	Fellow of Balliol College, Oxford.	Lord Justice of Appeal. Died 1894.
18. *H.S. Cunningham*	Henry Stewart Cunningham	M.A. of Trinity College, Oxford; and Barrister	K.C.I.E.; Judge of the High Court of Bengal; Author.
19. *L. Tollemache*	The Hon. Lionel Tollemache	M.A. of Balliol College, Oxford	Author.
20. *E. Chandos Leigh*	Hon. Edward Chandos Leigh	Fellow of Magdalen Coll., Oxford	Recorder of Nottingham.
21. *Horace Davey*	Horace Davey	Fellow of University Coll., Oxford; Barrister	Lord of Appeal; M.P. for Stockton.
22. *G.E. Thorley*	George Earlam Thorley	Fellow of Wadham Coll., Oxford	Warden of Wadham.
23. *T.G. Vyvyan*	Thomas Grenfell Vyvyan	Fellow and Dean, Caius College, Cambridge	Mathematical Master at Charterhouse; Author.

24. *Dr William Ogle*	William Ogle	Fellow of C.C.C., Oxford; M.D.	Superintendent of Statistics, Somerset House.
25. *Sir James Kay Shuttleworth*	James Kay Shuttleworth	Bart; High Sheriff of Lancashire.	Hon. D.C.L. Oxford. Died 1867.
26. *Mr Leatham*, M.P.	William Henry Leatham	M.P. for Wakefield	M.P. for South West Riding, Yorkshire. Died 1889.
27. *E. Caird*	Edward Caird	Fellow and Tutor, Merton Coll., Oxford	Professor of Moral Philosophy, Glasgow: Master of Balliol since 1893.
28. *W. Berkley*	William Berkley	Fellow of Trinity College, Oxford	Vicar of Navestock, Essex. Died 1906.
29. *T.H. Green*	Thomas Hill Green	Fellow of Balliol College, Oxford	Whytes's Professor of Moral Philosophy, Oxford. Died 1882.
30. *J. Bryce*	James Bryce	Fellow of Oriel College, Oxford	Right Hon.; M.P. for Aberdeen: Historian.
31. *Edward A. Freeman*	Edward Augustus Freeman	Late Fellow of Trinity College, Oxford	Regius Professor of Modern History, Oxford. Died 1892.
32. *William Stebbing*	William Stebbing	Fellow of Worcester Coll., Oxford	Assistant Editor of *The Times*; Author.
33. *Godfrey Lushington*	Godfrey Lushington	Late Fellow of All Souls Coll., Oxford	K.C.B.; G.C.M.G.; Permanent Under Secretary, Home Office.
34. *P. Cumin*	Patrick Cumin	M.A. of Balliol College, Oxford	Secretary of the Educational Department of the Privy Council. Died 1890.
35. *A.V. Dicey*	Albert Venn Dicey	Fellow of Trinity College, Oxford	Vinerian Professor of Law, Oxford.

Names as Written Down	Names in Full	In 1864	Subsequently
36. *T.E. Holland*	Thomas Erskine Holland	Fellow of Exeter Coll., Oxford; Chichele Prof. of International Law	Fellow of All Souls College, Oxford.
37. * *R. Ellis*	Robinson Ellis	Fellow of Trinity College	Corpus Professor of Latin, Oxford.
38. * *C. Cholmeley Puller*	C. Cholmeley Puller	M.A. of Balliol College, Oxford	Student of Lincoln's Inn.
39. *Leslie Stephen*	Leslie Stephen	Fellow of Trinity Hall, Camb.	Editor of *Dictionary of National Biography;* and Author of various works.
40. * *J.L. Strachan Davidson*	J.L. Strachan Davidson	M.A. of Balliol College, Oxford	Fellow, Classical Tutor, and Vice-Master, Balliol College
41. *Chas W. Goodwin*	Charles Wycliffe Goodwin	Fellow of St Catherine's Coll., Cambridge	Egyptologist: writer in *Essays and Reviews;* Judge in Shanghai and Yokohama. Died 1878.
42. *Charles H. Robarts*	Charles H. Robarts	Fellow of All Souls Coll., Oxford	Barrister; Remembrancer of the City of London.
43. *Kenelm E. Digby*	Kenelm Edward Digby	Fellow of C.C.C., Oxford	K.C.B.; Bencher of Lincoln's Inn; Permanent Under Sec., Home Office.
44. *J.L. Warren*	J. Locksdale Warren	B.A. of Trinity College, Cambridge	Barrister.
45. *Strangford*	Percy William Frederick Smythe, 8th Viscount Strangford	M.A. of Merton College, Oxford	Died 1869.
46. *H. Latham*	Rev. Henry Latham	Fellow and Tutor, Trin. Hall, Camb.	Master of Trinity Hall.

47. *C. H. Daniell*	Charles Henry Olive Daniell	Fellow of Worcester Coll., Oxford	Tutor and Vice-Provost of Worcester.
48. *Chas S. Miall*	Charles S. Miall	Nonconformist	Founder of Co-operative Societies. Died 1892.
49. *Mr Vansittart Neale*	Edward Vansittart Neale	M.A. of Oriel College, Oxford; Barrister	
50. *Bishop of Natal*	John William Colenso	Bishop of Natal; Author of book on *The Pentateuch.*	Died 1883.
51. *Professor Huxley*	Thomas Henry Huxley	F.R.S.; Prof. of Natural History, Royal School of Mines	P.R.S.: Privy Councillor; Author. Died 1895.
52. *William Ewart,* M.P.	William Ewart	M.P. for Dumfries Boroughs	Died 1869.
53. *B. Gray, Trin. Coll., Camb.*	Benjamin Gray	Late Fellow of Trinity Coll., Cambridge; Barrister	
54. *Ch. Neate,* M.P.	Charles Neate	Fellow of Oriel College, Oxford; M.P. for Oxford	Died 1879.
55. *E. P. Bouverie,* M.P.	Hon. Edward Pleydell Bouverie	M.A. of Trinity Coll., Cambridge; M.P. for Kilmarnock	Member of the Ecclesiastical Commission. Died 1889.
56. *Mr Cartwright*			
57. *H. Mansfield*	Horatio Mansfield	Late Fellow of Trinity College, Cambridge; Barrister	Stipendiary Magistrate for Liverpool. Died 1887.
58. *Will. Geo. Clark*	William George Clark	Fellow of Trinity Coll., Cambridge, and Public Orator	Part Editor of *Cambridge Shakespeare.* Died 1878.
59. *Arthur G. Watson*	Arthur George Watson	Fellow of All Souls Coll., Oxford; Assistant Master at Harrow	Retired.

251

Names as Written Down	Names in Full	In 1864	Subsequently
60. *E.C. Wickham*	Edward Charles Wickham	Fellow of New College, Oxford	Head Master Wellington College, 1873-93; Dean of Lincoln.
61. *Wm A. Fearon*	William Andrew Fearon	Fellow and Tutor of New Coll., Oxford	Head Master of Winchester College.
62. * *W.H. Fremantle*	Hon. William Henry Fremantle	Fellow of All Souls Coll., Oxford; Chaplain to the Bishop of London	Dean of Ripon.
63. *G.W. Hastings*	Graham W. Hastings	M.A. of Worcester Coll., Oxford; Barrister	
64. *John James Taylor*	John James Taylor	Professor of Ecclesiastical History in Manchester New College	Q.C.; Bencher of Lincoln's Inn.
65. *John Grey*	John Grey		Died 1869.
66. *Charles E.C.B. Appleton*	Charles E.C.B. Appleton	Fellow of St John's Coll., Oxford	First Editor of the *Academy* Newspaper; D.C.L. Oxford. Died 1879.
67. *Thomas Fowler*	Thomas Fowler	Fellow of Lincoln College, Oxford	Professor of Logic; President of Corpus Christi College, Oxford; Vice-Chancellor of Oxford University.
68. *C. Fortescue*, M.P.	Chichester Samuel Fortescue	M.A. of Ch. Ch., Oxford; M.P. for Louth	Created Lord Carlingford 1872: 2nd Lord Clermont 1887. Died 1898.
69. * *R.S. Wright*	Robert Samuel Wright	Fellow of Oriel College, Oxford	Sir R.S. Wright; Judge of the King's Bench.

252

70. *J. J. Sylvester*	James Joseph Sylvester	Professor of Mathematics, Virginia University, U.S.A.	Prof. of Mathematics, Johns Hopkins University; and Savilian Professor of Geometry, Oxford. Died 1897.
71. *John Bright*, M.P.	John Bright	M.P. for Birmingham	Right Hon.; President of the Board of Trade, etc. Died 1889.
72. *Rev. Prof. Wilson, C.C.C., Oxford*	John Matthias Wilson	Fellow of C.C.C., Oxford; Whyte's Professor of Moral Philosophy	President of C.C.C., Oxford. Died 1881.
73. *E. Charles*	Ebenezer Charles	Barrister	Died 1867.
74. * *H. Jenkyns*	Henry Jenkyns	M. A. of Balliol College, Oxford; Barrister	K. C. B.; Parliamentary Counsel to the Treasury. Died 1899.
75. *Thos Hughes*	Thomas Hughes	B.A. of Oriel College, Oxford; Barrister	Q.C.; County Court Judge: Author of *Tom Brown's Schooldays*, etc. Died 1896.
76. *Prof. Fawcett*	Henry Fawcett	Fellow of Trinity Hall, Camb.; Professor of Political Economy	M. P. for Brighton; Right Hon.; Postmaster-General. Died 1884.
77. *James E. Thorold Rogers, Prof. of Political Economy, Oxford*	James E. Thorold Rogers	M. A. of Magdalen Coll., Oxford Professor of Political Economy	M.P. for Southwark. Died 1890.
78. *E.S. Beesly*	Edward Spenser Beesly	M. A. of Wadham Coll., Oxford; Prof. of History, University Coll., Lond.	Author.
79. *Archer A. Clive*	Archer Antony Clive	Fellow of Lincoln College, Oxford	Barrister. Died 1877.
80. * *Henry J.S. Smith*	Henry John Stephen Smith	Fellow of Balliol Coll., Oxford; and Savilian Professor of Geometry	Vice-President of C. C. C. Oxford; Keeper of the University Museum; Mathematician. Died 1883.

Names as Written Down	Names in Full	In 1864	Subsequently
81. *W. Pollard-Urquhart,* M.P.	William Pollard-Urquhart	M.A. of Trinity College, Camb.; M.P. for Westminster	Author. Died 1871.
82. * *R.E. Bartlett*	Robert Edward Bartlett	Late Fellow of Trinity Coll., Oxford; Curate of St Mark's, Whitechapel	Vicar of Pershore; Bampton Lecturer.
83. *J.C.Mathew*	James Charles Mathew	Graduate of Trinity Coll., Dublin; Barrister	Judge of the King's Bench.
84. *J. Stirling*	James Stirling	M.A. of Trinity Coll., Cambridge; Barrister	Lord Justice of Appeal.
85. *H.M.Jackson*	Henry Mather Jackson	M.A. of Trinity College, Oxford; Barrister	Baronet; Q.C.; M.P.; appointed Judge and died 1881.
86. *W.B. Church*	W.B. Church	M.A. of Trinity Coll., Cambridge	
87. *A. Bailey*	Alfred Bailey	M.A. of Ch. Ch., Oxford; Barrister	
88. *Geo. Wood*	George Wood		
89. *John Rigby*	John Rigby	Fellow of Trinity College, Camb.; Barrister	Attorney-General and Lord Justice of Appeal.
90. * *Rev. W. Rogers*	William Rogers	M.A. of Balliol College, Oxford; Rector of St Botolph's, Bishops-gate; Prebendary of St. Paul's	Educationist. Died 1896.
91. * *The Dean of Westminster*	Arthur Penrhyn Stanley	Dean of Westminster, and Honorary Chaplain to the Queen	Author. Died 1881.
92. * *M.E. Grant Duff*	Mountstuart Elphinstone Grant Duff	M.A. of Balliol, Oxford; Barrister; M.P. for Elgin Boroughs	G.C.M.G.; Governor of Madras: Author.

254

93. *Rev. J. R. Byrne*	J. R. Byrne	M.A. of University College, Oxford	H.M. Inspector of Schools.
94. *Rev. F. D. Maurice*	Frederick Denison Maurice	M.A. of Exeter College, Oxford, formerly at Cambridge; Incumbent of St Peter's, Vere Street	Professor of Moral Philosophy, Camb.: Author. Died 1872.
95. *George C. Brodrick*	Hon. George Charles Brodrick	Fellow of Merton, Oxford; Barrister	Warden of Merton.
96. *Rev. G. D. Boyle*	George David Boyle	Incumbent of St Michael's, Handsworth	Dean of Salisbury.
97. *Alfred Wills*	Alfred Wills	B.A. of Lond. University; Barrister	Judge of the King's Bench Division.
98. *Henry Reeve*	Henry Reeve	Barrister: Editor of the *Edinburgh Review.*	C.B., D.C.L. Died 1895.
99. *M. S. Grosvenor Woods*	M. S. Grosvenor Woods	Fellow of Trinity College, Camb.	Barrister and Q.C.
100. *Montague H. Cookson*	Montague Hughes Cookson	Fellow of St John's Coll., Oxford; Barrister	M. H. Crackenthorpe. Q.C., Bencher of Lincoln's Inn.
101. *Charles E. Maurice*	Charles Edmund Maurice	B.A. of Ch. Ch., Oxford	Barrister.
102. *R. Bosworth Smith*	Reginald Bosworth Smith	Fellow Trinity College, Oxford	Assistant Master of Harrow School; Author.
103. *Ingram Bywater*	Ingram Bywater	Fellow of Exeter College, Oxford	Regius Professor of Greek, Oxford.
104. *Leonard Courtney*	Leonard Henry Courtney	Fellow of St John's Coll., Cambridge; Barrister	Right Hon.; M.P. for Bodmin.
105. *Charles C. Clifford*, M.P.	Charles Cavendish Clifford	Fellow of All Souls Coll., Oxford; Barrister; M.P. for Isle of Wight	Baronet. Died 1895.
106. *Frederic Harrison*	Frederic Harrison	Fellow of Wadham Coll., Oxford; Barrister	Honorary Fellow of Wadham; Author.

No.		Name	Position	Notes
107.	*W. L. Newman	William Lambert Newman	Fellow of Balliol College, Oxford	Reader in Ancient History, Oxford; Editor of Aristotle's Politics.
108.	*H. Merivale	Herman Charles Merivale	B.A. of Balliol College, Oxford; Barrister	Author and Playwright.
109.	*J. A. Symonds	John Addington Symonds	Fellow of Magdalen Coll., Oxford	Author. Died 1893.
110.	Sir Edward Strachey	Sir Edward Strachey, Bart	High Sheriff of Somerset	Author.
111.	*R. B. D. Morier	Richard Barnet David Morier	B.A. of Balliol College, Oxford; Diplomatic Service	G.C.B., G.C.M.G., Ambassador to St Petersburg. Died 1893.
112.	*B. Jowett	Benjamin Jowett	Regius Professor of Greek, Oxford	Master of Balliol. Died 1893.
113.	*A. Vernon Harcourt	Augustus George Vernon Harcourt	Senior Student of Ch. Ch., Oxford	Tutor of Ch. Ch. and Lee's Reader in Chemistry, Oxford.
114.	Jas. Cotter Morison	James Angustus Cotter Morison	M.A. cᵒ Lincoln Coll., Oxford; Student of Lincoln's Inn	Author of *Life of St Bernard*; one of the founders of *Fortnightly Review*. Died 1888.
115.	W. M. Kerr			
116.	*E. H. Bradby	Edward Henry Bradby	Late Fell. of Balliol, Oxford; Assistant Master in Harrow School	Head Master of Haileybury; Canon of St Albans. Died 1893.
117.	E. Miall	Edward Miall	M.P. for Rochdale	
118.	*C. S. Roundell	Charles Savile Roundell	Fellow of Merton Coll., Oxford; Barrister	Private Secretary to Earl Spencer, M.P. for Grantham.
119.	J. Carvell Williams	John Carvell Williams	Secretary to Liberation Society	Chairman of Liberation Society; M.P. for Nottingham.
120.	George J. Goschen	George Joachim Goschen	M.P. for City of London	Right Hon. Viscount Goschen.
121.	Goldwin Smith	Goldwin Smith	Fellow of University Coll., Oxford; Regius Prof. of Modern History	Professor of History at Cornell University; Author.

*indicates a member of Balliol College

Appendix 3

Religious Tests in Force at Oxford and Cambridge, 1866

(From G.C.Brodrick, *Report of Speeches on the Abolition of Tests*, pp. 3-5.)

The Tests now in force at Oxford and Cambridge are of two classes. I. University Tests; and II. College Tests.

I. At Oxford, every candidate for a M.A. degree is required to subscribe the XXXIX Articles, and the three Articles of the 36th Canon, and no person who has not submitted to this Test can be a member of the governing bodies (Congregation and Convocation), or receive a license to open a private hall, or become eligible for most academical offices. No subscription has been exacted on taking the Bachelor's degree since the Oxford Reform Act of 1854, but "offices" theretofore always held by Churchmen, and by virtue of that degree, were expressly excepted from the operation of the Act. Candidates for such offices, which include certain Professorships, are still compelled to sign the XXXIX Articles.

At Cambridge, no religious Test is imposed upon candidates for the M.A. or any lower degree, but no one can be a member of the governing body (the Senate), or hold any office always held by a Churchman by virtue of such degrees, without declaring that he is a *bona fide* member of the Church of England. He may, however, obtain a license to open a private hall ('hostel'), unless procluded by regulations to be made by the University itself.

Both at Oxford and Cambridge all Professors are required by the Act of Uniformity to make a declaration of conformity to the Liturgy of the Church of England, upon their admission.

II. The same declaration must be made by all Heads and Fellows of Colleges, at both Universities, under the provisions of the same Act. This is the only legislative enactment against the enjoyment of College endowments by Nonconformists; but, in many Colleges, the Fellows are obliged, under the College Statutes, to proceed to the M.A. degree within a certain time, on pain of forfeiting their Fellowships.

No person is compelled at either University to sign the Articles, or to make any profession of faith, on matriculation. There is no legal obstacle, therefore, to the admission of Dissenters, *as students*, at either. Under the present system, however, every student must be a member of some College or Hall. It is entirely within the discretion of the College authorities, in the one case, and of the Head in the other, to enforce or to dispense with attendance on chapel-services and divinity lectures, and otherwise to prescribe the terms upon which they may consent to receive Dissenting undergraduates.

The objects of Mr Coleridge's Bill for the Abolition of Tests in connection with Academical Degrees and Offices in the University of Oxford, may be shortly stated as follows:-

1. The Abolition of all Religious Tests now attached to any Non-Theological Degree in the University of Oxford.

2. The admission of all persons duly qualified by Degrees so enfranchised to Congregation and Convocation, that is to say, to the governing bodies of the University.

3. The Abolition of all Theological Tests as (directly or indirectly) qualifications for Non-Theological Professorships.

The object of Mr Bouverie's Bill to repeal certain portions of the Act of Uniformity relating to the Declaration made by Fellows of Colleges is –

> To abolish the Declaration now required from Fellows of Colleges, and from Professors, of conformity to the Liturgy of the Church of England as by law established, and thus to enable any College, if so disposed, to admit Nonconformists to their Fellowships.

Taken together, these two Bills will introduce in both Universities a Religious Equality almost complete in the matter of Lay Degrees,* and the tenure of Lay Fellowships and Professorships.

Neither Bill will affect the Religious Teaching, or the Theological Degrees of Professorships, or the Clerical Fellowships of either University.

G.C.BRODRICK.

---

*The Cambridge Senate will still be confined to those who are willing to make a Declaration of *bona fide* Church membership, but this restriction can hardly be maintained, if Mr Coleridge's Bill should pass into law.

Appendix 4

Membership of the Essay and Old Mortality Societies, Oxford

THE ESSAY SOCIETY

Founder-members in the autumn of 1852:
Hon. G.C.Brodrick
A.G.Butler
Hon. W.H.Fremantle
G.J.Goschen
H.N.Oxenham
C.S.Parker
C.H.Pearson

Joined 1853-54
W.L.Newman
H.S.Cunningham
Frederic Harrison
Godfrey Lushington

Joined after 1855
A.V.Dicey
James Bryce
Charles Bowen

Members by 1860
T.H.Green
A.O.Rutson
C.C.Puller
J.A.Symonds

THE OLD MORTALITY SOCIETY

Founder-members in the autumn of 1856
A.V.Dicey
A.S.Grenfell
G.B.Hill
G.R.Luke
J.Nichol
A.C.Swinburne

Joined 1857
R.Broughton
R.S.Wright

Joined 1858
James Bryce
A.Brown
T.H.Green

Joined 1861
F.L.Latham
J.Lee-Warner
A Robinson
C.L.Shadwell
E.C.Boyle
William Berkley
H.A.Giffard
J.R.Magrath
C.P.Ilbert
Robinson

259

Joined 1859
T.E.Holland
Aeneas Mackay

Joined 1860
J.W.Hoole
W.Esson
Henry Nettleship
J.F.Payne
Edward Caird

Joined 1862-6
J.A.Symonds
H.l.Thompson
I.Bywater
W.H.Pater
H.Ll.Brown
A.A.Clive
J.Wordsworth
S.R.Brooke
W.Wallace
H.W.G.Markheim

Information on Essay Society from G.C.Brodrick, *Memories and Impressions*, p. 100, and Horatio F.Brown, *John Addington Symonds*, 1895, p. 125; information on Old Mortality Society from a list compiled by T.E.Holland, dated 29 May 1895, in Bodleian.

Appendix 5

Membership of the Century Club, 1866-80

Lord Amberley
Lord Airlie
Walter Bagehot
Professor E.S.Beesly
Charles Bowen
Lord Brassey
Hon. G.C.Brodrick
James Bryce
Samuel Butler
Edward Caird
Thomas Chenery
Dr Andrew Clark
Arthur Cohen
Charles Cookson
Professor Leonard Courtney
Hon. Henry Cowper
Montague Crackanthorpe
H.S.Cunningham
G.W.Dasent
Horace Davey
Rev. J.Llewellyn Davies
A.V.Dicey
Sir Charles Dilke
Professor Henry Fawcett
A.O.Rutson
Lord St Maur
George Shaw-Lefevre
Professor H.J.S.Smith
Herbert Spencer
Hon. E.L.Stanley
James Stansfeld
Leslie Stephen

J.G.Fitch
Lord Edmond Fitzmaurice
Sir Alexander Grant
M.E.Grant Duff
Frederic Harrison
Frank Harrison Hill
Lord Houghton
Thomas Hughes
A.C.Humphreys-Owen
Professor T.H.Huxley
C.P.Ilbert
Sir Wilfred Lawson
Godfrey Lushington
Vernon Lushington
John MacDonell
George Osborne Morgan
Walter Pater
Herbert Paul
Thomas Bayley Potter
Rev. S.H.Reynolds
John Rigby
Professor Thorold Rogers
Rev. William Rogers
C.S.Roundell
J.A.Symonds
Henry Yates Thompson
Sir George Otto Trevelyan
John Westlake
James Woolner
R.S.Wright
Sir George Young

List compiled from information in Frederic Harrison,
'The Century Club' in *Realities and Ideals*, pp. 369-77.

Appendix 6

Membership of the Radical Club, 1871

M.P.s

Beaumont
Henry Campbell
(later Campbell-Bannerman)
(Stirling)
William Cornwallis Cartwright
(Oxfordshire)
Sir Charles Dilke (Chelsea)
Professor Henry Fawcett (Brighton)
Lord Edmond Fitzmaurice
(Calne)
Hon. Auberon Herbert
(Nottingham)
Thomas Lea (Kidderminster)
Edward Aldam Leatham
(Huddersfield)
Walter Morrison (Plymouth)
A.J.Mundella (Sheffield)
Lord Arthur Russell (Tavistock)
Peter Taylor (Leicester)
W.T.McCullagh Torrens
(Finsbury)
Sir George Otto Trevelyan
(Hawick Burghs)

Lay Members

Arthur Arnold
Professor John Elliot Cairnes
F.W.Chesson
Professor Leonard Courtney
Mrs Millicent Garrett Fawcett
Thomas Hare
Frederic Harrison
Lady Florence Herbert
Frank Harrison Hill
T.H.Huxley
Sir Louis Mallet
John Stuart Mill
John Morley
George Odger
Henry Sidgwick
William Carr Sidgwick
Leslie Stephen
Miss Harriet Taylor
Sir George Young

List compiled from names in Gwynn and Tuckwell, *Sir Charles Dilke,* vol.i, p.100, and correspondence in the Dilke MSS at the British Museum. If the full membership of forty were taken up, the identity of six members still remains unknown. I have not identified 'Beaumont', as there were four Liberals with this surname in the Commons in 1870.

Appendix 7

Contents of and Contributors to the Reform Essays, 1867

1.ESSAYS ON REFORM, London, Macmillan & Co., 1867

List of Subjects and Authors

Essay I — '*The Utilitarian Argument against Reform, as Stated by Mr Lowe*' by the Hon.G.C.Brodrick, M.A., Fellow of Merton College Oxford, p.1

Essay II — '*The Political Character of the Working Classes*' by R.H.Hutton, M.A., p.27

Essay III — '*On the Admission of the Working Classes as Part of our Social System; and on their Recognition for all Purposes as Part of the Nation*' by Lord Houghton, M.A., Trinity College, Cambridge; *and* Hon.D.C.L., Oxford, p.45

Essay IV — '*The Balance of Classes*' by Albert Venn Dicey, M.A. Fellow of Trinity College, Oxford, p.67

Essay V — '*On the Choice of Representatives by Popular Constituencies*' by Leslie Stephen, M.A., Fellow of Trinity Hall, Cambridge, p.85

Essay VI — '*Redistribution of Seats*' by John Boyd Kinnear, p.127.

Essay VII — '*The Analysis of the House of Commons, or Indirect Representation*' by Bernard Cracroft, M.A., Trinity College, Cambridge, p.155.

Essay VIII — '*On the Working of Australian Institutions*' by C.H.Pearson, M.A., Fellow of Oriel College, Oxford, p.191

Essay IX — '*The Experience of the American Commonwealth*' by Goldwin Smith, M.A., Fellow of University College, Oxford, p.217

Essay X — '*The Historical Aspect of Democracy*' by James Bryce, B.C.L., Fellow of Oriel College Oxford, p.239

Essay XI — '*Opportunities and Shortcomings of Government in England*' by A.O.Rutson, M.A., Fellow of Magdalen College, Oxford, p.279

Essay XII — '*The House of Commons in 1833*' by Sir George Young, Fellow of Trinity College, Cambridge, p.309

2. QUESTIONS FOR A REFORMED PARLIAMENT, London,
Macmillan & Co., 1867

List of Subjects and Authors

Essay I   'Ireland' by Frank Harrison Hill, p.1.

Essay II   'Workmen and Trade Unions' by Godfrey Lushington, M.A.,
           Barrister-at-Law, late Fellow of All Souls' College, Oxford,
           p.37.

Essay III 'The Poor' by Meredith Townsend, p.65.

Essay IV   'The Land-Laws' by W.L.Newman, M.A., Fellow of Balliol
           College, Oxford, p.79

Essay V   *'Popular Education'* by Charles Stuart Parker, M.A., Fellow of
           University College, Oxford, p.131.

Essay VI   *'Law Reform'* by John Boyd Kinnear, Advocate and Barrister-
           at-Law, p.199.

Essay VII *'The Army'* by George Hooper, p.219

Essay VIII *'Foreign Policy'* by Frederic Harrison, M.A., Barrister-at-Law,
           Fellow of Wadham College, Oxford, p.233

Essay IX   *'Bribery'* by Rev. James E.Thorold Rogers, M.A., Professor of
           Political Economy, Oxford, p.259

Essay X   *'The Progress of the Working Classes'* by J.M.Ludlow, Barrister-
           at-Law, and Lloyd Jones, p.277.

Appendix 8

The Reform Essays: Relationships of Contributors

	Oxford Essay Society, 1852-60	Tests Abolition Meeting, Freemasons' Tavern 1864	Ad Eundem Club, 1865	Century Club, 1866	Jamaica Committee, 1866	University Attended
Brodrick	x	x		x		Ox
Hutton						Lo
Houghton				x		Ca
Dicey	x	x		x	x	Ox
Stephen		x	x	x	x	Ca
Kinnear					x	Ed
Cracroft						Ca
Pearson	x					Ox
Smith		x	x		x	Ox
Bryce	x	x	x	x		Ox
Rutson	x	x		x	x	Ox
Young		x	x	x	x	Ca
Hill				x		Lo
Lushington	x	x	x	x	x	Ox
Townsend						
Newman	x	x			x	Ox
Parker	x					Ox
Hooper						
Harrison	x	x		x	x	Ox
Rogers		x		x	x	Ox
Ludlow					x	
Jones						

Appendix 9

OXFORD ACADEMIC CANDIDATES

Academic Liberals' Election Contests, 1868-92

*Italics represent constituences won

	pre-1868	1868	1874	1880	1885	1886	1892
Clifford, C.C.		*Newport* (1870)	*Newport*	*Newport*			
Freeman, E.A.	Cardiff (1857) Wallingford (1858)	Mid. Somerset					
Rogers, J.E.T.			Scarborough	*Southwark*	*Bermondsey*	Bermondsey	
Maskelyne, N.				*Cricklade*	*Wilts. N.*	Wilts. N. (L.U.)	Wilts. N. (L.U.)
Morgan, G.O.		*Denbigh*	*Denbigh*	*Denbigh*			
Smith, H.J.S.			Oxford Univ. (1878)				
Roundell, C.S.		Clitheroe		Grantham			*Skipton*
Grant Duff, M.	*Elgin Burghs.* (1857, 59, 65)	*Elgin B.*	*Elgin B.*	*Elgin B.*			
Goschen, G.J.	*City of London* (1863, 65)	*London*	*London*	*Ripon*	*Edinburgh E.*	Edinb. E. (L.U.) Liverpool (L.U.) *St George's, Hanover Sq.* (L.U.) (1887)	*St George's* (Con.)
Harrison, F.						London Univ.	

267

	pre-1868	1868	1874	1880	1885	1886	1892
Beesly, E. S.					Westminster	Marylebone	
Brodrick, G. C.		Woodstock	Woodstock	Monmouth			
Otter, F.					*Louth*	Sleaford (1889)	Horncastle
Lushington, G.		Abingdon					
Cookson, M.					Kensington	Brixton	
Davey, H.				*Christchurch*	Christchurch	Ipswich Stockport	*Stockton*
Warren, J. B. L.		Mid-Cheshire					
Rutson, A. O.				Northallerton			
Herbert, A.	Newport 1865 as Con.	Berkshire *Nottingham* (1870)				Leeds N.	
Morley, J.		Blackburn (1869)		Westminster *Newcastle* (1883)	*Newcastle*	*Newcastle*	*Newcastle*
Bryce, J.			Wick Burghs	*Tower Hamlets*	*Aberdeen S.*	*Aberdeen S.*	*Aberdeen S.*
Stanley, E. L.				*Oldham*	Oldham		
Robarts, C. H.		Mid-Surrey					

	pre-1868	1868	1874	1880	1885	1886	1892
Wright, R. S.					Norwich	Stepney	
Anson, W. R.				Stafford			
Parker, C. S.		*Perthshire*	Perthshire *Perth Burgh* (1878)	*Perth Burgh*	*Perth Burgh*	*Perth Burgh*	Perth Burgh
CAMBRIDGE ACADEMIC CANDIDATES							
Harcourt, W. G.	Kirkcaldy (1859)	*Oxford*	*Oxford*	Oxford *Derby*	*Derby*	*Derby*	Derby
Westlake, J.					*S. Essex*	S. Essex (L.U.)	M. Cornwall (L.U.)
Stephen, J. F.	Harwick (1865)		Dundee (1873)				
Roby, H. J.						*Eccles* (1890)	*Eccles*
Courtney, L. H.			Liskeard *Liskeard* (1876)	*Liskeard*	*S.E. Cornwall* (L.U.)	*S.E. Cornwall* (L.U.)	*S.E. Cornwall* (L.U.)
Rigby, J.					*Wisbech*	Wisbech	*Forfarshire*

269

	pre-1868	1868	1874	1880	1885	1886	1892
Fawcett, H.	Southwark (1860) Cambridge (1863) Brighton (1864) *Brighton* (1865)	*Brighton*	Brighton *Hackney*	*Hackney*			
Bowen, E. E.				Hertford			
Young, G.		Chippenham	Plymouth	Plymouth Plymouth			
Browning, O.						Lambeth N.	Worcester E.
Trevelyan, G. O.	*Tynemouth* (1865)	*Hawick Burghs*	*Hawick B.*	*Hawick B.*	*Hawick B.*	Hawick B. (L.U.) Glasgow *Bridgeton* (1887)	*Glasgow Bridgeton*
Thompson, H. Y.	S. Lancs	S. E. Lancs		Preston (1881)			
Dilke, C. W.				*Chelsea*	*Chelsea*	Chelsea	*Dean Forest*

	pre-1868	1868	1874	1880	1885	1886	1892
Jebb, R.C.						*Cambridge Univ.* 1891 as Con.	*Cambridge Univ.* (Con.)
Stuart, J.				Cambridge Univ. (1882) *Hackney* (1884)	*Shoreditch*	*Shoreditch*	*Shoreditch*
Moulton, J.F.					*Clapham*	Clapham	Nottingham
Fitzmaurice, E.		*Calne*	*Calne*	*Calne*			Deptford
Elliot, A.R.D.					*Roxburghsh.*	*Roxburghsh.* (L.U.)	Roxburghsh. (L.U.)
Kenny, C.S.		Pontefract			*Morley*	*Morley*	

Notes

PREFACE   pp. 9-10

1. 'The Nadir of Liberalism, in *Nineteenth Century*, vol. xix May 1886, p. 645.
2. G.C.Brodrick, 'The Utilitarian Argument against Reform' in *Essays on Reform*, Macmillan, 1867, p. 7.

1. BRAINS AND NUMBERS   pp. 11-18

1. Robert Lowe (unsigned article), review of *Essays on Reform* and *Questions for a Reformed Parliament* in *Quarterly Review*, vol. cxxiii, no. 245, July 1867, p. 245.
2. ibid.
3. See also the reviews of the two volumes in the *Athenaeum*, 23 March and 11 May 1867; *Contemporary Review*, vol. v, June 1867.
4. See the reviews in *Macmillan's Magazine*, vol. xv, April 1867, written but not signed by Leslie Stephen; *Saturday Review*, vol. xxiii, 6 April 1867 also unsigned, by J.R.Green; *British Quarterly Review*, vol. xlvi, July 1867.
5. Green op. cit., p. 438.
6. John Morley, review of *Essays on Reform* in the *Fortnightly Review*, new series, vol. ii, 1 April 1867, p. 492.
7. ibid.
8. ibid.
9. cf. R.Rhodes James, *Rosebery*, Weidenfeld, 1963, p. 52; A.L. Armstrong; 'Sir William Harcoourt, 1827-1904' in *Dictionary of National Biography*; J.A.Spender, *The Life of the Right Hon. Sir Henry Campbell-Bannerman*, vol. i, Hodder & Stoughton, 1923, pp. 19-20.
10. Speech at McGill University, Montreal, 1913, quoted in obituary in the *Scotsman*, 23 February 1922.
11. Bryce MSS., Bodleian Library, Oxford: G.O.Trevelyan – Bryce, 6 December 1900.
12. Quoted in John Wilson, *C-B*, Constable, 1973, p. 462.
13. cf. the essays in Gillian Sutherland, ed., *Studies in the Growth of Nineteenth-Century Government*, Routledge, 1972, and P.F.Clarke, *Lancashire and the New Liberalism*, Routledge, 1971.
14. Bryce MSS.: Bryce – A.V.Dicey, 16 April 1916.
15. Between 1948 and 1963 81 per cent of entrants to the administrative

grade of the civil service came from Oxford or Cambridge; the Labour Government which took office in October 1964 had thirteen graduates in a cabinet of twenty-three: eleven were from Oxford. In February 1974 there were sixteen graduates, nine from Oxford and two from Cambridge, in a cabinet of twenty.

16. cf. T.Bottomore, *Elites and Society*, 1964; Pelican, 1967, chapter iii; C.T.Harvie, 'Concepts of Elites' and 'Intellectuals and Society' in *British Elites, 1750-1870,*Open University, 1974.

17. Noel Annan, 'The Intellectual Aristocracy' in *Studies in Social History*, J.H.Plumb, ed., Longmans, 1955, p.244.

18. This assumption is implicit in the behaviourist analysis of British politics associated with the Nuffield College studies of successive general elections; cf. David Butler and Donald Stokes, *Political Change in Britain*, 1969; Pelican, 1971, pp.20-22.

19. cf. Sheldon Rothblatt's discussion of university history in *The Revolution of the Dons*, Faber, 1968, pp.15-26.

20. cf. Noel Annan, *The Curious Strength of Positivism in English Political Thought*, Oxford, 1959.

21. A cogent left-wing indictment of this was Gareth Stedman Jones, 'The Pathology of English History' in the *New Left Review*, no.46, November-December 1967.

22. For example, J.W.Burrow, *Evolution and Society*, Cambridge, 1966, concentrated on the extent to which concern with social evolution predisposed mid-Victorian society to sanction theories of biological evolution.

23. This concern effectively dates from John Vincent's *The Formation of the Liberal Party, 1857-1868,* Constable, 1966; subsequent developments are discussed in P.F.Clarke, 'The Electoral Sociology of Modern Britain' in *History*, vol.lvii, 1972, pp.31-55.

24. *Communist Manifesto*, 1848; Allen & Unwin, 1960, p.24.

25. Antonio Gramsci, 'The Intellectuals' in *Prison Notebooks*, trans. Quintin Hoare and Geoffrey Nowell-Smith, Lawrence & Wishart, 1971, p.18.

26. ibid., p.20.

2. THE LIBERAL INTELLECT   pp. 19-49

1. Presidential address at inaugural meeting, 26 June 1903, in *Proceedings of the British Academy*, vol.i, 1903-4, pp.14-15.

2. Of the first forty-eight fellows, I have identified the politics of forty; of these thirty-four were Liberals before 1886, although seventeen subsequently became Unionists. Thirty-seven of the forty-eight were Oxford or Cambridge graduates. (List in *P.B.A.*, vol.i.)

3. W.E.Gladstone: speech in the House of Commons in the debate on the third reading of Joseph Hume's Universities Admissions Bill, 28 July 1834, *Hansard*, 3rd series, vol.xxv, col.636.

4. Green MSS., Balliol College, Oxford: R.L.Nettleship's manuscript notes for Green's life, p.47.

5. This charge could be levelled, in a qualified way, against otherwise

excellent accounts like W.R.Ward, *Victorian Oxford*, Cass, 1965; V.H.H.Green, *Oxford Common Room*, Arnold, 1957; J.F.A.Mason and E.G.W.Bill, *Christ Church and Reform*, O.U.P., 1970.

6. For instance, Brian Simon, *Studies in the History of Education*, Lawrence & Wishart, 1960.

7. Quoted in Phyllis Grosskurth, *Leslie Stephen*, Longmans, 1968, p.8.

8. For instance, Gillian Sutherland, in *Policy-Making in Elementary Education*, Oxford, 1973, has described the older tradition of educational history as 'a kind of treasure house for twentieth-century studies of educational theory and practice' (p.3). Melvin Richter's *The Politics of Conscience: T.H.Green and his Age*, Weidenfeld & Nicholson, 1964 and John Vincent's *The Formation of the Liberal Party, 1857-1868*, Constable, 1966, are significant examples of the new departure in intellectual and political history.

9. Lewis Campbell, *The Nationalisation of the Old English Universities*, Chapman & Hall, 1901.

10. Noel Annan, *The Curious Strength of Positivism in English Political Thought*, Hobhouse Lecture, delivered 7 May 1958; O.U.P., 1959, p.9.

11. ibid., p.11. See also H.Stuart Hughes, *Consciousness and Society*, 1958; MacGibbon & Kee, 1967.

12. See, for instance, J.L.Talmon, *Romanticism and Revolution*, Thames & Hudson, 1967, p.124.

13. Leslie Stephen, *English Thought in the Eighteenth Century*, vol.ii, Smith Elder, 1876. *chapter xii, section vi*.

14. Noel Annan, *Leslie Stephen*, MacGibbon & Kee, 1951, p.110.

15. Leslie Stephen, *English Literature and Society in the Eighteenth Century*, Duckworth, 1904, p.97.

16. Victor Kiernan, 'Evangelicalism and the French Revolution' in *Past and Present*, vol.i, 1952, pp.49-50.

17. ibid., p.46.

18. ibid., p.47.

19. Goldwin Smith, *Reminiscences*, Macmillan, 1911, p. 4; and Sidney Lee, 'Goldwin Smith, 1823-1910' in *D.N.B.*

20. Goldwin Smith, *Lectures On Modern History 1854-1861*, Parker, 1861, p.9. The inaugural lecture was delivered in 1859.

21. Goldwin Smith, whose own beliefs were more or less agnostic, used to describe his political ideal as Christianity, by which he meant 'social affection and spontaneous combination for the public good'. See *The Civil War in America*, Manchester Union and Emancipation Society, 1866, pp.27-8; see also James Bryce, 'The Historial Aspect of Democracy' in *Essays on Reform*, Macmillan, 1867, p.272.

22. See R.L.Nettleship, 'Memoir of T.H.Green' in *Works of T.H.Green* vol.iii, Longmans, 1885, p.xix, and James Bryce, 'T.H.Green' in *Studies in Contemporary Biography*, Macmillan, 1903, p.87. Virginia Stephen noticed the same characteristics in her father, even in his conservative old age: see Virginia Woolf, 'Leslie Stephen' in *Collected Essays*, vol.iv, Hogarth Press, 1967, p.78.

23. Leslie Stephen, *Life of Sir James Fitzjames Stephen*, Smith Elder, 1895,

pp.309-10. Bunyan, as E.P.Thompson has remarked, combined the spirit of the religious revival with a powerful democratic charge: see *The Making of the English Working Class*, Gollancz, 1963, pp.31-5. His influence has strangely been neglected by Annan and Richter, but *The Pilgrim's Progress* was venerated by Chartist and Whig alike, and all who disagreed with Mr Worldly Wiseman's warning against 'weak men ... meddling with things too high for them' (p.32).

24. Quoted in R.Rait, *Memorials of A.V.Dicey*, Macmillan, 1925, p.13.
25. Quoted in Annan, *Leslie Stephen*, p.113.
26. ibid., p.108.
27. Austin Harrison, *Frederic Harrison: Thoughts and Memories,* Heinemann, 1926. Much more than a biography, this is a fine, shamefully neglected, study of the mid-Victorian mind, comparable to G.M.Young's *Portrait of an Age*, Oxford, 1936.
28. Harrison, op. cit., p.98.
29. ibid., p.129.
30. Sir Henry Cunningham, *Lord Bowen*, privately printed, 1896, pp.6-7.
31. *University Teaching* from *The Idea of a University,* part i, 1858; Longmans, 1908, p.186.
32. Ostrogorski, *Democracy and the Organisation of Political Parties*, Constable, 1908, pp.126-7.
33. Stephen, *English Thought in the Eighteenth Century,* vol.ii, p.428.
34. D.A.Hamer, *John Morley: Liberal Intellectual in Politics*, Oxford, 1968, pp.1-2.
35. Written in 1878; quoted in F.W.Hirst, *Early Life and Letters of John Morley*, vol.i, Macmillan, 1927, p.10.
36. Stephen, *English Thought in the Eighteenth Century,* vol.ii, p.428.
37. Stephen, *Fitzjames Stephen*, pp.107-8.
38. F.W.Maitland, *The Life and Letters of Leslie Stephen*, Duckworth, 1906, p.116.
39. William Hanna, *Memoirs of the Life and Writings of Thomas Chalmers D.D.*, vol.ii, Sutherland & Knox 1850, p.271.
40. Kiernan, op.cit., p.44.
41. Robert Lowe M.P., *Speeches and Letters on Reform*, Bush, 1867, p.105.
42. Matthew Arnold, *Culture and Anarchy*, delivered 1867, published 1869; Murray 1924, p.viii.
43. ibid. p.107.
44. Henry Sidgwick, 'The Prophet of Culture' in *Macmillan's Magazine*, vol.xvi, 1867, reprinted in *Miscellaneous Essays and Addresses*, Macmillan, 1904, pp.56-7.
45. Jackson MSS., Trinity College, Cambridge: Francis Thornton (father-in-law of Henry Jackson) to his father, 21 November 1836.
46. G.M. Trevelyan, *Sir George Otto Trevelyan*, Longmans, 1932, p.7; see also Stephen, *Fitzjames Stephen*, p.55.
47. Leslie Stephen, *Some Early Impressions, National Review,* 1903; Hogarth Press, 1924, p.56; Campbell, op.cit., p.61.
48. Mark Pattison, *Memoirs,* Macmillan, 1885, p.79.
49. R.W.Church, *The Oxford Movement, 1833-1845,* Macmillan, 1891, p.13.
50. ibid., p.338.
51. Annan, *Leslie Stephen*, p.121.

52. Church, op. cit., p.1; see also Harold Laski, 'The Political Theory of the Oxford Movement' in *Studies in the Problem of Sovereignty,* 1917; Allen & Unwin, 1967.

53. *Tracts for the Times: No. 1,* 1833.

54. John Morley, *On Compromise,* 1874; Watts, 1933, p.56.

55. ibid.

56. Mark Pattison, 'Philosophy at Oxford' in *Mind,* vol.i, 1877, p.85.

57. Goldwin Smith – Evelyn Abbott, 24 May 1894 in Arnold Haultain, ed., *A Selection from Goldwin Smith's Correspondence,* Werner Laurie, 1913, pp.268-70.

58. E.B.Pusey, *Collegiate and Professorial Teaching and Discipline,* Parker, 1854, pp.213-15.

59. Speech on 3rd reading of Joseph Hume's Universities Admission Bill, 28 July 1834, *Hansard,* 3rd series, vol.xxv, col.636.

60. Church, op. cit., p.340.

61. Quoted in Campbell, op. cit., p.52.

62. ibid.

63. Geoffrey Faber, *Jowett: A Portrait with Background*, Faber & Faber, 1957, p.197.

64. F.Meyrick, *Memories,* John Murray, 1905, p.26.

65. Pattison, *Memoirs,* p.238.

66. John Morley, 'On Pattison's *Memoirs*' in *Miscellanies,* vol.iii, Macmillan, 1886, p.149.

67. Church, op.cit., p.340.

68. Published in 1853.

69. Henry Sidgwick, 'Clough's Poems' in the *Westminster Review,* August 1869, reprinted in *Miscellaneous Essays,* p.65.

70. Henry Sidgwick – Graham Dakyns, 8 December 1866, quoted in A.S. and E.M.S., *Henry Sidgwick, a Memoir,* Macmillan, 1906, p.158. See also Sidgwick MSS., Trinity College, Cambridge: Henry Sidgwick – Mrs B.A.Clough, 27 April 1866.

71. Pattison, *Memoirs,* pp.234-5.

72. Speech of 16 March 1864, *Hansard,* 3rd series, vol.clxiv, cols.117-18.

73. Evelyn Abbott and Lewis Campbell, *Life and Letters of Benjamin Jowett,* vol.i, John Murray, 1896, pp.135-6.

74. William Stebbing, ed., *Memorials of Charles Henry Pearson,* Longmans, 1900, p.38.

75. Bryce MSS., A.V.Dicey – James Bryce, 12 November 1918.

76. cf. Stephen, *Some Early Impressions*, pp.74-5.

77. Church, op. cit., p.338.

78. Goldwin Smith, *Reminiscences,* pp.67-8.

79. R.T.Davidson and W.Benham, *Life of Archbishop Tait,* vol.i, Macmillan, 1891, p.152.

80. H.W.C.Davis, *Balliol College,* Blackwell, 1899, p.187.

81. Abbott and Campbell, op. cit. vol.i, pp.126-30.

82. ibid., p.412.

83. M.R.D.Foot, ed., *The Gladstone Diaries,* vol. i (1825-32), O.U.P., 1968; see also Frederic Harrison, *The Creed of a Layman,* Macmillan, 1907, pp.15-18.

84. Thomas Carlyle on John Sterling, quoted in Campbell, op. cit., p. 23.

85. Henry Scott Holland, 'Henry Parry Liddon, 1829-1890' in the *D.N.B.*

86. Max Beer, *History of British Socialism* vol. i, Bell, 1919, pp. 273-4.

87. *Annual Report* of O.S.S.M., 1836.

88. ibid., 1886.

89. Duncan Forbes, *The Liberal Anglican Idea of History*, Cambridge, 1952, p. 101.

90. ibid., p. 39.

91. ibid., p. 82.

92. ibid., p. 99.

93. Abbot and Campbell, op. cit., vol. i, pp. 135-6.

94. W.A.S. Hewins, 'Edward Vansittart Neale, (1810-1892)' in the *D.N.B.*

95. Including Maurice, Whately, Chenevix Trench, Thirlwall, Conington and Stanley: see Beer, op. cit., vol. i, p. 186.

96. *The Working Men's College*, 1854-1904, 1904, pp. 15-17.

97. A.S. and E.M.S., op. cit., p. 61.

98. *Programme* of The Oxford Working Men's Education Institution in Oxford local history collection, Bodleian Library, 1854.

99. See Torben Christensen, *Christian Socialism*, Aarhus, 1962, chapter 1.

100. Beer, op. cit., vol. i, p. 182.

101. Stephen, *Some Early Impressions*, pp. 63-4.

102. Stephen MSS., University Library, Cambridge: Fitzjames Stephen, *Autobiographical Fragment*, p. 36; see also M.E. Grant Duff, *Notes from a Diary, 1851-1872*, vol. i, John Murray, 1897, p. 78.

103. A.V. Dicey, *Law and Public Opinion in England during the Nineteenth Century*, 1904; Macmillan, 1914, p. 184; Stephen, *Some Early Impressions*, pp. 74-5.

104. Forbes, op. cit., p. 119.

105. Pattison, *Memoirs*, pp. 165-7.

106. Quoted in Annan, *Leslie Stephen*, p. 307.

107. Sir Henry Jones and J.H. Muirhead, *The Life and Work of Edward Caird*, Maclehose, 1921, pp. 22, 25-6, 59; Nettleship, 'Memoir of T.H. Green', p. xxv.

108. Frederic Harrison, 'Froude's Life of Carlyle' in the *North American Review*, January 1885, reprinted in *The Choice of Books*, Macmillan, 1886, p. 191.

109. Maitland, op. cit., p. 230.

110. cf. Raymond Williams, *Culture and Society*, Chatto & Windus, 1958, chapter 4.

111. John Stuart Mill, *Autobiography*, 1873; Oxford, 1924, p. 191.

112. Sidgwick MSS.: *Autobiographical Fragment*, dictated 13 August 1900.

113. Stephen, *Some Early Impressions*, pp. 75-6; F.W. Hirst, *Early Life and Letters of John Morley*, vol. i, Macmillan, 1927, p. 22.

114. Pattison, *Memoirs*, p. 208.

115. cf. Sheldon Rothblatt, *The Revolution of the Dons*, Faber, 1968, chap. 3.

116. Mill, op. cit., chapter 1, though the home education given by evangelical parents could produce similar precocity (see p. 54).

117. Mill, op. cit., p. 166.

118. cf. John Passmore, *A Hundred Years of Philosophy*, 1957, Pelican, 1968, p. 17.

119. Mill, op.cit., p.190.

120. ibid., p.134.

121. Rothblatt, op. cit., p.102.

122. Mill, op. cit., p.191.

123. William Whewell to James Garth Marshall, 27 December 1842 in Mrs Stair Douglas, *Life of William Whewell, D.D.*, Kegan Paul, 1881, p.280.

124. Mill, op. cit., p.176.

125. Robert Robson, 'Trinity College in the Age of Peel' in *Ideas and Institutions of Victorian Britain*, Bell, 1967, pp.332, 335.

126. Dicey, op. cit., p.431.

127. ibid., p.430 (quoting Sidgwick, *Miscellaneous Essays and Addresses*, pp.241-2, and Leslie Stephen, *The English Utilitarians,* vol.iii, Duckworth, 1900, pp. 224-37).

128. cf. Henry Fawcett, who talked of Mill's 'noble ... almost holy ideas', yet remained a firm adherent of wages-fund economics after the master had given them up: see Leslie Stephen, *The Life of Henry Fawcett,* Smith Elder, 1885, pp.102, 157.

129. See Henry Parris, 'The Nineteenth-Century Revolution in Government: a Re-appraisal Re-appraised' in *The Historical Journal* vol.iii, no.1, 1960, for a summary of the case against Dicey as a historian of nineteenth-century political thought.

130. Mill, op. cit., p.139.

131. ibid., p.140.

132. ibid., pp. 140-41.

133. ibid., p.179.

134. ibid., p.180.

135. For the ambiguities this produced in his politics, see Vincent, op. cit., pp.183-94.

136. Rothblatt, op. cit., pp.131-2.

137. Susan Liveing, *J.H.Bridges: A Nineteenth-Century Teacher*, Kegan Paul, 1926, p.56.

138. J.M.Rigg, 'Richard Congreve, 1818-1899' in *D.N.B.*

139. Frederic Harrison, *The Creed of a Layman,* Macmillan, 1907, p.14.

140. Royden Harrison, 'The Positivists: a Study of Labour's Intellectuals' in *Before the Socialists*, Routledge, 1965, p.251 ff.

141. Sidgwick MSS.: Leslie Stephen – Henry Sidgwick, 10 October 1882; see also Frederic Harrison MSS., London School of Economics: Edward Caird – Harrison, 16 April 1885, Goldwin Smith – Harrison, 9 May 1900.

142. Jackson MSS.: William Everett – Henry Jackson, 28 March 1873.

143. Annan, *Leslie Stephen,* p.215.

144. Goldwin Smith, *Lectures on Modern History,* Lecture 1, p.26.

145. Sidgwick MSS: Henry Sidgwick, *Account of the Development of his Ethical View, 1900;* and Goldwin Smith, *Lectures on Modern History,* p.16.

146. Sidgwick, *Account of the Development of his Ethical View,* p.10; Goldwin Smith, *Lectures on Modern History,* pp.18-19.

147. Goldwin Smith, *Lectures on Modern History,* p.27.

148. Rait, op. cit., p.182.

149. Goldwin Smith, *Lectures on Modern History,* p.12.

150. Henry Sidgwick, *'Alexis de Tocqueville'* in *Macmillan's Magazine*, vol. v, November 1861, reprinted in *Miscellaneous Essays and Addresses*, p. 369.

151. James Bryce in *English Historical Review*, vol. i, 1886.

152. Quoted in E. H. Carr, *What is History?*, 1961; Penguin, 1964, p. 1.

153. For Acton's opinion of Smith see the *Chronicle*, 31 August 1867.

154. Goldwin Smith, *Lectures on Modern History*, p. 27.

155. cf. J. R. Seeley's Inaugural as Regius Professor of History at Cambridge, 1869 in Seeley, *Lectures and Essays*, 1870; and Richter, op. cit. chapter 5.

156. Annan, *Leslie Stephen*, p. 122; Harrison MSS: John Morley – Harrison 25 July 1873.

157. Thorold Rogers MSS., Magdalen College, Oxford: Rogers – Leslie Stephen, 8 December 1869; file of letters to J. T. Hibbert, M.P.

158. For Green see Leslie Stephen, *Letters of J. R. Green*, Macmillan, 1901, p. 71; E. I. Carlyle, 'A.H.D.Acland, 1847-1926' in *D.N.B.* According to R. B. Haldane, Gladstone never forgave him for this act: see *An Autobiography*, Hodder & Stoughton, 1929, p. 93; G. C. Moore Smith, 'Edward Carpenter, 1844-1929, in *D.N.B.;* for Venn see Annan, *Leslie Stephen*, p. 122 ; H. Tedder, 'Charles Kegan Paul. 1828-1902' in *D.N.B.*

159. Richter, op. cit., p. 36.

160. Phyllis Grosskurth, *John Addington Symonds*, Longmans, 1964, p. 55.

161. Bryce MSS.: Bryce – A. V. Dicey, 14 November 1913.

162. Bryce MSS.: Henry Nettleship – James Bryce, 20 August 1865.

163. Bryce MSS.: Robinson Ellis – Bryce, 1 July 1860; Stephen, *The Letters of J. R. Green*, P. 44.

164. cf. Stephen, *Henry Fawcett*, p. 99.

165. Pattison, 'Philosophy at Oxford', p. 87.

166. Jowett – Stanley, 15 August 1858, quoted in Abbott and Campbell, op. cit., vol. i, p. 275.

167. Ward, op. cit., p. 240.

168. Stanley – Jowett, undated, 1863, quoted in Abbott and Campbell, op. cit., vol. i, p. 368.

169. Quoted in Faber, op. cit., p. 245.

170. R. E. Prothero, *Life of Dean Stanley*, vol. ii, Murray, 1893, p. 30; A. Vidler, *The Church in an Age of Revolution*, Penguin, 1961, chapter 11.

171. Sidgwick MSS.: E. E. Bowen – Sidgwick, 29 October 1860.

172. Harrison MSS.: T. H. Huxley – Thomas Chapman, 10 October 1860.

173. F. Harrison 'Neo-Christianity', reprinted in *The Creed of a Layman* as 'Septem contra Fidem', p. 98.

174. ibid., p. 99.

175. ibid., p. 114.

176. Campbell, op. cit., pp. 116-19. The credibility of the Broad Church party was shaken by the condemnation of the essayists by its most promising bishops, Tait, Hampden and Thirlwall.

177. Fitzjames Stephen defended Wilson and Williams before the Court of Arches and the Privy Council: see Stephen, *Fitzjames Stephen*, p. 184; Harrison, op. cit., p. 30.

178. Sidgwick MSS.: Apostolic paper, 'Is prayer a permanent function of humanity?' delivered 20 February 1864.

179. Sidgwick MSS.: Diary-letter written for J.A.Symonds, 27 August 1886. A general survey of Sidgwick's letters shows, however, that his theological preoccupations of the 1860s were replaced in later life by explicitly political concerns.
180. Stephen, *Fitzjames Stephen*, p.221.
181. cf. Bryce MSS.: Bryce – Dicey 1900-1922; H.A.L.Fisher, *Life of James Bryce, Viscount Bryce of Dechmont.* vol.ii, Macmillan, 1927, p.241.
182. Richard Cobden, speech of 23 November 1864 in John Bright and Thorold Rogers, eds., *Speeches on Questions of Public Policy*, vol.ii, Macmillan, 1870, p.364.
183. Arnold, op. cit., p.1.
184. Goldwin Smith, *An Inaugural Lecture*, Parker, 1859, p.12.
185. Cobden, op. cit. Two years earlier, he had tried to get a university-based review started which would provide intellectual support for radicalism. See Thorold Rogers MSS.: Cobden – Thorold Rogers, 22 May 1862.

3. THE UNIVERSITY CONTEXT pp. 50-73

1. Cyril Bibby, 'Thomas Henry Huxley and University Development' in *Victorian Studies*, vol.iii, December 1958, p.98.
2. Walter Bagehot, 'Review of the Report of the Commissioners on Oxford' in the *Economist*, 1852, reprinted in *Works and Life*, vol.i Longmans, 1915, p.151.
3. Obituary in the *Scotsman*, 23 January 1922, quoting a speech at McGill University, 1913. R.B. Haldane found Bryce condescending to the new civic universities, which he called 'Lilliputian': see *Autobiography,* Hodder & Stoughton, 1929, p.139.
4. Leslie Stephen, *The Life of Henry Fawcett,* Smith Elder, 1885, p.133. Leslie described his friend with significant ambiguity as 'a typical Cambridge man, whether as moulded by Cambridge or as one of the class by which Cambridge has itself been moulded', p.75.
5. Leslie Stephen, *Some Early Impressions, National Review,* 1903; Hogarth Press, 1924, pp.56-63.
6. Sidgwick MSS.: Henry Sidgwick, Diary–Letter to J.A.Symonds, 31 May 1888.
7. Jackson MSS.: A.V.Dicey – Henry Jackson, 8 November 1917.
8. Maurice Bowra, *Memories*, Weidenfeld, 1966, pp.137-8.
9. Bryce MSS.: Bryce – Dicey, 27 April 1909.
10. For this see Mrs E.M.Sellar, *Recollections and Impressions*, Blackwood, 1907, chapter 5.
11. See A.C.Chitnis, 'The Edinburgh Professoriate 1790-1826', unpublished Edinburgh Ph.D. thesis, 1968.
12. Sir James Stephen on Trinity Hall, quoted in J.P.C.Roach, 'Victorian Universities and the National Intelligentsia' in *Victorian Studies*, vol.iv, December 1959, p.133.
13. Gladstone's 'uttermost and last' prayers, on his deathbed, were for Oxford: see John Morley, *The Life of William Ewart Gladstone,* 1903; Lloyd's ed., vol.ii, 1908, p.576.

14. G.C.Brodrick, 'The Universities and the Nation' in the *Contemporary Review*, vol.xxiii, 1875, pp.79-80.
15. ibid., p.79.
16. Bryce remarked to Dicey in 1914 that German universities had more social influence because 'their people mixed more'. Bryce MSS.: Bryce – Dicey, 24 August 1914.
17. cf. G.M.Trevelyan, *Sir George Otto Trevelyan*, Longmans, 1932, p.146.
18. Sidgwick MSS.: Henry Sidgwick – J.A.Symonds, 20 May 1888.
19. Bryce MSS.: Roundell – Bryce, 24 June 1865.
20. For Arnold see p.28, and F.W.Maitland, *The Life and Letters of Leslie Stephen*, Duckworth, 1906, p.170; for Pattison see p.29, and Jackson MSS.: Henry Jackson – Mrs Jackson 30 October 1912.
21. Bryce MSS.: Freeman – Bryce, 20 October 1867 21 and 26 November 1865. Freeman, with some shrewdness, argued that the intellectual inflexibility of some of the younger men would, in the long run, make them conservative.
22. cf. Frederic Harrison, *Realities and Ideals*, Macmillan, 1908, pp.390-96.
23. cf. Jackson MSS.: 'Memorandum on Henry Sidgwick', 1900, pp.13-14.
24. Jackson MSS.: Sir George Young – Colonel Henry Jackson, 19 January 1922.
25. Beesly MSS., University College, London: Beesly – Crompton, 21 November 1864.
26. G.M.Young, *Victorian England: Portrait of an Age*, 1936; O.U.P., 1969, p.71. In appendix 1 of my thesis *University Liberals and the Challenge of Democracy* I compared the social and educational backgrounds of the seventy-eight Oxford liberals who attended the Freemasons' Tavern meeting on Tests Abolition with a sample of 126 Balliol undergraduates over the period 1853-8. 55 per cent attended one of the seven 'Clarendon' schools (62 per cent Balliol sample), 8 per cent attended other boarding schools (18 per cent Balliol sample).
27. cf. A.P.Stanley, *Life of Dr Arnold*, 1844; Hutchinson, 1903, p.62.
28. cf. Harvie, op. cit.: 10 per cent were educated at home, 9 per cent at day schools, 12.5 per cent at institutes of higher education, like Scottish universities, Kings College, London (Balliol sample, respectively 5 per cent, 5 per cent, 6·5 per cent).
29. A.V.Dicey, contribution to the *Bicentenary Record of the Northampton Mercury*, Mercury Press, Northampton, 1920, p.51. See also A.S. and E.M.S., *Henry Sidgwick: A Memoir*, Macmillan, 1906, p.6.
30. Leslie Stephen, *Life of Sir James Fitzjames Stephen*, Smith Elder, 1895, p.86.
31. Report of the Royal Commission on Cambridge University, *Parliamentary Papers*, vol.xliv, 1852-3, p.28.
32. cf. Hannah More's opinion in E.M.Forster, *Marianne Thornton, a Domestic Biography*, Harcourt Brace, 1956, p.75.
33. Susan Liveing, *A Nineteenth-Century Teacher*, Kegan Paul, 1926, p.53.
34. Goldwin Smith, *Reminiscences*, Macmillan, 1911, p.98.
35. cf. E.G.W.Bill and J.F.A.Mason, *Christ Church and Reform*, O.U.P., 1970, chapter ii.
36. Quoted in Lewis Campbell, *The Nationalisation of the Old English Universities*, Chapman & Hall, 1901, pp.13-14.

37. T.E.Kebbel, 'Edward Coplestone 1776-1849' in the *D.N.B.*
38. A.I.Tillyard, *A History of University Reform*, Heffer, 1913, p.40.
39. cf. John Roach, *Public Examinations in England*, Cambridge, 1971, chapter vii for a discussion of the examination question in the 1870s and 1880s.
40. J.H.Newman, *Apologia Pro Vita Sua*, 1864; Everyman, 1912, p.39.
41. Sir Henry Cunningham, *Lord Bowen*, 1896, pp.40-41.
42. W.R.Ward, *Victorian Oxford*, Cass, 1965, p.238; Leslie Stephen, 'Jowett' in *Studies of a Biographer*, Duckworth, 1898, pp.133-4; Frederic Harrison, 'Neo-Christianity', reprinted in *The Creed of a Layman*, Macmillan, 1907, as *'Stephen contra Fidem'*. p.100.
43. Brodrick, op. cit., p.64; Stephen, *Henry Fawcett,* p.106.
44. Ward, op. cit., p.210.
45. Stephen, *Henry Fawcett,* p.75.
46. *University of Cambridge Election Pollbook, November 1882.*
47. H.A.L.Fisher, *Life of James Bryce, Viscount Bryce of Dechmont*, Macmillan, 1927 vol.i, p.45.
48. Harvie, op. cit., p.102.
49. Evelyn Abbott and Lewis Campbell, *Life and Letters of Benjamin Jowett*, vol.i, John Murray, 1897, pp.57-8; Cunningham, op. cit., p.34.
50. cf. David Newsome, *Godliness and Good Learning*, John Murray, 1961.
51. Noel Annan, *Leslie Stephen,* MacGibbon & Kee, 1951, p.28; F.W.Maitland – Henry Jackson 29 May 1905 in C.H.S.Fifoot, ed., *The Letters of Frederic William Maitland,* Selden Society: Cambridge, 1965, p.340.
52. Pearson MSS., Bodleian Library, Oxford: Draft Manifesto of Tugendbund, c.1853.
53. William Stebbing, ed., *Memorials of Charles Henry Pearson,* Longmans, 1900, p.74.
54. ibid., p.51.
56. cf. Mallet, *The University of Oxford,* vol.iii, Methuen, 1927, chapter 26.
56. Abbott and Campbell, op. cit., vol.i, pp.125-32.
57. Harrison MSS.: Harrison – E.S.Beesly, n.d., 1854-5; Sheldon Rothblatt, *The Revolution of the Dons*, Faber, 1968, p.215.
58. cf. G.C.Brodrick, ed., *Report of Speeches on the Abolition of Tests*, Longmans, 1866, p.4.
59. Noel Annan, 'The Intellectual Aristocracy' in J.H.Plumb, ed., *Studies in Social History*, Longmans, 1955.
60. The genealogical details here were taken from the *D.N.B.;* Rait, *Memorials of A.V.Dicey,* Macmillan, 1925; Stephen, *Fitzjames Stephen*; C.H.Pearson, 'Memoir of H.J.S.Smith' in *The Collected Mathematical Writings of H.J.S.Smith,* vol.i, Clarendon Press, 1894; Stebbing, op. cit.; Pearson MSS.: Tugendbund manifesto, and John and J.A.Venn, *Alumni Cantabrigiensis*, 9 vols., Cambridge, 1922.
61. Jackson MSS.: Sir George Young – Colonel Jackson 17 January, 1922.
62. Obituary by E.S.Beesly, *Positivist Review*, no. 231, March 1912.
63. Jackson MSS.: Sir George Young – Henry Jackson, 12 June 1907; William Everett – Henry Jackson, 28 March 1873.
64. A.S. and E.M.S., op. cit., p.9; Stebbing, op. cit., p.16; Richter, *The Politics of Conscience: T.H.Green and his Age*, Weidenfeld & Nicholson, 1964, p.46.

65. Cunningham, op. cit., p.16.
66. Trevelyan, op. cit., p.24.
67. G.C.Brodrick, *Memories and Impressions* Nisbett & Co., 1900., pp.23-30; Basil Williams 'Sir George Young, 1837-1930' in the *D.N.B.*
68. Stebbing, op. cit., p.33; Stephen, *Henry Fawcett*, p.15.
69. Mark Pattison, 'Philosophy at Oxford' in *Mind*, vol.i, 1877, p.89.
70. Brodrick, *Memories and Impressions*, p.79; Fisher, op. cit., vol.i, p.47.
71. Rothblatt, op. cit., pp.207-11.
72. cf. Abbott and Cambell, op. cit., vol.i, pp.138-9; A.S. and E.M.S., op. cit., p.20.
73. Fisher, op. cit., vol.i, p.59.
74. Green MSS.: Chronology compiled by Mrs Green, 1883.
75. Phyllis Grosskurth, *John Addington Symonds*, Longmans, 1964, p.35.
76. 'In Memoriam' quoted by Leslie Stephen in *Sketches from Cambridge, by a Don*, Macmillan, 1865, p.73.
77. ibid.
78. Sidgwick MSS.: Autobiographical fragment, 1900.
79. ibid.
80. Mrs Charles Brookfield, *The Cambridge Apostles*, Pitman, 1906, pp.4-5.
81. Abbott and Campbell, op. cit., vol.i, p.173.
82. Christopher Hollis, *The Oxford Union*, Evans, 1965, pp.102-3.
83. James Osborne, *Arthur Hugh Clough*, Constable, 1908, pp.76-7.
84. Stebbing, op. cit., pp.72-4; Brodrick, *Memories and Impressions*, p.100.
85. Fisher, op. cit., vol.i, p.49; and *Minute Book of Old Mortality* in Bodleian Library, 1855.
86. Pearson MSS.: Tugendbund manifesto.
87. The Cabinet Ministers were Goschen and Pearson (in Victoria); the professors H.J.S.Smith and Pearson; and the M.P.s Grant Duff, Goschen, Pearson and Parker; the Deans G.D.Boyle (Salisbury) and W.H.Fremantle (Ripon); the Legal Member Fitzjames Stephen and the Assistant Secretary George Miller. As a tribute to its successor, the Essay Society, Goschen can be quoted. On entering Parliament in 1863 he wrote to Frederic Harrison: 'It has been a wonderful chance for me – the thing is how to keep my seat, and above all to do credit to the Essay Society and my friends.' (Harrison MSS.: G.J.Goschen – Harrison, May 1863.)
88. Green MSS.: T.H.Green's Balliol essay-books, 1856-7.
89. *Minute-book of Old Mortality*.
90. *Record of the Debates of the Oxford Unions*, Oxford, 1869. Debate of 8 March 1858.
91. Hollis, op. cit., p.113.
92. ibid; and Brodrick, *Memories and Impressions*, p.93.
93. Hollis, op. cit., p.80; W.Fraser Rae, 'Edward Hugessen Knatchbull-Huguessen, Lord Brabourne, 1829-1893' in the *D.N.B.*; S.H.Harris, *Auberon Herbert: Crusader for Liberty*, Williams & Norgate, 1943, p.84.
94. Hollis, op. cit., pp.124-5.
95. Palmerston Club membership lists in Bodleian.
96. Rothblatt, op. cit., chapter 7.
97. Newsome, op. cit., chapter 1.
98. Political Economy Club membership lists in Bodleian.

99.   Jackson MSS.: Young – Jackson, 12 June 1907.

100. Sidgwick MSS.: Cowell – Sidgwick, 9 April 1864.

101. Jackson MSS.: Young – Colonel Jackson, 19 January 1922.

102. ibid.

103. Printed list in Sidgwick MSS. 1865; Jackson MSS.: Young – Jackson, 17 June 1907.

104. Jackson MSS.: Young – Jackson, 17 June 1907.

105. Trevelyan, op. cit., p. 70.

106. Jackson MSS.: Dicey – Jackson, 8 November 1917.

107. *The Woodforde Diaries, 1758-1781*, vol. i, ed. John Beresford, 1924, pp. 11-32, 178-80.

108. Trinity Hall, Cambridge, had most of its fellows at the bar. They were generally non-resident which 'doubtless gave some of them a wider outlook on affairs; but was dangerous to the collegiate life, and might make a fellowship little more than a humble but agreeable sinecure': C. W. Crawley, 'Trinity Hall' in John Roach, ed., *The City and University of Cambridge*, vol. iii of the *Victorian County History of Cambridgeshire*, Oxford, 1959, p. 368.

109. Leslie Stephen, 'University Organisation' in *Fraser's Magazine*, vol. xxxii, February 1868, p. 141.

110. Quoted in Roach, op. cit., p. 247.

111. Stephen, 'University Organisation', p. 140.

112. Sidgwick – H. G. Dakyns, 24 August 1861 in A.S. and E.M.S., op. cit., p. 68.

113. Biographical information on the following has been taken from the *D.N.B.:* W. W. How, 'G. C. Brodrick, 1831-1903'; R. S. Rait, 'A. V. Dicey, 1835-1922,' and see Rait, op. cit., p. 42; A. Cochrane, 'Frederic Harrison, 1831-1923'; A. W. Pickard-Cambridge, 'C. S. Parker, 1829-1910'; W. A. S. Hewins, 'J. E. Thorold Rogers, 1823-1890'; Sidney Lee, 'Goldwin Smith, 1823-1910', and 'Leslie Stephen, 1832-1904'. *Who was Who*: 'Godfrey Lushington, 1832-1907'. *Modern English Biography*, vol. iii: 'A. O. Rutson, 1836-1890'.

114. Sidgwick MSS.: John Conington – Henry Sidgwick, 16 August 1869.

115. See biographical notes.

116. Brodrick, 'The Universities and the Nation', p. 80.

117. J. P. C. Roach, 'Victorian Universities and the National Intelligentsia' in *Victorian Studies*, vol. iii, December 1959, pp. 136-7.

118. See Charles Pearson's attempt to study science at Oxford in 1853 in Stebbing, op. cit., p. 77.

119. See James Stuart, *Reminiscences*, Cassell, 1912, pp. 155-6.

120. Quoted in Fisher, op. cit., vol. i, p. 62.

121. Stephen, *Fitzjames Stephen*, p. 140; Cunningham, op. cit., p. 90.

122. Stephen, *Some Early Impressions*, p. 114.

123. E. M. Everett, *The Party of Humanity*, North Carolina, 1939, p. 3.

124. M. M. Bevington, *The 'Saturday Review', 1855-1868*, Columbia, 1941, p. 43.

125. Stephen, *Some Early Impressions*, p. 120.

126. See M. Pinto-Duschinsky, *The Political Thought of Lord Salisbury*, Constable, 1967, chapters i and ii.

127. Maitland, op. cit., p. 163.

128. Stebbing, op. cit., p.91.
129. Everett, op. cit., p.75.
130. Charles L.Graves, *Life and Letters of Alexander Macmillan,* Macmillan, 1910, p.214. For the *Spectator* see the *D.N.B.* articles for the two editors, D.C.Lathbury, 'Richard Holt Hutton, 1826-1897', C.L.Graves, 'Meredith White Townsend, 1831-1911'.
131. Brodrick, *Memories and Impressions,* p.222.
132. Though in fact Cook organized regular breakfasts for his contributors. See Grant Duff, *Notes from a Diary,* vol.i, John Murray, 1897, p.136.
133. See Graves, *Alexander Macmillan,* p.199, and F.W.Hirst 'John, Viscount Morley, 1838-1923' in the *D.N.B.*
134. Goldwin Smith, op. cit., p.166.
135. Cunningham, op. cit., p.94.
136. Fisher, op. cit., vol.i., p.15.
137. Stebbing, op. cit., p.93.
138. Cunningham, op. cit., p.93.
139. Geoffrey Faber, *Jowett: A Portrait with Background,* Faber & Faber, 1957, p.197.
140. Campbell, op. cit., p.136.

4. THE TESTS AGITATION pp.74-96

1. Quoted in Mallet, *The University of Oxford,* vol.iii, Methuen, 1927, p.332.
2. Liberation Society, *Jubilee Restrospect,* 1894, p.37.
3. G.M.Trevelyan, *Sir George Otto Trevelyan,* Longmans, 1932, p.70.
4. There is no reference to the Act, or the agitation, in Brian Simon's *Studies in the History of Education,* Lawrence & Wishart, 1960, or in Sheldon Rothblatt's *The Revolution of the Dons,* Faber, 1968.
5. *Hansard,* 3rd Series, vol.cx, cols 691-6.
6. Lewis Campbell, *The Nationalisation of the Old English Universities,* Chapman & Hall, 1901; see also Winstanley, *Later Victorian Cambridge,* Cambridge, 1947, pp.36-7
7. Gladstone MSS., British Museum: Goldwin Smith – Gladstone, 27 June 1854, B.M. Add. MSS. 44303.
8. Leslie Stephen, *Some Early Impressions, National Review,* 1903; Hogarth Press, 1924, p.65.
9. See Duncan Forbes, *The Liberal Anglican Idea of History,* Cambridge, 1952, p.102.
10. Goldwin Smith, *Reminiscences,* Macmillan 1911, p.201.
11. See Leslie Stephen, 'William Whewell, 1794-1866' in the *D.N.B.* and *Some Early Impressions,* p.33.
12. Gladstone MSS.: Goldwin Smith – Gladstone, 2 May 1855: a letter attempting to interest Gladstone in a Peelite-oriented newspaper proposed by Goldwin Smith and his friends, B.M.Add.MSS. 44303.
13. See, for instance, Bryce's discovery of Lancashire society in the mid-1860s in Bryce MSS.: Bryce – Freeman, 22 May 1865.

14. See Stephen, *Some Early Impressions*, p.97; A.S. and E.M.S., *Henry Sidgwick, a Memoir*, Macmillan, 1906, p.196; James Bryce, 'University Tests' *North British Review*, vol.lxxxiii, March 1865, p.117.
15. Leslie Stephen, *The Life of Henry Fawcett*, Smith Elder, 1885, p.246; Brodrick MSS., Merton College, Oxford: Memorial of Cambridge Celibacy Committee, 1859.
16. Stephen *Henry Fawcett*,, p.110.
17. ibid., p.246.
18. See G.C.Brodrick, 'The Universities and the Nation' in the *Contemporary Review*, vol.xxvi, June 1875, p.64.
19. Liberation Society, *Jubilee Restrospect*, p.38.
20. A.S. and E.M.S, op. cit., p.196.
21. See Jackson MSS.: 'Memorandum on Henry Sidgwick', 1901, pp.5-6.
22. Leslie Stephen, 'University Organisation' in *Fraser's Magazine*, vol. lxxvii, February 1868, p.153.
23. See Sidgwick MSS.: H.Brandreth – Henry Sidgwick, 21 October 1867; Henry Sidgwick – his mother, 13 November 1867: 'Don't be afraid, we have a fine old Conservative constitution which will resist many shocks of feeble individuals like myself.'
24. W.R.Ward, *Victorian Oxford*, Cass, 1965, p.210.
25. ibid., p.211.
26. ibid., p.212; see also E.G.W.Bill and J.F.A.Mason, *Christ Church and Reform*, Oxford, 1967.
27. Sidgwick MSS.: Henry Sidgwick – E.M.Young, 28 July 1858.
28. Gladstone MSS.: H.B.Liddon – Gladstone, 16 March 1864, B.M. Add. MSS. 44237.
29. A.S. and E.M.S., op. cit., p.106.
30. Mark Pattison, *Memoirs*, Macmillan, 1885, p.249.
31. Sidgwick MSS.: John Conington – Henry Sidgwick, 16 August 1869.
32. Bryce MSS.: Reuben John Bryce – James Bryce, 26 June 1865.
33. Mallet, op cit., vol.ii, p.326.
34. Ward, op. cit., p.193.
35. ibid., p.200.
36. Goldwin Smith, 'The Elections to the Hebdomadal Council', Oxford, 1866, p.6.
37. ibid., p.3.
38. Ward, op. cit., p.229.
39. Goldwin Smith, 'The Elections to the Hebdomadal Council', p.6.
40. Gladstone MSS.: Goldwin Smith – Gladstone, 25 October 1860, B.M.Add. MSS. 44303.
41. Ward, op. cit., p.223.
42. ibid., p.235; an explicit University Conservative Association was set up in 1864: see *The Times*, 13 June 1864.
43. Mallet, op. cit., vol.iii, p.303.
44. Sir Henry Cunningham, *Lord Bowen*, 1896, p.40.
45. Winstanley, op. cit., p.44.
46. Stephen, *Henry Fawcett*, p.110.
47. *Hansard* 3rd series, vol.clxx, cols.1228-31.
48. *Hansard* 3rd series, vol.clxxi, cols.1385-7.

49. *Hansard* 3rd series, vol.clxx, col.1240.
50. Speech of George Joachim Goschen, in *Hansard*, 3rd series, vol.cxlxxi, col.1394.
51. Campbell, op. cit., p.134.
52. *Hansard,* 3rd series, vol.clxxiii, col.543.
53. *Hansard,* 3rd series, vol.clxxiv, col.102.
54. *Hansard,* 3rd series, vol. clxxv, col.1383.
55. I am indebted to my friend, Mr George Cubie, Assistant Clerk to the House of Commons, for information about nineteenth-century parliamentary procedure.
56 Gladstone MSS.: J.D.Coleridge – Gladstone, 17 December 1868, B.M.Add.MSS. 44138.
57. *Hansard,* 3rd series, vol.clxxvi, cols.678-9.
58. A fairly typical speech by a member of this group would be that of Sir William Heathcote, M.P. for Oxford University, on the second reading of Dodson's bill, 16 March 1864. *Hansard,* 3rd series, vol. clxxiv, cols.116-7.
59. James Bryce, op. cit., p.132.
60. Lord Ripon, who managed the Bill in the Lords in 1870, thought Salisbury's opposition had 'a flavour of Dizzyism': see Lucien Wolf, *The Life of Lord Ripon*, vol.i, John Murray, 1921, p.227.
61. M.Pinto-Duschinsky, *The Political Thought of Lord Salisbury*, Oxford, 1967, p.71.
62. *Hansard,* 3rd series, vol. clxx, cols.1239-40.
63. Goldwin Smith, *A Plea for the Abolition of Tests,* Parker, 1864, pp.96-100.
64. *Hansard,* 3rd series, vol.cxii, col.1523 (division at end of debate on 18 July 1850).
65. *Hansard,* 3rd series, vol.clxx, col.1240.
66. Campbell, op cit. p.133.
67. Gladstone MSS.: Acland – Gladstone, 1 March 1863, B.M.Add. MSS. 44091.
68 Gladstone MSS.: Gladstone – Acland, 18 March 1863, B.M.Add. MSS. 44091.
69. ibid.
70. ibid.
71. Gladstone, speech on second reading of Tests Abolition (Oxford) Bill, 16 March 1864: see *Hansard* 3rd series, vol.clxxiv, col.121.
72. *Hansard,* 3rd series, vol.clxxv, col.1383.
73. *Hansard,* 3rd series, vol.clxxiv, col.121.
74. ibid., col.158.
75. Monk Bretton MSS., Bodleian Library: Goldwin Smith – J.G.Dodson, 10 April 1864.
76. *Hansard,* 3rd series, vol.clxxvi, col.679.
77. B.M.Add.MSS. 44752, f.311.
78. B.M.Add.MSS. 44755, f.206.
79. Memorandum of 6 July 1863.
80. For a favourable estimate of Gladstone from an academic liberal see Gladstone MSS.: Goldwin Smith – Gladstone, 21 July 1865 (B.M.Add.MSS. 44303), or Bryce MSS.: C.S.Roundell – James Bryce, 24 June 1865.

81. For an unfavourable estimate see G.C.Brodrick, *Memories and Im-pressions*, Nisbett & Co., 1900, p.238; or Stephen, *Henry Fawcett*, p.244.

82. Monk Bretton MSS.: abstract of letter from Edward Miall to Goldwin Smith made by J.G.Dodson, 29 March 1864.

83. Monk Bretton MSS.: Petition with covering letter dated 18 May 1864.

84. Campbell, op. cit., p.137.

85. Speech of 4 February 1867, in Warden Brodrick's *Press Cutting Book*, vol.ii, Merton College Library, p.157, col.4.

86. Bryce MSS.: Goldwin Smith – Bryce, 7 July 1869.

87. John Morley, 'Young England and the Political Future' in the *Fortnightly Review*, new series, vol.i, April 1867, p.492.

88. Speech of 1 June 1864, in *Hansard*, 3rd series, vol.clxxv, cols.1012-13.

89. G.S.Woods, 'Peter William Clayden, 1827-1902' in the *D.N.B.*

90. P.W.Clayden, 'The Ecclesiastical Organisations of English Dissent', *Fortnightly Review*, new series, vol.iii, 1 May 1868, p.504.

91. ibid., p.503.

92. Bryce MSS.: E.D.Darbishire – James Bryce, 3 July 1865.

93. Bryce MSS.: Bryce – Freeman, 22 May 1865.

94. ibid., 3 February 1866.

95. ibid., 22 May 1865.

96. ibid.

97. H.A.L.Fisher, *Life of James Bryce, Viscount Bryce of Dechmont*, vol.i, Macmillan, 1927, pp.104-5; see also Frederic Harrison's conclusions, after a visit to northern industrial areas in 1861, in *Autobiographic Memoirs*, Macmillan, 1907, p.257.

98. John Vincent, *The Formation of the Liberal Party, 1859-1868*, Constable, 1966, p.67.

99. Even after the favourable result of the election of 1865 the Liberation Society reckoned the 'nonconformist interest' at Westminster at no more than forty M.P.s. Liberation Society MSS. County Hall, London: Minutes of Council, 26 July 1865, A/Lib/3, p.268.

100. Liberation Society MSS.: Report: 'Parliamentary Action in 1862', A/Lib/3, p.14.

101. Liberation Society MSS.: 'Memorandum on Parliamentary Action', December 1863, A/Lib/3, pp.139-65.

102. Liberation Society MSS.: Minutes of Council, 4 and 18 March 1864, A/Lib/3, pp.190, 193.

103. I.S.Leadam, 'George Osborne Morgan, 1826-1897' in the *D.N.B.*

104. Stephen, *Henry Fawcett*, pp.81-2.

105. Green MSS.: R.L.Nettleship's notes for Green's life, 6 May 1864.

106. John Bright, *Diaries*, ed. R.A.J.Walling, Cassell, 1930, pp.279-80.

107. R.L.Nettleship, 'Memoir of T.H.Green in *Works of T.H.Green*, vol.iii, Longmans, 1885, pp.61-2.

108. See Sidney Lee, 'Goldwin Smith 1823-1910' in *D.N.B.*; and Justin McCarthy, *Portraits of the Sixties*, Unwin, 1903, pp.372-3.

109. Campbell, op. cit., p.136.

110. J.A.Hamilton, 'Edward Miall, 1809-1881' in the *D.N.B.*

111. Liberation Society MSS.: Minutes of Council, 16 June 1864, A/Lib/3, p.208.

112. Liberation Society MSS.: Minutes of Council, 26 July 1865, A/Lib/3, p.268.
113. Bryce MSS.: Darbishire – Bryce, 3 July 1865.
114. Liberation Society MSS.: Minutes of Council, 6 March, 7 April and 9 June 1854, A/Lib/2, pp.58-9, 73, 77, 86.
115. Bryce MSS.: Darbishire – Bryce, 11 July 1865.
116. G.C.Brodrick, *Report of Speeches on the Abolition of Tests*, Longmans, 1866, p.11.
117. See list of Brodrick's leaders in Merton College Library.
118. Bryce MSS.: C.S.Roundell – Bryce, 24 June 1865.
119. ibid., 22 March 1866.
120. Gladstone MSS.: C.S.Roundell – Gladstone, 7 January 1869, B.M.Add. MSS. 44418, f.76.
121. Bryce MSS: C.S.Roundell – Bryce, 24 June 1865.
122. ibid., 24 July 1865.
123. Ward, op. cit., p.231.
124. Gladstone MSS.: Goldwin Smith – Gladstone, 12 September 1865. B.M.Add. MSS. 44303.
125. John Morley, *William Ewart Gladstone*, vol.i, Lloyd's 2-volume edition, 1908, pp.709-10.
126. Ward, op. cit., p.254.
127. *Hansard*, 3rd series, vol.clxxxix, cols, 75-6.
128. *Hansard*, 3rd series, vol.clxxxix, col.1050.
129. *Hansard*, 3rd series, vol. clxxxv, cols. 296-7.
130. Stephen, *Henry Fawcett*, p.235.
131. Gladstone MSS.: Goldwin Smith – Gladstone, 19 June 1867.
132. ibid., 17 June 1867, both B.M.Add. MSS. 44303.
133. Stephen, *Henry Fawcett*, p.236; see also Gladstone MSS.; Henry Fawcett – W.E.Gladstone, 15 February 1868, B.M.Add. MSS. 44126.
134. Sidgwick MSS.: Sir George Young – E.M.Sidgwick, 28 February 1906.
135. Bryce MSS: Sir George Young – Bryce, 12 February 1892.
136. *Hansard*, 3rd series, vol.cxc, cols.926-7.
137. *Hansard*, 3rd Series, vol.cxciii, col.471.
138. *Hansard*, 3rd series, vol.cxciii, col.1614.
139. Gladstone MSS.: Goldwin Smith – Gladstone, 28 February 1868, B.M.Add.MSS.44303.
140. Winstanley, op. cit., p.60.
141. Ward, op. cit., p.255.
142. ibid., p.256.
143. Gladstone MSS.: Memorandum on University Tests Bill, 17 December 1868, B.M.Add.MSS.44138.
144. ibid.
145. *Hansard*, 3rd series, vol.cxcviii, cols.143-5.
146. A.S. and E.M.S., op. cit., p.196; Auberon Herbert resigned his fellowship at St John's, Oxford, in December, for similar reasons: see S.H.Harris, *Auberon Herbert, Crusade for Liberty*, Williams & Norgate, 1943, p.94.
147. Campbell, op. cit., p.160.
148. Gladstone MSS.: C.S.Roundell – Gladstone, 9 November 1869,

B.M.Add. MSS. 44423, f.69.

149. Gladstone MSS.: Gladstone – C.S.Roundell, 10 November 1869 (copy), B.M.Add. MSS. 44423. f.75-6.

150. Liberation Society MSS.: Minutes of Council, 17 December 1896, A/Lib/4, p.211.

151. Gladstone MSS.: Gladstone – Roundell, 10 November 1869 (copy), B.M.Add. MSS. 44423. f.75-6

152. Winstanley, op. cit., p.78.

153. Ward, op. cit., p.260.

154. Report of the Select Committee, *Parliamentary Papers* vol.ix, 1871, p.91.

155. Winstanley, op. cit., p.87.

156. Leslie Stephen the *Nation*, 8 July 1870; and see, for instance, the evidence of the Rev.E.H.Perowne, interviewed on 28 July 1870: question no.516, *Parliamentary Papers*, vol.ix, 1871, p.43; this was commented on by Stephen in a despatch to the *Nation*, 11 August 1870.

157. Bryce MSS.: Benjamin Jowett – Bryce, 21 January 1871.

158. Winstanley, op. cit., p.86.

159. Liberation Society MSS.: Minutes of Council, 19 June 1871, A/Lib/4, p.347.

160. Gladstone MSS.: C.S.Roundell – Gladstone, 4 May 1871, B.M. Add. MSS. 44430. f.180.

161. Brodrick, 'The Universities and the Nation', p.63.

162. Gladstone MSS.: J.D.Coleridge – Gladstone, 11 December 1871, B.M.Add. MSS. 44138.

163. ibid., enclosed memorandum.

164. Mark Pattison, *Suggestions on Academical Organisation*, Edmonston, 1868, p.1.

165. Bryce MSS.: Bryce – Henry Sidgwick, 4 January 1868; see also Harrison MSS.: Pattison – Frederic Harrison, 18 February 1868.

166. Pattison, *Suggestions on Academical Organisation* section 5: 'Of the Re-Distribution of the Endowments Fund'.

167. J.S.Cotton, 'Charles C.B.Appleton, 1841-1879' in *D.N.B.*

168. See Noel Annan, *Leslie Stephen*, MacGibbon & Kee, 1951, pp.37-8; Bryce MSS.: Henry Nettleship – Bryce, 6 January 1868; Melvin Richter, *The Politics of Conscience: T.H.Green and His Age*, Weidenfeld & Nicholson, 1964, p.150.

169. Stephen, *Henry Fawcett*, p.114; and Brodrick, *Memories and Impressions*, p.355.

170. Brodrick, 'The Universities and the Nation', p.64.

171. Campbell, op. cit., p.211.

172. Brodrick, *Memories and Impressions*, p.182.

173. For Oxford see Ward, op. cit., p.198; for Cambridge see Rothblatt, op. cit., chapter 7: 'The Ideal of a College'.

174. James Bryce, *Studies in Contemporary Biography*, Macmillan, 1903, p.409.

5. UNIVERSITY MEN AND
FOREIGN POLITICS   pp.97-115

1. J.R.Green, unsigned review of *Essays on Reform* in the *Saturday Review*, vol.xxiii, 6 April 1867, p.438.

2. Bryce MSS.: Dicey – Bryce, 27 July 1917.

3. Bryce MSS.: Bryce – Dicey, 14 November 1913.

4. See Richard Garnett, 'John Sterling, 1806-1844'; and Ronald Bayne, 'Richard Chenevix Trench, 1807-1886' in the *D.N.B.*

5. Both became fervent Unionists after 1886. For Swinburne see his poem 'The Commonwealth' with its philippic against 'Judas Gladstone', *The Times*, 1 July 1886. For Nichol see William Knight, 'John Nichol' in *Some Nineteenth-Century Scotsmen*, Oliphant, 1903, p.229.

6. For instance, many of their fathers were special constables at the time of the Chartist assembly on Kennington Common on 10 April 1848. The same went for a good many of them as well. All the students save one of King's College were enrolled as specials: see William Stebbing, ed., *Memorials of Charles Henry Pearson*, Longmans, 1900, p.38.

7. *Cavour e l'Inghilterra*, vol.ii, part i, 1913, quoted in D.E.D.Beales, *England and Italy, 1859-1860*, Nelson, 1960, p.24.

8. Edmund Gosse, *Father and Son*, 1907; Heinemann, 1941, p.76.

9. Bryce MSS.: Dicey – Bryce, 12 November 1918.

10. H.A.L.Fisher, *Life of James Bryce, Viscount Bryce of Dechmont*, vol.i, Macmillan, 1927, p.51.

11. H.W.Rudman, *Italian Nationalism and English Letters*, Allen & Unwin, 1940, p.97.

12. James Stuart, *Reminiscences*, Cassell, 1912, p.57.

13. Evelyn Abbott and Lewis Campbell, *Life and Letters of Benjamin Jowett*, vol.i, John Murray, 1897, p.135.

14. Leslie Stephen, 'Arthur Hugh Clough, 1819-61' in the *D.N.B.*

15. See Frederic Harrison, *National and Social Problems*, Macmillan, 1908, p.116.

16. Fisher, op. cit., vol.i, p.51.

17. ibid., pp.180-85.

18. W.Hunt, 'Edward Augustus Freeman, 1823-1892' in *D.N.B.*.

19. A.V.Dicey *et al.*, *Memories of John Westlake*, Smith Elder, 1914, pp.28, 118.

20. R.Rait, *Memorials of A.V.Dicey*, Macmillan, 1925, p.220.

21. Leslie Stephen, *The Life of Henry Fawcett*, Smith Elder, 1865, pp.341-52.

22. J.M.Tregenza, *Professor of Democracy*, Melbourne U.P., 1968, chapter 2.

23. James Bryce, *Modern Democracies*, Macmillan, 1921, p.13.

24. ibid., p.19.

25. ibid., p.21

26. Graham Wallas, *Human Nature in Politics*, Constable, 1908, p.126.

27. See the essays by Leslie Stephen, Goldwin Smith, James Bryce in *Essays on Reform*, Macmillan, 1867; and by Frederick Harrison in *Questions for a Reformed Parliament*, Macmillan, 1867.

28. Beales, op. cit., p.21.

29. ibid., p.26.

30. ibid., p.34.

31. Jowett – Miss M.Elliot, 4 August 1861, quoted in Abbott and Campbell, op. cit., vol. i, p.353.

32. Symonds MSS., Bristol University: Henry Sidgwick – J.A.Symonds, n.d. (probably June 1868).

33. John Morley, *Recollections*, vol.i, Macmillan, 1917, p.80.

34. ibid., p.78.
35. E.J.Hobsbawm, *The Age of Revolution*, Mentor, 1962, p.164.
36. ibid., p.165.
37. Morley, op. cit., p.78.
38. Harrison, *National and Social Problems*, p.124.
39. See chapter 3 and G.M.Trevelyan, 'Englishmen and Italians' in *Clio, a Muse*, Longmans, 1930, p.111.
40. Rudman, op. cit., pp.17-21.
41. Quoted in Morley, op. cit., p.80.
42. See *Lettere di Guiseppe Mazzini ad Auerlio Saffi*, Rome, 1905.
43. Harrison, *National and Social Problems*, p.114.
44. Beesly MSS.: Saffi – Beesly, 28 May 1858.
45. For instance A.V.Dicey, quoted in William Knight, ed., *John Nichol*, Maclehose, 1896, p.140.
46. Fisher, op. cit., vol.i, p.51; see also F.Harrison, *Autobiographic Memoirs*, Macmillan, 1911, vol.i, p.186.
47. A.V.Dicey in Knight, ed., *John Nichol*, p.140; and Trevelyan, op. cit., p.118.
48. Bryce MSS.: Bryce – Dicey, 16 February 1909.
49. Bryce – Minnie Bryce, 14 April 1864, quoted in Fisher, op. cit., vol.i, p.120.
50. ibid.
51. Bryce MSS.: Bryce – Freeman, 25 April 1864.
52. Royden Harrison, *Before the Socialists*, Routledge, 1965, p.261.
53. The Crimean War witnessed a great increase in popular interest in foreign policy, through David Urquhart's Foreign Affairs Committees, which, in some ways, anticipated the rigours of the University Extension classes; some of the 150 or so formed in 1854-6 survived for twenty years: see Olive Anderson, *A Liberal State at War*, Macmillan, 1967, p.150.
54. Bolton King, *The Life of Mazzini*, Everyman, 1902, p.256; see also F.Harrison, *National and Social Problems*, pp.124-5.
55. ibid., p.269; see also John MacCunn, 'Joseph Mazzini' in *Six Radical Thinkers*, Arnold, 1907, pp.190-92.
56. For Green see R.L.Nettleship, 'Memoir of T.H.Green', in *Works of T.H.Green*, vol.iii, Longmans, 1885, p.xiii; for R.L.Nettleship see the 'Memoir' by A.C.Bradley in *Philosophical Lectures and Remains of Richard Lewis Nettleship*, vol.i, Macmillan, 1897, p.xxix; for Toynbee see F.C.Montague, *Arnold Toynbee*, Johns Hopkins, 1889, p.32.
57. Sidgwick MSS.: 'An account of the development of his ethical view'.
58. Joseph Mazzini, 'Duties towards the Country in *The Duties of Man*, 1858 in *Life and Writings*, vol.iv, Smith Elder, 1867, pp.276-81; King, op. cit., p.301.
59. James Bryce, 'The Historical Aspect of Democracy' in *Essays on Reform*, pp.266-7.
60. See F.Harrison, *National and Social Problems*, pp.124-5.
61. Goldwin Smith, *Reminiscences*, Macmillan, 1911, pp.319-21.
62. Henry Pelling, *America and the British Left*, Black, 1956, p.7.
63. Sidgwick MSS.: J.J.Cowell – Sidgwick, 15 September 1863. Cowell's father, who had been a Bank of England agent in the United States,

1837-9, was a prominent publicist for the South, which indicates a
reason for Cowell's attitude. See John Welsford Cowell, *France and the
Confederate States*, Hardwicke, 1865, etc.

64. Sidgwick – H.G.Dakyns, November 1863, quoted in A.S. and E.M.S.,
Henry Sidgwick: A Memoir, Macmillan, 1906, p.102.

65. G.M.Trevelyan, *Sir George Otto Trevelyan*, Longmans, 1932, p.62.

66. A.S. and E.M.S., op. cit., p.129; Trevelyan, *Sir George Otto Trevelyan*,
p.62.

67. See, for instance, Charles Roundell's address to the Social Science
Association on the Jamaica affair, with its assumption of negro
'inferiority' (my chapter 6, p.127), and James Bryce, *The American
Commonwealth*, vol.ii, Macmillan, 1888, chapters civ 'Present and
Future of the Negro' and xcv 'Reflections on the Negro Problem'.

68. Nettleship, op. cit., p.xlii.

69. John Morley, *William Ewart Gladstone*, vol.i, Lloyds, 1908, p.527; see
also Harrison MSS.: John Morley – Frederic Harrison, 26 April 1871.

70. Leslie Stephen, *'The Times' and the American War*, Ridgway, 1865,
chapter iii, 'Slavery and the War'.

71. ibid., chapter vi, *'The Times* and the Slavery Question'.

72. ibid., p.35

73. Goldwin Smith, op. cit., p.319.

74. James Bryce, 'The Historical Aspect of Democracy' in *Essays on Reform*,
p.242.

75. Stephen *'The Times' and the American War*, p.62, quoting *The Times*, 27
May 1863.

76. ibid., p.59, quoting *The Times*, 29 January 1862.

77. Goldwin Smith, 'The Experience of the American Commonwealth' in
Essays on Reform. p.223; and Leslie Stephen, 'On the Choice of
Representatives by Popular Constituencies', in the same volume, p.89.

78. Stephen, 'On the Choice of Representatives', p.72.

79. Justin McCarthy, *A History of Our Own Times*, vol.ii, Chatto & Windus,
1887, pp.116-17; E.D.Adams, *Great Britain and the American Civil War*,
vol.ii, Longmans, 1925, p.282.

80. Stephen, *'The Times' and the American War*, p.4.

81. Robert Lowe, review (unsigned) of *Essays on Reform* in the *Quarterly
Review*, vol.cxxii, July 1867, p.263. George Brodrick was also a *Times*
leader-writer, but, because of his Federal views, was kept well away
from the subject: see Stanley Morison, *The History of 'The Times'*, vol.ii,
The Times, 1935-52, p.450.

82. Quoted in Pelling, op. cit., pp.10-11.

83. ibid., p.10; see also Goldwin Smith, *Reminiscences*, pp.319-20.

84. Bryce MSS.: Bryce – Freeman, 3 February 1863.

85. Goldwin Smith, *Reminiscences*, chapter xii.

86. For T.H.Green see Bryce MSS.: Dicey – Bryce, 27 July 1917; for the
Positivists see Royden Harrison, op. cit., pp.257-8.

87. A telegraph link was opened in 1860, but soon broke down and was
not restored until 1865.

88. C.P.Lucas 'Edward Dicey, 1832-1911' in the *D.N.B.*; T.B.Saunders,
'Monckton Milnes, Lord Houghton, 1809-1885', in the *D.N.B.*
F.W.Maitland, *The Life and Letters of Leslie Stephen*, Duckworth, 1906,

chapter vi; Goldwin Smith, *Reminiscences,* chapter xix; and Henry Yates Thompson, *An Englishman in the American Civil War* in the *Diaries,* ed. Christopher Chancellor, Sidgwick & Jackson, 1971.

89.   Maitland, op. cit., p. 113; Goldwin Smith, *Reminiscences,* p. 329. See also Edmund Ions, *James Bryce and American Democracy,* Macmillan, 1968, p.45, and Rait, op. cit., p.64. In 1870 Dicey found Boston 'essentially English' and described his host, President C.W.Eliot of Harvard, as having an Oxford 'tone'.

90.   Stephen's intimacy with Lowell and Norton lasted for life: see Maitland, loc. cit. Armed with introductions from him, Bryce and Dicey went over in 1870, and established similarly close relations, especially with C.W.Eliot and Oliver Wendell Holmes Junior: see Fisher, op. cit., vol. i, p. 136.

91.   Ions, loc. cit.

92.   Henry Adams, *The Education of Henry Adams,* Houghton Mifflin, 1918; Modern Library Edn, 1931, p.120.

93.   ibid., p.186.

94.   ibid., p.205.

95.   ibid., p.204.

96.   J.A. Venn, *Alumni Cantabrigiensis,* Cambridge, 1922; Jackson MSS.: file of letters from William Everett.

97.   Sidgwick MSS.: Cowell – Sidgwick, 15 September 1863.

98.   Macmillan MSS., British Museum, Goldwin Smith – Alexander Macmillan, 29 May 1864.

99.   C.L.Graves, *Life and Letters of Alexander Macmillan,* Macmillan, 1910, p.184.

100.   James Bryce, 'E.L.Godkin' in *Studies in Contemporary Biography,* Macmillan, 1903, p.374.

101.   Henry Adams, op. cit., p.120.

102.   Leslie Stephen, *Some Early Impressions, National Review,* 1903; Hogarth Press, 1924, p.86.

103.   James Bryce, 'T.H.Green' in *Studies in Contemporary Biography,* p.90.

104.   Graves, op. cit., pp.201-2.

105.   See *A Bibliographical Catalogue of Macmillan and Company's Publications from 1843 to 1889,* 1891, and Macmillan MSS.: Goldwin Smith – Macmillan, 29 May 1864, *et seq.*

106.   John Stuart Mill, *Autobiography,* 1873; Oxford 1924, p.229.

107.   See *D.N.B.* articles on Hutton and Townsend.

108.   Rait, op. cit., pp.49-50; Stebbing, op. cit., pp.94-5.

109.   See *D.N.B.* article on Townsend.

110.   Lionel Robinson, 'Frank Harrison Hill, 1830-1910' in the *D.N.B.;* for the Darbishires see p.86.

111.   See my article, 'John Boyd Kinnear: Passages in the Life of a Scottish Radical' in the *Journal of the Scottish Labour History Society,* no.3, 1970.

112.   See Gladstone MSS.: correspondence with Goldwin Smith, B.M. Add. MSS. 44304.

113.   Goldwin Smith, *An Inaugural Lecture,* Parker, 1861, p.12.

114.   Macmillan MSS.: Goldwin Smith – Alexander Macmillan, n.d., (1864).

115. Lord Acton, review in the *Chronicle*, 31 August 1867; reprinted in *Essays on Church and State*, Hollis & Carter, 1952, p.407.

116. Goldwin Smith, 'The Manchester School' in the *Contemporary Review*, vol.lxvii, March 1895, pp.377-88.

117. Goldwin Smith, *Inaugural Lecture*, p.32.

118. Goldwin Smith, *Reminiscences*, p.322. Thomas Bayley Potter was, however, an errant pupil of the Manchester School, having supported the Crimean War and helped unseat Bright at the election which followed: see Eliza Orme, 'Thomas Bayley Potter, 1817-1898' in the *D.N.B.*

119. Bryce MSS.: Bryce – Freeman, 22 May 1865.

120. Bryce MSS.: Goldwin Smith – Bryce. 7 July 1869.

121. Justin McCarthy, *Portraits of the Sixties*, T.Fisher Unwin, 1903, p.382.

122. Goldwin Smith, *Reminiscences*, p.322; E.D.Adams, op. cit., vol.ii, p.136.

123. McCarthy, *Portraits of the Sixties*, p.381.

124. John Bright, diary entry for 15 May 1864 in R.J.Walling, ed., *The Diaries of John Bright*, Cassell, 1930, p.279.

125. ibid.

126. Green MSS.: Green – sister, 16 May 1864.

127. Bright, *Diaries*, 9 March 1864, p.271.

128. Henry Adams – John G.Palfrey, 16 November 1864, quoted in Harold Dean Cater, ed., *Henry Adams and his Friends*, Houghton Mifflin, 1947, p.27.

129. E.D.Adams, op. cit., vol.ii, p.109; but see also Mary Ellison, *Support for Secession, Lancashire and the American Civil War*, University of Chicago Press, 1973.

130. Green MSS.: 'R.L.Nettleship's notes for Green's life'.

131. Melvin Richter, *The Politics of Conscience: T.H.Green and His Age*, Weidenfeld & Nicholson, 1964, p.94.

132. Richard Holt Hutton, 'The Political Character of the Working Classes' in *Essays on Reform*, pp.30-31.

133. *Hansard*, 3rd series, vol.clxxxii, col.204. For a retrospective view of working-class 'soundnesss' on the issue see James Bryce, *Modern Democracies*, vol.ii, pp.413-14.

134. Royden Harrison, op. cit., p.75.

135. ibid., 'British Labour and American Slavery'.

136. See John Vincent, *The Formation of the Liberal Party, 1857-1868*, Constable, 1966, p.196; and E.D.Adams, op. cit., vol.ii., p.112.

137. E.D.Adams, op. cit., p.107; see also Macmillan MSS.: Goldwin Smith – Alexander Macmillan, 24 April 1864.

138. J.R.Green, review of *Essays on Reform* in the *Saturday Review*.

6. THE UNIVERSITY LIBERALS AND THE REFORM AGITATION pp. 116-40

1. In Mark de Wolfe Howe, ed., *Holmes – Laski Letters*, vol.i, Oxford, 1953, p.283.

2. W.L.Guttsman edited an abridged edition of the two volumes *A Plea*

for Democracy, MacGibbon & Kee, 1967; his introduction is perfunctory and rather inaccurate.

3. H.L.Beales, 'Centenary Tribute to an Appeal for Modernisation' in *Essays on Reform 1967*, ed. Bernard Crick, Oxford, 1967; this was a collection of essays on administrative reform by thirteen left-of-centre academics.

4. G.C.Brodrick, *Memories and Impressions*, Nisbett & Co., 1900, p.108.

5. G.C.Brodrick, 'On the different principles on which the chief systems of popular government have been based in ancient and modern times', T.&G.Shrimpton, 1855, p.15.

6. ibid., p.23.

7. *Debates of the Oxford Union*, Oxford, 1895.

8. Meeting of 23 March, reported in *Oxford Chronicle*, 30 March 1866.

9. John Stuart Mill, *Autobiography*, 1873; Oxford, 1924, pp.219-24

10. G.P.Gooch, *Lord Courtney*, Macmillan, 1920, p.83; A.V.Dicey *et al.*, *Memories of John Westlake*, Smith Elder, 1914, p.60; Courtney MSS., London School of Economics: J.E.Cairnes – Courtney 19 March 1863.

11. Leslie Stephen, *The Life of Henry Fawcett*, Smith Elder, 1885, p.186.

12. ibid., p.191.

13. Mill-Taylor MSS., London School of Economics: Mill – Fawcett, 5 February 1860.

14. Stephen, op.cit., p.118.

15. ibid, pp.205-14.

16. Mill-Taylor MSS.: Mill – Fawcett, 2 December 1864, commenting on Fawcett's speech of 13 September.

17. cf. F.B.Smith, *The Making of the Second Reform Bill*, Cambridge, 1966, p.52.

18. G.M.Trevelyan, *Sir George Otto Trevelyan*, Longmans, 1932, p.62.

19. cf. Sidgwick MSS.: file of letters to his mother.

20. F.W.Maitland, *The Life and Letters of Leslie Stephen*, Duckworth, 1906, p.107; Leslie Stephen, *Some Early Impressions*, *National Review*, 1903; Hogarth Press, 1924 p.91.

21. *Inaugural Proceedings of the Cambridge Union*, Cambridge, 1866.

22. Harrison MSS.: Harrison – Beesly, n.d. (1859).

23. Rogers MSS.: Richard Cobden – Rogers, 22 May 1862.

24. Goldwin Smith – Cobden, 27 October 1862, quoted in Elizabeth Wallace, *Goldwin Smith, Victorian Liberal*, Toronto University Press, 1957, p.145.

25. See Henry Adams, *The Education of Henry Adams*, Houghton Mifflin, 1918, Modern Library Edn, 1931, pp.158-61.

26. Gladstone MSS.: Goldwin Smith – Gladstone, 21 July 1865.

27. John Vincent, *The Formation of the Liberal Party, 1857-1869*, Constable, 1966, p.145.

28. Goldwin Smith, *Reminiscences*, Macmillan, 1911, pp.242-5; 'J.E.Thorold Rogers 1823-1890' in the *D.N.B.;* Vincent, op.cit., pp.225, 191; Stephen, *Henry Fawcett*, p.83.

29. cf. Rogers's introduction to Richard Cobden's *Speeches on Questions of Public Policy*, Macmillan, 1870, pp. xii-xiv.

30. *Daily News*, 12 October 1866; see also T.H.Green's reaction in

R.L.Nettleship, 'Memoir of T.H.Green' in *Works of T.H.Green*, vol.iii, Longmans 1885, p.xxii.

31. Bryce MSS.: Bryce – Freeman, 22 May 1865 and 3 February 1866.
32. F.M.Leventhal, *Respectable Radical: George Howell and Victorian Working-Class Politics*, Longmans, 1971, p.68.
33. Vincent, op. cit., p.190. Bright, for instance, did not start his speaking tour until the middle of 1866.
34. James Bryce, 'Robert Lowe' in *Studies in Contemporary Biography*, Macmillan, 1903, p.306.
35. James Winter, 'The Cave of Adullam and Parliamentary Reform' in *English Historical Review*, vol.lxxxi, 1966, p.46.
36. M. Pinto-Duschinsky, *The Political Thought of Lord Salibury*, Constable, 1967, p.149.
37. Asa Briggs, *Victorian People*, 1954; Penguin, 1965, p.240.
38. Bryce, op. cit., p.305.
39. Walter Bagehot, *The English Constitution*, Chapman & Hall, 1867, p.6.
40. Goldwin Smith, op. cit., pp.310-11; Bryce, op. cit, p.305.
41. Letter quoted in Evelyn Abbott and Lewis Campbell, *Life and Letters of Benjamin Jowett,*, vol.i, John Murray, 1897, p.421.
42. *The Times*, 28 July 1892.
43. Richard Garnett, 'Matthew Arnold, 1822-1888' in the *D.N.B.*
44. Briggs, op. cit., p.265.
45. Pinto-Duschinsky, op. cit., p.187.
46. Vividly described in Goldwin Smith, op. cit., p.310.
47. Courtney MSS.: J.E.Cairnes – Courtney, 22 April 1869.
48. A.Patchett Martin, *The Life of Robert Lowe, Viscount Sherbrooke*, vol.ii, Longmans, 1893, p.283.
49. ibid., p.285.
50. Leslie Stephen, *The English Utilitarians,* vol.ii, Duckworth, 1900, p.319.
51. Bryce, op. cit, pp.296-7.
52. ibid., p.298; and H.A.L.Fisher, *James Bryce, Viscount Bryce of Dechmont*, vol.i, Macmillan, 1927, p.15.
53. Adams, op. cit., p.25.
54. Bryce, op. cit., pp.296-7.
55. Harrison MSS.: Harrison – Beesly, 22 February 1867.
56. G.C.Brodrick, 'The Utilitarian Argument against Reform, as stated by Mr Lowe' in *Essays on Reform*, Macmillan, 1867, p.2.
57. ibid.
58. Frederic Harrison, 'Parliament before Reform' in *Fortnightly Review*, new series, vol.i, March 1867, reprinted in *Order and Progress*, Longmans Green, 1875, p.128.
59. A.O.Rutson, 'Opportunities and Shortcomings of Government in England' in *Essays on Reform*, p.287
60. Vincent, op. cit., p.153.
61. Martin, op. cit., p.273.
62. Robert Lowe, *Speeches and Letters on Reform*, Bush, 1867, p.54; Royden Harrison, *Before the Socialists*, Routledge, 1965, p.124.
63. F.Harrison, op. cit., p.128.
64. Leventhal, op. cit., pp.73-4; F.B.Smith, op. cit., p.140.
65. Vincent, op. cit., p.192.

66. Leslie Stephen in the *Nation,* 23 October 1866.
67. *The Times,* 17 June 1867.
68. Minute Books of the Reform League in the Howell Collection, Bishopsgate Institute; the *Daily News,* 26 September 1866, gives a comprehensive account of the Reform Union's supporters.
69. See the *Oxford Chronicle,* April 1866-July 1867.
70. *Cambridge Independent Press,* 21-8 April 1866.
71. Houghton MSS., Trinity College, Cambridge: Rutson – de Grey, 6 January 1867.
72. John Morley, *William Ewart Gladstone,* vol. i, Lloyds, 1908, p. 634.
73. Stephen in the *Nation,* 23 October 1866, p. 332.
74. Fisher, op. cit., vol. i, p. 119; Sir Henry Cunningham, *Lord Bowen,* 1896, p. 100; F. Harrison, *Autobiographic Memoirs,* Macmillan, 1911, p. 299.
75. E. im Thurn 'Edward John Eyre, 1815-1901' in the *D.N.B.* Bernard Semmel, *The Governor Eyre Controversy,* MacGibbon & Kee, 1962, chapter 3.
76. See list of members of the Committee on 1 January 1867 in *Jamaica Papers,* vol. v.
77. Vincent, op. cit., p. 196.
78. *Daily News,* 6 October 1866.
79. See *D.N.B.* article on Eyre; Semmel, op. cit., chapter 5.
80. The Tests demonstration at Manchester in April 1866 had to compete with a speech by Gladstone at Liverpool; see Bryce MSS.: Goldwin Smith – Bryce, 17 April 1866.
81. Bryce MSS.: Bryce – Freeman, 2 December 1865.
82. Bryce MSS.: Freeman – Bryce, 11 June, 1 July 1866; Bryce – Freeman, 24 June 1866.
83. Bryce MSS.: Freeman – Bryce, 16 September 1866.
84. Sidgwick MSS.: Henry Sidgwick – mother, 7 November 1866; and Sidgwick – Seeley, 9, 10, 12 and 15 May 1866.
85. Leslie Stephen in the *Nation,* 23 October 1866.
86. R. T. Shannon, 'John Robert Seeley and the Idea of a National Church' in Robson, ed., *Ideas and Institutions of Victorian Britain,* Bell, 1967, p. 242.
87. Bryce MSS.: Freeman – Bryce, 26 November 1865; Goldwin Smith, op. cit., p. 365.
88. Beesly MSS.: E. S. Beesly – Henry Crompton, 21 November 1864.
89. Frederic Harrison, 'The Century Club' in the *Cornhill,* 1903, reprinted in *Realities and Ideals,* Macmillan, 1908, p. 376.
90. ibid., p. 371.
91. ibid., p. 376.
92. ibid., p. 374.
93. *Saturday Review,* 23 February-27 April 1867.
94. Bryce MSS.: Roundell – Bryce, 29 November 1866.
95. C. L. Graves, *Life and Letters of Alexander Macmillan,* Macmillan, 1910, p. 200.
96. Graves, op. cit., p. 214.
97. Cunningham, op. cit., pp. 93-4.
98. Phyllis Grosskurth, *John Addington Symonds,* Longmans, 1964, p. 106.
99. ibid., p. 105.

100. Houghton MSS.: Rutson – Houghton, 8 January 1876.
101. Boase, *Modern English Biography,* vol.iii, privately published, 1892; Cass, 1965, p.360.
102. Grosskurth, op. cit., p.106.
103. Symonds MSS.: Rutson – J.A.Symonds, 20 February 1865.
104. The Rutsons were a Liverpool merchant family who had bought land: see *Burke's Landed Gentry, 1952,* under Rutson-Fife; *Victoria History: Yorkshire (North Riding),* vol.i. pp.179, 380, 546, 548; W.A. Munford, *William Ewart,* Grafton, 1960, pp.xiv, 18.
105. Bryce MSS.: Rutson – Bryce, 10 December 1866.
106. Houghton MSS.: Rutson – Houghton, 15 January 1867.
107. Macmillan MSS.: Bryce – A.Macmillan, 4 and 6 December 1866; and Harrison MSS.: Harrison – E.S.Beesly, n.d., 1859.
108. Bryce MSS.: Rutson – Bryce, 10 and 11 December 1866.
109. Bryce, op. cit., p.88.
110. Houghton MSS.: Rutson – Houghton, 17 January 1867.
111. Deduced from comparison of list of contributors in the *Saturday Review,* 11 February 1867, with published book.
112. Houghton MSS.: Rutson – Houghton, 15 January 1867; Bryce MSS.: Bryce – Freeman, 2 January 1867.
113. Lucien Wolf, *The Life of Lord Ripon,* John Murray, 1921, vol.i, p.221.
114. Houghton MSS.: Rutson – de Grey/Houghton, 4 January 1867.
115. *Daily News,* 18 March 1867.
116. Bryce MSS.: Rutson – Bryce, 5 March 1867.
117. Robert Blake, *Disraeli,* 1966; Methuen, 1969, pp.456-7.
118. Dicey did not meet Goldwin Smith until 1871, so cannot have been in the original group: see Bryce MSS.: Dicey – Bryce, 25 July 1909; on 15 January Rutson was still looking for someone to write what became Stephen's essay: see Houghton MSS.: Rutson – Houghton, 15 January 1867.
119. Rutson gave the later date in his letter to Houghton of 16 January.
120. R.S.Rait, 'A.V.Dicey, 1835-1922' and C.P.Lucas, 'E.J.S.Dicey, 1832-1911' in the *D.N.B.*
121. William Stebbing, ed., *Memorials of Charles Henry Pearson,* Longmans, 1900, p.94.
122. Sidney Lee, 'Goldwin Smith, 1823-1910' in the *D.N.B.*
123. Frederic Harrison, letters on 'Martial Law', *Daily News,* 1866, *Jamaica Papers,* vol.v.
124. Account of events and descriptions of measures from F.B.Smith, op. cit., unless otherwise stated.
125. cf. Briggs, op. cit., p.261; Royden Harrison, op. cit., p.109: F.B.Smith, op. cit., pp.2, 230.
126. Houghton MSS.: Rutson – de Grey/Houghton, 4 January 1867.
127. Bagehot 'Introduction to the Second Edition' of *The English Constitution,* 1872, p.266.
128. *Hansard,* 3rd series, vol.clxxxviii, cols.1086 ff.
129. *Daily News,* 18 March 1867.
130. Bryce MSS.: Alexander Macmillan – Bryce, 14 March 1867.
131. *The Times,* 3 May 1867.

132. Macmillan MSS.: Bryce – Macmillan, 13 March 1867, Goldwin Smith was a regular contributor to the *Examiner.*

133. A.Tilney Bassett, *Gladstone's Speeches*, Cassell, 1916, pp.36-7.

134. Vincent, op cit., pp.190-94.

135. Leventhal, op. cit., p.80.

136. Royden Harrison,op. cit., p.136.

137. Report in the *Bee-hive*, 13 May 1867.

138. The academics, on the whole, cared little for Thorold Rogers: cf. Bryce MSS.: Bryce – Freeman, 24 December 1886; for his Reform League career see the *Oxford Chronicle*, April 1866-August 1867.

139. Royden Harrison, op. cit., p.141.

140. *Oxford Chronicle*, 18 May 1867.

141. cf. the tone of Smith's article 'Securities for Reform' in *Manchester Examiner*, 1 April 1867.

142. Robert Lowe, anonymous review in the *Quarterly Review*, vol.cxxiii, July 1867, p.277.

143. John Morley, review in the *Fortnightly Review*, vol.i, new series, 1 April 1867, p.469.

144. W.R.W.Stephens, *The Life of Edward Augustus Freeman*, vol.i, Macmillan, 1895, p.257; Bryce MSS.: Bryce – Freeman, 4 April 1867.

145. Leslie Stephen, *The Letters of J.R.Green*, Macmillan, 1901, p.500.

146. *Guardian*, 3 April 1867.

147. 'The Republicanism of Young England' in the *Contemporary Review*, vol.v, June 1867, p.238.

148. Lowe, anonymous review in the *Quarterly Review*, p.244.

149. ibid., p.253.

150. J.R.Green, anonymous review of *Essays on Reform* in the *Saturday Review*, 6 April 1867, p.437.

151. ibid.

152. e.g. the *Westminster Review*, vol.lxxxviii, July 1867, p.162.

153. Beales, op. cit., p.10; the *Athenaeum*, 23 March 1867.

154. *Daily News*, 28 March 1867.

155. F.B.Smith, op. cit., p.182.

156. Bryce MSS.: Bryce – Freeman, 4 April 1867.

157. *Daily News*, 9 April 1867.

158. H.J.Hanham, *Elections and Party Management*, Longmans, 1959, p.39.

159. *Manchester Examiner*, 5 April 1867.

160. Briggs, op. cit., p.189.

161. Leslie Stephen, 'The Political Situation in England' in the *North American Review*, October 1868, p.548.

162. Bryce MSS.: Goldwin Smith – Bryce, 22 July 1866.

163. cf. John Morley's comments in the *Fortnightly Review*, p.492.

164. *Oxford Chronicle*, 20 April 1867.

165. cf. F.Harrison, 'The Transit of Power' in the *Fortnightly Review* vol.iii, May 1868, republished in *Order and Progress*, pp.147 ff.

166. Gooch, op. cit., p.84.

167. Maitland, op. cit., p.203.

7. THE SCIENCE AND ART OF POLITICS pp.141-73

1. The Positivists were explicit elitists, and commentators on their political thought have tended to attribute their ideas to their colleagues, e.g. D.A.Hamer in *John Morley: Liberal Intellectual in Politics*, Oxford, 1968, p.78; C.Kent, 'Academic Radicalism in Mid-Victorian England', D.Phil. thesis, Sussex, 1969.

2. cf. Goldwin Smith's disparaging reference to the venality of the eighteenth century in his *Inaugural Lecture*, Parker, 1859, or A.V. Dicey's article 'Legal Etiquette' in the *Fortnightly Review*, vol.viii, 1 August 1867, which argued that lawyers' privileges were contingent on their utility to society.

3. Leslie Stephen, 'On the Choice of Representatives by Popular Constituencies' in *Essays on Reform*, Macmillan, 1867, p.106.

4. Mosca, Pareto and Weber (on the Prussian bureaucracy) were not translated into English until the 1920s. For a discussion of the application of elite theory to British politics in the nineteenth century see my essay 'Theories of Elites' in *British Elites, 1750-1870*, Open University Press, 1974.

5. In *Essays on Reform*, p.85.

6. ibid., p.91.

7. ibid., p.116.

8. Goldwin Smith, op. cit., p.12; and Seeley, 'The Teaching of Politics' in *Lectures and Essays*, Macmillan, 1870, p.296. Seeley's argument is so close to Smith's that conscious borrowing seems likely.

9. Goldwin Smith, op. cit., p.12.

10. Schools Inquiry Commission: Evidence, *Parliamentary Papers*, vol.xxviii, 1867-8, part ii, p.81.

11. Arnold Haultain, ed., *The Life and Opinions of Goldwin Smith*, Werner Laurie, 1913, pp.52-4.

12. G.S.Kitson Clark, 'History at Cambridge, 1873-1973' in the *Historical Journal*, vol.xvi, no.3, 1973, pp.541-2.

13. ibid., p.538; and Audrey Cunningham, *William Cunningham, Teacher and Priest*, S.P.C.K., 1950, p.67.

14. Green MSS.: Essay-book I: 'The Duties of the University to the State'.

15. C.S.Parker 'On the History of Classical Education' in F.W.Farrar, *Essays on a Liberal Education*, Macmillan, 1867, p.78.

16. *The Times*, 18 December 1862 (cutting in Brodrick MSS.).

17. Bryce MSS.: Bryce – Freeman, 22 May 1865; and see pp.85-6.

18. A.O.Rutson, 'Opportunities and Shortcomings of Government in England' in *Essays on Reform*, pp.289-90.

19. ibid.

20. Leslie Stephen, *The English Utilitarians*, vol.iii, Duckworth, 1900 p.280.

21. For instance, see Leslie Stephen, 'On the Choice of Representatives', pp.119-20. Professor H.J.Hanham has commented on this recognition as a sign of greater radical maturity in the 1860s as compared with the 1830s: see *Elections and Party Management*, Longmans, 1959, p.xv.

22. *The Working Men's College, 1854-1904*, p.17.

23. For biographical information see the *D.N.B.*, save for Lushington, for whom see *The Times*, 6 February 1907, and Royden Harrison, 'The

Positivists: A Study of Labour's Intellectuals' in *Before the Socialists*, Routledge, 1965, p.251.

24. Frederic Harrison, 'Parliament before Reform', an article published in March 1867 in the *Fortnightly Review*, and reprinted in *Order and Progress*, Longmans Green, 1875, pp.147, 151.

25. A.O.Rutson, op. cit., pp.293-4.

26. For instance, see A.V.Dicey, 'The Balance of Classes' in *Essays on Reform*, p.76. The 'incorporation' argument was also used by Godfrey Lushington in his essay on 'Workmen and Trade Unions' in *Questions for a Reformed Parliament*, Macmillan, 1867, p.56. Professor Royden Harrison, in his study of the Positivists and the Labour Movement in *Before the Socialists*, pp.251-342, has tended, I feel, to be led by their violence of language – notably in the cases of E.S.Beesly and Frederic Harrison – to over-emphasize their proletarian consciousness and neglect their basic economic orthodoxy and close connections with middle-class liberal intellectuals.

27. John Malcolm Ludlow and Lloyd Jones, 'The Progress of the Working Classes' in *Questions for a Reformed Parliament*, p.328.

28. Richard Holt Hutton, 'The Political Character of the Working Class' in *Essays on Reform*, pp. 38-9.

29. Leslie Stephen, 'On the Choice of Representatives', p.121.

30. James Bryce, 'The Historical Aspect of Democracy' in *Essays on Reform*, p:270.

31. ibid., p.272.

32. ibid., p.277. Bryce never departed, throughout his career, from this diagnosis. Despite his later disillusion with the effects of democratic government, he could still write to A.V.Dicey in 1921 that 'the extension of the franchise has not heated the boiler further, but may rather have been a safety valve': see Bryce MSS.: Bryce – Dicey, 9 May 1921.

33. Lord Houghton, 'On the Admission of the Working Classes' in *Essays on Reform*, p.63.

34. G.C.Brodrick, review of John Stuart Mill, *Thoughts on Parliamentary Reform*, Parker, 1859 in *The Times*, 1859, republished in *Political Studies*, Kegan Paul, 1879, p.139 (afterwards cited as 'Review of Mill.')

35. Green MSS.: R.L.Nettleship's notes for Green's life: 'Almost the last words he said were, "Mill was such a *good* man" '; see also Melvin Richter, *The Politics of Conscience: T.H.Green and His Age*, Weidenfeld & Nicholson, 1964, p.165.

36. See R.L.Nettleship, 'Memoir of Green', in *Works of T.H.Green*, vol.iii, Longmans, 1885, p.xliv.

37. G.C.Brodrick, 'The Utilitarian Objection to Reform' in *Essays on Reform*, p.7.

38. ibid. (Echoed by Houghton, op. cit. p.47.)

39. ibid., p.8.

40. ibid., p.11 (see also Rutson, op. cit., p.293).

41. ibid. (See also Stephen, 'On the Choice of Representatives', p.121.)

42. J.S.Mill, *Considerations on Representative Government*, Longmans Green, 1861, p.100.

43. Brodrick, 'Review of Mill', p.141.

44. ibid., p.143. (By and large, throughout their careers, the academics were resolute opponents of women's suffrage. Fawcett, Henry Sidgwick and Edward Caird were exceptions to the general rule. The Positivists seem to have been the most enthusiastic anti-suffragists of the lot. An interesting statement of their case against Mill is given by Frederic Harrison in a letter to John Morley in 1871: see Harrison MSS.: Harrison – Morley, 20 February 1871.)

45. ibid.

46. ibid., p.143.

47. ibid., p.146 (see also Stephen, 'On the Choice of Representatives', p.106).

48. ibid., p.151.

49. Stephen, 'On the Choice of Representatives', p.96.

50. ibid., p.104.

51. Rutson, op. cit., p.279.

52. ibid., p.293. This seems diametrically opposed to the picture of cabinet government given by Bagehot in *The English Constitution*, Chapman & Hall, 1867, which contributors to the reform essays could have read in the *Fortnightly Review* in 1865 and 1866. Although Bryce and Dicey venerated him in their pessimistic later years – see Bryce MSS.: Bryce – Dicey, 27 April 1916 – I can find no mention of his work in the reform essays, and no sign that any of the contributors was at all influenced by it. The fact that, at a period when partisan feeling ran high, he was so often found on the 'other side', may account for this.

53. cf. Basil Willey, *Nineteenth-Century Studies*, 1949; Penguin 1964, pp.152-9.

54. As were most liberals during the 1860s, to whom Mill's intellectual innovations made little sense. They seem to have included Mill himself: see John Vincent, *The Formation of the Liberal Party 1857-1868*, Constable, 1966, p.190.

55. cf. Duncan Forbes, *The Liberal Anglican Idea of History*, Cambridge, 1952, p.123.

56. For instance, Dicey continued to condemn him until he died in 1873: see R.Rait, *Memorials of A.V.Dicey*, Macmillan 1925, p.56; and Henry Sidgwick's poem, 'The Despot's Heir', was published in *Macmillan's Magazine*, March 1861, quoted in A.S. & E.M.S., *Henry Sidgwick: A Memoir*, Macmillan, 1906, p.64.

57. John Stuart Mill, *Autobiography*, 1873; Oxford 1924, p.201.

58. Rutson, op. cit., p.281.

59. Noel Annan, 'The Curious Strength of Positivism in English Political Thought' L.T.Hobhouse Lecture delivered 7 May 1958; O.U.P., 1959, p.15.

60. See James Bryce, 'The Historical Aspect of Democracy', p.266; see also Bryce MSS.: Bryce – Freeman, 2 January 1867, and Freeman – Bryce, 3 and 24 February 1867; also Stephen, 'On the Choice of Representatives', p.92.

61. Stephen, 'On the Choice of Representatives', p.92.

62. Rutson, op. cit., p.285.

63. cf. Bryce, op. cit., pp.243-50.

64. Forbes, op. cit., p.142.
65. See L.P.Curtis Jnr, *Anglo-Saxons and Celts*, University of Bridgeport, 1968, chapter vi.
66. Frederic Harrison, *National and Social Problems*, Macmillan, 1908, pp.124-9, 146-62.
67. Bolton King, *The Life of Mazzini*, Everyman, 1902, pp.269-75; and my pp.101-4.
68. Rutson chose de Tocqueville's chapters as the model for the reform essays: see Houghton MSS.: Rutson – Houghton, 5 January 1867.
69. Brodrick, 'The Utilitarian Objection to Reform', pp.19-20; and see Hugh Brogan, 'Tocqueville and the Liberal Moment' in *Historical Journal*, vol.xiv, no.2, 1971, pp.289-303.
70. James Bryce, 'The Historical Aspect of Democracy', p.241.
71. ibid., p.272.
72. Vincent, op. cit., p.153.
73. Stephen, 'On the Choice of Representatives', pp.119-20.
74. Brodrick, 'Review of Mill', p.153.
75. Vincent, op. cit., p.153.
76. Rutson, op. cit., p.304.
77. Brodrick, 'Review of Mill', p.153.
78. Goldwin Smith, op. cit., p.17.
79. Brodrick, 'Review of Mill, p.152.
80. Goldwin Smith, op. cit., p.33.
81. Bryce MSS.: Bryce – Dicey, 14 November 1913.
82. Leslie Stephen's chapter on 'Political Economy' in his *The Life of Henry Fawcett*, Smith Elder, 1885, pp.136-74, is, I think, probably the best account of the economic beliefs held by Fawcett's generation. See also G.C.Brodrick, 'The Socialistic Tendencies of Modern Democracy' in *Macmillan's Magazine*, vol.liii, March 1886. Henry Sidgwick, latterly prepared to make heretical suggestions about government control of large areas of the economy, nevertheless insisted that he did so on accepted economic principles, and, on the same grounds, found it very difficult even to accept the distortion of the market implied by the operation of the Poor Law: see Sidgwick MSS.: Sir Louis Mallet – Sidgwick, 8 April, 16 September 1886, 14 July, 5 October 1887, and Sidgwick – Mallet, 23 July 1887; also papers prepared for the Political Economy Club and the Charity Organisation Society during the 1870s and 1880s.
83. G.C.Brodrick, 'On the different principles on which the chief systems of popular government have been based in ancient and modern times', T. & G.Shrimpton, 1855, pp.17-18.
84. Bryce, op. cit., p.239.
85. Brodrick, 'On the principles of popular government', p.140.
86. Sir George Young, 'The House of Commons in 1833' in *Essays on Reform*, p.320.
87. B.Cracroft, 'The analysis of the House of Commons, or Indirect Representation' in *Essays on Reform*, p.162.
88. Houghton MSS.: Rutson – Houghton, 15 January 1867.
89. Young, op. cit., pp.321-3
90. Young, op. cit., p.309.

91. Brodrick, 'On the principles of popular government', pp. 149-50.
92. Dicey, 'The Balance of Classes' in *Essays on Reform* p. 83; see also Stephen, 'On the Choice of Representatives', p. 121.
93. Brodrick, 'On the principles of popular government', p. 146; this was also echoed by Stephen, 'On the Choice of Representatives', p. 113.
94. Sidgwick MSS.: Dicey – Mrs Sidgwick, 7 November 1902.
95. A.V.Dicey, *Law and Public Opinion*, Macmillan, 1905, p. 219.
96. ibid.
97. Statistics from Geoffrey Best, *Mid-Victorian Britain, 1851-1873,* Weidenfeld & Nicholson, 1971, pp. 6-7.
98. cf. Olive Anderson, *A Liberal State at War*, Macmillan, 1967, pp. 130-40; and Vincent, op. cit., p. 117.
99. Stephen, 'On the Choice of Representatives', p. 110; Rutson, op. cit., p. 304.
100. Charles Pearson, *National Life and Character,* Macmillan, 1893, p. 265; cf. also James Bryce, *The American Commonwealth*, Macmillan, 1889, vol. ii, p. 628; and Leonard Courtney, 'The Swarming of Men' in *Nineteenth Century*, vol. xxiii, March 1888.
101. J.R.Green, 'The East End and its Relief Committees' in the *Saturday Review*, 11 January 1868, reprinted in *Stray Studies*, Macmillan, 1903, pp. 137-48.
102. W.L.Newman, 'The Land Laws' in *Questions for a Reformed Parliament.*
103. Stephen, *Henry Fawcett*, p. 156.
104. ibid., p. 155.
105. ibid., p. 163: for Sidgwick see Sidgwick MSS.: John Malcolm Ludlow – Sidgwick, 13 July 1869 (describing five cooperative workships which would welcome investment, in response to an offer of help from H.S.); Edward Meads – Sidgwick, 20 September 1871 (letter from the Secretary of one of the five, the London Co-operative Cabinet Manufacturing Society, appealing to H.S. for a message of encouragement to the workers, as the business was in difficulty and the men discouraged). In addition see *The Oxford Industrial and Cooperative Society: An Historical Sketch, 1872-1909,* for the involvement of academics in it, including Goldwin Smith, H.J.S.Smith and A.H.D.Acland; James Stuart at Cambridge tried to link the cause of University Extension with that of Cooperation (p. 208); his Trinity colleague, Sedley Taylor, wrote sympathetically on *Profit-Sharing*, Macmillan, 1884; see also Thorold Rogers, *The Industrial and Commercial History of England*, Unwin, 1891, pp. 146-50.
106. Goldwin Smith, *Reminiscences,* Macmillan, 1911, pp. 280-81.
107. Paraphrased by G.P.Gooch in *Lord Courtney,* Macmillan, 1920, p. 109.
108. T.H.Green, *Lectures on the Principles of Political Obligation,* delivered 1879; Longmans Green, 1921, pp. 227-8; Frederic Harrison's New Year address to the Positivist Association, 1880, shows that the Positivist line was much the same: see F.Harrison, *National and Social Problems*, pp. 250-51.
109. Goldwin Smith, 'The Experience of the American Commonwealth' in *Essays on Reform*, p. 218.
110. Goldwin Smith, *The Civil War in America*, Manchester Union and Emancipation Society, 1866, pp. 27-9.

111.   'Mr Goldwin Smith and the American Example for England' in the *Economist*, 23 March 1867. On grounds of style and content, I would attribute this review to Walter Bagehot, but I lack definitive proof.

112.   Rutson, op. cit., p.295; see also G.C.Brodrick's extended study of land and the land laws, undertaken for the Cobden Club, *English Land and English Landlords*, Cassell, 1881; for a critique of the old orthodoxy by a younger academic of collectivist leanings, see C.A.Fyffe, *The Land Question: a Lecture given at the Oxford Reform Club, November 26, 1884*.

113.   Henry Fawcett, *The Economic Position of the British Labourer*, Cambridge, 1865, pp.40-43.

114.   Newman, op. cit., p.119; see also Dicey, *Law and Public Opinion*, p.1xxv.

115.   Matthew Arnold, *Culture and Anarchy*, Murray, 1869, p.134.

116.   Rutson, op. cit., pp.298-9. cf. Harold Perkin's calculation of the apparently secure wealth of the mid-century aristocracy in *The Origins of Modern English Society*, Routledge, 1969, p.416.

117.   Quoted in Alan Harding, *A Social History of English Law*, Penguin, 1966, p.334.

118.   A.V.Dicey, 'The Legal Boundaries of Liberty' in *Fortnightly Review*, no.xxiii, 1 January 1868, p.8.

119.   Fawcett, op. cit., pp.174-5.

120.   Lushington, 'Workmen and Trade Unions' in *Questions for a Reformed Parliament*, p.50. The Positivist patronage of trade unions had its roots in their political and legal interests; Austin Harrison regarded his father's, Frederic Harrison's, grasp of economics as 'decidedly weak', despite his influential position: see Austin Harrison, *Frederic Harrison: Thoughts and Memories*, Heinemann, 1926, p.154.

121.   Dicey, 'The Legal Boundaries of Liberty', p.6.

122.   Dicey, 'The Balance of Classes' in *Essays on Reform*, p.72.

123.   Lushington, op. cit., p.56.

124.   *The Times*: obituary of Lushington, 6 February 1907; Bryce MSS.: Bryce – Dicey, 24 November 1908.

125.   Young, op. cit., p.319.

126.   cf. Dicey, *Law and Public Opinion*, pp.146-62.

127.   S.Webb, 'The Basis of Socialism: Historic' in *Fabian Essays in Socialism* Fabian Society, 1889, p.65.

128.   Leslie Stephen, *Life of Sir James Fitzjames Stephen*, Smith Elder, 1895, pp.376-81; see also John Boyd Kinnear, 'Law Reform' in *Questions for a Reformed Parliament*.

129.   Royden Harrison, op. cit., p.310.

130.   Harding, op. cit., p.349; and A.V.Dicey, 'Law Teaching, Oral and Written', in H.H.Henson, ed., *A Memoir of the Right Honourable Sir William Anson*, Oxford, 1920, pp.84-103.

131.   Stephen, *Fitzjames Stephen*, pp.376-81.

132.   See Harding, op. cit., p.349 and F.H.Lawson, *The Oxford Law School*, Oxford, 1968.

133.   See Bryce, 'Robert Lowe' in *Studies in Contemporary Biography*, Macmillan, 1903, p.305.

134.   Commons Preservation was a most un-Benthamite activity, according to Dicey in *Law and Public Opinion*, p.249, yet Fawcett was an ardent preservationist – see Stephen, *Henry Fawcett*, p.293 – and Leslie

Stephen first secretary of the C.P.S.: see F.W.Maitland, *The Life and Letters of Leslie Stephen*, Duckworth, 1906, p.172. Bryce tried to apply the principle of endowment redistribution to charity in 1883 with his City Charities Bill, transferring traditional benefactions from the depopulated centre of London to the East End: see H.A.L.Fisher, *James Bryce, Viscount Bryce of Dechmont,* vol.i, Macmillan, 1927, p.188.

135. Quoted in Asa Briggs, *Victorian People,* 1954; Penguin, 1965, p.262.
136. Charles Stuart Parker, 'Popular Education' in *Questions for a Reformed Parliament,* p.131.
137. ibid., pp.177-84.
138. ibid., p.191; see also Stephen, *Henry Fawcett,* p.163.
139. Parker, op. cit., p.165.
140. Schools Inquiry: Royal Commission, The Taunton Commission, *Parliamentary Papers,* vol. xxviii, 1867-8, part 1, Report.
141. Secondary Education: Royal Commission, The Bryce Commission, *Parliamentary Papers,* vol. xliii, 1895, part 1, Report, pp.9, 133.
142. Taunton Commission Report, p.613.
143. Bamford, *Rise of the Public Schools,* Nelson, 1967, p.184.
144. Bryce Commission Report, pp.10 ff.
145. For the development of this see Gillian Sutherland, *Policy-Making in Elementary Education, 1870-1895,* Oxford, 1973.
146. ibid., p.43.
147. cf. Roach, *Public Examination in England,* Cambridge, 1971, chap. 11.
148. Bamford, op. cit., pp.183 ff.
149. Parker, op. cit., p.134.
150. See table in Bamford, op. cit., p.172.
151. G.C.Brodrick, 'The Influence of the Older English Universities on National Education', lecture delivered to the Social Science Congress, Brighton, October 1875, reprinted in *Literary Fragments,* Spottiswoode, 1891, pp.30-31.
152. Dicey, 'The Balance of Classes', p.76.
153. For Bryce see Fisher, op. cit., vol.i, p.110; for Green see Taunton Commission Report, p.307; for Stuart see his *Reminiscences,* Cassell, 1912, p.177; for Stanley see *Oxford University Reform,* 1869, pp.18-19. While the distinction between classical and modern education remained, the step-ladder was virtually a non-starter: see Bryce Commission Report p.63.
154. cf. J.R.Green's review of *Essays on Reform* in the *Saturday Review,* 6 April 1867.
155. John Vincent, *Pollbooks: How Victorians Voted,* Cambridge, 1967, p.50.
156. G.C.Brodrick, *Memories and Impressions,* Nisbett & Co., 1900, pp.222-3.

8. PRACTICAL POLITICS 1868-86 pp.174-217

1. G.M.Trevelyan, *Sir George Otto Trevelyan,* Longmans, 1932, p.124.
2. J.Roach 'Liberalism and the Victorian Intelligentsia' in *Cambridge Historical Journal,* vol.xiii, 1957, p.71.
3. Gladstonian: Bryce, Rutson, Young, Lushington, Parker, Harrison and Rogers. Unionist: Brodrick, Hutton, Dicey, Leslie Stephen,

Kinnear, Cracroft, Pearson, Goldwin Smith, Hill, Townsend and Ludlow. Politics not known: Newman and Hooper.

4. cf. F.M.L.Thompson, *English Landed Society in the Nineteenth Century*, Routledge, 1963, pp.303-15, and Harold Perkin, *The Origins of Modern English Society*, Routledge, 1969, p.416.

5. James Bryce, extract from speech to students of McGill University, Montreal, 1913, quoted in obituary in the *Scotsman*, 23 February 1922.

6. B.Cracroft, 'The Analysis of the House of Commons' in *Essays on Reform*, Macmillan, 1867, p.177.

7. H.J.Hanham, *Elections and Party Management*, Longmans, 1959, p.211.

8. ibid., p.212.

9. *Nation*, vol.vii, 8 August 1868, written 18 July pp.109-110. Fawcett's opinion was similar: see Fawcett – J.E.Cairnes, 23 August 1868, quoted in Leslie Stephen, *The Life of Henry Fawcett*, Smith Elder, 1885, pp.238-9.

10. *Fortnightly Review*, vol.iii, new series, 1 July 1868, p.112.

11. ibid., p.114.

12. Goldwin Smith – Frederic Harrison, 26 October 1868, in Arnold Haultain, ed., *Goldwin Smith's Correspondence*, Werner Laurie, 1913, p.13.

13. Hanham, op. cit., pp.252, 262; the most corrupt boroughs tended to be of medium size.

14. F.W.Maitland, *The Life and Letters of Leslie Stephen*, Duckworth, 1906, pp.106-7.

15. Stephen, the *Nation*, vol.vii, 8 August 1868, pp.109-10.

16. Bryce MSS.: Joshua Girling Fitch – James Bryce, n.d., 1867.

17. Harrison MSS.: A.O.Rutson – Frederic Harrison, 3 and 4 September 1868.

18. G.C.Brodrick, *Memories and Impressions*, Nisbett & Co., 1900, p.147.

19. ibid., p.198.

20. Bryce MSS.: Freeman – Bryce, 22 November 1868; S.H.Harris, *Auberon Herbert, Crusader for Liberty*, Williams & Norgate, 1943, pp.85-6; *The Times*, 19 September 1868.

21. *D.N.B.*

22. Dilke dropped out of academic liberal society after the Crawford divorce case in 1885. He was expelled from the Ad Eundem – see Jackson MSS.: Sir George Young – Henry Jackson, 12 June 1907 – and from various remarks of Bryce and Trevelyan it is evident that he was subsequently regarded with intense hostility. Donald Crawford, the 'injured party' was a friend of Bryce and T.H.Green; one imagines that Dilke's intrigues with Mrs Pattison and Mrs Crawford were construed as an assault on the mores of the group: see Bryce MSS.: Bryce – G.O.Trevelyan, 4 February 1918.

23. Stephen, *Henry Fawcett*, p.216.

24. ibid., pp.195-6. In Stephen's MSS. of the biography, at Trinity Hall, Cambridge, there is an interesting series of annotations by Mrs Fawcett in which, usually successfully, she attempts to tone down the instances of her husband's political acumen.

25. Brodrick, op. cit., p.264.

26. Hanham, op. cit., p.250.

27. ibid., p. 252.
28. ibid., p. 258.
29. ibid., p. 252.
30. ibid., p. 40.
31. Trevelyan, op. cit., pp. 72-3.
32. Royden Harrison, 'The Reform League and the General Election of 1868' in *Before the SOCIALISTS,* Routledge, 1965, p. 174.
33. ibid., p. 182; Hanham, op. cit., p. 330.
34. *Oxford Chronicle,* 18 May 1867.
35. 'The Exclusion of the Clergy from the House of Commons' in *Fraser's Magazine,* vol. lxxv, June 1867.
36. *Spectator,* 5 September 1868.
37. ibid., 14 November 1868.
38. Bryce MSS.: Roundell – Bryce, 4 August 1868.
39. *The Times,* 12, 15 and 23 August 1868.
40. ibid., 23 September 1868.
41. ibid., 20 October 1868.
42. Bryce MSS.: Freeman – Bryce, 25 October 1868.
43. Harrison MSS.: Rutson – Harrison, 4 September 1868.
44. Howell MSS.: Constituency Reports: Chippenham.
45. *The Times,* 24 August 1868.
46. Howell MSS.: Constituency Reports: Woodstock.
47. *The Times,* 3 November 1868.
48. Howell MSS.: Constituency Reports: Woodstock.
49. *The Times,* 19 August, 10, 19, 24 and 29 October, 3, 7 and 17 November 1868.
50. ibid., 1 and 29 October 1868.
51. ibid., 1 October 1868.
52. ibid., 7 November 1868; Bryce MSS.: Freeman – Bryce, 31 October, 22 November 1868; Sir George Young – Bryce, 12 February 1892.
53. He was particularly active in Sheffield, where he promoted A. J. Mundella's candidature, and in Marylebone, where he supported Dr Humphry Sandwith: see *The Times,* 19, 21 August; the article on Goldwin Smith in the *D.N.B.,* supp. ii; and Howell MSS.: Letter-book for 1868.
54. Thorold Rogers MSS.: S. Morley – Rogers, 27 June 1868; *The Times* 1, 24 October, 14 November 1868.
55. Bryce MSS.: Roundell – Bryce, 4 August 1868.
56. ibid.
57. Hanham, op. cit., p. 215.
58. *The Times,* 24 August 1868.
59. Howell MSS.: Constituency Reports: Chippenham.
60. ibid.: Woodstock.
61. Bryce MSS.: Freeman – Bryce, 9 December 1868; see also Charles Robarts's declaration speech in Mid-Surrey, *The Times,* 27 November; Sir George Young's at Chippenham, *The Times,* 21 November 1868; Brodrick, op. cit., pp. 151-2.
62. Bryce MSS.: Freeman – Bryce, 2 November 1868; W. R. W. Stephens, *Life and Letters of Edward Augustus Freeman,* vol. i Macmillan, 1895, p. 354.

63. Green MSS.: Green – Charlotte Symonds, 29 November 1868, from R.L.Nettleship's notes for Green's life.

64. *The Times*, 18 November 1868.

65. *Fortnightly Review*, vol.iii, 1 December 1868, p.692.

66. J.R.Green – Edward Denison, 21 September 1868, quoted in Leslie Stephen, *The Letters of J.R.Green*, Macmillan, 1901, p.201.

67. ibid., 19 November 1868, p.205.

68. *Saturday Review*, vol.xxiii, 6 April 1867, p.438.

69. Sir George Young – Herbert, 23 February 1870, quoted in Harris, op. cit., p.98.

70. James Bryce – Herbert, 25 February 1870, quoted in Harris, op.cit., p.98. In March 1869 John Morley attempted to get in for Blackburn at a by-election. He campaigned on a 'moderate liberal' address, wildly at variance with the impatient radicalism of his *Fortnightly* line but in character with his enduring enthusiasm for the game of politics. He lost heavily: see F.W.Hirst, *The Early Life and Letters of John Morley*, vol.i, Macmillan, 1927, pp.132-54.

71. Most of the details here are taken from the *D.N.B.*, with the exception of those from: Brodrick, op. cit., p.162; Sir Henry Cunningham, *Lord Bowen*, 1896, pp.118-19; and Roundell – Gladstone, 20 December 1868 and 7 January 1869, B.M.Add. MSS. 44418, and 27 December 1871, B.M.Add. MSS.44432.

72. 'The first of our lot', Auberon Herbert soon wearied of parliament and resigned his Nottingham seat in 1874 to devote himself to the propagation of his extreme individualist view of government: see Mill MSS.: Herbert – J.S.Mill, 29 May 1872; Harris, op. cit., p.144.

73. *The Times*, 10 February 1874.

74. Brodrick, op. cit., p.152.

75. Winston Churchill, *Lord Randolph Churchill*, vol.i, Macmillan, 1906, p.55.

76. Brodrick, op. cit., p.154.

77. ibid., pp.152, 154.

78. Hanham, op. cit., p.222.

79. *McCalmont's Parliamentary Poll Book; Burke's Landed Gentry*.

80. The *Glasgow Herald*, 28 January 1874, reported that Bryce was expected to come north 'to see how the land lies'. For Courtney see G.P.Gooch, *Lord Courtney*, Macmillan, 1920, p.119.

81. Bryce MSS.: J.Annan Bryce – Reuben John Bryce, 1 January 1872.

82. ibid., Alexander Douglas – Bryce, 21 April 1873.

83. ibid., Edward Caird – Bryce, n.d., 1874.

84. ibid., Bryce – Alexander Douglas, 28 November 1873.

85. ibid., Alexander Douglas – Bryce, 21 April 1873.

86. ibid., Edward Caird – Bryce, n.d., 1874.

87. H.A.L.Fisher, *James Bryce, Viscount Bryce of Dechmont*, vol.i, Macmillan, 1927, p.147.

88. Gooch, op. cit., p.119.

89. Bryce MSS.: Bryce – Freeman, 22 March 1874.

90. *John o'Groats Journal*, 9 February 1874.

91. *Caithness Chronicle*, 9 February 1874.

92. *Glasgow Herald*, 12 February 1874.

93. Bryce MSS.: Freeman – Bryce, 14 February 1874.

94. Gooch, op. cit., p.122.

95. Fawcett got back in for Hackney in April 1874 in a campaign run by Dilke and supported financially by many of his university colleagues: see Dilke MSS.: Edmond Fitzmaurice – Charles Dilke, 12 March, 18 and 22 April, 1 May 1874.

96. Bryce MSS.: Bryce – Freeman, 22 March 1874.

97. Hanham, op. cit., p.230; J.P.Mackintosh, *The British Cabinet*, Methuen, 1968, p.197.

98. Green's last speech was a call for an Oxford caucus on the Birmingham pattern: see Green MSS.: Notes for speech of 15 March 1882.

99. Letter in *Manchester Examiner and Times,* 19 April 1880.

100. Letter in *Manchester Examiner and Times*, 24 April 1879. Auberon Herbert, on libertarian grounds, was violently opposed to the caucus system: see Harris, op. cit., p.180.

101. Leventhal, *Respectable Radical: George Howell and Victorian Working-Class Politics,* Longman, 1971, p.200; D.A.Hamer, *Liberal Politics in the Age of Gladstone and Rosebery,* Oxford, 1972, p.81.

102. Bryce MSS.: Bryce – Freeman, 23 March 1879; H.O.Barnett, *Canon Barnett, His Life, Work and Friends*, Murray, 1918, p.216.

103. Bryce MSS.: Gladstone – Bryce, 23 March 1880.

104. Leventhal, op. cit., p.201.

105. Barnett, loc. cit.

106. Stephen, *Henry Fawcett,* p.196.

107. Jackson MSS.: Dicey – Henry Jackson, 21 February 1917.

108. James Bryce, preface to Mosei Ostrogorski, *Democracy and the Organisation of Political Parties,* vol.i, Macmillan, 1902, p.xlv.

109. Hamer, op. cit., chapter 3.

110. Gooch, op. cit., p.109.

111. Leventhal, op. cit., p.102.

112. Stephen Gwynn and Gertrude Tuckwell, *The Life of Sir Charles Dilke,* vol.i, Murray, 1917, p.100.

113. ibid.

114. Dilke MSS., British Museum: Frederic Harrison – Dilke, 7 July 1870, 8 February 1872; Mrs Fawcett – Dilke, 12 February 1871.

115. Dilke MSS.: Sir Louis Mallet – Dilke, 10 February 1871.

116. Harrison MSS.: Harrison – John Morley, 20 February 1871.

117. Royden Harrison, op. cit., pp.231, 274; Mill–Taylor MSS.: Mill – Fawcett, 26 July 1870. Outside the Radical Club, the only other pro-French voice I can find was Charles Henry Pearson – see William Stebbing, *Memorials of Charles Henry Pearson,* Longmans, 1900, p.182 – although Dilke and Herbert, who had started on the Prussian side, were later drawn to support a republican France: see Roy Jenkins, *Sir Charles Dilke, A Victorian Tagedy,* Collins, 1958, p.66. Freeman, Goldwin Smith and Bryce, though latterly with some misgivings, were pro-Prussian throughout: see Bryce MSS.: Bryce – Freeman, 26 September 1870; Bryce – G.O.Trevelyan, 9 June 1919; Goldwin Smith – Max Muller, 18 July 1870 in Haultain, ed., op. cit., p.23.

118. Harrison MSS.: Harrison – Morley, 20 February 1871.

119. Dilke MSS.: Dilke – Mrs Fawcett, 24 January 1871; Mrs Fawcett – Dilke, 27 January 1871. Though Dilke, as a Secularist, disapproved of the sectarianism of the N.E.L.: see Jenkins, op. cit., p.56.
120. Jenkins, op. cit., pp.69-76. (George Otto Trevelyan attacked the Queen's revenue anonymously.)
121. ibid., p.76.
122. Dilke MSS.: Harrison – Dilke, 9 February 1872.
123. Dilke MSS.: Auberon Herbert – Dilke, 31 January 1873.
124. Jenkins, op. cit., p.52.
125. Gwynn and Tuckwell, op. cit., vol. i, p.159.
126. John Morley, *Recollections*, vol. i, Macmillan, 1917, p.147; Harrison MSS.: Morley – Harrison, 17 July 1873.
127. Morley, op. cit., p.157.
128. Harrison MSS.: Morley – Harrison, 9 November 1875.
129. ibid., 23 August 1876.
130. Charles Stuart Parker, 'Popular Education', in *Questions for a Reformed Parliament*, Macmillan, 1867, p.165.
131. ibid., p.196.
132. James Murphy, *The Education Act, 1870: Text and Commentary*, David & Charles, 1972, p.28.
133. Sidgwick MSS.: Henry Sidgwick – Roche Dakyns, 5 August 1867.
134. G.O.Trevelyan resigned from the government over the Bill. Gladstone took a long time to forgive him: see Trevelyan, op. cit., p.91.)
135. Quoted in A.S. and E.M.S., *Henry Sidgwick: a Memoir*, Macmillan, 1906, p.254.
136. *Nation*, 9 July 1870, written on 24 June 1870.
137. *Nation*, 27 June 1870, written on 10 June 1870.
138. See J.W.Derry, *The Radical Tradition*, Macmillan, 1967, p.311.
139. Houghton MSS.: A.O.Rutson – Lord Houghton, 28 January 1872.
140. *The Times*, 6 February 1874.
141. T.H.Green, who had considered entering the Nonconformist ministry in the 1860s, had by 1880 moved back to accept the principle of establishment, subject to a broad-based theology and democratic participation by congregations: see Green MSS.: 'Notes for a Speech on Church Reform', Merton College, 7 December 1881; 'Arnold Toynbee 1852-1883' in the *D.N.B.*
142. Frank Harrison Hill, in *Questions for a Reformed Parliament*, pp.15-16.
143. Bryce MSS.: Bryce – Freeman, 1 May 1872. Cardinal Cullen was the Primate of all Ireland.
144. John Morley, *William Ewart Gladstone*, vol. ii, Lloyds, 1908, pp.33-5.
145. ibid.
146. Gooch, op. cit., p.112; the *Daily News* under Hill's editorship, also opposed the Bill: see Justin McCarthy, *A History of our Own Times*, vol. i, Chatto & Windus, 1887, p.401.
147. Gladstone MSS.: Report of Fawcett's speech, 11 March 1873, B.M.Add. MSS. 44156.
148. Morley, *Gladstone*, vol. ii, p.39.
149. ibid., p.53.
150. *The Times*, 9 December 1876.

151. Stephens, op. cit., vol. ii, pp. 110-24.
152. James Bryce, 'J.R.Green' in *Studies in Contemporary Biography,* Macmillan, 1903, p. 141.
153. A.J.P.Taylor, 'Gladstonian Foreign Policy' in *The Trouble Makers,* 1957; Panther 1969, p. 71.
154. ibid., p. 64; R.T.Shannon, *Gladstone and the Bulgarian Agitation,* Nelson, 1963, p. 273.
155. Taylor, op. cit., p. 71.
156. James Bryce, 'Russia and Turkey', and A.O.Rutson, 'Turkey in Europe' in the *Fortnightly Review,* vol. xx.
157. Fisher, op. cit., vol. ii, p. 314; Houghton MSS.: Rutson – Lord Houghton, 10 January 1876.
158. Bryce MSS.: Freeman – Bryce, 23 November 1876.
159. Stephens, op. cit., vol. ii, p. 106.
160. Bryce, *Modern Democracies,* vol. ii, Macmillan, 1921, pp. 414-15
161. R.H.Hutton, 'The Political Character of the Working Class' in *Essays on Reform,* p. 33.
162. James Bryce, 'Benjamin Disraeli, Earl of Beaconsfield' in *Studies in Contemporary Biography,* pp. 52-3.
163. ibid., p. 53.
164. Shannon, op. cit., p. 182.
165. See Frederic Harrison, *et. al., Essays on International Policy,* Chapman & Hall, 1866; Frederic Harrison, 'Foreign Policy' in *Questions for a Reformed Parliament,* p. 256.
166. 'Note by Mr Alfred Robinson' in *The Collected Mathematical Papers of H.J.S.Smith,* vol. i, Clarendon Press, 1894, p. iv.
167. *The Poll for the Election of a Burgess for the University of Oxford,* 1878.
168. 'Note by Mr Alfred Robinson', p. lviii.
169. Goldwin Smith – Emma Winkworth, 20 May 1878, in Haultain, ed.,op. cit., p. 63.
170. Bryce MSS.: Bryce – Dicey, 9 May 1921.
171. Shannon, op. cit., p. 213.
172. Roach, op. cit., p. 71.
173. Despite his energetic criticism of Disraeli's policy, Freeman was not adopted by any constituency, which saddened him: see Freeman – Henry Allon, 29 April 1880 in Stephens, op. cit., vol. ii, p. 201.
174. Hanham, op. cit., p. 220.
175. Several academics, notably James Stuart and A.O.Rutson, were active in Mrs Butler's National Association: see James Stuart, *Reminiscences,* Cassell, 1912, p. 166. The same tendency can, I think, be observed in the Positivists' involvement in their own religious organization in the mid-1870s – see Royden Harrison, op. cit., pp. 315-17 – and, indeed, in the growing involvement of men like Bryce and Freeman in the rights of the subject races of the Turkish Empire.
176. T.H.Green, George Rolleston and Thorold Rogers were active in the Oxford Temperance Association: see *Report* of the Association, no. 6, 1874, p. 5. Rolleston, according to the *D.N.B.,* 'wasted much energy in municipal politics', chiefly to do with public health: Jowett devoted a great deal of energy during his Vice-Chancellorship, 1882-6, to municipal reforms.

177. Henry Sidgwick, Mrs Fawcett and James Stuart were among those who founded a Reform Club with this purpose in Cambridge in 1872: see *Cambridge Reform Club Essays,* 1873.

178. See Oxford School Board pamphlets in Bodleian.

179. Charles Loch Mowat, *The Charity Organisation Society,* Methuen, 1961, p.23. The one parish in which, according to Mowat, C.O.S. ideals enjoyed a temporary triumph during the 1870s was St George's, Hanover Square, where the vicar was an Oxford liberal, the Rev.W.H.Fremantle.

180. L.R.Phelps, *The Administration of the Poor Law in Oxford,* Oxford, 1900, p.2; obituary of Henry Sidgwick in the *Charity Organisation Review,* October 1900, p.256.

181. Phelps, loc. cit.; *The Administration of Poor Relief in the Oxford Incorporation,* pamphlet of 1900 in Bodleian.

182. I established this by comparing lists of Guardians from the report of the Oxford Incorporation and the Oxford C.O.S. with the pollbook for the 1878 election.

183. Phelps, op. cit., p.3.

184. *History of the Oxford Incorporation of Guardians,* Oxford 1910, p.8.

185. *Reports* of the Oxford Incorporation, 1870-1910.

186. A.S. and E.M.S., op. cit., p.430.

187. *Oxford Magazine,* vol.v, 19 January 1887.

188. See, for instance, Henry Sidgwick, 'On the Economic Exceptions to *Laissez Faire*' in *Miscellaneous Essays and Addresses* Macmillan, 1904; Alfred Milner, *Arnold Toynbee,* Arnold, 1895, pp.15-16; Helen Bosanquet, *Bernard Bosanquet,* Macmillan, 1924, pp.97-9.

189. For a socialist view of the C.O.S. see Beatrice Webb, *My Apprenticeship,* Penguin, 1938, pp.221-34.

190. Sidgwick, preface to P.F.Aschrott, *The English Poor Law System,* Knight, 1888, p.viii.

191. A.S. and E.M.S., op. cit., pp.418-19; see also A.V.Dicey, *Law and Opinion,* Macmillan, 1905, p.294.

192. Bryce MSS.: Dicey – Bryce, 30 September 1902.

193. Dicey – Mrs R.B.Litchfield, 10 October 1897, in R.Rait, *Memorials of A.V.Dicey,* Macmillan, 1925, p.142.

194. Noel Annan, *Leslie Stephen,* MacGibbon & Kee, 1951, p.60.

195. Morley, *Recollections,* vol.i, p.121.

196. Leslie Stephen, 'Order and Progress' in the *Fortnightly Review,* vol.xvii, July 1875, p.828.

197. ibid., p.824.

198. ibid., p.823.

199. ibid., p.826; see also Leslie Stephen, 'The Value of Political Machinery' in the *Fortnightly Review,* vol.xviii, December 1875, p.849.

200. Stephen, 'Order and Progress', p.827.

210. ibid., p.834.

202. Leslie Stephen – R.C.Webb, 12 May 1875, quoted in Mary Reed Bobbitt, *With Dearest Love to All,* Faber, 1960, p.133.

203. Although there were eight Oxford men in the Cabinet of 1905, none, save of course Morley and Bryce, was deeply influenced by academic liberalism. Grey and Tweedmouth left without taking their degrees:

see Trevelyan, *Grey of Falloden*, Longmans, 1937, p.17; 'Lord Tweedmouth, 1849-1909' in the *D.N.B.* Herbert Gladstone was a Keble High Churchman; Asquith believed himself influenced neither by Jowett nor Green: see Jenkins, *Asquith*, Collins, 1964, pp.21-2; 'Lord Gladstone, 1854-1930' in the *D.N.B.* R.B.Haldane claimed to be a disciple of Green. He went to Edinburgh: see Haldane, *An Autobiography*, Hodder & Stoughton, 1929, pp.7, 214.

204. See, for instance, Bryce MSS.: Goldwin Smith – Bryce, 10 April 1905 and 6 February 1908; Bryce – Dicey, December 1910 and 9 May 1921; Dicey – Bryce, 23 July 1911; R. St J.Parry, *Henry Jackson*, Cambridge, 1926, p.203.

205. Bryce MSS.: Bryce – G.O.Trevelyan, 29 April 1916.

206. See P.F.Clarke, *Lancashire and the New Liberalism*, Cambridge, 1971, pp.170-75.

207. See Sheldon Rothblatt, *The Revolution of the Dons*, Faber, 1968, chapter 7.

208. ibid., pp.215-16.

209. A.S and E.M.S., op. cit., pp.371-8, 511.

210. *Cambridge University Calendar*, 1881.

211. Sidgwick MSS.: Journal-letter to J.A.Symonds, 22-6 December 1884.

212 ibid.

213. Fisher, op. cit., vol.i, pp.132-5; Dicey, who made a determined attempt to raise the level of Oxford legal studies while Vinerian professor (1882-1909), confessed himself, on his retirement, disappointed at their neglect: see Bryce MSS.: Dicey – Bryce, 16 January 1910.

214. James Bryce, *Studies in Contemporary Biography*, p.95.

215. Sidgwick MSS.: Journal-letter to J.A.Symonds, 6 August 1888.

216. G.W.Kitchin, *Ruskin in Oxford*, Murray, 1904, p.40.

217. ibid., p.43.

218. Leslie Stephen 'Mr Ruskin's Recent Writings' in *Fraser's Magazine*, June, 1874, quoted in E.T.Cook, *The Life of John Ruskin*, vol.ii, Allen, 1911, p.323. For a more sympathetic view, but one which nevertheless comes to the same conclusion, see Frederic Harrison, *'Fors Clavigera'* in *Realities and Ideals*, Macmillan, 1908, pp.364-8.

219. Goldwin Smith, *Reminiscences*, Macmillan, 1911, p.358; Stephen, 'Mr Ruskin's Recent Writings'; Kitchin, op. cit., p.49.

220. John Ruskin, *Fors Clavigera*, no.civ, 1871-84, p.362.

221. Cook, op. cit., p.176.

222. For Toynbee, Cook and Milner see Cook, op. cit., p.187; for Hobson see J.A.Hobson, *Confessions of an Economic Heretic*, Allen & Unwin, 1938, p.42; for Sadler see Michael Sadler, *Sir Michael Sadler: A Memoir*, Constable, 1949, p.37.

223. Hobson, op. cit., p.42.

224. ibid., p.50.

225. F.C.Montague, *Arnold Toynbee*, John Hopkins University, 1889, p.37.

226. See Bryce, 'Intellect and Education in English Politics' in the *Nation*, vol.36, 25 January 1883, p.76; Dicey, 'The Social Movement in England' in the *Nation*, vol.38, 10, 17 January, 6 March, 17 April 1884, pp.29, 49, 272, 337.

227. Bryce, 'The Late Mr Fawcett' in the *Nation*, vol.39, 27 November 1884, p.457.

228. Bryce, 'The Deaths of Professors Balfour and Jevons' in the *Nation*, vol. 35, p. 217, 14 September 1882.

229. See Sidgwick, *The Principles of Political Economy*, Macmillan, 1883, esp. chapter 3; and A.S. and E.M.S., op. cit., pp. 398, 442, for his own (low) estimate of the work and his attitude to collectivism.

230. Bryce, 'British Home Politics' in the *Nation*, vol. 40, 11 June 1885, p. 479.

231. See N. Jha, *The Age of Marshall*, Cass, 1968, chapter v.

232. cf. Melvin Richter, *The Politics of Conscience: T.H. Green and His Age*, Weidenfeld and Nicholson, 1964, chapter 5.

233. For the unity of the two on the issue of free inquiry see Sidgwick MSS.: Green – Sidgwick, 27 May 1867 and 28 December 1868.

234. Lewis Farnell, *An Oxonian Looks Back*, Hopkinson, 1934, p. 44.

235. cf. J.M. Keynes's opinion of Sidgwick, cited in Annan, op. cit., p. 319.

236. Bryce, *Modern Democracies*, vol. ii, p. 367.

237. See F.M.L. Thompson, op. cit., p. 276.

238. A.V. Dicey, 'Fifty Years of Reform in England', in the *Nation*, vol. 35, 20 July 1882, p. 49.

239. cf. James Bryce, 'The Parliament of 1880 – Causes of its Failure' in the *Nation*, vol. 41, 10 September 1885, p. 213.

240. G.C. Brodrick, 'On the different principles on which the chief systems of popular government have been based in ancient and modern times', T. & G. Shrimpton, 1855, p. 18.

241. See Hamer, op. cit., pp. 81-7; Andrew Jones, *The Politics of Reform, 1884*, Cambridge, 1972, p. 94.

242. Fisher, op. cit., vol. i, p. 191.

243. *Cambridge Reform Club Papers*, especially nos. 1-3.

244. ibid., p. 6; see also James Bryce, 'An Ideal University' in *The Contemporary Review*, vol. 45, June, 1884, p. 856.

245. Stuart, op. cit., p. 171.

246. *University Extension: Reports of the Sub-Committees*, 1867.

247. Goldwin Smith, 'The Oxford Reports on University Extension', *Macmillan's Magazine*, vol. xv, 25 January 1867, p. 226.

248. W.R. Ward, *Victorian Oxford*, Cass, 1965, p. 263.

249. Mallet, *A History of the University of Oxford*, Methuen, 1927, vol. iii, pp. 426-7.

250. Ward, op. cit., pp. 267-8.

251. ibid., p. 269.

252. ibid., p. 267.

253. Costs at Keble were computed at £80 p.a. In 1900 the minimum costs of a year's residence was £100 p.a. In the same year Ruskin Hall was set up; its costs were £52 p.a.: see Mallet, op. cit., pp. 430, 473, 479.

254. Ward, op. cit., p. 285.

255. Oxford established an extension delegacy in 1878, but it was only effective after 1885; in 1875 both universities combined with London to launch, under Goschen's presidency, the London Society for the Extension of University Teaching: see R.D. Roberts, *Eighteen Years of University Extension* Cambridge, 1891, pp. 1, 97-103.

256. M.E. Sadler and H.J. Mackinder, *University Extension, Past, Present and Future*, Cassell, 1891, p. 18; Stuart, op. cit., p. 162.

257. Stuart, op. cit., p.166. Stuart owed his introduction to the Rochdale Pioneers to A.O.Rutson, who had been associated with them through Mrs Josephine Butler's various campaigns for women's rights.

258. ibid., pp.170-71; see also A.S. and E.M.S., op. cit., p.271: 'I am considering a scheme for educating the whole country, at least as far as it is willing to be educated, and has left school.'

259. Stuart, op. cit., p.173.

260. ibid., p.57. Despite his distinguished Cambridge career as Professor of Mechanism, 1875-89, and subsequent political career as a Liberal M.P. and Privy Counsellor, he lacks a notice in the *D.N.B.*

261. ibid., pp.132-3. The ratio of university students per head of population in Scotland 1875-1900 was 1:1,000 compared with 1:2,600 in Germany and 1:5,800 in England; of the 882 students in the first year of the Arts course at the four Scottish universities in session 1866-7, 20 per cent came from parochial schools: see Newman A.Wade, *Post-Primary Education in the Primary Schools of Scotland*, University of London Press, 1939, pp.25-33; see also N.A.Jephson, *The Beginnings of English University Adult Education*, Michael Joseph, 1973, pp.74-8.

262. Pattison, *Suggestions on Academical Organisation*, Edmonston, 1868, pp.160, 326.

263. Sadler and Mackinder, op. cit., p.74.

264. Roberts, op. cit., p.12.

265. R.G.Moulton, *The University Extension Movement*, Bemrose, 1887, pp.15-21.

266. Roberts, op. cit., p.17.

267. ibid., p.13.

268. ibid., p.26 (Roberts calculated that an acceptable fee for a working man was 1s.6d. – 7½p).

269. ibid., p.55.

270. ibid., p.22.

271. Geoffrey Best, *Bishop Westcott and the Miners*, Cambridge, 1966, pp.13-15.

272. Roberts, op. cit., p.60.

273. ibid., p.75; Stuart, op. cit., p.166.

274. Edwin Welch, *The Peripatetic University*, Cambridge, 1973, p.67. Browne, who later became Bishop of Peterborough, drew a salary of £700 p.a., Roberts £50: see Welch, op. cit., pp.75, 78.

275. Roberts, op. cit., p.65. Stuart attempted to get Trinity to allocate fellowships to extension lecturers, but failed. Trinity also refused to allow extension lecturers to retain their fellowships: see Stuart, op. cit., p.174.

276. *Young Oxford*, vol.ii, December 1901, p.458.

277. Edward Carpenter, *My Days and Dreams*, Allen & Unwin, 1916, p.81. This was also evident to the economic historian William Cunningham, at that time a Liberal, who taught at Liverpool: see Audrey Cunningham, *William Cunningham, Teacher and Priest*, S.P.C.K., 1950, p.31.

278. Roberts, op. cit., p.99.

279. Stuart, op. cit., p.174.

280. Sadler was Professor of Education at Manchester, 1903-11. Mackinder

was Principal of Reading College and later Director of the London School of Economics, whose first Director, W.A.S.Hewins, was also an Oxford extension lecturer.

281. Mallet, op. cit., vol.iii, p.469; Browne, callously but fairly accurately, defended extension as a sort of outdoor relief for unemployed graduates: see Welch, op. cit., p.76.

282. Statistics taken from *Whitaker's Almanac*, 1886.

283. Quoted in Asa Briggs, ed., *William Morris, Selected Writings and Designs,* Penguin, 1962, p.243.

284. Thomas Hardy, *Jude the Obscure,* St Martin's Library Edn, 1957, pp.125-7; after his rebuff by the Master of Biblioll College, Jude Fawley chalks on the College wall 'I have understanding as well as you; I am not inferior to you: yea, who knoweth not such things as these?' – Job 12:3.

285. Stuart, op. cit., p.166; A.S. and E.M.S., op. cit. p.380.

286. Lewis Campbell, *The Nationalisation of the Old English Universities,* Chapman & Hall, 1901, p.270; Parry, op. cit., p.88.

287. Perry Anderson, 'Components of the National Culture' in Alexander Cockburn, ed., *Student Power,* Penguin, 1969, p.226.

288. ibid., p.228.

289. ibid., p.219.

290. See also Noel Annan, 'The Curious Strength of Positivism in English Political Thought', and Gareth Stedman Jones, 'The Pathology of English History' in *New Left Review,* no.46, November-December, 1967.

291. Mosei Ostrogorski, *Democracy and the Organisation of Political Parties,* 2 vols., Macmillan, 1902.
A.Lawrence Lowell, *The Government of England,* 2 vols., Macmillan, New York, 1908.
Elie Halévy, *La Formation du Radicalisme Philosophique,* 3 vols., S.T.E.M., Paris, 1901-4; *Histoire du Peuple Anglais au XIX Siècle,* 5 vols., S.T.E.M., 1912-32.
Paul Mantoux, *La Révolution Industrielle au XVIIIe Siècle,* Gallimard, 1906.

292. Charles Booth, *Life and Labour of the People in London,* 17 vols., Macmillan/Williams & Norgate, 1889-1903.
Sidney and Beatrice Webb, *The History of Trade Unionism,* Longmans, 1894; *English Local Government from the Revolution to the Municipal Corporations Act,* 8 vols., Longmans, 1906-29.
Graham Wallas, *Human Nature in Politics,* Constable, 1908.
Patrick Geddes, *City Development,* Geddes & Co., 1904; *Cities in Evolution,* Williams & Norgate, 1915.

293. Sidgwick MSS.: 'Professor Sidgwick's Account of the Development of his Ethical View', pp.10-11.

294. R.L.Nettleship, 'Memoir of T.H.Green', p.xliv.

295. Green, 'Popular Philosophy and its Relationship to life' in *Works* , vol.i, 1868, p.117; and Richter, op. cit., p.175.

296. For Stephen see Maitland, op. cit., p.171; for Bryce see Fisher, op. cit., vol.i, p.226; for Rutson see Houghton MSS.: Rutson – Lord Houghton, 9 January 1876.

297. Stephen, 'Order and Progress', p.832.
298. ibid., p.834.
299. Richter, op. cit., pp.148-57.
300. J.R.Seely, 'Liberal Education in Universities' in *Essays on a Liberal Education*, Macmillan, 1867, p.164.
301. ibid., p.129.
302. ibid., pp.140, 170.
303. Henry Sidgwick, 'The Theory of Classical Education' in *Essays on a Liberal Education*, p.123.
304. ibid., p.103.
305. T.W.Bamford, *The Rise of the Public Schools*, Nelson, 1967, p.63.
306. ibid., pp.63, 116-19; James Bryce 'E.E.Bowen' in *Studies in Contemporary Biography*, p.347.
307. Ward, op. cit., pp.288-9; for Cambridge see A.S. and E.M.S., op. cit., p.511.
308. *D.N.B.*
309. Parry, op. cit., p.81.
310. Bryce, *Studies in Contemporary Biography*, pp.287-90.
311. Audrey Cunningham, op. cit., pp.67-8; A.S. and E.M.S., op. cit., p.320.
312. Audrey Cunningham, op. cit., p.31.
313. Alan Harding, *A Social History of English Law*, Penguin, 1966, p.349; F.H.Lawson, *The Oxford Law School*, Oxford, 1968, chapters 1-4.
314. See George Haines IV, 'German Influence upon Victorian Science Education' in *Victorian Studies*, vol.i, 1956, p.229; and Cyril Bibby, 'Thomas Henry Huxley and University Development' in *Victorian Studies*, vol.iii, 1958, pp.100-104.
315. Jackson MSS.: 'Memoranda on Henry Sidgwick', p.13.
316. Henry Sidgwick – H.G.Dakyns, 27 February 1884 in A.S. and E.M.S., op. cit., p.380.
317. John Sparrow, *Mark Pattison and the Idea of a University*, Cambridge, 1967, p.139.
318. Mark Pattison, *Memoirs*, Macmillan, 1885, p.320.
319. See *D.N.B.* entries; also Farnell, *An Oxonian Looks Back*, pp.103-9.
320. Rothblatt, op. cit., p.176.
321. H.A.L.Fisher, *Frederic William Maitland*, Cambridge, 1910, p.20.
322. ibid., p.19.
323. C.H.S.Fifoot, *Law and History in the Nineteenth Century*, Quaritch, 1956, p.18.
324. ibid., p.8.
325. ibid., p.12.
326. *Victoria History of the Counties of England: General Introduction*, Oxford, 1970, pp.12-13.
327. Unsigned prefatory note in the *English Historical Review*, vol.i, p.4.
328. Bryce MSS.: Bryce – Henry Sidgwick, 5 and 8 February 1900; A.S. and E.M.S., op. cit., p.581. Sidgwick died before the Academy received its Charter.
329. *Proceedings of the British Academy*, vol.i, 1903-4, p.12.
330. ibid., p.13.
331. Janet Beveridge, *An Epic of Clare Market*, Bell, 1960, pp.3, 16.

332.   Mark Pattison, 'Philosophy at Oxford' in *Mind*, vol. i, 1877, p. 84.

9. 1886 AND AFTER   pp. 218-42

1.   cf. J.L.Hammond's chapter on 'Gladstone and the Educated Classes' in *Gladstone and the Irish Nation*, Longmans, 1938, pp. 523-52; Roach, 'Liberalism and the Victorian Intelligentsia' in *Cambridge Historical Journal*, vol. xiii, 1957; and two monumentally inaccurate articles by Trowbridge H.Ford, 'Dicey as a Political Journalist' in *Political Studies*, vol. xviii, no. 2, 1970, and 'Dicey's Conversion to Unionism' in *Irish Historical Studies*, vol. xxviii, September 1973, pp. 552-82.

2.   Alastair B.Cooke and John R.Vincent, *The Governing Passion: Cabinet Government and Party Politics in Britain, 1885-6*, Harvester Press, 1974, section 1.

3.   cf. the blurb on *Dicey's Letters on Unionist Delusions*, Macmillan, 1887. Bryce edited two symposia on Home Rule: *The Handbook of Home Rule*, Kegan Paul, 1887, and *Two Centuries of Irish History*, Kegan Paul, 1888. Gladstone's encouragement apparently included financial help, although Morley, who had been Chief Secretary, did not think the projects worthwhile: see Bryce MSS.: Bryce – Gladstone, 10, 26 July, 12 August, 8 October 1886; Gladstone – Bryce, 8 July 1886.

4.   cf. A.V.Dicey, 'A Sign of the Times in England' in the *Nation*, vol. xxxvii, 12 July 1883, p. 30; and James Bryce, 'The Progress of Democracy' in the *Nation*, vol. xl, 12 February 1885, p. 134.

5.   Diary-letter to J.A.Symonds, quoted in A.S. and E.M.S., *Henry Sidgwick: A Memoir*, Macmillan, 1906, p. 448.

6.   A.V.Dicey, 'On the Eve of Gladstone's Speech' in the *Nation*, vol. xlii, 22 April 1886, p. 336.

7.   *Oxford Magazine*, vol. iv, 16, 23 June 1886, pp. 253, 270.

8.   See 'Note by Mr Alfred Robinson' (on the election) in *The Collected Mathematical Papers of H.J.S.Smith*, Oxford, 1894, p. lviii.

9.   Reported in the *Liberal Unionist*, 20 July 1887, vol. i. p. 257.

10.   Bryce MSS.: Leslie Stephen – Bryce, 15 June 1886.

11.   Bryce MSS.: Dicey – Bryce, 18 May 1886; Sidgwick MSS.: Diary-letter for J.A.Symonds, 26 February 1887; John Morley, *Recollections*, vol. i, Macmillan, 1917, p. 122.

12.   A.S. and E.M.S., op. cit., pp. 453-63; *Oxford Liberal Association, Annual Reports, 1867-1906*.

13.   Quoted in Noel Annan, *Leslie Stephen*, MacGibbon & Kee, 1951, p. 206.

14.   'Ireland' in *Questions for a Reformed Parliament*, Macmillan, 1867, pp. 34-6.

15.   cf. Leslie Stephen, 'On the Choice of Representatives by Popular Constituencies', and Goldwin Smith, 'The Experience of the American Commonwealth' in *Essays on Reform*, Macmillan, 1867, pp. 99 and 220.

16.   J.S.Mill, *England and Ireland*, Longmans, 1868, p. 26; Bolton King, *The Life of Mazzini*, Everyman, 1902, p. 107; cf. Bryce's statement of

his own position in 'How we became Home Rulers' in *The Handbook of Home Rule*, pp. 24-7.

17. Stephen, loc. cit.

18. ibid.; Goldwin Smith, loc. cit.; James Bryce, 'The Historical Aspect of Democracy' in *Essays on Reform*, p. 266.

19. Bryce, 'How we became Home Rulers', p. 39; see L. P. Curtis, Jnr, *Anglo-Saxons and Celts*, University of Bridgeport, 1968, p. 81, for his relations with the Anglo-Saxonist Home Rulers J. R. Green and E. A. Freeman. A further cause for anti-Irish feeling was Irish opposition to Italian unity in the 1860s: cf. Bryce MSS.: Freeman – Bryce, 9 December 1868.

20. S. H. Harris, *Auberon Herbert, Crusader for Liberty*, Williams & Norgate, 1943, p. 278.

21. cf. 'The Social Movement in England' in the *Nation*, vol. xxxviii, 10 January 1884, p. 29; and 'On the Eve of Gladstone's Speech' in the *Nation*, vol. xlii, 22 April 1886, p. 336.

22. Speech of 17 June 1887, reported in *Cambridge Chronicle*.

23. G. P. Gooch, *Lord Courtney*, Macmillan, 1920, p. 221; Goldwin Smith, *Reminiscences*, Macmillan, 1911, p. 439; Ray Strachey, *Millicent Garrett Fawcett*, John Murray, 1931, p. 87.

24. Milner MSS., Bodleian Library, Oxford: Milner – Goschen, 25 April 1886.

25. Bryce MSS.: Bryce – Freeman, 18 February 1887.

26. Bryce MSS.: Freeman – Bryce, 15 November 1886.

27. ibid., 22 May, 1887.

28. Stephens, *Life and Letters of Edward Augustus Freeman*, vol. ii, Macmillan, 1895, p. 236; Curtis, op. cit., p. 78.

29. Bryce MSS.: Dicey – Bryce, 3 January 1885.

30. R. Rait, *Memorials of A. V. Dicey*, Macmillan, 1925, p. 100.

31. Frederic Harrison, 'Parliamentary Candidature' in *Realities and Ideals*, Macmillan, 1908, p̄. 237; Royden Harrison, *Before the Socialists*, Routledge, 1965, p. 335.

32. Leslie Stephen, 'The Political Situation in England' in the *North American Review*, October 1868, p. 553.

33. A. V. Dicey, 'Why do People hate Mr Gladstone?' in the *Nation*, vol. xxxv, 14 September 1882, p. 219.

34. G. C. Brodrick, *Memories and Impressions*, Nisbett & Co., 1900, p. 159; A. S. & E. M. S., op. cit., p. 434; James Bryce, 'The Vote of Censure' in the *Nation*, vol. xl, 19 March 1885, p. 237.

35. Bryce MSS.: Bryce – Gladstone, 24 May 1886; Bryce – Dicey, 9 May 1921.

36. cf. Stephen, 'On the Choice of Representatives', p. 114.

37. D. A. Hamer, *John Morley, Liberal Intellectual in Politics*, Oxford, 1968, pp. 176-8.

38. See *Lord Carlingford's Journal*, A. B. Cooke and J. R. Vincent, eds., Oxford, 1971, p. 20.

39. Trevor Jones, *The Politics of Reform, 1884*, Cambridge, 1972, p. 260.

40. See *The Diary of Sir Edward Walter Hamilton*, Dudley Bahlmann, ed., Oxford, 1972, especially entries for 22 November and 2 December 1884, pp. 740, 745.

41. He was expelled from the Ad Eundem. See Jackson MSS.: Sir George Young – Henry Jackson, 12 June 1907. In a letter of 15 February 1918 Bryce described him to Dicey as 'repellent'.
42. Hamilton Diary, 20 November 1884, p.737.
43. Jones, op. cit., pp.258, 260.
44. See Hansard, 1880-85.
45. Hamilton Diary, entry for 15 January 1883, p.379.
46. Cooke and Vincent, The Governing Passion, p.150; Bryce MSS.: Sidgwick – Bryce, 19 May 1886; Dicey – Bryce, 18 May 1886.
47. Quoted in Morley, op. cit., p.218.
48. ibid.
49. Cutting from New York Evening Post (for which Bryce was London correspondent) in Bryce MSS.: H.A.L.Fisher, James Bryce, Viscount Bryce of Dechmont, vol. i, Macmillan, 1927, p.200.
50. James Bryce, 'England and Ireland: an Introductory Statement', Committee on Irish Affairs, paper no.1 , 1884.
51. 'B.F.C.Costelloe, 1855-99' in M.E.B., supp.4; see also Beatrice Webb, Our Partnership, Longmans, 1948, pp.64, 501.
52. Jones, op. cit., p.95.
53. James Bryce, 'The Irish Elections and the Struggle in Ulster' in the Nation, vol.xlii, 7 January 1886, p.8.
54. Cooke and Vincent, The Governing Passion, p.150.
55. cf. H.H.Henson, Sir William Anson, Oxford, 1920, pp.142-3; Cambridge Review, vol.vii, 26 May 1886, p.345; and Oxford Magazine, vol.iv, 26 May 1886, p.119.
56. John A.Stevenson, 'Reminiscences of the Hon. George Brodrick', typescript memoir in Merton College Library, Oxford, p.1; Brodrick, 'The Past and Future Relation of Ireland to Great Britain', Macmillan's Magazine, 1871, reprinted in Political Studies, Kegan Paul, 1879, p.355.
57. Brodrick, Memories and Impressions, p.234.
58. Seeley, The Expansion of England, Macmillan, 1883, p.50; and see R.T.Shannon, 'John Robert Seeley and the Idea of a National Church' in Robson, ed., Ideas and Institutions of Victorian Britain, Bell, 1967, p.266.
59. Sidgwick MSS.: Diary-letter to Symonds, 4 April 1885 and 8 December 1886.
60. ibid., 29 November 1884 and 17 March 1886.
61. ibid., 7 April 1886.
62. ibid., 2 June 1886.
63. ibid., 3 and 9 July 1886.
64. Ethel Sidgwick, Mrs Henry Sidgwick, Sidgwick & Jackson, 1938, p.102.
65. Sidgwick MSS.: Diary-letter to Symonds, 28 March 1887.
66. ibid., 8 January 1888.
67. Sidgwick, op. cit., p.104.
68. cf. Henry Sidgwick – A.V.Dicey, 1 March 1893, in A.S. and E.M.S., op. cit., p.526; Sidgwick MSS.: Diary-letter to Symonds, 4 July 1892.
69. A.V.Dicey's review (unsigned) of England and Ireland by C.G.Walpole, in the Nation , vol.xxxv, 28 September 1882, p.267; this went further than a slightly earlier article 'Home Rule from an English Point of

View' in the *Contemporary Review*, vol.xlii, July 1882, pp.66-86, which, while rejecting Home Rule (for reasons very similar to Dicey's post-1886 position), implied a moral presupposition in favour of outright independence, in the argument that this would be beyond the normal British conception of justice. I do not think that I make overmuch use of the conspiracy theory of history (though Trowbridge H.Ford's articles on Dicey provide an unhappy precedent) in suggesting that the unsigned Dicey's Irish sympathies were probably, at that time, closer to his own mind than his more qualified public utterances. By November, however, his remedy – though drastic – was not separatist: he wanted Parnell to be given Cabinet responsibility for Ireland, as 'a bona fide attempt to treat the Irish members as the persons entitled to decide on Irish legislation': see Bryce MSS.: Dicey – Bryce, 1 November 1882. His mature hostile view was stated in 'On the Eve of Gladstone's Speech' in the *Nation*, vol.xlii, 8 April 1886, p.336. But by 18 May, reconciled to Gladstone's success, he thought the issue ought to be settled by a plebiscite, followed by a constitutional convention: see Bryce MSS.: Dicey – Bryce, 18 May 1886.

70. Bryce MSS.: Dicey – Bryce, 18 May 1886.
71. Dicey, 'Home Rule from an English Point of View', p.85.
72. A.V.Dicey, 'What are the Causes of the Conservative Reaction in England?' in the the *Nation*, vol.xlii, 14 January 1886, p.30; his brother was a wholehearted Unionist: cf. Edward Dicey, 'The Unionist Vote' in the *Nineteenth Century*, vol.ii, August 1886.
73. A.V.Dicey, 'Can the English Constitution be Americanised?' in the *Nation*, vol.xlii, 28 January 1886, p.73.
74. cf. James Bryce's (unsigned) review of *England's Case against Home Rule*, Macmillan, 1886, in the *Nation*, vol. xliv, 20 January 1887, p.59.
75. Cooke and Vincent, *The Governing Passion*, pp.85-8.
76. *The Times*, 29, 30 June 1886.
77. Milner MSS.: Gell – Milner, 29 June 1886.
78. ibid., and Goldwin Smith – Milner, 15 January 1887.
79. cf. M.C.Hurst, *Joseph Chamberlain and Liberal Reunion*, Routledge, 1967; *The Times*, 27 June 1887; Bryce MSS.: Bryce – Freeman, 24 September 1887.
80. *Oxford Magazine*, vol.iv, 26 May 1886, p.198.
81. Quoted in A.S. and E.M.S., op. cit., p.463.
82. Cooke and Vincent, *The Governing Passion*, p.108.
83. cf. *Oxford Magazine*, vol.iv, 20 October 1886, p.287, vol.v, 23 February, 9 March, 27 April 1887, pp.93, 128, 147; and James Bryce, 'An Ideal University' in the *Contemporary Review*, vol.xlv, June 1884, pp.836-56.
84. W.R.Ward, *Victorian Oxford*, Cass, 1965, p.258; 'The Duke of Devonshire, 1808-1891' in *The Times*, 22 December 1891.
85. *Oxford Magazine*, vol.v, 19 January 1887, p.2.
86. ibid., vol.v, 19, 26 January, 2 February 1887, pp.3, 20, 35.
87. *The Times*, 27 June 1887.
88. *Liberal Unionist*, vol.i, 13 July 1887, p.250.
89. *Cambridge Review*, vol.ix, 9 November 1887, pp.65, 73.
90. cf. J.D.Duff 'Richard Claverhouse Jebb, 1841-1905' in the *D.N.B.*; Henson, op. cit., p.149.

91. Its first edition was published on 30 March 1887.

92. Bryce MSS.: Dicey – Bryce, 23 July 1886.

93. Speech at Dublin, 7 December 1893 in Rait, op. cit., p. 115.

94. James Bryce, 'Conditions of the Irish Problem' in the *Nation* vol. xli, 15 September 1885, p. 296; cf. also Sidgwick MSS.: Diary-letter to Symonds, 7 April 1886; and Fisher, op. cit., vol. i, p. 220.

95. For instance, the *Oxford Magazine* for November 1886 reported, besides an address on Home Rule by Brodrick and a meagrely attended lecture by Bryce on the American constitution, a meeting by the Toynbee Trustees to inaugurate a teaching and research programme in industrial areas, a talk by Prebendary Brereton on the Cavendish College project to attract needy students to Cambridge, reports from Toynbee Hall and the Oxford House in Bethnal Green, and conferences on educational reform and the poor law. This was typical enough of most months during term, and of Cambridge as well.

96. Hilaire Belloc, ed., *Essays in Liberalism*, Cassell, 1897, pp. 1-30.

97. Report of Liberal Unionist meeting at Oxford in *the Times*, 28 January 1888; A. V. Dicey, *Letters on Unionist Delusions,* Macmillan, 1887, p. 69.

98. See papers of Oxford University Home Rule Association in E. K. Chambers MSS., Bodleian Library, Oxford.

99. *Oxford Magazine,* vol. v, 22 February 1888, p. 243.

100. Brodrick, *Memories and Impressions*, p. 405.

101. See Peter Fraser, 'The Liberal Unionist Alliance: Chamberlain, Hartington and the Conservatives, 1886-1904' in *The English Historical Review*, vol. lxxvii, 1962, pp. 53-78.

102. Hamer, *Liberal Politics in the Age of Gladstone and Rosebery,* Oxford, 1972, chapter viii.

103. William Stebbing, *Memorials of Charles Henry Pearson,* Longmans, 1900, pp. 211-14, 245; and entry on 'C. H. Pearson, 1830-1894' in the *D.N.B.*

104. Pearson MSS.: Bryce – Pearson, 7 May 1892.

105. Charles Pearson, *National Life and Character,* Macmillan, 1893, pp. 355-7.

106. See R. C. K. Ensor, *England, 1870-1914*, Oxford, 1936, p. 332.

107. See H. Stuart Hughes, *Consciousness and Society,* MacGibbon & Kee, 1967, p. 34; Stebbing, op. cit., p. 182.

108. Pearson, op. cit., pp. 133-4, 106-10.

109. *D.N.B.* entry.

110. Pearson MSS.: Bryce – Pearson, 7 May 1892.

111. *National Review*, December 1894, p. 219.

112. ibid. Jowett was also impressed: see letter to John Nichol, 31 August 1893 in Evelyn Abbott and Lewis Campbell, *Life and Letters of Benjamin Jowett,* vol. ii, John Murray, 1897, pp. 473-4, and, in America, Theodore Roosevelt said that only Mahan's *Influence of Sea Power* had aroused more interest: see Pearson MSS.: Roosevelt – Pearson, 11 May 1894.

113. Harrison MSS.: Pearson – Harrison, n.d. (1893).

114. Bryce MSS.: Sidgwick – Bryce, 1 October 1888.

115. Brodrick, *Memories and Impressions*, p. 378.

116. Bryce MSS.: Bryce – Dicey, 19 September 1917; Fisher, op. cit., vol. i, p. 299.
117. Harrison MSS.: Leonard Courtney – Harrison, 15 February 1891, Gilbert Murray – Harrison, 24 October 1897.
118. cf. Gareth Stedman Jones, *Outcast London*, Oxford, 1972.
119. Melvin Richter, *The Politics of Conscience: T.H.Green and His Age*, Weidenfeld & Nicholson, 1964, p. 13.
120. Morley, op. cit., vol. i, p. 288.
121. Mark Pattison, *Memoirs*, Macmillan, 1885, p. 167; Brodrick, *Memories and Impressions*, p. 378; Lewis Campbell, *The Nationalisation of the Old English Universities*, Chapman & Hall, 1901, p. 8.
122. Fisher, op. cit., vol. ii, p. 270; Rait, op. cit., p. 166.
123. Dicey – Mrs R.B.Litchfield, 10 October 1897, quoted in Rait, op. cit., p. 143.
124. Sidgwick – Horatio F.Brown, 9 August 1900, quoted in A.S. and E.M.S, op cit., p. 596.
125. Courtney resigned from the Unionist party and lost his seat in the 'Khaki Election'; for Stephen see F.W.Maitland, *The Life and Letters of Leslie Stephen*, Duckworth, 1906, p. 453; for Maitland see Leslie Stephen – C.E.Norton, 21 September 1899 in C.H.Fifoot, ed., *The Letters of F.W.Maitland*, Cambridge, 1965, p. 258.
126. Bryce MSS.: Bryce – Goldwin Smith, 23 March 1900.
127. Bryce MSS.: Goldwin Smith – Bryce, 17 May 1903.
128. ibid., 18 May 1900.
129. *D.N.B.*, supp. ii.
130. For Pollock see Elliot MSS.: Letter-book of correspondence with A.V.Dicey, p. 20: for Maitland see Maitland – Jackson, 15 January 1906 in Fifoot, ed., op. cit., p. 464.
131. Rait, op. cit., p. 116. There is an interesting discussion of the intellectual drift from Unionism in the 1900s in Robert Blake, *The Conservative Party from Peel to Churchill*, Eyre & Spottiswoode, 1970, p. 187.
132. Rait, op. cit., p. 119.
133. Bryce MSS.: Dicey – Bryce, 16 January 1910.
134. John Wilson, *C-B*, Constable, 1973, p. 461.
135. Jackson MSS.: Fitzmaurice – Jackson, 19 December 1905.
136. Wilson, op. cit., p. 509; see also John Morley, quoted by Harold Laski in a letter to Justice Holmes, 18 October 1921: *Holmes – Laski Letters*, vol. i, Oxford, 1953, p. 375.
137. Wilson, op. cit., p. 570.
138. cf. Bradford Perkins, *The Great Rapprochement*, Gollancz, 1969, pp. 275-8.
139. Bryce MSS.: Bryce – Dicey, 24 November 1908, see also Goldwin Smith – Bryce, 13 August 1909.
140. Bryce MSS.: Bryce – Dicey, n. d., December 1910.
141. ibid., 14 November 1913.
142. Bryce MSS.: Morley – Bryce, 24 September 1914. Bryce MSS.: Bryce – Dicey, 24 August 1914.
143. *Report of the Committee on Alleged German Outrages*, H.M.S.O., 1915: Bryce's friends on the Committee were Sir Frederick Pollock, Sir Kenelm Digby and H.A.L.Fisher.

144. The notion that the events which the Bryce Committee investigated were fabricated seems to have become orthodoxy: e.g., see Arthur Marwick, *The Deluge*, 1965; Macmillan 1973, p.131. But most British criticism of atrocity stories has tended to elide a variety of the more outlandish examples, culled from later in the war, with the Belgian experience: see Francis Williams and Z.A.B.Zeman in *History of the Twentieth Century*, Purnell, 1968, part 29. The Bryce Committee certainly exaggerated the numbers involved. It reported 400 dead at Andenne, where the Belgians themselves claimed only 210. But in an official proclamation the German commander himself claimed that 100 civilians had been shot in reprisal: see *Report*, pp.14-16; Barbara Tuchman, *August 1914*, Constable, 1962, pp.306-14. Some of the worst instances were verified by American witnesses, a fact which must have had a considerable effect in overcoming Bryce's resistance.

145. Bryce MSS.: Bryce – Freeman, 24 September 1870; see also Keith Robbins, 'Lord Bryce and the First World War' in the *Historical Journal*, vol.x, 1967, pp.255-72.

146. Bryce MSS.: Trevelyan – Bryce, 8 September 1914.

147. G.H.Hardy, *Bertrand Russell and Trinity*, privately published 1942, pp.24-5.

148. Bryce MSS.: Harrison – Bryce, 30 October 1917.

149. Rait, op. cit., p.228.

150. Jackson MSS.: Dicey – Jackson, 9 October 1914.

151. Bryce MSS.: Bryce – Dicey, 1 August 1916.

152. ibid., 19 September 1917.

153. ibid., 21 November 1917.

154. Bryce MSS.: Dicey – Bryce, 31 January 1916. Incidentally Dicey subsequently castigated 'the silliness of sending workmen who couldn't speak a word of Russian, and did not know even the outlines of Russian history, to confer with Russian Socialists': Jackson MSS.: Dicey – Jackson, 3 November 1917.

155. Bryce MSS.: Bryce – Dicey 12 December 1919.

156. ibid., 28 January 1919.

157. Courtney MSS.: Charles Roden Buxton – Lady Courtney, 19 May 1918.

158. Jackson MSS.: Henry Yates Thompson – Jackson, 1 September 1918.

159. Significantly, a memorial for Russell's reinstatement at Trinity was signed by nearly all the fellows under fifty, including many who had participated in the war, and opposed, unsuccessfully, by nearly all the older men. See Hardy, op. cit., pp.49-51, 59-60.

160. Bryce MSS.: Bryce – Dicey, 28 January 1917.

161. ibid., 21 October 1919.

162. Bryce MSS.: Dicey – Bryce, 23 August 1920.

163. Bryce MSS.: Bryce – Dicey, 4 April 1921.

164. Fisher, op. cit., vol.ii, p.170; Arnold J.Toynbee, *Acquaintances*, Oxford, 1967, chapter 11; Robbins, op. cit., pp.265-71.

165. Jackson MSS.: Annotated letter of Bryce – Colonel Jackson, 20 January 1922.

166. G.M.Trevelyan, *Sir George Otto Trevelyan*, Longmans, 1932, pp.148-51.

167. *The Times*, 5 July 1930.

Index

Benthamism, 38, 40, 124, 151, 154;
Mill's revolt, 39, 41
Berkley, William, 190
Boards of Guardians, 195
Booth, Charles, 210
Bosanquet, Bernard, 44, 196
Bouverie, Edward Pleydell, and
abolition of Tests, 79-80, 81, 83,
89, 91
Bowen, Charles, 11, 57, 60, 72, 126;
portrait-sketch, 24-5; legal
career, 70, 129; and abolition of
Tests, 88; Bribery Commissions,
183
Bowen, Edward, 61; at Harrow, 212
Bradlaugh, Charles, 135
Bradley, A.C., 211
Bradley, F.H., 44, 203
Bramwell, Lord, jurist, 168
Brand, Lt, and Jamaica revolt, 126,
139
Bridges, J.H., 36, 55, 60; religious
positivism, 42
Bright, Frank, 60
Bright, Jacob, 89
Bright, John, 102, 114; university
reform, 75, 84, 87; in Oxford,
112-13; ineffective leadership,
115; and political reform, 119,
120, 125, 126, 135; on Reform
Bill 1867, 134
British Academy, philosophy and
aims, 19, 215, 216
British Association, Wilberforce-
Huxley clash, 45-6
Broad Church Movement, 147;
theology and leaders, 35-7, 47;
breakdown, 75; and Eastern
Question, 193
Broadhurst, Henry, 186
Brodrick, Hon. G.C., 11, 36, 60,
138; lay Fellowships, 54; liberalism, 61, 62, 66, 84; journalism,
69, 71, 72, 89, 134; abolition of
Tests, 89; university reform, 94,
95, 124, 171; land expert, 141;
reviews his political ideas, 173;
Parliamentary candidate, 177-81
passim, 184, 185-6; Fenian
Commission, 183; Home

Rule–Unionism issue, 225, 228,
232; death, 239; quoted on,
prize-Fellowships, 51-2; good
government, 117, 151-2, 159-60,
204; northern isolation, 146;
Mill, 152, 157, 158-9; Parliamentary representation, 161; Fawcett, 178; socialism 235
Browne, Rev. G., and University
Extension, 208
Browning, Oscar, 62, 145
Bruce, H.A., and Education Bill,
189, 190
Bryce, James, Viscount, 44, 52, 60,
126; secular Evangelicalism, 25,
45; and Newman, 31-2; democratic government, 48, 104, 107,
108, 130, 221; university reform,
50, 94; loyalty to his university,
50, 51; character, 62-3, 66; later
career, 69, 70, 72, 86; in the
North, 86, 111-12; school inspec-
tor, 86, 88, 146; and abolition of
Tests, 88-9, 91; interest in minority rights, 99, 100; and Italy,
102-3; American Civil War, 108,
110; parliamentary reform, 121;
'tea-room' threat, 139; historian,
141 ('comparative method'),
215; nationalism, 156; Regius
Professor, 169, 183, 200; educational reform, 170; Parliamentary candidate, 177, 184, 185,
186, 224-5; foreign affairs, 192,
194; and 1880-85 Parliament,
203, 204; extension movement,
206; Ireland, 219, 221, 222, 224,
225, 231, 238; imperialism 222;
enters the Cabinet, 232; radicalism, 236; ambassador in America, 238-9; Committee on
German atrocities, 239-40; last
years, 241-2; quoted on university liberalism, 12-13; Lowe, 122,
123; upper-class government,
150; democracy, 152, 159;
government, 160; political life,
175, 183; lack of a policy, 185,
186-7; Irish educational issue,
191; Fawcett, 202; Pearson, 234;

Clough, Arthur H., 59, 99; his Oxford, 32, 63, 64
Cobden, Richard, 87-8; and American Civil War, 105, 114; radicalism, 108, 112, 145; on university studies and students, 48-9
Colenso, Bishop J., 81, 91
Coleridge, J.D., 61, 92; and abolition of Tests, 89, 91, 92, 254
Coleridge, Samuel T., 98; 'romantic conservatism', 35, 36, 39, 41
Collectivism, 162
Committee on Irish Affairs, 204, 224-5
Commons Preservation Society, 169
Comte, Auguste, Positivism, 40-41; totalitarian elitism, 41; denial of free will, 43
Congreve, Richard, 42
Conington, John, 52-3, 67, 78; reading parties, 63
Cook, E. T., 201
Cook, John D., ed. *Saturday Review,* 71
Cooperative movement, 36, 148, 149, 164; liberal, academic support, 195, 206; idea of a 'University', 208
Coplestone, Edward, 29, 56
Cory, W. Johnson, 36
Costelloe, B. F. C., 224
Courtney, Lord Leonard H., 11, 71, 224, 237; and political reform, 118, 129; Parliamentary candidate, 184, 185, 231; radicalism, 187, 189, 191; imperialism, 222; Unionism, 230; in the First World War, 240-41
Cowell, John Jermyn, and American Civil War, 105, 106, 109
Cracroft, Bernard, 130-31, 133, 175; and power of aristocratic government, 138
Cranborne, Lord, 121, 133, 134
Crompton, Henry, 53
Cunningham, Sir Henry, 60, 72; on Charles Bowen, 24-5
Cunningham, William, economist, 145, 212-13, 215

Dale, Alfred, 228
Dale, Rev. R. W., Radical, 228
Darbishire, R. D., 86; Tests abolition campaign, 88-9
Darwin, Charles, 45, 46, 120
Davey, Lord, 11, 239
Democracy, democratic government, 11, 13, 48; academic liberals and, 48, 101, 117, 174, 175; American Civil War context, 106-8, 109; and foreign policy, 193; socialist content, 221
Denison, Archdeacon, 229
Derby, Lord, 17, 127
Devonshire, Duke of, 229
Dicey, Albert Venn, 12, 44, 51, 66, 168; and 1848 revolution, 34, 99; and political life, 186; in later years, 52, 69, 213, 215, 236-7; family ramifications, 59-60; foreign interests, 100, 101, 102, 108; journalism, 111, 132, 134, 202, 219, 227; and *Reform Essays,* 132, 139, 171; and Parliamentary representation, 161, 203-4; collectivism, 162; Home Rule, 219, 222, 226-7; death, 242; quoted on: T. H. Green, 20, 97; Evangelicalism, 23, 54; Smith, 45; Bryce, 62-3; Poor Law and poverty, 196-7; Gladstone, 223; Unionism, 230-31, 232; *Digest of the Law of England,* 169; *England's Case against Home Rule,* 227; *Law and Public Opinion,* 13-14, 40, 162, 210; *Law and Working of the Constitution,* 226, 230; 'Legal Boundaries of Liberty', 167; *Six Months in the Federal States,* 110
Dicey, Edward, 132, 227
Dickson, Col, 135
Digby, Kenelm, 169
Dilke, Sir Charles W., 178, 183, 188; policy/unity process, 187; Eastern Question, 194; divorce case, 224
Disraeli, Benjamin, Earl of Beaconsfield, 192; and Parliamentary reform, 121, 132, 133,

331

143; and middle-class Nonconformity, 193

Dod's Electoral Facts, 133, 138

Dodson, John G., and abolition of
Tests (Oxford Bill), 80, 82-3, 85,
90, 91

Durheim, Emile, 21

Eastern Question, 192-4

Edinburgh Review, 72; attacks Oxford, 56

Education, link with reform, 11, 15,
170-71; public schools, 34, 54,
60; liberal academic commitment, 164, 169, 204; role of endowments, 169, 170; Taunton
Commission, 170-71; cause of
dissension, 189-92; sectarianism,
189-90; extension of higher sec-
tor, 204-5, 208, 212; provincial
colleges, 208-9; Act of 1870, 184,
188, 189

Ellis, Robinson, 60; on Huxley, 45-
6

English Historical Review,
programme, 44, 215

Enlightenment, rationalism, 22, 35,
154

Essays on the Endowment of Research,
94

Essays on a Liberal Education, 211

Essays in Liberalism, 231

Essays in Philosophic Criticism, 203

Essays on Reform, and democratic
government, 11, 157-8; contributors, 11-12, 52, 69, 72, 111, 116,
129-32, 239, 261-2, 263; reviews,
97, 115, 131, 134, 136; publication, 110, 116, 129-31; conflict
over, 120, 130, 131; editorship,
130-32, 133; involvement of
Daily News, 131, 134, 138; professional journalists, 132-3; impact
and reception, 133, 134-5, 136,
138; ideology, 158; projected
'Tracks', 181; contents and contributors, 261-2

Essays and Reviews, counter-attack to

clericalism, 46-7, 72, 77

Essay Society, 60, 65, 67, 73; membership, 255

Evangelicalism, 21-2, 28, 59; individualistic ethic, 22, 25, 105, 154;
social advantages, 22-3, 25-6, 48,
55, 234; personal toll, 24-5; and
civil disorder, 26-7; and university reform, 46, 47, 55; and public
schools, 54-5; universities, 55;
decline in sectarian fervour, 85-
6; and Catholic liberalism, 98-9;
and slavery, 106; academic inheritance, 142; distinction
between rational and vital religion, 154; continuing appeal,
230

Everett, William, 109; and Comtism, 42, 60

Ewart, William, M.P., 130

Eyre, Governor, and negro revolt,
90; Jamaica Commission, 126-7

Faber, George S., 29

Farnell, Lewis, 203, 214

Farrar, F. W., 145, 211

Fawcett, Henry, 11, 44, 45, 61, 110;
academic conservatism, 50;
Tests abolition campaign, 79,
87, 89, 91; M.P., 88; university
finance, 94, 95; foreign political
interests, 100; and a reformed
Parliament, 114, 118, 126, 134,
139; ideological vacillations,
118-19, 224; and classical economics, 159, 202; and cooperatives,
164; trade unions, 167; Parliamentary candidate, 178, 180,
183, 185, 186; Radical Club,
187; alliance with Irish Catholics, 191; in isolation, 192; *Nation*
obituary, 202; on a 'rural middle
class', 166

Fawcett, Dame Millicent, 187, 188,
189, 222

Financial Reform Association, 117

Fisher, H. A. L., on Bryce, 44, 53,
57; on Maitland, 214

191; separatism, 221, 225; nationalists, 222, extinction of Liberalism, 225; Free State, 242

Italy, 97, 143; unification crises, 98; Catholicism, 99; focus of university interest, 100-105 *passim,* 113, 120, 156, 193; Piedmont liberalism, 101, 105; London exiles, 102; nationalism, 156

Jackson, Henry, 12, 52, 58, 209; university reform, 62, 199-200; First World War, 240

Jacobitism, 25, 29

Jamaica, native revolt, 90; Governor Eyre and, 126-7, 187

Jebb, Sir Richard, 230

Jeune, F. H., 66

Jevons, W. S., 202; *The Coal Question,* 164

Jex-Blake, T. W., 60

Jones, Lloyd, 147

Jowett, Benjamin, 130; Broad Churchman, 31, 33; in Paris, 1848, 33, 99; at Balliol, tutor, 34, 37, 58, 64; at Balliol, Master, 95, 211, 213; university reform, 46, 52-3, 73, 84, 211; prosecution, 47; quoted on: *Essays and Reviews,* 46; a new liberal periodical, 72-3; Mazzini, 101; Lowe, 121; university liberalism, 194

Keble, John, 35

Kenny, Courtney S., 213

Kiernan, Prof. V., on Evangelicalism, 23

Kinnear, John Boyd, 111, 138; education and career, 132; journalism, 132-3; power of aristocracy, 160

Kitchin, Dean G. W., 200

Kitson Clark, G. S., 16

Knatchbull-Huguessen, Edward, Lord Brabourne, 66

Kossuth, Lajos, in Britain, 99, 100

Labour Party, 241-2

Laing, Samuel, 184, 185

Lake, William C., at Balliol, 34

Leatham, E. A., and Dodson's Bill, 85

Liberal Unionism, 225-6, 238; in universities, 227-30; Tory support, 231, 232; Birmingham movement, 228, 231

Liberalism, academic, sociopolitical influence, 12, 13, 18; causes of failure and neglect, 13, 15, 18, 37, 182-3, 185, 186; isolation from Liberal party, 18, 194; variable characteristics, 19-20; effect of loss of faith, 25; sectarianism, 31, 32, 35, 38, 47; critical dilemma, 32-3; intellectual character in 1860s, 48-9, 54, 73; collegiate differences, 57; activist membership, 65, 66, 255-6; and future role of universities, 94, 95, 146, 198; and working-class politics, 135, 137-8, 147-9, 231; failure to analyse British political system, 142, 144, 150; and nature of government, 158-60; unbalanced representation, 160-62; priorities for 'positive' government, 162-3; and industrialization, 163-5; land ownership, 165-7, 169; legal reforms, 167, 168-9; and educational reform (elitism–participation debate), 169-71, 189, 190-91; secession from liberal democracy, 174-5, 194; numbers in Commons 1868-86, 196; number of candidates 1868-86, 175-6; electioneering, 177-82; chances of high office, 183; government patronage, 183-4; and campaigns of 1874, 1880, 184-6; civic interests, 194-5; desertion of propertied classes, 202; new philosophical interpretations, 202-3, 211-12; failure of social role and analysis, 209-11, 216-17; effect of Home Rule division, 218-19; Parliamentary ineffectiveness, 224-5; young right-wing mobilization, 227, 231, 232, 235; lack of a social philosophy, 235;

Election Contests 1868-92, 265-9
Liberalism, party, 48, 26; role of
  intellectuals, 12, 14; complex
  commitment, 21; and abolition
  of Tests, 75, 79-84, 87; and
  American Civil War, 105; collapse of discipline, 138, 175, 184;
  rejection of democracy, 174-5;
  first association, 180; defection
  of property, 194; 'new' ideology,
  199; and Unionism 218, 219
Liberty and Property Defence League, 222
Liddell, H. G. Dean of Christ
  Church, 77
Liddon, Henry P., 92; and New
  Poor Law, 35
Lincoln, Abraham, 103, 107, 109,
  113
London, accessibility to university
  towns, 33; academic liberalism,
  53, 73; lay Fellowships, 53, 68;
  journalism, 89; and European
  capitals, 98; political exiles, 100,
  102
London Ethical Society, 201-2
London School of Economics, 216
London University, 59; King's College, 33-4, 36, 61, 213
Lowe, Robert (Viscount Sherbrooke), 62, 143, 178; university
  radicalism, 11, 14; and franchise,
  27, 125; and Reform Bill 1867,
  71, 121, 125, 133-4; American
  Civil War, 107, 156; utilitarianism, 121-2, 123, 151; abilities,
  122, 123; economics, 122, 124,
  139; reproves Mill, 122-3;
  attacks working classes, 124-5;
  and endowments, 169; on *Essays
  on Reform*, 136, 137; *Speeches and
  Letters on Reform*, 123-4, 132
Lowell, J. R., 108, 210
Lucraft, Benjamin, and the International, 186
Ludlow, John M., 110-11, 147; cooperatives, 149
Luke, G. R., 65
Lushington, Sir Godfrey, 11, 60, 77,
  131; career, 69; political reform,

139, 167-8; Positivist, 167; Parliamentary candidate, 178;
  death, 239
Lushington, Vernon, Comtism, 60
Lytton, Sir Edward Bulwer, 107-8

McCarthy, Justin, on university
  scholars, 112
Macaulay, Lord, 39, 167
Mackay, Thomas, *English Poor Law*,
  196
Mackinder, Halford, and new institutions, 208
Macmillan, Alexander, publisher to
  the universities, 71, 110; and his
  authors, 110; and *Essays on
  Reform*, 129, 130; *Letter to a Whig*,
  109; *Magazine*, 109-10
Maine, Sir Henry, 174, 213, 225-6
Maitland Frederick W., 145, 237;
  biographer of Stephen, 53; Cam-
  bridge career, 213, 214; death,
  239
Mallet, Sir Louis, on Radical Club,
  187-8
Manchester, and Tests abolition cam-
  paign, 84-6, 88-9; social isolation,
  146; Owen's College, 202, 205
Manchester Reform Club, 84-5
'Manchester School', Smith's ideal,
  111-12
Mansel, Henry L., 46
Market economies, academic liber-
  als and, 195-6, 197
Marlborough, Duke of, 173, 178
Marrett, R. R., 53
Marriott, Charles, 35
Marshall, Alfred, 202, 215; attacks
  Sidgwick, 200
Martineau, James, Unitarian, 86,
  111, 132
Marxism, 231; and ideology, 16;
  view of the intelligentsia, 17,
  209; historical inquiry, 214
Masterman, C. F. G., 199
Maurice, Frederick, Broad Church-
  manship 28, 35, 63, 75; social
  projects, 36, 39, 127-8; his ap-
  peal, 36-7; remedy for class
  alienation, 155-6

Mazzini, Giuseppe, 100; university interest, 101-2, 156; modern assessment, 102; ideology, 103-4; 156; veneration, 104; concept of nationality, 104; Ireland, 221

Meyrick, Frederick, on Newman, 31-2

Miall, Edward, 88; Liberation Society, 88

Mill, James, utilitarianism, 39; *Essay on Government*, 39; *History of India*, 154

Mill, John Stuart, 37, 65, 110, 116; university influence, 38-40, 151; and Comte, 41; franchise reform, 118, 134; and Fawcett, 118-19; and Jamaica revolt, 126, 154; political ideas, 143, 152; concept of democracy, 147, 154; utilitarianism, 151-2, 153-4; function of Parliament 152; and European liberalism, 154; wages-fund theory, 164, 167; radicalism, 187, 188; Ireland, 221; *Autobiography*, 154; *On Liberty*, 40, 46, 122, 155; *Parliamentary Reform*, 152, 157; *Political Economy*, 153; *System of Logic*, 38, 40, 41, 153

Mills, Wright, elite sociology, 143

Milnes, Richard Monckton: *see* Lord Houghton

Milner, Alfred, Viscount, 201, 222; at Oxford, 228; state socialism, 231

Montalembert, Charles René de, 117

Moore, George E., 53, 203

Morgan, George Osborne, 87, 94, 177-8

Morgan, Henry Arthur, 87

Morley, John, Viscount, 38, 44, 66, 71, 215; and university liberalism, 11, 12; loss of faith, 26; 'great issues' policy, 187, 188; and educational reform, 190, 191; rank and file support, 224; Irish Secretary, 232; quoted on: radicalism – vested interest conflict, 11; Evangelicalism as social control, 26; Oxford Movement,

29-30, 32; Mazzini, 101-2; American Civil War, 106; *Essays on Reform*, 136, 137; new legislation, 176-7, 182; Stephen, 197; Oxford Anglicanism, 236; *Fortnightly* leaders, 177, 189, 197

Morris, William, 51, 186; *News from Nowhere*, 209

Morrison, Walter, 134, 187

Mosca, Gaetano, elite sociology, 143

Moulton, John Fletcher, 204-5

Müller, Max, rejected for Sanscrit Chair, 46

Murray, Gilbert, 53

Namier, Sir Lewis, 20; and ideology, 15-16

National Education League, 188, 194

National Liberal Club, 128

National Liberal Federation, 186, 190, 194

National Liberal League, 186, 204

National Reform Union, 135; centred in Manchester, 125, 126

Neale, Edward Vansittart, 36, 149

Nelson, Col (Gen.), and Jamaica revolt, 126, 139

Nettleship, Edward, 94

Nettleship, Henry, 45, 62, 94; and research, 213-14

Nevinson, H. W., on Ruskin, 201

Newcastle Commission on Popular Education, 88

Newdegate, Charles, M.P., 80, 134

Newman, Francis, 53; on his Evangelicalism, 24

Newman, John Henry, 53, 201, 223; and agnostical reserve, 25; High Churchmanship, 29; conversion, 30, 37, 55; responsibility for change, 31-2; definition of an authority, 45; and university reform, 56

Newman, William L., 60, 69, 130; 'The Land Laws', 163; on land-ownership, 166

Nichol, John, 98, 102; and political reform, 117-18

Nichol, John Pringle, 99

Noetics, 29, 56

Nonconformists, relationship with Liberals, 31, 84-8, 89-93; and abolition of Tests, 74, 75, 81, 83-7; academic ignorance, 75-6; admission to degrees, 76; educational background, 76; crisis of belief, 85-6; elite membership, 86-7; and Education Bill, 189, 190

North of England Council for Promoting Higher Education of Women, 205

Norton, Charles Eliot, 108

Oakley, Frederick, at Balliol, 34

Odger, George, trade unionist, 187, 188

Old Mortality Society, 64-5, 65-6, 67, 97, 99, 102, 199; founder members, 256

Ostrogorski, 210; Bryce's Preface to his work, 25

Oxford Home Rule Association, 232

Oxford Magazine, 219-20

Oxford Movement, Tract 1, 29-30; and role of universities, 31; reactions to, 32, 64; rout, 33, 48, 64; and academic thought, 48

Oxford Reform League, 118

Oxford Society for the Suppression of Mendacity, 35

Oxford University, 11; creation of governing elite, 13-14, 50, 58; religious opinions, 28-9; High Church conservatism, 29; modern liberalism, 31-4, 52; Railway Mania, 33; college tuition, 34, 58; and Mill, 38; allegiance to, 50-51; a total experience, 51, 59; financial and status benefits, 51-2; in early nineteenth century, 55-6; reforms, 56, 145; election of Fellows, 57, 77, 94; Tugendbund, 58, 60, 65; private tuition, 61-2; undergraduate societies, 64-6; honours course, 65; political clubs, 66-7; college reforms, 77,

95; politico–religious controversy, 77-9; Italian Republicans, 102, 104; Union debates, 117; domestic upheavals, 127; northern disregard, 146; numbers in Commons 1867, 175; candidates 1864 and 1868-86, 175-6; university extension, 205, 231; Balliol 'radicalism', 211; classical Fellowships, 211; and Home Rule, 219-20; Unionism, 227-32

Paley, William, 27, 37

Palmer, Edwin, at Balliol, 34

Palmerston, Lord, William Temple, 81, 121, 143

Panizzi, Sir Arthur, 102

Pareto, Vilfredo, 21; elite sociology, 143

Parker, Charles Stuart, 60, 61, 131; and curricula reform, 145-6; on 'Popular Education', 169-70, 171, 189; M.P., 183, 185

Pattison, Mark, 29, 38, 52, 67, 78; and Railway Mania, 33; clerical domination, 37, 46; cynicism, 53; foreign affairs, 192; scholarship, 213; on Newman, 30; Oxford Movement, 32; private tutors, 61; Oxford liberals, 217, 236; *Academical Organization*, 94, 206

Paul, Charles Kegan, 44

Pearson, Charles, 11, 36, 60, 61, 66, 138; ex-University career, 69, 72, 233; foreign interests, 100; journalism, 111, 132; and extension movement, 206; in Australia, 233, 234; *Early Age of English History*, 131; *National Life and Character*, 163, 233-4; assessments, 234-5

Pelham, Henry, 214

Pelling, Dr Henry, on American Civil War, 108

Pender, John, 184, 185

Politics, political science, manipulative component, 15; failure of traditional theories, 15-16; new role of ideology, 16-17; concept

provincial colleges, 208-9; at a distance from mass society, 209; demands of new disciplines, 212-16; academic relationships, 220-21; and Parliamentary representation, 228-9; Unionism, 230-32; *see also* Cambridge *and* Oxford

Utilitarianism, utilitarians, 20, 39; university following, 37, 40, 43, 48-9, 104, 151-3, 155; rationalism, 75; individualism, 104; Mill and, 151-2, 153-4; liberal academic modification, 151-2, 172

Vaughan, C. V., headmaster of Harrow, 63

Venables, George S., Bryce on, 72; on Lowe, 123

Venn, John, 44

Victoria County Histories, 214-15

Vincent, John, attacks liberal intellectuals, 124, 157, 158; *Pollbooks,* 172

Wallace, Alexander R., 45

Wallace, Donald McK., 193

Wallace, William, 203

Wallas, Graham, 210; attacks university teaching, 25

Ward, Mrs Humphry, *Robert Elsmore,* 200

Ward, James, 215

Ward, William G., Catholic manifesto to *The Ideal of a Christian Church,* 31; at Balliol, 34

Warren, Leicester, 179

Watson, A. G., 77

Weber, Max, 21; elite sociology, 143

Wedderburn, Sir David, 187

Wesley, John, 23

Westlake, John, 100, 118

Whately, Richard, 29, 35

Whewell, William, 39, 40, 68; defence of Cambridge, 56; conservatism, 75; *Inductive Sciences,* 39

White, Joseph Blanco, 29

Whitehead, Alfred N., 203

Wilberforce, Bishop Samuel, 29; attacks evolutionary theory, 45-6; clerical party, 47, 92

Wilberforce, William, 29; secession of his children, 59

Williams, Rowland, 47

Williams, R. E., 180

Wilson, Bristowe, 47

Wilson, Cook, 203

Wordsworth, William, 98

Working classes, and national politics, 18, 97, 147; and foreign politics, 103, 108, 147, 193; relationship with academics, 97, 147, 164, 196, 209; and American Civil War, 113, 114; socioeconomic conditions, 124, 125; assaulted by Lowe, 124-5, press and *Essays on Reform,* 134-5; and Parliamentary representation, 161-2; and the law, 167; radical club, 187, 188; and university extension, 206-7, 209; pitmen's classes, 207, 208, 209; belief in Gladstone, 231; Agricultural Union, 180

World War, First, 239-40

Wright, R. S., 126, 170; on Truck Commission, 183

Young, Sir George, 11, 61, 69; inertia in reform, 161; Parliamentary candidate, 178, 180, 181; British Guiana Commission, 183; Eastern Question, 192; *Times* obituary, 242; on Ad Eundem Club, 67; Law Reform, 168; *University Tests,* 90

Young, George M., sketch of 'Arnoldians', 54